EXPERIMENTAL ANIMATION

Experimental Animation: From Analogue to Digital, focuses on both experimental animation's deep roots in the twentieth century and its current position in the twenty-first century media landscape.

Each chapter incorporates a variety of theoretical lenses, including historical, materialist, phenomenological and scientific perspectives. Acknowledging that process is a fundamental operation underlining experimental practice, the book includes not only chapters by international academics, but also interviews with well-known experimental animation practitioners such as William Kentridge, Jodie Mack, Larry Cuba, Martha Colburn and Max Hattler. These interviews document both their creative process and thoughts about experimental animation's ontology to give readers insight into contemporary practice.

Global in its scope, the book features and discusses lesser-known practitioners and unique case studies, offering both undergraduate and graduate students a collection of valuable contributions to film and animation studies.

Miriam Harris is an experimental animator and Senior Lecturer at the Auckland University of Technology, New Zealand. She completed postgraduate study in Digital Animation and Visual Effects at Sheridan College, Toronto, and her experimental animated films have won awards at international film and animation festivals. Her essays have been published in the books *Animated Worlds* (2007), *The Jewish Graphic Novel: Critical Approaches* (2008) and *24 Czech and Polish Animators* (2011). She is on the editorial board of the animation journal *Animation Practice, Process, & Production*, edited by Paul Wells.

Lilly Husbands is a lecturer in Animation and Visual Culture at Middlesex University, United Kingdom. Her research is broadly concerned with the legacy and evolution of experimental animation in the context of contemporary multimedia practice. She has published numerous book chapters and articles on experimental animation in journals such as *Moving Image Review & Art Journal (MIRAJ)*, *Frames Cinema Journal* and *Alphaville: Journal of Film and Screen Media*. She is an associate editor of *Animation: An Interdisciplinary Journal*.

Paul Taberham is a senior lecturer at Arts University Bournemouth, United Kingdom. He has published on topics such as film cognition, evolutionary theories of art, avant-garde film and animation, film sound and aesthetics. He is the co-editor of *Cognitive Media Theory* (2014) and author of *Lessons in Perception: The Avant-Garde Filmmaker as Practical Psychologist* (2018). In addition, he has spoken internationally at conferences and published articles for several edited collections and journals including *Projections: The Journal for Movies and Mind* and *Animation Journal*. He is a fellow of The Society for Cognitive Studies of the Moving Image.

EXPERIMENTAL ANIMATION

From Analogue to Digital

*Edited by Miriam Harris, Lilly Husbands
and Paul Taberham*

Routledge
Taylor & Francis Group

LONDON AND NEW YORK

First published 2019
by Routledge
2 Park Square, Milton Park, Abingdon, Oxon OX14 4RN

and by Routledge
52 Vanderbilt Avenue, New York, NY 10017

Routledge is an imprint of the Taylor & Francis Group, an informa business

British Library Cataloguing-in-Publication Data
A catalogue record for this book is available from the British Library

Library of Congress Cataloging-in-Publication Data
A catalog record has been requested for this book

ISBN: 978-1-138-70296-7 (hbk)
ISBN: 978-1-138-70298-1 (pbk)
ISBN: 978-1-315-20343-0 (ebk)

Typeset in Bembo
by Deanta Global Publishing Services, Chennai, India

MIX
Paper from
responsible sources
FSC
www.fsc.org
FSC™ C013985
Printed in the United Kingdom
by Henry Ling Limited

CONTENTS

List of figures   viii
Foreword by Janeann Dill   ix
Acknowledgements   xi
List of contributors   xii

Introduction   1
Miriam Harris, Lilly Husbands and Paul Taberham

PART I
Definitions, histories and legacies   **15**

1   It is alive if you are: Defining experimental animation   17
    Paul Taberham

2   A consideration of the absolute in visual music animation   37
    Aimee Mollaghan

3   Experimental animation and motion graphics   51
    Michael Betancourt

PART II
Interviews A   **69**

A1 Georges Schwizgebel   71

A2 Rose Bond   73

A3 William Kentridge   77

A4 Robert Sowa   79

PART III
From analogue to digital   **83**

4   Materiality, experimental process and animated identity   85
    Dan and Lienors Torre

5   'Meticulously, Recklessly, Worked Upon': Direct animation,
    the auratic and the index   102
    Tess Takahashi

6   Digital experimentation: Extending animation's
    expressive vocabulary   114
    Miriam Harris

7   Beyond a digital Écriture Féminine: Cyberfeminism and
    experimental computer animation   132
    Birgitta Hosea

PART IV
Interviews B   **151**

B1 Jodie Mack   153

B2 Maya Yonesho   158

B3 Larry Cuba   161

B4 Max Hattler   164

PART V
Close analysis of individual artists   **167**

8   A hermeneutic of polyvalence: Deciphering narrative
    in Lewis Klahr's *The Pettifogger* (2011)   169
    Lilly Husbands

9   How to be human: The animations of Jim Trainor   186
    Steve Reinke

PART VI
Interviews C   197

C1 Martha Colburn   199

C2 Masha Krasnova-Shabaeva   202

C3 Diego Akel   205

PART VII
Science and the cosmos   209

10 Animating the cosmological horizon: Between art
    and science   211
    Janine Randerson

11 Where do shapes come from?   228
    Aylish Wood

12 NASA's voyager fly-by animations   246
    Sean Cubitt

PART VIII
Interviews D   259

D1 Tianran Duan   261

D2 David Theobald   263

D3 Gregory Bennett   267

Index   *271*

FIGURES

1.1   Still: *Kebab World*   29
1.2   Still: *Black Lake*   32
3.1   Synchronisation of Sound: Image   55
4.1   *The Collagist*   88
4.2   *Rippled*   93
4.3   Frame grabs from *Power*   94
6.1   Still: *Ugly*   128
8.1   Still: *The Pettifogger*   175
8.2   Still: *The Pettifogger*   175
8.3   Still: *The Pettifogger*   176
10.1 Janine Randerson, *Remote Senses, Storms Nearby*   221
10.2 Janine Randerson, *Albedo of Clouds*   223
11.1 The 2D rainfall pattern is the foreground with the 3D
      rain curtain in the background of the image   233
11.2 Still: *Where Shapes From*   238

FOREWORD

Even more interesting than the correspondence between certain sounds
and colors is the analogous reflections of the artistic tendencies of certain
'epochs' in the structure both of music and painting.

Sergei Eisenstein (1947, 94)

Sergei Eisenstein's quest for a language of montage in photographic cinema is
strikingly similar to Viking Eggeling's quest for a dynamic language of visual
symbols for painting, scroll and abstract animation. Both artists sought their
answers in a formal relationship of the Horizontal–Vertical; both were concerned
with singular units of time for projection (frame by frame timing); and both
founded their respective theories of a visual language of time in musical counterpoint on form *as* content. Essentially, both artists were two of our first critical
theorists in film. Eisenstein's theories are the early roots of film criticism as a
whole; and Eggeling's theories, alongside experiments by Leopold Survage and
Walter Ruttmann, exemplify our first critical roots in experimental animation
as a fine art mode and aesthetic discipline.

Embedded in the historical and cultural Soviet Union of the 1930s, film as
a cinematic recording of events opened the door for sociopolitical theory to
eclipse Eisenstein's quest for a cinematic language, effectively removing experimental film as a critical discipline in cinema history. Rescued by twentieth
century experimental film critics (Lawder 1975), experimental film, ironically,
was framed as an outgrowth of art history. Correspondingly, following Viking
Eggeling's premature death just days after his abstract animation film, *Diagonal
Symphony*, was exhibited at the Absolute Film Show in Berlin in May 1925,
experimental animation as a critical and aesthetic discipline and praxis was
aborted *in total*.[1] Art historians failed to grasp the mantle for the evolution of
Eggeling's seven to eight years of concentrated experimentation and research

that shaped his "Theory and Counterpoint of Visual Elements", so that high art culture served to annihilate the whole of experimental animation as a viable trajectory for a critical art history and mode of art. Subsequently subsumed into film history in the 1970s, experimental animation was regarded as single frame-by-frame experimental film (Dill 2006). This critical substation initially served to welcome experimental animation into the fold of a shared art history with experimental film. Doubly, it served to subvert, distract and marginalise experimental animation's singular contributions to an aesthetic mode of fine art worthy of a singular canon of literature to equal its earliest art historical roots. Rectifying this predicament is our twenty-first century calling.

It would seem to me to be any scholar's pleasure to write a foreword for any book in their field of study. Speaking as its author here, it has been a particular pleasure to receive the editors' invitation and to have the opportunity to write a foreword for this book. I thank the editors, the publisher and the contributing authors of this anthology for doing their part to rectify the historical distractions and submersion of our field with this collection of critical scholarship in experimental animation and interviews with its artists. At its Latin root, to animate is *to give life to* ... experimentation has long been understood in the sciences as a method for research and investigation ... conclusively, *Experimental Animation: From Analogue to Digital* converses well with both topics.

—Janeann Dill, Doktor der Philosophie, MFA

Notes

1 Although Eggeling died in 1925, there is evidence that Eisenstein saw Eggeling's, Rutmann's and Richter's abstract films in 1929 when he played a part in a film by Hans Richter. If or how these films may have had an impact on Eisenstein is not clear. Moritz, William, "Restoring the Aesthetics of Early Abstract Films," Research paper presented at Society for Animation Studies Conference, California Institute for the Arts, Los Angeles County, October 1991, 9.

References

Dill, Janeann. "Philosophy of Experimental Animation: Towards A Neo-Aesthetic Discipline," Doktor der Philosophie Dissertation. Interview, P. Adams Sitney, Getty Scholar and Fellow, and Professor, Princeton University, USA, 2006.

Eisenstein, Sergei. *The Film Sense*, Edited and Translated by Jay Leyda. New York: Harcourt, Brace & World, 1947, 94.

Lawder, Standish. "Eisenstein and Constructivism" in Sitney, P. Adams (Editor), *The Essential Cinema: Essays on Films in the Collection of Anthology Film Archives*, vol. 1, series 2. New York: Anthology Film Archives, 1975.

ACKNOWLEDGEMENTS

In addition to all of the wonderful contributors to this collection, the editors would like to thank: Suzanne Buchan, Harriet Cann, Nikita Diakur, Janeann Dill, Anne McIlleron, Stella Freud Harris, Norman, Zoe and Gil Harris, Madhavi Menon, Christopher Holliday, Cole Husbands, Lewis Klahr, Lili Mei, Michele Pierson, Edwin Rostron, Noelle, Atticus, Ezra and Bast Taberham.

The editors would also like to thank Steve Reinke, Chris Gehman and YYZ Books for allowing us to reprint Tess Takahashi's chapter, which was originally published in their edited collection *The Sharpest Point: Animation at the End of Cinema*.

CONTRIBUTORS

Michael Betancourt is an artist/theorist concerned with digital technology and capitalist ideology who has published in *The Atlantic, Millennium Film Journal, Leonardo* and *CTheory*; who has been translated into Chinese, French, German, Greek, Italian, Japanese, Persian, Portuguese and Spanish; and who has authored many books, including *The Critique of Digital Capitalism, The History of Motion Graphics, Semiotics and Title Sequences, Synchronization and Title Sequences* and *Title Sequences as Paratexts*. His work can be found online at michaelbetancourt.com. He teaches as The Savannah College of Art & Design.

Sean Cubitt is a Professor of Film and Television at Goldsmiths, University of London, United Kingdom, and a Professor Grade II at the University of Oslo, Norway, and Honorary Professorial Fellow of the University of Melbourne, Australia. His publications include *Timeshift: On Video Culture* (Routledge, 1991), *Videography: Video Media as Art and Culture* (Palgrave, 1993), *Digital Aesthetics* (Sage, 1998), *Simulation and Social Theory* (SAGE, 2001), *The Cinema Effect* (MIT Press, 2004), *EcoMedia* (Rodopi, 2005), *The Practice of Light: A Genealogy of Visual Technology from Prints to Pixels* (MIT Press, 2014) and *Finite Media: Environmental Implications of Digital Technologies* (Duke University Press, 2017). He is also series editor for Leonardo Books at MIT Press; his research focuses on the history and philosophy of media, political aesthetics, media art history and ecocriticism.

Birgitta Hosea is a London-based artist, animated filmmaker and Reader in Moving Image at the Animation Research Centre, University for the Creative Arts. Her practice combines animation, performance, installation and drawing to engage with themes arising from the female condition including sexuality – *Hot Pussy* (1993), the performance of 'femme' identity – *Dog Betty* (2007), confronting the voyeuristic male gaze – *Out There in the Dark* (2008) and reclaiming the night, *dotdot* *dash* (2018). Most recently, she has exhibited at the Hanmi Gallery in Seoul, the Venice Biennale, the Karachi Biennale and Chengdu Museum of Contemporary Art. Working with digital arts since 1995, she was awarded a MAMA Award for Holographic Arts (2009) and an Adobe Impact Award (2010). She has been Head of Animation at the Royal College of Art as well as Course Director of MA Character Animation at Central Saint Martins, London, the United Kingdom, where she completed her PhD in animation as a form of performance.

Aimee Mollaghan is the programme leader for undergraduate Film Studies and Film Studies with Film Production at Edge Hill University in the United Kingdom. She is the author of *The Visual Music Film* (2015). Her current research is centred on music and psychogeography, landscape and soundscape in contemporary cinema and artist's film and she has published several articles on this topic. Her book chapter on the audiovisual compositions of British artist Lis Rhodes was recently published in *The Music and Sound of Experimental Film*. She is also the reviews editor for *Animation: an Interdisciplinary Journal*.

Janine Randerson is a New Zealand-based media artist and Associate Professor at the Auckland University of Technology, Auckland, New Zealand. Randerson has collaborated with environmental scientists on residencies and projects with NIWA, BoM (Bureau of Meteorology) in Melbourne and NERI (National Environmental Research Institute) in Denmark. Her current projects situate media art in relation to water, weather and politics both locally and internationally. She is the author of *Weather as Medium: Toward a Meteorological Art* (MIT Press, 2018; edited by Sean Cubitt and Doug Sery).

Steve Reinke is an artist and writer best known for his monologue-based video essays. He is Associate Professor of Art, Theory & Practice at Northwestern University. He is represented by Galerie Isabella Bortolozzi Berlin. www.myrectumisnota grave.com

Tess Takahashi is an independent, Toronto-based scholar, writer and programmer who focuses on experimental moving image arts. She is currently working on two books, *Impure Film: Medium Specificity and the North American Avant-Garde* (1968–2008), which examines artists' work with historically new media, and *Magnitude*, which considers artists' work against the backdrop of Big Data and data visualisation. She is a member of the experimental media programming collective Ad Hoc and the editorial collective for *Camera Obscura: Feminism, Culture, and Media*. Takahashi's writing has been published there as well as in *Cinema Journal*, the *Millennium Film Journal*, *Animation*, *MIRAGE* and *Cinema Scope*.

Dan Torre is a Lecturer in the School of Media and Communication at RMIT University in Melbourne, Australia. He has written widely on animation, media and popular culture.

Lienors Torre is a Lecturer in the School of Communication and Creative Arts at Deakin University, Australia.

Aylish Wood is a Professor of Animation and Film Studies at the University of Kent, Canterbury, the United Kingdom. She has published articles in *Screen*, *New Review of Film and Video*, *Journal of Film and Video*, *Games and Culture*, *Film Criticism* and *Animation: An Interdisciplinary Journal*. Her books include *Technoscience in Contemporary American Film* (Manchester University Press, 2002), *Digital Encounters* (Routledge, 2007) and *Software, Animation and the Moving Image: What's in the Box* (Palgrave Macmillan, 2014), a study of intersections between software and the production of moving images, encompassing games, animations, visual effects cinema and science visualisations.

INTRODUCTION

Miriam Harris, Lilly Husbands and Paul Taberham

The explosion of discourse surrounding animation over the last several decades has made very clear the difficulty of defining animation in any satisfactorily comprehensive or cohesive way. This challenge is compounded when it comes to trying to pin down the heterodoxies of what is called experimental animation. Throughout its long history, experimental animation has been associated with a wide range of innovative forms and techniques such as painting or scratching directly onto celluloid, collage, stop-motion, hand drawing, analogue computer graphics and others. More recently artists have made use of 2D and 3D computer animation, spatial projection and interactive installation to create works that disrupt conventions and expand the potentialities of moving image art. Experimental animation is predominantly aligned with non-industrial production contexts that foreground the role of the individual artist, and it can also be identified by particular modes of circulation and distribution.

When discussed in largely aesthetic terms, experimental animation is often characterised by what it is not. 'Non-objective', 'non-narrative', 'non-linear', 'non-normative' and 'unconventional' are some of the words central to a vocabulary that is used to describe this multifarious art form. And although in some ways negation feels like a frustratingly indirect and imprecise way of defining it, avoiding a circumscriptive definition is a way of allowing for the wide range of aesthetic and conceptual approaches, styles, techniques, materials and media that have been identified as experimental animation since the beginning of the twentieth century. This definitional flexibility is part of what has enabled the category to persist into the twenty-first century. As a method of art making, animation harbours an immense capacity for formal experimentation and creative expression, and the various artists and works that are examined in this book are testaments to this freedom and the complex heterogeneity that results from it.

Experimental Animation: From Analogue to Digital proposes some ways of distinguishing and defining both historical and contemporary experimental animation (see Paul Taberham's chapter in particular); however, the collection's approach is not intended to be delimiting. In the contemporary context especially, identifying experimental animation as a coherent category entails the semi-contradictory task of signalling the art form as distinct whilst also acknowledging its interconnectedness with and inseparability from other forms of moving image art and animation. One of the primary aims of *Experimental Animation: From Analogue to Digital* is to investigate some of the aesthetic and cultural territories that experimental animation occupies in the current multimedia landscape. Across the chapters, authors adopt diverse methods to explore various instantiations of experimental animation, from more traditional forms such as abstract visual music, hand drawn and collage animation to 3D animation, web-based projects, multi-channel installations and data visualisation. The collection's 14 interviews with contemporary experimental animators who are situated in different parts of the globe provide revealing details about their individual artistic processes, offering insights as to the forces at work that differentiate experimental animation from mainstream modes and even other forms of experimental filmmaking.

What's in a name?

To use the term 'experimental' in the collection's title is to take on a descriptor that is by no means universally adopted amongst practitioners working with animation outside of the commercial animation industry, nor is it invariably acknowledged as a distinct category of moving image art. We as editors have chosen it in preference to 'avant-garde', 'independent', 'alternative', 'artist' or any number of freshly coined terms because it directly acknowledges the significance of the seminal, and for many years the only book-length work devoted exclusively to the subject, Robert Russett and Cecile Starr's *Experimental Animation: Origins of a New Art*. This 1976/1988 text was instrumental in establishing a foundation for the understanding and appreciation of experimental animation as a multifaceted art form that includes a range of media, formal techniques, figurative features and approaches to narrative.[1] Russett and Starr (1988) explained that despite its 'obvious limitations', the term 'experimental' was chosen to indicate 'individual techniques, personal dedication, and artistic daring' (9). As a term, it was 'broad and elastic enough to embrace the extraordinary range of cinematic works' (ibid.) that they saw belonging to the category.

'Experimental' appeals for several other reasons as well. Firstly, it emphasises an acknowledgement of the form's historical alignment with avant-garde and experimental cinema and signals these disparate works as part of an evolving lineage of experimental moving image practice. Many experimental animators see their work in relation to this history, even as they engage with new technologies and diverse artistic and cultural influences. Other artists who may not strictly identify themselves as experimental animators may nevertheless be ascribed such a categorisation by curators, critics and scholars. This, in turn, points to the significant roles that historiography, curation and criticism continue to play in shaping the ways experimental animation circulates in the world and is conceived of as an art form. Indeed, for many years, experimental animation was subsumed historiographically and critically into related (and themselves interconnected) fields of practice such as experimental cinema and artists' film and video. While it is not necessary (or practicable) to draw firm distinctions between experimental filmmaking and experimental animation, this collection acknowledges subtle differences between the two approaches in terms of the materiality of studio arts practices and their attendant skillsets, as well as the particular emphasis on process in fine-arts-based work. It also recognises the importance of foregrounding examinations of the specific conceptual and formal concerns of animation inasmuch as they differ from live-action (e.g., regarding qualities of abstraction, graphicness, visualisation, formal experimentation, among others).

Another reason we use the term 'experimental' is because, although the encapsulating terms 'artists' moving image' or 'moving image art' would technically cover both the analogue and digital works that are covered in this collection, they de-emphasise animation as a specific technique (and 'artists' animation' seems particularly redundant). In addition, 'experimental' and its connotations of countercultural ideology are also not out of place, with many works maintaining the critical, anti-hegemonic ethos of the avant-garde (as well as its marginalised status). Furthermore, as many of the artist interviews presented in this collection demonstrate, 'experimental' communicates the importance of creative processes that involve exploration, play and discovery and that allow for the embrace of the unexpected and non-prescriptive. Finally, when 'experimental' is considered according to its etymology, it is shown to be a particularly apt and illuminating descriptor of these particular kinds of animated works. The word 'experiment' shares a Latinate root with 'experience'. This etymological connection points to the role experience plays in distinguishing what makes experimental animation 'non-normative' and 'unconventional'. It highlights the significance of the ways that artists use various formal techniques to explore creative possibilities that often destabilise habitual perception and cognition, often challenging viewers to make sense of experiences that are uniquely made possible by the special illusionistic capacities of animation as a technique (Husbands 2014, 7).

From its earliest days the term 'experimental animation' implied an ungovernable multiplicity of forms, media and approaches, and this has only become more complex since the emergence of digital technologies and the Internet. Russett and Starr's formative book did not attempt to offer a comprehensive theorisation of the art form but rather concentrated on the backgrounds, techniques and practices of individual artists. Because it was the only text devoted to the subject for so many years, the book nevertheless established a canon of experimental animators and a loose set of characteristics by which experimental animation would come to be known. The first edition of *Experimental Animation* omitted numerous alternative forms of experimental animation (including hand drawn and puppet animation) and focused solely on early European and North American contexts. The authors acknowledged these limitations in their preface and introduction, including an essay in the 1988 edition of the book that called attention to the evolution and development of experimental animation, and which briefly mentioned the many (predominantly) American artists who were working with animation in the 1970s and 1980s.[2] Russett and Starr called for more scholarly work to be done on the various overlooked areas of the art form. However, decades later this developmental period of experimental animation's history remains under-investigated.

The book was somewhat oddly timed because the late 1960s and 1970s saw the expansion and diversification of many forms of moving image art that defied notions of medium specificity. In many ways, experimental animation was at the forefront of these changes. Russett and Starr acknowledged this with the inclusion of pioneering computer animators such as Lillian Schwartz, John Whitney and Larry Cuba, as well as artists like Ed Emshwiller and Reynold Weidenaar, who were experimenting with image processing and analogue computer animation/video synthesiser techniques like Scanimate that blurred the boundaries between animation and forms of video art. Experimental animators had begun exploring expanded forms of cinema as early as the 1950s, with artists like Robert Breer introducing flipbooks and mutoscopes into the art gallery (Uroskie 2014), as well as Stan VanDerBeek's multimedia project the *Movie-Drome* in the 1960s (Sutton 2015). Many artists working with animation in the latter quarter of the twentieth century were interested in a different set of artistic criteria than many of their forebears, engaging with influences drawn from a variety of popular and fine art practices including Pop art, psychedelia, underground comix, cartoons, graffiti art and album cover art. During this period, experimental animation's formal and aesthetic innovations increasingly fed into the visual language of popular media by way of commercialised forms like film and television title sequences, animated idents, advertisements, music videos and motion graphics (Betancourt 2013; Husbands 2019; Spigel 2008).

Further changes in animation production practices during this period such as the rise in the number of animation programmes at universities, the founding of the International Animated Film Association (ASIFA) in 1960 and the increase in animation festivals around the world (Annecy (1960), Zagreb (1972), Ottawa (1976), Hiroshima (1985) and the non-ASIFA affiliated Cambridge Animation Festival (1981)) resulted in more independent, 'creator-driven' works being produced that were not strictly adherent to the traditions of either experimental or cartoon animation (Bendazzi 2016; Furniss 2016). The proliferation of independent short form narrative animations during this period further served to expand existing categories and to blur boundaries between experimental animation and other independent forms. In the United States, programmes like the Children's Television Workshop's (CTW) 'Sesame Street' (1968–present) and cable television channels like MTV (1981–present) exposed audiences to alternative and experimental animation techniques. In Britain, the Animate! Channel 4 collaborations spearheaded in 1990 by Clare Kitson and Paul Madden funded and disseminated experimental forms of animation to a wide audience on television (Cook and Thomas 2006; Kitson 2008). The proliferation of animation across diverse cultural sectors over the next few decades (leading to what Suzanne Buchan (2013) has called the 'pervasiveness of animation' in contemporary moving image culture) contributed to an ever-increasing instability of formal categories within experimental cinema, animation and contemporary art more broadly.

The expansion of the field of animation studies since the 1990s has increasingly included closer examinations of more experimental forms of animation. Journals such as *Animation Journal, Animation: An Interdisciplinary Journal, AP3, Leonardo, Screen, Cinema Journal, Millennium Film Journal, Moving Image Review & Art Journal (MIRAJ), The Underground Film Journal, INCITE Journal of Experimental Media* and others regularly feature articles on experimental animation that draw from a variety of theoretical and methodological approaches. Over the years, numerous monographs have been published on visual music (Brougher and Mattis 2005; Mollaghan 2015) and various individual experimental animators (Buchan 2010; Dobson 2006; Dobson 2017; Keefer and Guldemond 2012; Hames, 2008; Horrocks 2010), and the more recent collections *Animated 'Worlds'* (2006) and *Pervasive Animation* (2013) (both edited by Suzanne Buchan) and *The Sharpest Point: Animation at the End of Cinema* (2005) (edited by Chris Gehman and Steve Reinke) feature discussions of experimental animations within their broader discursive scopes.

Buchan has rightly claimed that a range of conceptual frameworks is needed to address the extraordinary heterogeneity of animation as an art form and medium. As she suggests, 'an effective approach to this complexity is to use pluralist and interdisciplinary methods' (Buchan 2013, 2). Whilst these are entirely appropriate approaches that fully serve animation's multiplicity, this insistence on plurality has perhaps discouraged discussions of the continuities between experimental forms of animation and experimental animation as a critical mass. However, the number of arts university programmes, festivals and curated screenings devoted to experimental animation, as well as recent publications like Vicky Smith and Nicky Hamlyn's edited collection *Experimental and Expanded Animation* points to a continued relevance of and interest in the form. We are encouraged by the persistence of a desire to group artists and animated works under such a category, however porous. In drawing together essays and interviews exclusively devoted to experimental animation into one volume, this collection aims to contribute to the carving out of a critical space for examining the art form in all its diversity.

Accessibility, circulation and distribution

As Erika Balsom (2017) has noted with regard to film and video art more broadly, distribution channels deeply influence how we encounter, conceive of and write the history of these art forms. She argues that 'distribution participates in the generation of value and canon formation, as particular works may be widely available to be seen and written about, while others remain inaccessible' (8). With the exception of a few organisations exclusively devoted to (mostly abstract) experimental animation such as the Center for Visual Music (CVM) and the Iota Center, experimental animations have historically been collected and distributed by the same organisations that distribute, promote and preserve experimental cinema and artists' moving images. Experimental animations can be found scattered across various university, museum and personal archives, co-ops and artist collectives around the world such as the UK's LUX and Animate Projects, Canyon Cinema, the Academy Film Archive, The New York Film-Makers' Cooperative, Anthology Film Archives, and the Video Data Bank in the United States, Light Cone, Cinédoc and Paris Films Coop in France, Austria's sixpackfilm, Canadian Filmmakers Distribution Centre (CFMDC), the National Film Board of Canada (NFB) and many others.

The traditional rental model adopted by many of these organisations and cooperatives has had to adapt to changes brought about by digitisation and the easy circulation of both sanctioned and bootlegged versions of works online. Over the years many of these organisations have produced various VHS, DVDs and, more recently, video on demand (VOD) services featuring classic and contemporary experimental animations. In addition, experimental animations have at points been distributed by specialist DVD labels such as Other Cinema, Index, Re:Voir, Kinetica Video Library (part of the Iota Center) as well as grant-based or individually funded limited edition DVDs. The exposure that this kind of distribution generates plays a role in which artists receive critical attention and affects the ways in which experimental animation is categorised as a moving image art form.

Awareness of traditional works of experimental animation has grown considerably over the last two decades, and we are currently witnessing a proliferation of new works that draw from a variety of older and newer media, styles and techniques. Access to historical experimental animated work continues to increase as websites like UbuWeb are expanded and artists upload their older works to their websites and other online platforms (in some cases these works have been restored and digitised using arts and cultural grants). Since the mid-2000s especially, experimental animation has thrived thanks to online platforms like YouTube, Vimeo and Tumblr, where search terms and tags enable artists from around the world to categorise their work for themselves. Both inside and outside of the classroom, more young artists than ever before are being exposed to traditional and contemporary examples of experimental animation. There has been a significant growth in the number of festivals, screenings and gallery and museum exhibitions devoted to forms of experimental animation, steadily shifting its cultural weight and presence.[3] Short, single-channel works continue to be shown in curated screenings and specialist film and animation festivals while others manifest as multi-channelled gallery installations, loops, site-specific projections, live performances, gifs, Virtual and Augmented Reality and video games. These newer forms further stretch the boundaries of what might be seen to constitute contemporary experimental animation (or at least to form part of its legacy). To further complicate matters, some multi-channel experimental animated works created for installation exist simultaneously in expanded and single-channel versions.

The roles of the curator, festival coordinator and artist collective remain vital in terms of identifying and cataloguing significant new experimental animations as well as discovering and recirculating overlooked or forgotten works. Some significant ongoing curated screenings and festivals include Edwin Rostron's Edge of Frame screenings in London; Alexander Stewart and Lilli Carré's curated Eyeworks Festival in Chicago and Los Angeles; Giant Incandescent Radiating Animation Festival (GIRAF) in Calgary; Punto y Raya Festival in Madrid and Barcelona; Ars Electronica in Linz; Georama festival in Tokyo; Animasivo Festival in Mexico; the Wrocław Media Art Biennale in Poland, among others.[4] Online and real world collectives like Peter Burr's Cartune Xprez (2006–2013), Casey Jane Ellison's Aboveground Animation, Edwin Rostron's Edge of Frame, Late Night Work Club, Ghosting.TV, Seattle Experimental Animation Team (SEAT), Latin America's Moebius Animación and others offer places for artists to connect, exhibit work and for viewers to discover new and older works of experimental animation. The international reach of experimental animation – supported by the technological dissemination of works – is, however, also entirely reflective of the form's global expressions and international filmmaking contexts.

A global phenomenon

English-language accounts and analyses of experimental animation have reflected somewhat of an imbalanced history in terms of the dominance of Western European and North American animators in the twentieth century. This is in part due to the historical and cultural contexts out of which specific practices arose (e.g., European modernism and the diasporic shifts that took place during and after the Second World War). However, artists in many other parts of the world have produced animated works that can be seen to contribute to a wider conception of the expressive potential of experimental animation as an art form (this is not to ignore or conflate certain culturally specific influences and practices but to highlight the commonalities and cross-fertilisations that have taken place in particular over recent decades). For example, Eastern Europe forged rich animation cultures of experimentation and subversion from the 1930s to the 1980s – films by Franciszka and Stefan Themerson, Julian Antonisz, Daniel Szczechura and Jan Švankmajer are examples – and this continues in the work of experimental animators such as Krakow-based Marta Pajek, despite changes in funding structures in the formerly communist countries. In Japan, the rise of experimental film and anime is evidenced in the work of artists such as Takashi Ito, Keiichi Tanaami, Osamu Tezuka, Yōji Kuri, Yoriko Mizushiri, Atsushi Wada, Tabaimo and others. Experimental animation enjoys a lively presence in

Latin America – Luis Bras, Bibiana Rojas, Julian Gallese, Víctor Iturralde Rúa, Tania de León and Juan Camilo González are examples – and in the Pacific, Lisa Reihana and Veronica Vaevae have created experimental animations that incorporate references to Len Lye, from a feminist, Maori and Cook Island perspective.

In this anthology, we have attempted to address this imbalance by acknowledging the work of a range of animators from different parts of the globe, rather than just concentrating on the terrain of Europe and the United States. The animator interviews within this compilation take the reader into the heart of experimental creative practices from Poland to Japan, China to New Zealand, Brazil to South Africa, while also focusing a keen eye on animators operating in the zones that have been more typically accorded academic attention. For several decades, experimental film and animation festivals have enabled animators from diverse geographies to mix and mingle, as have artist residencies, and gallery opportunities. The proliferation of digital media, together with the ubiquitous nature of the Internet, facilitates more than ever the viewing and transmission of creative work between different corners of the world. The question may be asked as to whether experimental animation possesses distinctive features that collapse national boundaries, or whether the provenance of the work markedly affects the creator's outlook and outcome.

Perhaps the answer to such a question lies in a combination of influences. Len Lye, for instance, absorbed different aesthetic modes based on his place of residence and areas of interest, from the pattern and symbolism of indigenous Oceanic cultures to the modernist abstract artists that he encountered in New York. Yet his creative expression was filtered through a perspective that bears commonalities with other experimental animation practitioners: A seeking of alternatives to linear narratives, the combining of media in non-traditional ways, and a use of reflexivity that exposes materiality and a sense of process. This kind of multifaceted exploration infiltrates the work of all the animators interviewed in this book. For example, US animator Jodie Mack welcomes 'the blurring of any and all lines between genres', Brazilian animator Diego Akel notes that he is 'constantly experimenting with different art media', and New Zealand animator Gregory Bennett seeks to preserve 'a creative spontaneity in the making process while acknowledging the medium itself rather than effacing the base digital aesthetic behind the lure of the photoreal'.

Although signatures exist in their animations that tie them to specific social and political geographies, a pot-pourri of influences can be perceived in the work of the experimental animators interviewed for this anthology. One of the reasons perhaps for such variety is the locational mobility chosen by many of these artists. For instance, Russian animator Masha Krasnova-Shabaeva currently lives in Rotterdam, and Max Hattler grew up in Germany, completed his Masters in London at the Royal College of Art and is currently an Assistant Professor at the City University of Hong Kong. Maya Yonesho grew up in Japan, lives in Stuttgart, but also lectures at Kyoto Seika University. Robert Sowa is Head of The Animation Film Studio at the Academy of Fine Arts in Krakow and was taught by renowned Polish experimental animator Jerzy Kucia. Several aspects of Sowa's work – the use of stop-motion puppets and poetic narratives – can be equated with Eastern European experimental animators who worked behind the Iron Curtain, such as Jan Švankmajer. But Sowa is of a generation who has been able to travel without impediment and has ready access to the Internet, and he also cites Len Lye and Australian filmmaker Paul Cox as influences. Certain sensibilities associated with Eastern European animation can be identified in the animations and installations of Beijing-based Tianran Duan, who lectures at Renmin University, completed his MFA in the animation and digital arts pro-gramme at USC, and cites Polish animator Piotr Kamler as a profound influence.

Some of the animators explore more modernist, universalist concerns, some have brought a politicised attention to social and cultural issues, whereas others have intertwined the two spheres. Larry Cuba's pioneering digital abstractions are resolutely linked with abstract painting and sculpture; a relationship shared with experimental animators he admires such as Norman McLaren, Jordan Belson and John Whitney. Georges Schwizgebel similarly describes his work as 'animated painting that deals with poetry'. William Kentridge, Martha Colburn and Rose Bond work with fine art media that includes drawing, printmaking and paint-ing, but a number of their animated sequences traverse areas with strong social content: racism in South Africa, the US invasion of Iraq, climate change and the changing face of urban centres. Rose Bond brings the last category to life by projecting animated drawings from inside architectural spaces, detailing the historical and social layers residing in that particular space.

Experimental animation: From analogue to digital

The scholarly articles in this collection are divided into four separate subsec-tions. The first is called 'Definitions, histories and legacies' and it deals with broader themes in relation to experimental animation, such as defining the field, proposing categories and examining the influence of experimental ani-mation on commercial practice. It begins with Paul Taberham's 'It is alive if you are: Defining experimental animation', which outlines some of the major historical figures in the field. It also offers a working definition of experimental animation by detailing some of its central tenets, such as the free exposure of the materials used to make the film, the discernible presence of the artist, the centrality of surface detail and the tendency to evoke ideas rather than explicitly state them.

Aimee Mollaghan's 'A consideration of the absolute in visual music animation' connects the Romantic ideals of eighteenth and nineteenth century music to visual music of the early twentieth century, suggesting that both were characterised in their respective periods as a supreme universal language. Non-figurative in nature and operating without any overt narrative, the absolute film as defined in Mollaghan's chapter is divided into two separate but overlapping concepts: *Formal absolutism*, in which meaning was created through visual form rather than extra-visual elements such as story or character; and *spiritual absolutism*, in which the film operates as an agent of spiritual transcendence.

Michel Betancourt's 'Experimental animation and motion graphics' illustrates the way in which the aesthetics of visual music intercepted the commercial realm by way of motion picture title sequences. A direct link is forged between experimental animators like John Whitney and contemporaneous graphic designers such as Saul Bass. Betancourt suggests that this connection between visual music and title sequences continues up to the present day, in a more familiar and sanitised form.

The second subsection is entitled 'From analogue to digital' and it focuses on the materials used in experimental animation in relation to their historical, aesthetic, ideological and social contexts. It begins with Dan and Lienors Torre's 'Materiality, experimental process and animated identity' which focuses on experimental animation's engagement with unconventional production techniques and physical materials. These include found objects, three-dimensional puppets, paper cut-outs, sand, clay and oil paint. Torre and Torre argue that while technologies have developed dramatically in recent years, it is the use of low-tech materials that have helped to characterise experimental animation, differentiating it from the dominant commercial animation productions and giving rise to unique forms and receptions.

Tess Takahashi's '"Meticulously, Recklessly, Worked Upon": Direct animation, the auratic and the index' discusses the resurgence in popularity of direct animation from the 1990s onwards. She suggests that the proliferation of the digital image has caused a crisis in which the old medium of film is being encroached upon by a new representational technology. In opting for celluloid over the digital image, Takahashi suggests that more than being shaped purely by formal or decorative concerns, direct animation artists wish to express a physical presence in their work and avoid resorting to automated digital images that risk obscuring artistic intention.

In 'Digital experimentation: Extending animation's expressive vocabulary', Miriam Harris offers a counter-argument to the assumption that digital animation is cold, mechanical, lacking a human touch and should be more closely associated with spectacle than creative innovation. She explores emotionally resonant experimental digital animations which feature conceptual depth and imagination, and proposes that digital animation extends the vocabulary and expressive power of experimental work.

Birgitta Hosea's 'Beyond a digital écriture féminine: Cyberfeminism and experimental computer animation' examines female artists who contributed to the earliest forms of computer animation and cyberfeminist discourses from the turn of the millennium. She also considers the possibilities of what a feminist approach to experimental computer animation might be. Observing that the majority of female animation students prefer to employ handmade aesthetics over more technical processes such as CGI, Hosea ends with a call for action, suggesting that there needs to be more research into why women are underrepresented in the tech sector, and how this can be counteracted.

The third subsection focuses on individual artists, playing a part in remedying the scarcity of in-depth, close analyses that experimental animation often demands. In 'A hermeneutic of polyvalence: Deciphering narrative in Lewis Klahr's *The Pettifogger*', Lilly Husbands focuses on Lewis Klahr's enigmatic and polyvalent feature-length collage animation *The Pettifogger*, and the cryptic way in which it engages with narrative. Husbands suggests that the nebulous qualities of Klahr's film should be embraced as part of the experience, and that the goal is not to decode a linear narrative, but rather to respond imaginatively to recurring patterns and expressive tropes featured therein.

In 'How to be human: The animations of Jim Trainor', Steve Reinke recounts the way in which his relationship with the work of Jim Trainor deepened, the more closely he engaged with it. While it initially seemed simple and humorous with a mischievous approach to morality and transgression, Reinke claims that on closer scrutiny, Trainor's films offer a radical new approach to making and engaging with cartoons. Moreover, they may also illustrate new ways of being in the world. Reinke unpacks six of Trainor's films, coaxing out interpretations that are hidden beneath the surface.

The final subsection is called 'Science and the cosmos', and it focuses on scientific and cosmological concerns which sometimes motivate the work of experimental animators. Janine Randerson's 'Animating the cosmological horizon: Between art and science' examines a body of techniques used by artists for engaging with cosmological representation. The first section focuses on Jordan Belson's astronomical imagery, and the latter part positions contemporary artists Joyce Hinterding and David Haines, along with artists Sarah and Joseph Belknap as inheritors of Belson's cosmological visual language. In addition, Randerson discusses her own artistic connection to Belson through her video installation artworks that animate remote satellite images.

Aylish Wood's 'Where do shapes come from?' explores the concept of digital materiality, and the way in which algorithms are used by artists. This is discussed in relation to Semiconductor's *Where Shapes Come From*. Wood illustrates how the material arrangements of data alters our experience of information, and also how algorithms are active in cultural politics.

Sean Cubitt's 'NASA's Voyager fly-by animations' offers an eco-poetic reading of James Blinn's NASA animations of the Voyager space mission, tracing some of the missing theological genealogies of modern science. He suggests that Blinn's animations continue to reverberate as some of experimental animation's most moving expressions of what lies beyond the human.

Taken as a whole, this collection is designed to offer an overview of current thinking about experimental animation from a diverse range of scholars and artists. We hope it serves as an inspirational springboard for those who love to create, think or write about this elusive art form.

Notes

1 The 1977 edition of Russett and Starr's book was titled *Experimental Animation: An Illustrated Anthology.*
2 To further complicate matters, in his 2009 book Russett called experimental computer animation 'hyperanimation', despite citing such work as a direct descendent of earlier experimental animation practices.
3 A growing minority of experimental animations circulate in the art world where they are exhibited and sold through galleries as single and limited editions. See for instance Chicago-based Western Exhibitions and the website Artsy.net, which offers links between collectors and art works.
4 Others include Herb Schellenberger's series of screenings *Independent Frames: American Experimental Animation in the 1970s + 1980s* at the Tate Modern in 2017; Northwest Animation Festival in Portland, Oregon, Ann Arbor Film Festival, the London International Animation Festival (LIAF) and GLAS Animation Festival in Berkeley.

References

Balsom, Erika. *After Uniqueness: A History of Film and Video Art in Circulation.* New York: Columbia University Press, 2017.

Bendazzi, Giannalberto. *Animation: A World History*, Volumes 1–3. Boca Raton: CRC Press, 2016.

Betancourt, Michael. *The History of Motion Graphics: From Avant-garde to Industry in the United States.* Maryland: Wildside Press, 2013.

Brougher, Kerry and Olivia Mattis, eds. *Visual Music: Synaesthesia in Art and Music Since 1900.* London: Thames & Hudson, 2005.

Buchan, Suzanne. *Animated 'Worlds.'* Eastleigh: John Libbey Publishing, 2006.

Buchan, Suzanne. *The Quay Brothers: Into a Metaphysical Playroom.* Minneapolis: University of Minnesota Press, 2010.

Buchan, Suzanne. *Persuasive Animation.* London: Routledge, 2013.

Cook, Benjamin and Gary Thomas, eds., *The Animate! Book: Rethinking Animation.* London: LUX, 2006.

Dobson, Terence. *The Film Work of Norman McLaren.* Herts: John Libbey Publishing, 2006.

Dobson, Nichola. *Norman McLaren: Between the Frames.* London: Bloomsbury Academic, 2017.

Furniss, Maureen. *A New History of Animation.* London: Thames & Hudson, 2016.

Gehman, Chris and Steve Reinke, eds., *The Sharpest Point: Animation at the End of Cinema.* Toronto: YYZ Books, 2005.

Hames, Peter. *The Cinema of Jan Svankmajer: Dark Alchemy.* New York: Columbia University Press, 2008.

Horrocks, Roger and Shirley. *Art that Moves: The Work of Len Lye.* Auckland: Auckland University Press, 2010.

Husbands, Lilly. 'Animated Experientia: Aesthetics of Contemporary Experimental Animation.' PhD dissertation, King's College London, 2014.

Husbands, Lilly. 'The "Quasi-Artistic Venture": MTV Idents and Alternative Animation Culture.' In *Animation and Advertising.* Edited by Malcolm Cook and Kirstin Thompson. London: Palgrave MacMillan, forthcoming.

Keefer, Cindy and Jaap Guldemond. *Oskar Fischinger 1900–1967: Experiments in Cinematic Abstraction.* Amsterdam: EYE Filmmuseum, 2012.

Kitson, Clare. *British Animation: The Channel 4 Factor.* London: Parliament Hill Publishing, 2008.

Mollaghan, Aimee. *The Visual Music Film.* London: Palgrave Macmillan, 2015.

Russett, Robert. *Hyperanimation: Digital Images and Virtual Worlds.* Herts: John Libbey Publishing, 2009.

Russett, Robert and Cecile Starr. *Experimental Animation: Origins of a New Art.* New York: Da Capo, 1988.

Spigel, Lynn. *TV by Design: Modern Art and the Rise of Network Television.* Chicago: University of Chicago Press, 2008.

Sutton, Gloria. *The Experience Machine: Stan VanDerBeek's Movie-Drome and Expanded Cinema.* Cambridge, Mass.: The MIT Press, 2015.

Uroskie, Andrew V. *Between The Black Box and The White Cube: Expanded Cinema and Postwar Art.* Chicago: University of Chicago Press, 2014.

PART I

Definitions, histories and legacies

1

IT IS ALIVE IF YOU ARE

Defining experimental animation

Paul Taberham

To the uninitiated, experimental animation may seem willfully difficult. The artist Stuart Hilton observes that the field is aggressively uncompromising, difficult to fund, difficult to watch and difficult to explain. Yet when it is well executed, it can create 'the right kind of wrong' ('Edges: An Animation Seminar' 2016). As uncompromising as it may be, learning to appreciate experimental animation yields a world of provocative, visceral and enriching experiences. We may ask, what does one need to know when first venturing into this style of animation? What are the first principles one should understand? This chapter will outline some of the underlying assumptions that can serve as a springboard when stepping into this wider aesthetic domain.

The basic premises of experimental animation hark back to the early twentieth century avant-garde. Ad Reinhardt said the following of modern art in 1946: '[it] will react to you if you react to it. You get from it what you bring to it. It will meet you half way but no further. It is alive if you are.' (Reinhardt, quoted in Bell and Gray [1946], 2013, 35).[1] The same idea applies to experimental animation. The richness of one's response will determine the value of the artwork, and so a willing and imaginative mind is a necessary precondition.

Experimental animation need not be understood as a 'genre' with its own set of iconographies, emotional effects or recurring themes like westerns, horrors or romantic comedies. Rather, it may be understood as a general approach with a number of underlying premises. A common assumption is that experimental animation is concerned with pushing boundaries, though within the boundary-pushing, there are norms and conventions which emerged that have been revisited and refined over time. Examples include the tendency towards evocation rather than the explicit statement of ideas; freely exposing the materials used to make the film; a staunch aesthetic and thematic individualism of the artist who produced the work; and on some occasions, the visualisation of music. All of these themes will be discussed in the course of this chapter.

Instead of offering traditional narratives like those found in the commercial realm, experimental animation typically offers formal challenges to the spectator. In commercial cinema, the spectator is ordinarily compelled to speculate on how the story will resolve, and it may invite viewers to reflect on the behaviour of the characters and themes raised by the story. The underlying question viewers must ask when engaging with an experimental animation is more likely to be how should they engage with the given material.

In the commercial realm, implicit assumptions about what determines a film's value can go unnoticed. One may ask, what makes a movie compelling to begin with? A typical answer for mainstream filmmaking is that it needs an engaging plot, compelling characters and it should provoke an emotional investment on the part of the viewer. However, there is no all-pervading rule that says these are essential criteria a film must follow in order to provide a meaningful or valuable experience. A film might be appealing because it presents unique formal challenges, it might offer an intense visceral experience, challenge traditional standards of beauty, or it might frame a philosophical question in a provocative way. There are a variety of ways in which a film may be engaging or memorable. Thus, underlying assumptions about filmic experience are called into question when engaging with experimental animation.

A common misconception is that experimental animation, along with other artforms which directly challenge a spectator's habits of engagement such as contemporary dance, atonal music or abstract painting, should be understood as elite, intended only for a specialised audience. Thanks to websites like Edge of Frame, the Experimental Animation Zone page on Vimeo and the websites for the NFB, the Iota Center and the Center for Visual Music, experimental animation is easy to discover and explore. It also need not be considered an elite art because of all types of film, it is the cheapest to produce – experimental animation has traditionally been created by a single artist without a team of staff members. High production values aren't as important as original ideas, and thanks to home computers and online streaming, they can be produced and distributed inexpensively. In this sense, it is the most inclusive of all types of filmmaking.

Motivation for creating experimental film (and animation by extension) varies from artist to artist. Some think of the field as *reactive*, possessing an oppositional relationship to commercial filmmaking and the values of mainstream society. Malcolm Le Grice, for instance, offers a reactive model of experimental film, suggesting that its aesthetic challenges take on a political dimension by prohibiting the audience from being lulled into a passive state of reception, unlike commercial film (Le Grice 2009, 292). It serves as an antidote to the mainstream. Others endorse a *parallel* understanding of experimental film, in which the mainstream and avant-garde operate in different realms without influencing one another (Smith 1998, 396). Within this conception, the films may be enjoyed without the confrontational polemics sometimes implied by avant-garde filmmakers. Ultimately, the reason artists produce work in the way they do can be taken on a case-by-case basis, but both are legitimate motivations.

Those who create experimental animation may be considered first and foremost artists in a more generalised sense, for whom animation fulfils their creative needs. They might also be painters, sculptors or multimedia artists. In this instance, why might an artist turn to animation instead of live action filmmaking or other forms of expression? Creative freedoms granted to animators include the ability to manipulate motion down to the smallest detail – movement (smooth and jarring) is an aesthetic concern for experimental animators, in addition to form, colour and sound. One may also create an entire, self-contained environment without real-life actors or locations. Conversely, one may also 'coax life' out of physical inanimate objects through stop-motion animation. Artists who express themselves through abstraction may also extend their craft to animation, bringing movement to their non-figurative imagery.

Major figures

There are major figures of classical experimental animation who have received a notable amount of critical attention within the field. These may be divided into four broad waves. The first wave featured European abstract painters working in the silent era who turned to animation, inspired by musical analogies to imagery. These are Hans Richter (1888–1976), who broke the cinematic image into its most basic components (darkness and light) with simple motions. Viking Eggeling (1880–1925) used more elaborate shapes than Richter, which would swiftly transform in a variety of permutations. Walter Ruttmann's (1887–1941) abstract shapes were loosely evocative of figurative imagery, with triangles jabbing at blobs of colour, waves crashing across the bottom of the screen, and the like.

The second wave continued to work with sound-image analogies, but their work was also accompanied by (and sometimes synchronised with) music. The best-known artists of this era are Oskar Fischinger (1900–1967) and Len Lye (1901–1980). Both are comparable in their use of image-sound equivalents, but Fischinger's style was shaped by classical music, traditional cel animation and a graphic formalism. Lye's style was looser, making use of 'direct animation' (scratching directly onto the celluloid) techniques and up-tempo popular music of the time. Two other noted figures who emerged around the same period are Mary Ellen Bute (1906–1983), who pioneered the use of electronic imagery in her abstract films, and Jules Engel (1909–2003), a multi-disciplinary fine artist and teacher who was the founding director of the Experimental Animation program at CalArts.

The third wave began to pull away from direct musical analogies. Norman McLaren (1914–1987) was arguably the most varied and prolific of experimental animators, owing to his long-running employment at the National Film Board in Canada. McLaren worked with a wide range of animation techniques and produced films that both harked back to previous experimental animators and also innovated new approaches. John Whitney Sr. (1917–1995) initially collaborated with his brother James, and later went on to pioneer computer animation, combining his mutual interests in abstraction, mathematics and visual harmony. Harry Smith (1923–1991) produced cryptic collage animations, and also painted abstractions directly onto film strips that were reportedly made while under the influence of hallucinogens. Jordan Belson (1926–2011) drew inspiration from meditation and spiritual practices to create abstractions that were suggestive of macro-cosmic and micro-cosmic imagery. Robert Breer (1926–2011) developed a loose, sketch-like style whose steam-of-consciousness images sit on a threshold between abstract and figurative, moving and static.[2]

The final wave works more consistently with referential imagery instead of abstraction, and occasionally includes spoken word. Lawrence Jordan (1934–) creates phantasmagorial evocations with the use of cut-out animation, resembling the collages of Max Ernst. Jan Švankmajer (1934–) and is a self-described surrealist (though his work began after the heyday of the surrealist movement), who uses stop-motion animation on everyday objects to unsettling effect. Stephen and Timothy Quay (known together as The Quay Brothers (1947–)) are also stop-motion artists, who were influenced by Švankmajer, amongst other Eastern European artists. Like their Czech precursor, they also create unsettling film-poems, reanimating abandoned dolls and other detritus. Their films are notably pristine, with smooth motion and delicate layers of dust and grime.

This list of prominent artists is not intended to be exhaustive, nor does it lead us up to the present. It only covers artists which have been canonised in western texts and made (for the most part) commercially available. However, it covers some of the most widely cited figures who came to prominence between the 1920s and the 1980s. In part, this is because from the vantage point of the time in which this chapter was written, the domain of experimental animation has become more difficult to define and organise into canonical figures from the 1990s onwards. This may be due to the growth of the Internet and increased freedom for artists to share their work with the public. In any case, the artists listed above serve as exemplars when first discovering experimental animation.

Single-screen animations will be the focus of this chapter, rather than multi-screen works, gallery-specific animation rather than site-specific (e.g., projecting onto the side of buildings). Nor will the recent adoption of .gif files (brief, looped digital films) as found in the work of artists like Lilli Carré and Colin MacFadyen be considered, or David O'Reilly's recent forays into videogame development. These are exciting new developments in the field however, which deserve vigorous discussion of their own.

Previous definitions

There are two seminal books from the field of animation studies which offer their own definitions of experimental animation: Paul Wells' *Understanding Animation*, and Maureen Furniss' *Art in Motion: Animation Aesthetics*. Both formulate their definitions by contrasting the tendencies of commercial animation with those of experimental animation. As well as helping to identify what makes a film experimental, they also help us to understand how to engage with such works.

Wells defines commercial (or 'orthodox') animation as consisting of configuration (as opposed to abstraction), temporal continuity, narrative form, a singular style and an 'invisible' creator. He notes that the materials used to create the imagery in these kinds of animation are hidden, and they are driven by dialogue. By contrast, experimental animation tends towards the abstract over the figurative, non-continuity, creative interpretation over traditional storytelling, exposure of the materials used to make the animation, multiple styles applied in the same film, the artist who produced the work feels present and the film will be driven by music instead of dialogue. (Wells 1998, 36)

Each contrasting point (e.g., configuration – abstraction) is placed on a continuum and animations may sit between the various poles. Between orthodox and experimental animation sits "developmental" animation, which serves as a conceptual catchall for films that don't belong in the other two categories. Wells' typology productively indicates that there is a continuum between orthodox and experimental films. The model also usefully places animations within the commercial and independent realm on the same continuum, though they are typically kept separate. His definition of orthodox animation is satisfying, but the list of characteristics which pertain to the experimental raises as many questions as it resolves.

If the canonical artists listed above are to be taken as typical examples of experimental animators, then there are a high number of counter-examples to his characteristics of experimental animation which should be considered intrinsic to the form. For instance, abstraction in experimental animation arguably reigned supreme from the 1920s to the 1940s, but less so after that. As such, the claim that using figurative imagery pulls away from the realm of the experimental is contentious.

Wells also suggests that 'experimental animation often combines and mixes different modes of animation' (1998, 45). This is true of Len Lye and Robert Breer (both listed above), but it is atypical of some of the others such as Viking Eggeling, Oskar Fischinger, Jules Engel or John Whitney. It can, however, be found in commercial animation such as the combination of cel and CG in Disney's *Treasure Planet* (2002, Dir. Ron Clements and John Musker), or the more recent *Legend of the Boneknapper Dragon* (2010, Dir. John Puglisi) in which the present is represented with 3D animation, while flashbacks switch to 2D. *The Amazing World of Gumball* (2011–) also combines 2D, CG and stop-motion. Mixed-media is increasingly intercepting commercial animation, so it is possible that Wells' typology (which was first published in 1998) would need to be revised today in this respect.

Finally, Wells suggests that experimental films are motivated by dynamics of musicality rather than dialogue. He presumably has visual music artists like Len Lye and Oskar Fischinger in mind when making this claim, though musical analogies to imagery have become less relevant to the field of animation since the

1950s. One may also bear in mind the centrality of music to commercial anima- tions during the 1930s, like Disney's *Silly Symphonies* series (1929–1939). In addi- tion, there are animations that are arguably driven by *action* rather than music or dialogue, such as *Tom and Jerry* or the Road Runner cartoons.

In essence, I suggest that abstraction, the blending of animation techniques and dynamics of musicality should not necessarily be considered intrinsic to experimental animation. Or rather, making animations figurative, using a sin- gular animation method and not structuring your film around music do not diminish a film's status as 'experimental'.

Maureen Furniss' comparable series of dichotomies separates 'traditional/ industrial/hegemonic forms' with 'experimental/independent/subversive forms'. (Furniss 2008, 30) It cites several similar elements to Wells' tabulation as being indicative of experimental animation such as that they tend to be non-narrative, abstract and non-linear. It also raises additional issues regarding the contexts in which they are created, funded, exhibited and interpreted. Furniss productively comments that experimental films are typically produced with small budgets, by individuals and they are made for small-scale exhibitions. In addition, they chal- lenge dominant beliefs and reflect concerns of marginalised groups.

These are all useful issues to raise. What might be queried is the way in which experimental form is clustered together with independent and 'subversive' forms (the latter of which isn't a term with a wide currency), since these approaches can take notably different shapes. An 'independent film', as it is generally understood, is more likely to directly challenge dominant beliefs and reflect concerns of a mar- ginalised group. The canonical 'experimental' artists cited in this chapter are white, largely male and either American or European. In this respect, they are not margin- alised unless one considers artists generally (as counter-culturalists) to be outsiders. In addition, abstract and surrealistic films need not be understood as representing the concerns of marginalised groups (such as people identifying as LGBT+, ethnic minorities or the disabled), so much as creating 'evocations' or film-poems.[3]

Both Wells and Furniss prudently make the point that these categories exist on a continuum. Furniss rightly comments that both of her categories represent extremes 'to which few cultural products could adhere completely; but, evaluat- ing a particular text in terms of the various paradigms, it is possible to see a given work as generally being related to one mode of production or the other' (ibid.). This is a suitable way to think about categories such as commercial or experi- mental animation, since it is seldom a tidy distinction.

The role of narrative

What may be productive to add to both definitions of experimental and commer- cial animation is a brief consideration of what narrative is, since it is an important component that divides the commercial from the experimental. To offer a bare- bones definition, we may say that a narrative consists of a chain of events which are causally linked, that occur in a defined passage of time and space (Bordwell and Thompson 2008, 75). They also typically feature protagonists. In addition, the generic convention for commercial filmmaking and animation is that they are built around conflict and resolution, with a central protagonist who achieves a defined goal while overcoming an obstacle. These are the sorts of narratives one encounters when watching a Disney, Pixar or Dreamworks movie.

Some animations feature narratives which don't fit that pattern. They tend to be funded via arts grants which aren't expected to make the same amount of profit as the major studios, and sometimes do represent marginalised groups. This moderate position between the extreme poles of commercial and experimental is what would typically be defined as 'independent'. Examples would include feature films like *Persepolis* (2007, Dir. Marjane Satrapi and Vincent Paronnaud), *Mary and Max* (2009, Dir. Adam Elliot), *The Illusionist* (2010, Dir. Sylvain Chomet) and *It's Such a Beautiful Day* (2012, Dir. Don Hertzfeldt) though there are many more.

Like conventional narratives, independent animations normally feature discernible characters and involve a chain of events occurring in cause and effect relationship. Beyond this, they also negotiate storytelling in a different way to commercial animations; they might lack a disruption and subsequent resolution in a traditional sense, protagonists may drift instead of driving towards a defined goal, and there are no easy divisions between heroes and antagonists. Also, obstacles are not necessarily overcome in the way they are in commercial animations. These are stories that, like life itself, lack the tidiness of conventional narratives. They offer insight into the human condition, but the meaning of the film is left open for audiences to ponder.[4]

Experimental animation doesn't typically feature causally linked events which occur in a defined time and space. It may be conceived as an *enchantment*, rather than a story. If there is a character at all, they would ordinarily be psychologically opaque. Or a human figure might appear, but it's in the same manner as a life drawing, not to be understood as an agent with internal thoughts and intentions, but as an aesthetic object such as those featured in Ryan Larkin's *Walking* (1968) or Erica Russell's *Triangle* (1994).

Of course, even between these three categories (commercial, independent and experimental) there are borderline cases. David O'Reilly's *The External World* (2012), for instance, features a network of recurring characters in a staged enactment. Causal links between scenes are either tenuous or non-existent and the humour is absurdist, dark and irreverent. It 'feels' like an experimental film, even though it features a loose narrative in a manner that is more typical of an independent film. Ultimately, categories such as commercial, independent and experimental should be used to elucidate one's understanding of a work of art, not limit it. As such, they need only be used insofar as they are useful.

Setting parameters

With previous definitions and distinctions in mind, a series of tendencies that pertain to the field of experimental animation may be detailed. Like Wells and

Furniss' models, I hasten to add that these are not essential characteristics but rather *tendencies*.

First, the context of distribution and production may be outlined in the following way:

- It may be created by a single person or a small collective.
- The film will be self-financed or funded by a small grant from an arts institution, without expectation to make a profit.
- Instead of undergoing commercial distribution, experimental films are normally distributed independently online, or through film co-operatives to be exhibited by film societies, universities and galleries.

Second, the aesthetics of experimental animation may be characterised thus:

- They *evoke* more than they *tell*, and don't offer a single unambiguous 'message'.
- Surface detail typically plays a more significant role in the experience of the film than the content.
- The materials of animation may be consciously employed in a way that calls attention to the medium.
- Psychologically defined characters with discernible motivations and goals do not feature.

Third, the role of the artist may also be considered:

- The personal style and preoccupations of the artist will be readily discernible.
- The artist may try to express that which cannot be articulated by spoken word, such as abstract feelings or atmospheres. In a sense, they try to express the inexpressible by calling upon their non-rational intuitions.
- Instead of pre-planning a film and then executing that plan in the same manner as a commercial film, the entire act of creation may be a process of discovery.

With a working definition of experimental animation in place, some of these tendencies will be considered in closer detail.

Art as an imaging board

An experimental animator creates meaning in a different way to a traditional storyteller. In conventional stories, events can be interpreted unambiguously. For instance, in *Snow White and the Seven Dwarfs* (1937) a young maiden is pursued by a jealous Queen. She hides with kindly Dwarfs, but the Queen tricks her into eating a poisoned apple and she falls into a death-like coma. The Queen subsequently falls off a cliff while being chased by the Dwarfs, and Snow White is revived by her true love's first kiss. An underlying message is easy to identify: It is better to be gentle and kind than jealous and cruel.

In experimental animation, a film might defy straightforward description and not necessarily feature an explicit take-away moral or message. Experimental animators don't express ideas in a direct way. They *provoke* rather than *tell* and in turn, the spectator is free to interpret the work as they will. The goal isn't to unravel the hidden meaning set up by the artist, but rather respond to the experience imaginatively, as if the work was a mirror reflecting back what the spectator brings to the experience. If a viewer is concerned that they don't 'get it', they may instead ask themselves how it made them *feel*. It might create a mood of ambient entrancement, agitation, relaxation or disorientation, for instance. This is an adequate and legitimate response. In this collection, Lilly Husbands comments on how the appeal of experimental animation is in part rooted in the way it resists straightforward interpretation:

> Their indeterminacy is one of their most stimulating and productive aspects because it invites the viewer to actively participate in their comprehension of the animation. Rather than coming across as vague or confused, inde-terminacy in experimental works is often what immediately piques our curiosity, urging us to discover all the various ways of understanding them.
>
> *(Husbands 2019, 190)*

The critic Jonathan Rosenbaum also comments on this, highlighting the risk of looking for a straightforward answer to films that don't offer explicit messages:

> One way of removing the threat and challenge of art is reducing it to a form of problem-solving that believes in single, Eureka-style solutions. If works of art are perceived as safes to be cracked or as locks that open only to skeleton keys, their expressive powers are virtually limited to banal pronouncements of overt or covert meanings – the notion that art is supposed to say something as opposed to do something.
>
> *(Rosenbaum 2018)*

One may allow the feeling of mystery, then, to be embraced and appreciated as part of the experience when engaging with experimental animation. Instead of being held captive by the film for its duration and then promptly forgetting it afterwards, a work may instead leave you with an itch, or a feeling that there was something you missed that compels you to revisit it days, weeks or years later. You might not solve the film in subsequent viewings, but may still settle into the mysteries.

Instead of thinking about experimental animation from the perspective of a viewer, one may also consider it from the perspective of the artist. During the creative process, an artist might reflect on a given subject and a series of images will come to mind. Using a form of non-rational intuition, the meaning might be highly internalised and various references won't necessarily be discernible to the general viewer (although the title can sometimes offer a clue). Even if the spectator is not privy to whatever motivated the images, one may nonetheless understand that there was some form of rationale or reasoning behind the imagery, and that understanding informs the experience.

For example, consider Robert Breer's *Bang!* (1986) which on the surface appears to feature a string of dissociated images, but there is a discernible theme to those who look for it. Broadly speaking, the film is autobiographical, and it deals with Breer's childhood and adolescence. Instead of telling a linear story, the film is more like a daydream in which images 'skip around the way thoughts do'. (Breer, quoted in Coté 1962/63, 17)

We see familiar fascinations of a boy growing up in the 1930s and 1940s – outdoor activities (the forest, rafting, a waterfall), sport (football and baseball), Tarzan and airplanes. We also see images evoking pubescent, burgeoning sexuality (drawings of a nude woman, a drooling man and sperm swimming) and a female voice utters 'such a male fantasy'. Adolf Hitler also momentarily appears on the screen alongside German fighter aircrafts – Breer was 13 years old when the Second World War broke out. His early interest in vision also appears in the film, featuring optical toys such as the thaumatrope. Reference to personal regret is also made, with the words 'don't be smart', 'don't be stupid' and 'don't be crazy' flashing across the screen, all phrases one is often told during childhood and teenage years.[5]

Presented with these images, the spectator is free to ruminate on themes raised in the film such as nostalgia, regret and conflict (both in war and sport). The notion of *meaning* in the film is distinctly internalised with Breer drawing from his own memories of youth. Yet with these sounds and images, viewers are free to either feel something, or feel nothing. Interpret it, or not. Artists accept that they create works, send them into the world and viewers will make their own readings and interpretations. As with all experimental animation, there is no single correct reaction to *Bang!*; indeed, the notion of a correct reading would be considered limiting. Without guidance, the theme of childhood is easily missed. Even if it passes unnoticed, the viewer may still be engaged by Breer's distinctive range of materials used to make the film such as felt-tip pen, pencil, filmed television, photographs and childhood drawings. His use of a loose sketch style and flickering imagery is also enough to hold the viewer's interest.

In the creation of art, an artist may enter a state of flowing free association where one must listen, and remain true to one's muse. Some artists, such as those during the Gothic period did not consider their work to be a form of personal expression; rather, they were channelling God's will. Today, the creative act is less commonly understood in these terms, but the notion of drawing from an exterior force (divine or otherwise) persists.

One artist who did consider his work to draw creatively from a sacred force is Jordan Belson. He drew inspiration by practicing meditation and then recreating his inner visions through film. In *Allures* (1961), the viewer's attention is continually drawn back to the centre of the frame. We see distant spirals and flicker effects, and drawing together scientific and religious imagery, we also see intersecting dots resembling atomic structures and revolving mandalas.[6] The soundtrack works with the imagery to create a unified experience of entrancement. An abstract work like this seems to defy interpretation altogether, so how does one talk about it? In a sense, the images may be understood and appreciated in a pre-conscious way; indeed, Belson encouraged this. He has commented that his films 'are not meant to be explained, analysed, or understood. They are more experiential, more like listening to music' (Belson quoted in MacDonald 2009, 77).

Nonetheless, images can be imaginatively interpreted, which may enrich one's experience. For instance, one may say that the opening images in *Allures* create the impression that the spectator is being pulled through a cosmic tunnel into the imaginative space of the film, or the screen awash with light represents enlightenment. Aimee Mollaghan has suggested that in *Allures*, a high-pitched electronic sound accompanied by a lower beating rhythm resembles the nervous and circulatory systems. In addition, the film features 'fields of dots and dashes super-imposed over each other [that] reflect the speed and activity of the neural pathways as they enter even deeper into the state of meditation' (Mollaghan 2015, 89). By looking at the specifics of this wholly abstract film, it is possible to discern the theme of inner-consciousness. Conversely, Gene Youngblood suggests that the film depicts the birth of the cosmos. (Youngblood 1970, 160) Suffice to say, both interpretations of this film – that it expresses the small and large, the micro and macro, are accommodated in the work. It is possible (and rewarding) to see it both ways.

To summarise this part of the discussion, we may say that experimental animation defies straightforward description, and is poetic and suggestive instead of concrete. Artists use non-rational intuition to create images which viewers can respond to imaginatively. There is no single correct reading of an experimental animation, and the film may be designed to create a feeling which can't be articulated through a conventional story.

Presence of the artist

Generally, commercial animations aren't intended to be interpreted as the work of an expressive individual. In part, this is because commercial animations are highly collaborative and require a large working crew. There are exceptions such as directors Hayao Miyazaki, Pendleton Ward and Genndy Tartakovsky – auteurs whose names bring a series of themes and stylistic tropes with them, even if their work is collaborative. More broadly this is not the case, general audiences don't tend to remember who directed *Lady and the Tramp* (1955, Dir. Clyde Geronimi, Wilfred Jackson and Hamilton Luske), *The Lion King* (1994, Dir. Rob Minkoff and Roger Allers) or *Frozen* (2013, Dir. Jennifer Lee and Chris Buck), to name a few examples. These studio-based films, moreover, also tend to have multiple directors.

The artist's creative presence can be more vividly felt when watching an experimental animation. We can suppose that experimental animators will express more personal visions than commercial directors since they generally work alone, and they do not produce animations commissioned by a studio with an expectation to make a profit. In experimental animation, the artist is the creative force who 'communicates' (what is the film *saying*?) and who 'expresses' themselves (what is the artist's *personal style*?) rather than striving to 'entertain' – though the film should be engaging on some level. Familiar viewers will watch films by an artist expecting certain themes and techniques the director has used previously. The film, in turn, becomes understood as a chapter in a larger oeuvre. The distinctiveness of individual voices may be in part accountable to the fact that the creation of art may often be more heavily conceived as a process of discovery, rather than a film that is pre-planned and then subsequently executed.

We have already considered how there are broad principles used to understand the field of experimental animation (they evoke more than tell, call attention to their own medium and feature an authorial presence). There are also more localised principles which apply to specific artists. Robert Breer, for instance, utilises a range of materials to create his films and images loosely relate to each other in a similar manner to a daydream; Jordan Belson works with abstract images that evoke impressions of inner-consciousness and also the larger universe.

Experimental animators are sometimes drawn to depicting extreme psychic states or madness. Jan Švankmajer for example associates himself with the surrealist art movement, in which the artist draws creatively from the *unconscious*, the part of the mind that remains untouched by rationality, social convention and the laws of nature, which is most readily accessed through dream. While experimental animators tend to look inwards and create something that feels internalised, as in the cases of Robert Breer and Jordan Belson cited above, they nonetheless try to create an experience that will offer a meaningful experience to others. Otherwise, there would be no reason to share it in the first place.

An artist may be unique in the way they question premises intrinsic to commercial animation. As previously stated, underlying assumptions about filmic experience are called into question – does a film need to tell a story? Does it need compelling characters or emotional investment? In addition, should animated movement always strive to be smooth? Do images need to be beautiful by conventional standards? In a comparable spirit to Jan Švankmajer, recent animators like Katie Torn and Geoffrey Lillemon express themselves with imagery that would typically be considered grotesque.

David Theobald's authorial presence can be vividly felt in his films since they frame a philosophical question in a distinctive way. He is known for producing high quality computer generated animation, but featuring minimal onscreen movement (challenging the assumption that an animated film needs to be full of activity).

Lilly Husbands explains:

> although his works might resemble the visual aesthetic of these commercial studios, Theobald's animations spend their entirety focusing on places and objects that would appear in a Pixar animation only very briefly and most likely somewhere in the background. The intensive labour that goes into Theobald's animations is perversely used to produce images of everyday objects and scenarios that would normally be deemed unworthy of prolonged attention.
>
> *(Husbands, 2015)*

Theobald's 3-minute *Kebab World* (2014) features a single, static shot that looks into a kebab takeaway shop window. Most of the frame remains motionless, though the kebab slowly rotates and the neon lights of the shop sign blink. A radio plays throughout, and the sound of a police siren briefly passes by, complete with blue and red flashing lights illuminating the contents of the frame, though we never see the car. For those attuned to Theobold's approach, the banality of subject matter and extended lack of narrative activity may be interpreted as humorous (why would anyone take the time to animate something as dull as this?), even if it tests the limits of the viewer's patience (see Figure 1.1).

Other films by the same artist operate in a similar way, such as *Jingle Bells* (2013) and *Night Light* (2016). As stated previously, Theobald's authorial presence is readily discernible in these films because they make a philosophical statement in an aesthetically provocative way. While humans, by their very nature, conceive of their surroundings in relation to themselves, in reality the exterior world has its own nature that is independent of human thought and intention. Husbands explains: 'Theobald's refusal to cater to conventional narrative expectations, denying spectators their attendant gratifications, serves to remind them of the

FIGURE 1.1   Still: *Kebab World*, David Theobald 2014.

fact that everything is not always selfishly, anthropocentrically, *for us*' (ibid.). The world, in other words, continues whether we are paying attention to it or not.

As briefly illustrated with Breer, Belson and Theobald, then, the creative force behind experimental animation is more vividly present than it typically is in a commercial animation.

Surface details

Outside the field of experimental animation, the surface details of the animated images are intended to be enjoyed – from Disney movies to anime action spectacles. In commercial animations, however, the function of the surface detail is always subordinated to the story that it serves, and won't play as big a part of the experience once it has been integrated into the larger, more 'meaningful' form of an over-arching story. By contrast, the sensuous appeal of some experimental animations, the colours, movements and visual textures more fully comprise the film's aesthetic appeal. Similarly, the attention to surface patterning is also central to poetry, in which the readers do not just decode its meaning; rather they pay attention to the ways in which the semantic features are patterned with rhyme, rhythm and alliteration.

This is notably the case when the animation is partially or wholly abstract. This can come in the form of visual music (which aspires to the dynamic and nonobjective qualities of traditional music), though not all experimental animations try to express an audio-visual equivalence. Abstraction warrants particular attention in this discussion however, since it played a key part in the development of experimental animation. In the early twentieth century, artists of the time were concerned about what was considered a 'misuse' of cinema. Robert Russett explains that they 'envisioned motion pictures not as a form of popular entertainment, but rather as a new and dynamic expression, one closely allied with the major art movements of the day'. (Russett 2009, 10).

Painter Wassily Kandinsky claimed in 1911 that visual art should aspire to the achievements of music; that is, he sought a visual equivalent to music in contemporary painting. This led to abstract art. In *Concerning the Spiritual in Art*, he argues, 'A painter [...] in his longing to express his inner life cannot but envy the ease with which music, the most non-material of the arts today, achieves this end. He naturally seeks to apply the methods of music to his own art. And from this results that modern desire for rhythm in painting, mathematical, abstract construction, for repeated notes of colour, for setting colour in motion' (Kandinksy 2000, 21). Contemporaries of Kandinsky such as František Kupka and Paul Klee posessed similar creative aspirations.

By the 1920s, European abstract painters Walter Ruttmann, Viking Eggeling and Hans Richter extended their craft to animation (thus pioneering experimental animation as a field), with the musical organisation of film time as their central concern. Concepts from musical composition such as orchestration, symphony, instrument, fugue, counterpoint and score were applied. In turn, this necessitated audiences to pay special attention to the surface details of their films, rather than having surface details subordinated to the larger narrative. Richter's *Rhythmus 21* (1921) strips visual information back to its core element – motion in time. An assortment of squares and rectangles (sometimes white on black, other times black on white) expand and contract on the screen at different speeds. Each visual articulation, like a series of musical motifs, repeats and makes variations. Like music, the movements are variously fast, slow, aggressive, smooth, graceful and abrasive. Just as two or more musical melodies can move in counterpoint, so too can shapes in motion move contrapuntally around one another.[7]

While more recent experimental animators tend to produce figurative instead of abstract imagery, the surface detail remains a significant part of that overall experience. The work of William Kentridge, for example, intentionally features both the gesture of his charcoal markings and their subsequent erasure as part of the overall aesthetic effect. Likewise, one of the attributes that makes Allison Schulnik's disquieting claymations compelling is the texture of the clay she uses to mould her figures.

Exposing the medium

In commercial animation, viewers aren't typically invited to actively contemplate the materials used to make the film (e.g., cel animation, stop-motion or CGI). By contrast, experimental animation sometimes foregrounds its own materiality.[8] This tendency harks back to modernist art in the early twentieth century. Clement Greenberg explains this by considering the transition from realistic paintings to modernist art:

> Realistic, naturalistic art had dissembled the medium, using art to conceal art; Modernism used art to call attention to art. The limitations that constitute the medium of painting – the flat surface, the shape of the support, the properties of the pigment – were treated by the old masters as negative factors that could be acknowledged only implicitly or indirectly. Under Modernism these same limitations came to be regarded as positive factors, and were acknowledged openly.
>
> *(Greenberg 1991, 112)*

Modernist paintings such as the works of Pablo Picasso, Henri Matisse and Piet Mondrian stressed the flatness of the canvas rather than concealing it with illusions of visual depth. Flatness was unique to pictorial art, and was thus embraced.

Exposing the materials of experimental animation is common, and it can be done in a variety of ways. Motion might be intentionally rough instead of smooth (undermining the illusion of natural movement), and in stop-motion the animator may choose to leave their fingerprints in the clay rather than smoothing them out. When artists like Len Lye scratch directly onto the film stock, their physical presence can be indelibly felt in the markings. Caleb Wood's *Plumb* (2014) begins

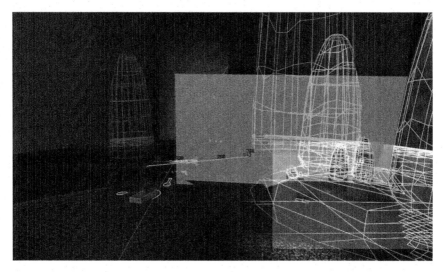

FIGURE 1.2   Still: *Black Lake*, David O'Reilly 2013.

with a hand drawing pictures on a wall with a marker pen. There is a wide shot of the various markings, and then each one is shown in close up in rapid succession which creates an animation. David O'Reilly's CG animated *Black Lake* (2013) pulls the viewer through an uncanny, hallucinatory underwater landscape with rocks, fish, a house and other objects. After a minute and a half, the same objects are seen in wire-frame form, exposing the way in which they were digitally generated (see Figure 1.2).

Another way of exposing the materiality of animation is to make the audience visually register the frame rate of the film they are watching. If successive images are sufficiently different, a flicker effect occurs in which the viewer can discern every frame rather than relaxing the eye into the impression of smooth motion. Robert Breer's *Recreation* (1956) applied the flicker effect, as did Paul Sharits' *T:O:U:C:H:I:N:G* (1968). The technique is still frequently applied today with more recent films like Thorsten Fleisch's *Energie!* (2007) and Jonathan Gillie's *Separate States* (2016). The techniques used to create an animation, thus are something that may be exposed and celebrated in a variety of ways.

Conclusion

The central aim of this chapter has been to elucidate the underlying viewing strategies needed when engaging with traditional experimental animation.[9] In doing so, I have outlined some of the major historical figures in the field and offered a working definition of experimental animation. In addition, some of the central principles have been detailed: The notion that these films evoke rather than tell, the discernible presence of the creative force behind the films, the centrality of surface details and exposing the materials used to make the film.

Before rounding this discussion off, a couple more issues may be briefly considered. First of all, it is also notable that experimental animation has received less critical attention than experimental film more broadly. Beyond visual music and synaesthetic film[10] (which are closely related), there are no widely acknowledged categories for experimental animation unlike their live action counterparts such as the psychodrama, lyric film, structural film or ecocinema.[11] Artist and curator Edwin Rostron suggests that this may be advantageous, commenting '[It's] perhaps the general lack of critical attention historically that has allowed this area of work to escape being theoretically defined and pigeonholed too much – and to be honest as an artist I see this as a blessing! I find it exciting and interesting to work in an ill-defined area where anything goes and expectations are less clear' (Rostron 2017).

The relationship between experimental animation and commercial films may also be explored in more detail. Just as the term *avant-garde* is of military origins, meaning 'advance garde', implying (in the artistic context) pioneers who lead the way for the commercial realm, experimental animators influence mainstream aesthetics. This can occur in the realm of special effects, where artists like Michel Gagné can produce abstract animations like *Sensology* (2010) and also use the same techniques for special effects in *Ratatouille* (2007). Title sequences can also be influenced by experimental animation such as the opening to *Scott Pilgrim Vs. the World* (2010), which is a homage to the scratch films of Len Lye and Norman McLaren. Animator Gianluigi Toccafondo also began his career producing experimental animations like *La Coda* (1989) and *La Pista* (1991) and later produced title sequences for feature films such as *Robin Hood* (2010) with an aesthetic adapted from his earlier style. Finally, music videos have also been influenced by experimental animation. Robyn's 2007 video to 'With Every Heartbeat' features a homage to Oskar Fischinger's *Composition in Blue* (1935), and the video to 'Where Are Ü Now' (2015) by Skrillex, Diplo and Justin Bieber draws straight from the sketchy, flicker aesthetic pioneered by Robert Breer.[12]

One may ask: When writing about experimental animation, what does one discuss? This question is particularly pertinent when considering this type of film – how does one talk about a film that often tries to express the inexpressible? This four-step plan may offer a helpful starting point:

- To begin with, vividly describe the artwork. This will show that you were sensitive to the details of the film rather than just experiencing them as a flurry of vague, generalised images.
- Summarise existing material on your chosen artist case study. Outline what their 'larger project' or general approach is. This has happened briefly in this essay in relation to Jordan Belson and David Theobald.
- Articulate the creative aspirations of the artist by matching it with specific moments of their film.
- If you can discern one, offer your own interpretation of the film which hasn't been expressed elsewhere.

In experimental animation, images come from the quick-of-the-soul. An artist listens to their muse, and shares their vision with the outside world. As the viewer, your principal duty is to relax, keep an open mind and let the film do its work.

Notes

1 Specifically, Reinhardt was referring to abstract painting. But the same principal may be applied to modernist and postmodernist art more generally.
2 There are a host of other important figures from this period that are detailed in Russett and Starr's *Experimental Animation: Origins of a New Art*, such as Lillian Schwartz and Stan Vanderbeek. But for the sake of brevity, they have been left out of my discussion. However, more can be learned about them, and others, in Russett and Starr's book.
3 It is, however, notable that some of the 1970s surrealist independent animations such as Suzan Pitt's *Asparagus* (1979) took on themes of feminism and identity politics.
4 See: Bordwell, David. 'The Art Cinema as a Mode of Film Practice.' *Film Criticism 4*, no. 1 (Fall 1979): 56–64.
5 See Fred Camper's 'On Visible Strings' and Miriam Harris' 'Drawing Upon the Unconscious: Text and image in two animated films by Robert Breer and William Kentridge' for more detailed analyses of this film.
6 Ying Tan insightfully comments that as well as absorbing all that have something to contribute to art such as all religions, cultures, science and technology, Belson's films emphasise the intuitive over the intellectual, they speak of experience as an earthly human being, and may be understood as sacred art. See: Tan, Ying. 'The Unknown Art of Jordan Belson'. *Animation Journal*. Spring 1999: 29.
7 See Aimee Mollaghan's article in this collection for a more detailed discussion of visual music.
8 Note that the articles in this collection from Miriam Harris, and Dan and Lienors Torre also discuss materiality in animation.
9 The word 'traditional' is used in this instance because the form has developed and extended into other fields such as motion graphics, music videos, multiple screen and site-specific projections and interactive platforms. Each of these warrant their own focused consideration.
10 See: Taberham, Paul. 'Correspondences In Cinema: Synaesthetic Film Reconsidered". *Animation Journal* 2013: 47–68.
11 For definitions of the psychodrama, lyric film and structural film, consult Sitney, P. Adams. *Visionary Film*. 3rd ed. Oxford: Oxford University Press, 2001. For ecocinema, see Scott MacDonald, 'The Ecocinema Experience,' in *Ecocinema Theory and Practice*, edited by Stephen Rust, Salma Monani and Sean Cubitt (New York: Routledge, 2013).
12 Michael Betancourt's article in this collection explores the intersection between experimental animation and the commercial realm in more detail.

References

'Edges: An Animation Seminar.' 2016. *edgeofframe.co.uk*. www.edgeofframe.co.uk/edges-an-animation-seminar

Allers, Roger and Rob Minkoff. *The Lion King*. US, 1994. Film.

Bell, Kristine and Anna Gray. *Ad Reinhardt: How to Look. Art Comics*. Hatje Cantz, 2013.

Belson, Jordan quoted in MacDonald, Scott. *A Critical Cinema 3: Interviews with Independent Filmmakers*. London: University of California Press, 2009.

Belson, Jordan. *Allures*. US, 1961. Film.

Bocqulet, Ben. *The Amazing World of Gumball*. UK and US, 2011–Present. Television series.

Bieber, Justin. *Where Are Ü Now*. US, 2015. Film.

Bordwell, David. 'The Art Cinema as a Mode of Film Practice.' *Film Criticism 4*, no.1 (Fall 1979): 56–64.

Bordwell, D. and Kristin Thompson. *Film Art: An Introduction*. 8th ed. New York: McGraw-Hill Higher Education, 2008.

Bird, Brad. *Ratatouille*. US, 2007. Film.

Breer, Robert. *Recreation*. France, 1956. Film.

_____. *Bang!* US, 1986. Film.

Buck, Chris and Jennifer Lee. *Frozen*. US, 2013. Film.

Camper, Fred. 'On Visible Strings'. *Chicago Reader* June 5, 1997, accessed November 2018. www.chicagoreader.com/chicago/on-visible-strings/Content?oid=893567

Chomet, Sylvain. *The Illusionist*. France and UK, 2010. Film.

Clements, Ron and John Musker. *Treasure Planet*. US, 2002. Film.

Coté, Guy. 'Interview with Robert Breer. *Film Culture 27* (Winter 1962/63): 17.

Disney, Walt. *The Silly Symphonies*. US, 1929–1939. Film.

Elliot, Adam. *Mary and Max*. Australia, 2009. Film.

Fischinger, Oskar. *Composition in Blue*. Germany, 1935. Film.

Fleisch, Thorsten. *Energie!* Germany, 2007. Film.

Gagné, Michel. *Sensology*. France, 2010. Film.

Gillie, Jonathan. *Separate States*. UK, 2016. Film.

Furniss, Maureen. *Art in Motion: Animation Aesthetics*. New Barnet Herts: John Libbey Cinema and Animation, 2009.

Geronimi, Clyde, Wilfred Jackson and Hamilton Luske. *Lady and the Tramp*. US, 1955. Film.

Greenberg, Clement. 'Modernist Painting.' In *Art Theory And Criticism: An Anthology Of Formalist Avant-Garde, Contextuaist And Post-Modernist Thought*, 1st ed., London: McFarland & Company, Inc., 1991, 112.

Hanna, William and Joseph Barbera. *Tom and Jerry*. US, 1940–1958. Film.

Hertzfeldt, Don. *It's Such a Beautiful Day*. US, 2012. Film.

Hand, David. *Snow White and the Seven Dwarfs*. US, 1937. Film.

Harris, Miriam. 'Drawing on the Unconscious: Text & image in two animated films by Robert Breer and William Kentridge.' CONFIA International Conference of Illustration & Animation in Barcelos, Portugal, June 2016, published proceedings: CONFIA 2016.

Husbands, Lilly. 'Animated Alien Phenomenology In David Theobald's Experimental Animations'. *Frames Cinema Journal 5*, 2015, accessed July 2014. http://framescinemajournal.com/article/animated-alien-phenomenology-in-david-theobalds-experimental-animations/

_____. In: M. Harris, L. Husbands and P. Taberham, eds., *Experimental Animation: From Analogue to Digital*. New York: Routledge, 2019.

Jones, Chuck. *Road Runner*. US, 1949–1965. Film.

Kandinsky, Wassily. *Concerning the Spiritual in Art*. New York: Dover Publications Inc., 2000.

Larkin, Ryan. *Walking*. Canada, 1968. Film.

Le Grice, Malcolm. *Experimental Cinema In The Digital Age*. London: British Film Institute, 2009.

Mollaghan, Aimee. *The Visual Music Film*. Hampshire: Palgrave Macmillan, 2015.

Paronnaud, Vincent and Marjane Satrapi. *Persepolis*. France and Iran, 2007. Film.

Puglisi, John. *Legend of the Boneknapper Dragon*. US, 2010. Film.

O'Reilly, David. *Black Lake*. Ireland, 2013. Film.

_____. *The External World*. Germany and Ireland, 2012. Film.

Pitt, Suzan. *Asparagus*. US, 1979. Film.

Richter, Hans. *Rhythmus 21*. Germany, 1921. Film.

Robyn. *With Every Heartbeat*. Sweden, 2007. Film.

Rosenbaum, Jonathan. 'ROOM 237 (and a Few Other Encounters) at the Toronto International Film Festival, 2012.' *jonathanrosenbaum.net*. 2018. www.jonathanrosenbaum.net/2018/01/room-237-and-a-few-other-encounters-at-the-toronto-international-film-festival-2012/

Rostron, Edwin. Letter to Paul Taberham. "Re: Edge Of Frame Seminar Audio". Email, 19th February 2017.

Russell, Erica. *Triangle*. UK, 1994. Film.

Russett, Robert. *Hyperanimation*. New Barnet: John Libbey, 2009.

Scott, Ridley. *Robin Hood*. UK and US, 2010. Film.

Sharits, Paul. *T:O:U:C:H:I:N:G*. US, 1968. Film.

Smith, Murray. 'Modernism and the Avant-Gardes.' *The Oxford Guide to Film Studies*. Edited by John Hill and Pamela Church Gibson. New York: Oxford University Press, 1998.

Taberham, Paul. 'Correspondences In Cinema: Synaesthetic Film Reconsidered.' *Animation Journal* 2013: 47–68.

Theobald, David. *Jingle Bells*. UK, 2013. Film.

_____. *Night Light*. UK, 2016. Film.

Toccafondo, Gianluigi. *La Coda*. San Marino, 1989. Film.

_____. *La Pista*. Italy, 1991. Film.

Wells, Paul. *Understanding Animation*. London: Routledge, 1998.

Wright, Edgar. *Scott Pilgrim Vs. the World*. UK, 2010. Film.

Wood, Caleb. *Plumb*. US, 2014. Film.

Youngblood, Gene. *Expanded Cinema*. USA: E.P. Dutton, 1970.

2

A CONSIDERATION OF THE ABSOLUTE IN VISUAL MUSIC ANIMATION

Aimee Mollaghan

The idea of the absolute film first emerged in the early part of the twentieth century, reinforcing the philosophical or aesthetic connection between a certain body of non-objective moving image productions and non-programmatic music. The term *absolute* in relation to the absolute film is drawn from the concept of absolute music. In his 1891 treatise *On the Musically Beautiful: A Contribution towards the Revision of the Aesthetics of Music*, German musicologist Eduard Hanslick uses the phrase 'absolute music' to refer to music that is free from extra-musical considerations; music that can be described as abstract in nature; music that does not have an overt programme; music that is not explicitly about anything; music for music's sake. Therefore, by virtue of drawing on this definition of absolute music, the absolute film might sensibly be defined as a moving image presentation that is abstract and non-figurative in nature without an overt programme or narrative.

Absolute music not only provided the ideal paradigm for a certain body of experimental animation in the twentieth century, but late-nineteenth-century musicological debates over absolute and programme music also established a theoretical precedent for the public discourse on experimental animation after 1900. A number of moving image artists were overtly inspired by the rhetoric, philosophy and metaphor of music. Drawing on the Romantic ideal of absolute music as the supreme universal language, these animators initially looked at the paradigm of absolute music to give a structure to their work and subsequently for spiritual expression. According to animation historian William Moritz, the term *absolute* was first appropriated from music and applied to the animated work of Hans Richter, Viking Eggeling and Walter Ruttmann by critics in the 1920s.

For the purposes of this chapter I wish to extend this analogy to draw on two distinct but overlapping musicological claims to the *absolute*, the *formal absolutism* of musicologist Eduard Hanslick and the *spiritual absolutism* of philosophers such as FWJ Schelling. The first was a formalist claim in which meaning is created through musical form rather than extra-musical elements. The second was a claim of transcendence from the world of the concrete and particular to that of the spiritual and universal. Philosophers such as Schelling and Arthur Schopenhauer reconciled these claims by contending that pure form in music could elevate it to a spiritual language and still contain purely musical meaning. Reducing the idea of the absolute to two overarching categories, the *formal absolute* and the *spiritual absolute*, not only allows for an overview of the changing trends and aesthetics of the absolute film but also provides a methodology for interrogating the moving image work of figures such as Richter, Eggeling, Jordan Belson, James Whitney and John Whitney, in the process illustrating how musical ideas can be applied conceptually to the moving image in order to elucidate both the musical and metaphysical characteristics of the text.

Absolute music

The idea of absolute music as a language that could be universally comprehended began to emerge in the nineteenth century. Influenced by Romanticism, philosophical ideas concerning music underwent a radical re-examination between the eighteenth and nineteenth century. Up until this point, in order for music to be regarded as a worthwhile contribution to society, thinkers and philosophers needed to attribute particular extra-musical meanings to it. Music needed to have a meaning outside of itself, in the form of a programme or narrative content, that influenced and was influenced by religious and moral beliefs. Consequently, purely instrumental music was almost completely rejected as a worthwhile mode of production. Ironically, according to Lydia Goehr, the abstract characteristics that led to this dismissal were those championed by later music critics and practitioners. (Goehr 1992, 148) This is not to say that this type of instrumental music replaced programme music entirely. Clearly, they have continued to coexist. There was, however, a distinct move by composers to legitimise instrumental or absolute music as a valid musical form, emancipating it from the need for an extra-musical programme. Further to this, Goehr asserts that the composers were also endeavouring to validate music as a sovereign art to be assessed on its own terms rather than those of painting and sculpture. They insisted that music was an art form that depended solely on itself and its specificity as a medium for its own significance (ibid.).

One could assert that a similar struggle occurred with the absolute film. A parallel can be drawn between music's struggle for emancipation as a self-sufficient art form and the absolute film's struggle for autonomy. Just as musicians felt the need to produce artefacts such as sheet music that allowed music to be reproduced, so too did experimental animators, drawing on the language of music to give form to their work. This, it can be posited, is one of the reasons why the colour organ or light show gave way to film as the medium of choice for artists such as Eggeling, Richter, Ruttmann and Fischinger for a period of time. Eventually, under the influence of the Romantic theorists, music came to be discussed in terms of unique forms such as the sonata and symphony that are peculiar to music itself. Musical form was now considered an independent cogent form, and in time, its formal qualities came to be appropriated by other art forms such as painting, sculpture, ballet and the film on a structural or metaphorical level.

Although it was Richard Wagner who first coined the term 'absolute music' in 1846, Hanslick was the first theorist to discuss it as a formal concept in 1891, ostensibly becoming an ideologue for the musical formalists. Theorists such as Nicholas Cook indicate that Hanslick's theories were in fact misread as a repudiation of music's ability to carry a transcendent meaning. Cook indicates that what matters in this circumstance is not what Hanslick meant but what he was understood to mean. By the early twentieth century the accepted reading of Hanslick was that music 'was to be understood in exclusively structural terms while issues of meaning were ruled out of court'. (Cook 2001, 174) Under these terms, it is the tone material of music – the basic notes and rests – that expresses the musical idea. Musical compositions were considered complete and self-subsistent in and of themselves. They were not a medium for the projection of the ideas and feelings of the composer.

The second claim for absolute music was grounded in the notion of transcendence from the world of the concrete and particular to the realm of the spiritual and universal. FWJ von Schelling, similar to Arthur Schopenhauer, reconciled these claims by contending that pure form in music could elevate it to a spiritual language and still contain purely musical meaning. Schelling's philosophy of music influenced both Schopenhauer and ETA Hoffmann. According to Mark Evan Bond, Hoffmann 'perceived music as occupying an altogether separate sphere beyond the phenomenal, thereby endowing musical works with the power to provide a glimpse of the infinite' (Evan Bond 1997, 412). He viewed musical harmony as 'the image and expression of the communion of souls, of union with the eternal, with the ideal that rules over us and yet includes us' (ibid.).

As I have argued, attempts to legitimise absolute music during the Romantic period left it in an ambiguous position. In addition to embodying itself as a formal musical structure, devoid of specific content, it could now embody everything. Ultimately, however, music's emancipation from the extra-musical, its being freed from an obligation to provide a meaningful contribution to society and its subsequent autonomy in the Romantic period, led to it becoming an ideal model for the other arts. It became a particularly pertinent model for the absolute film, as film is a medium with which it shares several distinctive attributes such as temporality, rhythm, movement and the idea of *fitting together*.

The formal absolute film

The formalist debate over programmatic and non-programmatic music may have created a theoretical framework for the absolute film, but it was the disillusionment with existing artistic structures in the wake of the First World War that made the model of absolute music the ideal structure to underpin a new regime in art, music and film. In his essay 'Towards a Newer Laocoon', American art critic and champion of modernism Clement Greenberg identifies this shift from ideas that were bound up in nationalism and ideology after the Great War to one where there was an emphasis on form (Greenberg 2003, 541). There was a sense that artists were searching for a new way forward, free from the weight of history and what had come before. What better model for moving forward than that of absolute music, which, in the words of music theorist Daniel K. L. Chua, has 'no history' and 'denies that it was ever born'? (Chua 1999, 9).

Artist Piet Mondrian encapsulated the prevailing mood in the post- First World War period when he stated: 'For let us not forget that we are at a turning point of culture, at the end of everything ancient: the separation between the two is absolute and definite' (Mondrian 2003, 290). There was a rejection of traditional concepts of beauty and a search for a new paradigm that would better serve the spirit of the age. The avant-garde search for a universal language that could provide a framework for the articulation of this spirit inevitably led avant-garde artists such as Paul Klee and Wassily Kandinsky to turn towards what Greenberg refers to as the 'pure form' of absolute music (Greenberg 2003, 565). Increasingly, there was a move towards an idea of *art pour l'art* and an increasing emphasis on form over content. As Guillaume Apollinaire states, 'The subject no longer counts, or if it counts, it counts for very little' (Apollinaire 2003, 187).

Greenberg proposes that the avant-garde arrived at this non-objective approach to art as a way of essentially imitating God by creating something original and irreducible in which '[c]ontent is to be dissolved so completely into form that the work of art or literature cannot be reduced in whole or in part to anything not itself' (Greenberg 2003, 541). Due to painting striving for autonomy as an art form, this two-dimensionality was the only characteristic that painting could possess that was not shared with other plastic arts. Sculpture and even painting up until this point had existed in three dimensions, through the use of perspective and reference to external objects. Artist Hans Hofmann echoes this assertion claiming that the 'essence of the picture is its two-dimensionality' (Hofmann 2003, 373). Hoffmann, as Maya Deren would later do in relation to film, is making a claim that each art has a defining and unique feature. For Deren, temporality, a characteristic also specific to the medium of music, was film's distinctive feature.

This emphasis on medium specificity in modernist theories of art and film can be considered analogous to the attempts musicians and philosophers made in the eighteenth and nineteenth centuries to claim legitimacy for instrumental music by suggesting that music was an art form that had distinct qualities. Moreover, it seems to have a counterpart in formalism, which was seemingly advocated by Hanslick in relation to music in the nineteenth century. Chua contends that the 'elevation of "Art" as some kind of divine utterance' divorced from content and function appeared to endow modernity with the meaning and legitimisation it needed'

(Chua 1999, 13). He writes, '"Art" became a religion of modernity, and absolute music, as the condition to which all art should aspire, was its God' (ibid., 13).

Filmmakers such as Richter and Eggeling were influenced not only by the formal qualities of absolute music but also by Kandinsky's ideas on the spiritual in art. Kandinsky considered music to have a direct access to man's soul due to the capacity of the abstract form to express inner longing. By the time Richter and Eggeling were introduced to each other by Dadaist Tristan Tzara in 1918, they were already separately pursuing the analogy between music and painting. Although Richter specifically wished to paint completely objectively, incorporating the principle of music in this work did not mean that he wished to create forms that imitated specific musical compositions or that either he or Eggeling were attempting to visualise music exactly. They were instead seeking a system or theory that would embody their philosophy. Richter asserts that such a system was to be found in the musical principle of counterpoint, which means 'point against point' or, more generally, 'melody against melody'.

Commensurate with Schopenhauer's proclamation that music 'is such a great and exceedingly fine art, its effect on man's inmost nature is so powerful, and it is so deeply and profoundly understood by him in his inmost being as an entirely universal language whose distinctiveness surpasses even that of the world of perception itself', (Schopenhauer 1969, 256) Richter and Eggeling, like their contemporaries in the neo-plastic arts, were not merely trying to explore formal relationships but were attempting to create a new universal language of visual art. They produced a pamphlet, since lost, entitled *Universelle Sprache*, which outlined the grammar for their new universal language of art. Goehr writes that Romantic theorists argued that instrumental music, free of particularised content, is the most conceivable aspirant for being the 'universal language of art' (Goehr 1992, 155). Music was a direct route to a truth that transcended time and transitory human feelings to become something more than the product of the time in which it is produced. Musical form was therefore the obvious syntax for Richter and Eggeling to pursue.

In their search for this new universal language, Richter and Eggeling were striving for an art form analogous to formal absolute music, in which it is not the individual forms (the content) that are important (hence the dissolution of representation) but the relationship that these elements have to each other in the wider construction of the film form. At times, however, it would appear that, unlike in a formal absolute music sonata or symphony, it is the primacy of the relationship between the formal elements that takes precedence over the overarching structure. Eggeling's *Symphonie Diagonale* (1921–24), for example, unites the formal visual elements of the animation through the standard of counterpoint and internal rhythm. This idea tallies with Hanslick's ideas about cogency in musical form.

According to Hanslick, the four musical movements that underpin musical form (such as the sonata or symphony) coalesce according to laws of musical aesthetics. This is distinct from ideas on programmatic 'feeling' theories, which purported that the movements represented four separate states of the composer's mind, which must be arranged into a coherent whole. Hanslick thought that if the movements of a composition appear unified, this unity could be considered to have its basis in musical determinants such as rhythm, harmony and melody. This is especially apparent in Richter's film, *Rhythmus 21* (1921–24). The form of the film is held together by the dynamism of the rhythm rather than a structured musical framework.

The first half of the twentieth century saw a progressive breaking down of musical structures that had prevailed in Western musical culture for over two hundred years. Traditional sonata and symphonic structure began to be abandoned in favour of new organisational forms. Just as music enjoyed a move from a purely formal aesthetic of the absolute (as seemingly advocated by formalists such as Hanslick) to one where absolute music could function on a formal and a spiritual level simultaneously, there was also a comparable move in the aesthetic and philosophical paradigm of the absolute film. R. Bruce Elder (2010) suggests that rather than celebrate the absolute film, the 1925 screening, *Der Absolute Film*, organised by the Novembergruppe in fact marked the end of the absolute film movement in Germany with the next substantial incarnation occurring in America (Elder 2010, 63–64).

Although there were artists such as Mary Ellen Bute engaging with the Absolute film and figures such as Hilla Von Rebay championing non-objective film and art on the East Coast of America, for the purposes of this chapter I am most interested in the more overt spiritual turn that it took on the West Coast of America in the post-war period. While the animations of John Whitney and Larry Cuba can visually be located within a graphic tradition, the strict formalism of Eggeling and Richter was to give way to a cinema of the spiritually absolute in this locale. Visually there was a marked shift from the geometric aesthetic to a more visceral *gaseous* one.

The spiritual absolute film

Music may have achieved legitimacy on a worldly level in the nineteenth century as an autonomous form that had value and meaning in itself, but it could also function on a spiritual level at the same time. It may have been freed from the *obligation* to embody the spiritual and infinite but it still retained the *possibility* of expressing these characteristics. During the 1950s and 1960s there was an evolution in the aesthetic and philosophical paradigm of the absolute film. Certainly, there was a progression from the silent hard-lined formal aesthetic of the German absolute filmmakers Richter and Eggeling to the graphic sound films of figures such as Fischinger, Bute and Norman McLaren, but the absolutism of these filmmakers ceded to a more nebulous, abstruse spiritualism when it made its way to the American West Coast. This was for several reasons: The influx into the United States of the European avant-garde artists and filmmakers (including figures such as Richter and Fischinger) following the impending outbreak of the Second World War; a philosophical shift by the American avant-garde away from what they viewed as a European conservatism; the establishment of the *Art in Cinema* screenings in San Francisco in the late 1940s; changing viewing contexts; a rise in the practice of Eastern religions; and the use of perception-altering drugs such as LSD, mescaline and peyote by the counterculture in their search for a transcendental experience.

Further to this, Eastern religions such as Buddhism became valuable sources of inspirations for filmmakers on the American West Coast in the 1960s. This is not only because they carried valuable cultural currency in that locale, but, as David E. James points out, the 'emphasis on vision in meditation' made it easy to adapt the spiritual function to the screen (James 1989, 128). Heavily influenced by the audiovisual relationship in the formal absolute films of Richter, Eggeling, Ruttmann and Fischinger, the West Coast filmmakers Jordan Belson and John and James Whitney began to adapt their moving image work in order to explore a tension between the mystical and the formal, extending the more graphic and hard-lined animation of Fischinger et al. to encompass a more halitous, gaseous style of animation that embodied more overtly metaphysical concerns.

James Whitney began to collaborate with his brother John on a series of short films entitled *Five Film Exercises* (1943–44). Composed of simple abstract shapes, these exercises were primarily a formal exploration of the audiovisual relationship. While John continued to pursue a predominantly formal agenda based on theories of harmony in his visual music, James Whitney and Belson began to make films that were influenced by interests in mysticism, Jungian psychology, alchemy, yoga, Taoism, quantum physics, Krishnamurti, Ramana Maharshi and consciousness expansion. William C. Wees refers to James Whitney's films as 'films for the inner eye', a categorisation that can be readily expanded to encompass the work of Belson too (Wees 1992, 136).

Just as contemporaneous composers who wished to embody the spiritual in their music turned East for inspiration, so too did filmmakers like Belson and James Whitney, not merely for visual inspiration but also for musical inspiration. There was a move towards a more minimal aesthetic in music and visual art in the 1960s, which in turn inspired a sparser, more formal appearance in the aesthetic of the absolute films by animators such as Norman McLaren in Canada.[1]

In addition, Eastern musical traditions had an influence on the work of minimalist composers such as Philip Glass, Lamonte Young, Steve Reich and Terry Riley. With the exception of Lamonte Young, who became a renowned teacher of Indian music, these composers adopt particular characteristics of Eastern music – for example, shunning harmony and using Eastern concepts of arranging rather than composing music – rather than entirely committing to Eastern music and its philosophical underpinnings. They instead assume aspects of it but still reside within the confines of a Western classical condition that continued to place an emphasis on the privileged role of the composer and instruments that are recognisable to the Western ear. In a similar manner, McLaren appropriated many of these characteristics for the structure of his three minimalist *Line* films (*Lines Vertical* (1960), *Lines Horizontal* (1962) and *Mosaic* (1965)) while aesthetically remaining within the margins of the formally absolute visual music film. However, in consonance with Schelling's Idealist notions of the cosmos and the arts being one, Whitney and Belson did not just incorporate elements of Indian music and its surrounding philosophy, but embraced it aesthetically as a whole.

Indian classical music, like Western classical music, has its basis in religion and spirituality, yet it enjoys a more explicit function within Hindu theology, equating sound (Nada) with a manifestation of the unifying Absolute (Brahman). This sacred sound, Nada-Brahman is carried through the ragas of Indian music. According to ancient Vedic scriptures there are two types of sound. The first is called *Anahata Nada* (the unstruck or unmanifested sound). This is what the ancient Pythagoreans referred to as the *music of the spheres*, the sound that the celestial bodies make as they move through the universe. Ravi Shankar notes that it is the 'vibration of ether, the upper or purer air near the celestial realm' (Shankar 2006). It is this sound that is sought by the 'great enlightened' yogis during their hours of meditation and contemplation. The second sound is referred to as *Ahata Nada* (struck sound). This type of sound encompasses any sound heard in general surroundings, whether musical or non-musical, man-made or natural.

Robert Sims writes that Indian music explicitly recognises 'the relationship existing between music and the spiritual dimension' (Sims 1992–93, 63). He also posits that almost all facets of Indian culture are founded on principles of the transcendent and are unified by an 'awareness of the cosmic hierarchy' (ibid., 65). Finally, he proposes that if cosmology refers to the hierarchical order of reality that is both microcosmic and macrocosmic in nature, then music, which by its very nature is the ordering of sound, is an 'appropriate' and natural cosmological symbol (ibid., 70). These are the very reasons why Eastern music is a particularly apt model for the structuring of images in the spiritually absolute films of Belson and Whitney. It both binds together the cycles of images that constitute their moving image work as a constant mantra as well as functioning as another spiritual element in the search for metaphysical transcendence and the Absolute.

There is a marked problem when one tries to articulate the ineffable. James Whitney clearly understood the limitations of existing language to express the inexpressible and asserts that he seeks to 'go beyond any language' (Whitney, quoted in Wees 1992, 112). Whitney designed his films as aids to meditation and used rhythmical abstraction in an attempt to induce a trance-like state in the observer. Essentially, the dot patterns on the screen in *Yantra* (1957) are functioning as an instrument to focus psychic forces by concentrating them on a pattern. By directing the viewer's eye towards this pattern at the centre of the screen, he is holding both the viewer's *outer* and *inner* eye captive, hypnotising them to carry them on their cosmic journey.

Both Belson and Whitney foreground the *circle* in their films through their appropriation of circular images derived from cosmology, such as clouds of nebulae, the circular form and movement of the images themselves, the overarching circular structure of the films and their use of cyclical musical forms such as the

Indian *raga*. The raga is a form of music fundamental to Indian music that does not have a direct equivalent within the Western classical tradition. Modal in character, it makes use of microtonal intervals (tones between the 12 tones of the Western keyboard). Indian classical musicians improvise on the form of the raga, assembling melodic sequences through playing rather than composing them in the Western classical music tradition. This central framework is undergirded by tradition and built on by the ability of musicians to improvise following years of dedicated study. Aesthetically, a raga is the 'projection of the artist's inner spirit, a manifestation of his most profound sentiments and sensibilities brought forth through tones and melodies. The musician must breathe life into each raga as he unfolds and expands it' (Shankar, 2006). As much as 90 per cent of Indian music may be improvised and depends on the musician's understanding of the nuances and subtleties of the raga on which he is extemporising.

A parallel can be made between this idea of an Indian musician and the manner in which Jordan Belson and James Whitney slowly assembled rather than composed their films over long periods of time. Belson dedicated himself to the study of Eastern religion, philosophy and practice before choosing a visual raga and improvising on it in real time. Temporally, *Yantra* loosely draws its structure from an Indian raga. The flicker in *Yantra* establishes a pulse to draw the audience into the rhythm of the film, working like a drone over which the melody of dot images is played. *Yantra* is arranged in a series of cycles in the same manner as a traditional Indian raga. As the film progresses the initial cycle of dot formations is repeated in subsequent cycles with subtle variations, just like a sitar player improvising around the central theme of a raga until it reaches the final cycle. The dot is the basic compositional form for all images in the film and recurs throughout. These clusters of dots continue to fluctuate and dance around the screen surface like subatomic particles racing around the nucleus of an atom. Whitney's dots, due to the simplicity of their structure, have an ambiguity to them, and it is this ambiguity that allows Whitney to make connections at microcosmic and macrocosmic levels. This idea harks back to the Neo-Platonic theory of microcosm and macrocosm in which identical patterns can be identified at all levels of the cosmos. It is also found in Eastern religions such as Taoism. Whitney's dots can embody the most minute atomic particles and cells while simultaneously exemplifying all of the celestial bodies in the universe.

Although the absolute film adopts music as its paragon, rather paradoxically, many of the early absolute films either eschewed the inclusion of a music soundtrack, appropriated pre-existing music or music composed on completion of the images of the film. The American West Coast animators (John Whitney specifically), however, were adamant that their films should be original audiovisual compositions in which the sound and image shared an equal partnership. This, as John Whitney's films *Permutations* (1968) and *Arabesque* (1975) and James Whitney's films *Yantra* and *Lapis* (1966) demonstrate, was not always borne out. Belson however, looked on music as an integral part of his work, assembling his own soundtracks in relation to the images. He adopted an approach to sound and image that was predicated on intersensory correspondence in a more evident manner than that of the Whitney brothers, determined that the audience would not know if they were 'seeing it or hearing it' (Youngblood 1970, 155). Belson firmly believed the two media 'to be connected in their strong relevance to the subconscious mind and to basic psychological and physiological phenomena' (Belson quoted in Polta and Sandal 1961). He claimed that electronic music makes use of reverberations of sound present in human perceptions when the brain does not repress them. This is reflective of the Indian spiritual belief that the vibrations in music correspond to the vibrations of the cosmos.

There are many reasons why Indian music is a particularly apt model for the 'cosmic cinema' (Youngblood 1970) of Jordan Belson and James Whitney. It is fundamentally impersonal. According to Ananda Coomaraswamy it 'reflects an emotion and an experience which are deeper and wider and older than the emotion or wisdom of any single individual'. (Coomaraswamy 1917, 164–65). On a surface level, however, Belson's films may seem personal. He is after all presenting his own personal experience of intense meditation, as in *Samadhi* (1967). He also confesses that he does not make up the images in his films but has already seen them either externally or internally (Youngblood 1970, 159). However, although Belson may have seen the images with his *inner* or outer eyes, these images are impersonal archetypal images associated with deep meditation, hallucination or drug use. He is also employing traditional Eastern imagery, representations of space and images from closed-eye vision that the viewer is most likely also familiar with and, like a classical Indian musician playing a raga on a sitar, he is creating an improvisation around a theme. Belson is not composing his film but is assembling it in order to reflect Coomaraswamy's idea of reflecting universal emotions and experiences that are greater than any single individual.

A synthesis between the formal and spiritual

Even though John Whitney's initial moving image offerings were composed in collaboration with his brother James, aesthetically his digital animations reside within the lineage of the German incarnation of the absolute film, featuring graphic geometric patterns against black space that are subject to defined mathematical parameters. He modified this earlier incarnation, however, to allow for more metaphysical concerns, while still functioning on a formal level. Echoing the clarion call of partisans for the avant-garde such as Richter and Eggeling in Germany, Greenberg, Barnett Newman and indeed Belson in America, John Whitney called for a new language for his expression of the absolute. In *Digital Harmony*, his treatise on this new language, he lauded music 'as most worthy of study among prior arts' (Whitney 1980, 44–45), asserting that the foundation for his new art was based on musical – and by extension mathematical – principles. These principles reflected a broader context wherein Pythagorean laws of harmony operate. He strove to produce a body of absolute animations in service to this.

The Pythagorean conception of harmony predicated on mathematics was to exert a profound influence on Whitney's ideas of digital harmony. The Pythagoreans, who were followers of ancient Greek Ionian philosopher Pythagoras, considered music, the cosmos and numbers to be synonymous. Idealist philosophers like Schelling, acknowledged Pythagorean ideas pertaining to the role of music in relation to the absolute. Schelling draws on Pythagorean ideas of reconciling the soul and number, stating that it is the temporality and arithmetical side of music that constitutes a 'universal form' which allows for the reconciliation of the 'infinite' into something, which can be comprehended by the human intellect (Schelling 1989, 117). Thus, Schelling postulates that 'rhythm, harmony, and melody', the 'first and purest forms of movement in the universe', elevate and allow the cosmic bodies to float in space (ibid.). Chua suggests that the absolute music articulated by the Romantics diverges from the ideals of the Pythagorean conception of music; the music of Pythagoras was one in which the world was composed by music whereas the music of the modern world was 'one manufactured by instrumental reason' (Chua 1999, 15). In fact, as Chua points out, that ancient world of the Pythagoreans was 'more rational in its organisation of the cosmos than the modern world, for its music was rationality itself' (ibid.).

In his call for a new language, Whitney echoed Richter's and Eggeling's earlier calls for a new audiovisual language based on the model of music. However, rather than simply appealing to the universal, absolute or temporal nature of music, Whitney was also interested in the movement and patterns associated with music. Furthermore, Whitney made clear the need for a new language and grammar to underpin his art but did not consider the contemporary arts at the time to be moving in a direction sufficient to this realisation. Whitney's vision for a new art, with a new language, also required a new technology. Whitney considered existing animation processes to be inadequate to the structure of this new language and appropriated the computer graphic with its underlying mathematical foundations as the generative building block and visual equivalent to the musical tone. The visual periodicity and harmonics of the computer graphic made it readily accessible to dynamic manipulation through the fledgling computer. Whitney came to use the Graphic Additions to FORTRAN (GRAF) programming language developed by Jack Citron at IBM.[2]

As with his earlier films made with his brother James on their self-engineered mechanical pendulum instrument, Whitney was resolute that the relationship of sight and sound would be best served through the utilisation of *motion* as the common aesthetic that allows the structure of music to be translated into moving images. In order for this concept to function, Whitney had to suppose that musically derived mathematical patterns functioned outside of music and could be applied in alternative contexts, in this case graphic pictorial forms. Whitney speculated that motion could become pattern if the objects are moved differentially, recalling Fischinger's claim that 'new motions and rhythms' which asserted themselves became increasingly important when 'acoustical laws' were applied to 'optical expression' (Fischinger 1946, 112). This is ostensibly the same as tones in music becoming melody through a movement from one tone to the next. As Whitney states, 'emotion from music derives from force-fields of musical structuring in tension and motion' (Whitney 1980, 40). This is also true in the visual world when motion is introduced to pictorial elements.

Although Whitney has stated that the content of music is motion, in actuality it is a series of tones arranged into a pattern that develops over time. Musical tones are the raw material of the structure of music. Whitney uses the computer pixel as his raw material to be sculpted temporally, just as musical tones dance across time to create music. In order for Whitney to create the *motion* of music he is using a visual equivalent of the musical tone. Just as his brother James adopted the dot, John employs the point to create patterns in animations such as *Permutations* and *Arabesque*, which are in a constant state of flux. With these computer-engendered works it is immediately clear that Whitney has borrowed from traditional Persian pattern construction. In *Matrix III* (1972) he uses simple geometric figures of triangles and hexagons but, more interestingly, he uses a series of points arranged into patterns resembling those found in Islamic art and, in both *Arabesque* and *Permutations*, the rose windows of the Gothic period. There is a precise harmonious geometry governing the distribution of constituent elements of Islamic designs and rose patterns, and through the use of these structuring elements in his new *digital* approach, he is making a visual connection between the origins of mathematics and geometry and the absolute.

Conclusion

In conclusion, drawing on the analogy of the *absolute* in music, this chapter has demonstrated the philosophical or aesthetic connection between a certain body of non-objective moving image productions and non-programmatic music. It has established that there were two main claims for music under the new Romantic ideals of the eighteenth and nineteenth centuries. The first, formalist claim, rested on the contention that music gained meaning through its specific form and content rather than extra-musical material. The second, spiritual claim, allowed for a shift from the tangible and concrete in order to facilitate metaphysical, universal considerations. This consideration of the absolute through these two categories, the *formal absolute* and the *spiritual absolute*, provided a way in which to examine how musical concepts can be applied as a framework for expounding the musical and ineffable qualities of a moving image text. Furthermore, by using the concept of the formal absolute and the spiritual absolute as a framework, it has allowed for an overview of changing trends and aesthetics of the absolute film.

There is a substantial transformation in aesthetic from the hard-lined minimalist expression of the formal absolute in the films of the modernist visual music filmmakers Eggeling, Ruttmann and Richter to the gaseous, amorphous, spiritually informed visual music practice of the American West Coast filmmakers. Given the intangibility and abstruseness of the absolute film, one must question what the next phase in its evolutionary history might be. To a certain extent, the underlying philosophy of absolute music has been taken up by contemporary figures such as Scott Draves and Bret Battey. Both Draves and Battey appear to be answering John Whitney's call for a technology and new language as an articulation of the absolute through their software-based audiovisual compositions often grounded in generative computer algorithms. The computer animated work of both artists, is like the canonical absolute films of figures such as Fischinger or John Whitney, undergirded by metaphysical concerns. Battey's work is influenced by Indian music and contemplative practice, and Draves writes that he is interested in 'throwing off the reins of the material world and entering into a more abstract or mathematical or even spiritual world, and making the connections' through his compositions (Draves 2013). However, rather than existing as discrete films, these works often function within expanded contexts or exist within a number of different iterations, with both artists using software as an audiovisual instrument, yet this progression in line with developments in technology and society seems like a natural evolution in absolute moving image practice.

Notes

1 For an example of this see Norman McLaren, *Lines Vertical* (1960), *Lines Horizontal* (1962) and *Mosaic* (1965).
2 GRAF was derived from FORTRAN, the programming language initially developed by IBM in the 1950s for engineering and scientific computing which also came to be used by composers such as Iannis Xenakis for musical composition.

References

Apollinaire, Guillaume. From 'The Cubist Painters.' *Art in Theory 1900–2000: An Anthology of Changing Ideas*. Edited by Charles Harrison and Paul Wood. Oxford: Blackwell Publishing, 2003.

Bond, Mark Evan. 'Idealism and the Aesthetics of Instrumental Music at the Turn of the Nineteenth Century.' *Journal of the American Musicological Society 50*, no. 2/3 (Summer–Autumn 1997): University of California Press.

Belson, Jordan. *Samadhi*. US, 1967. Film.

Chua, Daniel K. L. *Absolute Music and the Construction of Meaning*. Cambridge: Cambridge University Press, 1999.

Cook, Nicholas, 'Theorising Musical Meaning,' *Music Theory Spectrum 23*, no. 2, (Autumn 2001).

Coomaraswamy, Ananda, 'Indian Music.' *The Musical Quarterly 3*, no. 2 (1917).

Elder, Robert Bruce. *Harmony and Dissent: Film and Avant-garde Art Movements in the Early Twentieth Century*. CA: Wildrid Laurier University Press, 2010.

Fischinger, Oskar. 'My Statements are in My Work.' *Art in Cinema*. Edited by Frank Stauffacher. San Francisco: Art in Cinema Society-San Francisco Museum of Art, 1946.

Draves, Scott. 'New Ways to Dream Electric Sheep: An Interview with Scott Draves,' Interview by Nese Devenot. *Reality Sandwich*, 2013, accessed February 20, 2018. http://realitysandwich.com/167897/electric_sheep_interview_scott_draves/

Greenberg, Clement. 'Avant-Garde and Kitsch.' *Art in Theory 1900–2000: An Anthology of Changing Ideas*. Edited by Charles Harrison and Paul Wood. Oxford: Blackwell Publishing, 2003.

Goehr, Lydia. *The Imaginary Museum of Musical Work: An Essay in the Philosophy of Music*. Oxford: Clarendon Press, 1992.

Harrison, Charles and Paul Wod. *Art in Theory 1900–2000: An Anthology of Changing Ideas*. Oxford: Blackwell Publishing, 2003.

Hofmann, Hans. 'On the Aims of Art.' *Art in Theory 1900–2000: An Anthology of Changing Ideas*. Edited by Charles Harrison and Paul Wood. Oxford: Blackwell Publishing, 2003.

James, David E. *Allegories of Cinema*. Princeton: Princeton University Press, 1989.

McLaren, Norman. *Lines Vertical*. Canada, 1960. Film.

_____. *Lines Horizontal*. Canada, 1962. Film.

_____. *Mosaic*. Canada, 1965. Film.

Mondrian, Piet. 'Neo-Plasticism: The General Principle of Plastic Equivalence.' *Art in Theory 1900–2000: An Anthology of Changing Ideas*. Edited by Charles Harrison and Paul Wood. Oxford: Blackwell Publishing, 2003.

Polta H. R. and Roger Sandal. 'Outside the Frame.' *Film Quarterly 14*, no. 3 (Spring, 1961).

Richter, Hans. *Rhythmus 21*. Germany, 1921–24. Film.

Schelling, F. W. J. *The Philosophy of Art*. Minneapolis: University of Minnesota Press, 1989.

Schopenhauer, Arthur. *The World as Will and Representation, Vol. 1*. Translated by E.F. J. Payne. New York: Dover Publications Inc., 1969.

Shankar, Ravi 'On Appreciation of Indian Classical Music.' The Ravi Shankar Foundation, 2006, accessed February 2, 2018. http://www.ravishankar.org/indian_music.html

Sims, Robert. 'Aspects of Cosmological Symbolism in Hindustani Musical Form.' *Asian Music 24*, no. 1 (Autumn 1992–Winter 1993).

Wees, William C. *Light Moving in Time: Studies in the Visual Aesthetics of Avant-garde Film*. Berkeley: University of California Press, 1992.

Whitney, James. *Yantra*. US, 1957. Film.

_____. *Lapis*. US, 1966. Film.

Whitney, John. *Permutations*. US, 1968. Film.

_____. *Matrix III*. US, 1972. Film

_____. *Arabesque*. US, 1975. Film.

_____. *Digital Harmony: On the Complementarity of Music and Visual Art*. Peterboro, NH: Byte Books, 1980.

Whitney, John and James Whitney. *Five Film Exercises*. US, 1943–44. Film.

Youngblood, Gene. *Expanded Cinema*; Introduction by R. Buckminster Fuller. London: Studio Vista, 1970.

3

EXPERIMENTAL ANIMATION AND MOTION GRAPHICS

Michael Betancourt

Motion graphics encompasses a diversity of production techniques, ranging from ray-traced 3D computer animations to optically printed composite cinematography and traditional cel animation. Although the first designs produced in the United States that are recognisable as 'motion graphics' were made for the Hollywood studios at Leon Schlesinger's Pacific Art and Title Studio starting in 1919 (and called 'Art Titles') ('Pacific Title & Art Studio to be liquidated' 2009), the contemporary field emerged from the particular historical context in the United States after the Second World War as Modernism became the dominant approach to design (Betancourt 2013). While the range of applications on TV (broadcast design) includes station identity graphics and advertisements, and the use of motion graphics in commercial narrative films appears prominently as the title sequence, their vast scope also includes video games and interactive digital software, confounding any attempt to briefly survey them because contemporary digital animation/compositing software such as *Adobe AfterEffects* has lowered the production costs and technological barriers to entry, allowing motion graphics to become a common part of everyday experiences with *all* media, even billboards next to highways. These ubiquitous and prosaic, even banal designs – commercials, title sequences and various 'other' animated materials now appearing on TV, in video games and in film – are commercialisations of the historical avant-gardes as popular mass media. Literary critic Larry McCafferty called these transfers 'avant-pop' in the 1990s: The comingling of avant-garde aesthetics and techniques with commercial priorities of realism, accessibility and ease-of-comprehension (McCafferty 1995).

This chapter summarises how the 'avant-pop' transformation of the abstract traditions of 'visual music' became motion graphics, using the title sequence as an illustration. The choice of title sequences for this discussion is utilitarian: They offer abundant and readily accessible examples of these relationships for analysis;

unlike other applications of motion graphics, such as the ephemeral graphics of broadcast design and advertising that become inaccessible after their limited time of initial use, *only* the title sequence *remains* accessible over time, making these designs valuable for historical analysis since they continue to influence later designers long after more ephemeral animations are forgotten, and thus provide an on-going link to earlier, avant-garde sources.

The concept of 'avant-pop' reveals the role of film and television in promoting Modernist art in the 1950s and 1960s (MacDonald 2010, 214–215) through the commercial embrace of experimental animation, avant-garde film and video art (Jacobs 1975, 543–544). The realist and narrative meanings attached to motion graphics differentiate these uses from those of the avant-garde, beginning during the 1950s – for example, with John Whitney's graphic, spiralling forms used in Saul Bass' *Vertigo* title sequence (1958) to suggest a literal 'vertigo'; this conversion of abstraction-into-realism is what distinguishes the commercial design from its avant-garde sources. Commercial media converts the abstract into a stylised variant of familiar representational content (Betancourt 2016); the adaptation in *Vertigo* is typical. Whitney, who worked simultaneously on commercial design projects and his own abstract films (Sandhaus 2014, 158), promoted these adaptations, first at the *Aspen Design* conference in 1959, then on an on-going basis throughout the 1960s. His work directly makes aesthetic and technical transfers between avant-garde film/video and motion graphics. The video artist Ron Hays (Folkart 1991) also promoted the heritage of visual music for commercial production. Like Whitney, he initially developed his theory of music-image from avant-garde film making (Hays 1974), applying it in his video art (as with his tape *Space for Head and Hands*, 1975). He utilised the same imagery and techniques in commercial music videos (as in Earth, Wind and Fire's 'Let's Groove,' 1981).

The heritage of visual music as a formal arrangement of sound-image relations, as well as a set of visual techniques is abundantly apparent in both music videos and title sequences. However, it is not simply a question of synchronisation. Interlocking concerns with synaesthetic form, the painterly/graphic organisation of space, and experimental animators' use of optical printing and computer technology also occupy central positions in the commercialisation of motion graphics. This heritage is especially apparent in the design and organisation of feature film title sequences. Designs such as Saul Bass' *The Man With The Golden Arm* (1955), which adapts elements of Hans Richter's abstract film *Rhythmus 21* (aka *Film ist Rhythmus*, 1923), or Simon Clowes' design for *X-Men: First Class* (2011) that borrows from a range of historical films (such as Walter Ruttmann's absolute films of the 1920s[1] and the works of Mary Ellen Bute) are exemplars of the 'avant-pop' approach that defines how motion graphics engages with experimental animation. Clowes' title design makes this 'avant-pop' engagement with historical abstraction explicit through a transformation of Modernist experimentalism into a representation of genetics and gene sequencing. Similar quotations from Mary Ellen Bute's *Tarantella* (1940) organise the title design for the French film *Ça Ce Soigne?* (*Is It Treatable?* 2008). These references draw attention to the *established* character of the visual music imagery in experimental animation as a language for recombination and manipulation by motion graphics.

The title sequence for *The Man With The Golden Arm* (1954) designed by Saul Bass is a nexus assimilating these influences from historical animations that, in turn, became a central reference for future motion graphics designs. In mediating these transfers between experimental and commercial animation, this title sequence reveals the intersection of otherwise independent histories. In his 1961 introduction to 'The Title Makers,' an *Adventureland* segment on his TV show *Walt Disney Presents*, Walt Disney inadvertently explained how the prestige given to Bass' design links experimental animation to the innovations of motion graphics:

> Now, time was, you know, when you could open a motion picture merely by flashing its title on the screen, and listing the names of the people who helped put it together, but not anymore! We've reached the point where almost everybody wants to make a bid for the title as the "most ingenious" of the title makers. It has become a real challenge to devise a sequence that is fresh and interesting and entertaining. Also according to theory, it should also help to get the audience into the proper frame of mind.
>
> *(Disney 1961)*

The historical source for these 'ingenious' approaches to animation in title sequences was avant-garde film. The impact of this tradition is obvious in how it 'directs' what appears in title designs by Saul Bass. *The Man With the Golden Arm* makes the connections between visual music animations and motion graphics explicit. The 'birth' of the field as a commercial enterprise in the post- Second World War period depends on Bass's fusion of film titles with International ('Swiss') Style graphics (Spigel 2008) and the abstract animated films of the 1920s and 30s. The history of the abstract or 'absolute' film's technical-aesthetic development during the two decades prior to the general embrace of synchronous sound recording by the film industry in 1927 (Betancourt 2013) applied avant-garde experiments in abstract painting to motion pictures. Musical analogies (Tuchman 1985; Brougher 2005)[2] are common in all the 'silent' films that provide the sources for title designs such as *The Man With The Golden Arm*. This title sequence in particular provided a model to emulate and a standard to challenge over the next two decades.

Ralph K. Potter, Director of Transmission Research at Bell Laboratories, who collaborated with abstract film-maker Mary Ellen Bute in designing the oscilloscope control device she used to make her *Abstronics* films (Potter 1951), was closely involved in promoting avant-garde film to advertising directors as a source of innovation and aesthetics for their TV commercial designs in the 1950s. Potter writes:

Of all the film societies in the country none has influenced the creative television artist more than *Cinema-16*. Their experimental, avant-garde and new art forms pop up with amazing regularity. [...] While many of [Vogel's] highly volatile films evaporate into nothingness or obscure points of aesthetics, most are excellent visual barometers for the graphic artist. Agency Art Directors and film producers flock to view these private showings. Much of what they see eventually finds its way into TV commercials.

(Potter 1961, 63)

The title of Potter's article, 'Sources of Stimulus: TV Commercials Often Draw on Avant-Garde Films,' makes the connection between non-commercial experimental film and commercial motion graphics explicit. The embrace of Modernist approaches to art (Spigel 2008, 217–218), especially those employed by the avant-garde, were also engaged by graphic designers during this period as a way of demonstrating a collective embrace of Modernism (Whitney 1980, 156). The 'visual music film' is a pervasive foundation; contemporary motion graphics have been shaped by and continue to draw from this history, even as production technology has drastically changed. This embrace of Modernist design in a highly commercial medium where business concerns determined the aesthetic forms chosen is symptomatic of the transfers between the art world and commercial world that surrounded television production in the 1950s and 1960s (Currie and Porte 1967, 16). However, following Potter's suggestions and the readily accessible programmes at *Cinema-16* in New York, early television became the primary source of direct crossover from the independent productions of artists to the corporate productions of television (Sutton 2011), visible in the initial emergence of motion graphics as 'broadcast design' (Whitney 1980, 156).

Approaches to visual music are historically limited in scope and application to particular types of musical composition and only to arrangements of visual imagery evoking a synaesthetic experience based in a correlation between the sound and either an immanent form seen on screen, or through an emergent relationship between the visible sync-points and the audible sync-points provided by the beat, musical phrasing or the performance of individual instruments (see Figure 3.1). The range of artists influenced by how 'visual music' arranges sound and image cuts across the boundaries between movements, media, and decades of time to reveal a consistent interplay of abstract form, synaesthesia, and synchronisation (Tuchman 1985).

Visual music films use synchronisation to translate the cultural/ideological meaning common to abstraction (the visualisation of a transcendent spirituality) into a physical phenomenon comparable to 'lip-sync' in its immediacy of connection between sound and image. The role of 'visual music' in the abstract films made by Walter Ruttmann, Viking Eggeling, Hans Richter and Oskar Fischinger, as well as American Mary Ellen Bute, realise synaesthesia as an

SYNCHRONIZATION OF SOUND::IMAGE

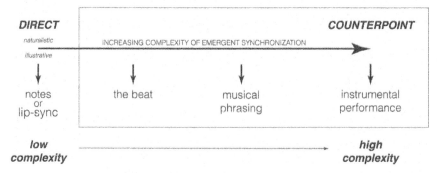

FIGURE 3.1   Synchronisation of Sound: Image. Diagram by Michael Betancourt.

immanent phenomenon, either through a direct analogy to music or by creating a counterpoint of sound and motion/editing, demonstrating visuals comparable to music. Many of their films were readily available for viewing during the formative years of motion graphic's emergence during the 1940s, either at movie theatres, or in specialised screenings. Baroness Hilla von Rebay, the first director of the *Museum of Non-Objective Painting* (later renamed the *Solomon R. Guggenheim Museum*), sponsored screenings of abstract films acquired from Hans Richter in 1940 and worked to make experimental animation generally more accessible to the public. The network of relationships between abstraction, synaesthesia and visual music reveal more than just a set of congruencies – it is a 'fine art approach' originating in the avant-garde that has been adapted for commercial use (the field of 'motion graphics' is this use). Considering this heritage illuminates the complex role and aesthetics of synaesthetic form for motion graphics – immediately apparent in how synchronisation (including music, sound effects and voiceover narration) is a definitive formal constraint. In motion graphics the visuals explicitly function as an illustration of the soundtrack.

Synchronisation links abstract forms to music, equally demonstrating and reinforcing the link between motion graphics and earlier visual music animations. The counterpoint synchronisation employed in title sequences such as the design for *The Seven Year Itch* (1955) by Saul Bass connects musical sync-points to the graphic animation/transitions between title cards. Their connections are metaphoric. The 'windows' that fold open and closed to present each credit in this design move simultaneously to musical cues provided by the score. When the audience hears a note, they see a simultaneously corresponding motion appear on-screen, creating an apparently 'natural' connection that masks the arbitrary nature of their construction. Abstraction and visual music present the ideo-cultural belief in a 'spiritual' reality made tangible-visible through a combination of visual form – whether graphic or typographic is irrelevant – creating a synaesthetic experience (Moritz 1999) where synchronisation with sound acknowledges its sources in earlier visual music animations.

Prestige via title design

When motion graphics employ music, they follow the model of visual music (Betancourt 2013) animations, linking the design directly to the score. *The Man With The Golden Arm* is a notable early example in which this synchronisation is looser, contrasting with Bass's later designs where the same formal idiom derived from International ('Swiss') Style graphic design is more precisely synchronised (Spigel 2016). The sequence runs approximately two minutes, which was the most common length for title sequences since the 1920s; his later designs have a longer running time that allows for more complex audio-visual relations and additional imagery not connected to individual credits. This sequence was Bass' first graphic animated title, composed from 16 static title cards with animated transitions. It begins clearly synchronised but gradually drifts into syncopation: The notes come slightly before or slightly after the visual sync-point in a reiteration of the syncopation common to jazz music. The syncopated drift only returns to a close synchronisation for the final animorph into a graphic arm at the conclusion of the sequence. Bass has connected his design to the film's narrative about a white Jazz musician's struggle with heroin addiction – summarised iconically by a twisted, graphic icon of an arm that is at the same time a literal visualisation of the film's title. The immediacy of connection between the imagery and the film's title is common to feature film title sequences (Betancourt 2018, 57–58). The series of white lines evoke needles, inviting an acknowledgement of the *syncopation* as the impact of intoxication and addiction. Thus the design can be understood as a literal restatement of the drama, addiction made apparent as the *in*ability of these elements to remain precisely synchronised, the animorph transforming this narrative information into the formal logo/decoration. This arm also appears prominently in the film posters and other advertising. It was the first time a post- Second World War film employed the same designs in both titles and advertising posters.

These same needles/lines also evoke Richter's first film, *Rhythmus 21*, a work crucial to the transfer between experimental animation and motion graphics. After the Second World War, Hans Richter engaged in historical revisionism, claiming his own film, *Film Ist Rhythmus* (1923, which he retitled *Rhythmus 21* and added a title card stating 'Realisé en 1921'), as the first abstract film ever produced. Showing an animation of white and grey lines, paper rectangles and squares moving against a black background, the film does not appear to have had a public screening prior to the last Paris Dada performance, the *Soirée du Cœur à Barbe* in 1923 where it appears on the programme (Elsaesser 1996, 15). The 'history' Richter contributed to the *Art in Cinema* catalogue that prioritised his work above that of Ruttmann would be repeated and expanded upon in the years following its publication, both by Richter and by other writers (Weinberg 1951). Richter helped secure this position by selling 35mm prints of his own films to both the *Museum of Modern Art* and the *Museum of Non-Objective Painting* along with a collection of works by Duchamp, Leger and Eggeling. These films enabled both institutions to promote Richter's version of history through their screening series. Museum of Non-Objective Painting Director Rebay's weekly screening of abstract animation made Richter's films both readily accessible and highly visible in New York starting in the 1940s; they would also figure prominently in Frank Stauffacher's 1946 programme *Art in Cinema* (MacDonald 2010, 3). From 1942 to 1956, Richter was the director of the Film Institute of the City College of New York, a position he used to promote his revisionist history of avant-garde and abstract film that gave his work priority (Lukach 1983). Being first meant that Richter's film was guaranteed prestige in any programme that showed it. It is precisely this elevated status that his revisionist history was intended to produce, and the impact of this prestige function is readily apparent in Bass's design-animation for *The Man With The Golden Arm*, which emulates the first abstract film.

The pioneer of Modernist broadcast design, William Golden, was appointed Creative Director of Advertising and Sales Promotion in 1951, making him the designer and art director responsible for CBS's print and on-air designs from their head office in New York. He was also responsible for the Modernist transformation of broadcasting that began immediately with his assumption of the role in 1951. His view that design was not art, but a specific variety of craft, is apparent in the organisation of a small department of 39 employees that embraced innovation and functioned autonomously within the corporate structure of CBS (Spigel 2008). Golden explained his views at the Aspen Design conference in 1959:

> Once he stops confusing Art with design for Business and stops making demands on the business world that it has neither the capacity nor obligation to fulfill, [the designer will] probably be all right. In fact I think he is pretty lucky. In the brave new world of Strontium-90 – a world in which craftsmanship is an intolerable deterrent to mass production – it is a good thing to be able to practice a useful craft.
>
> *(Golden 1962, 63)*

Golden used Modernist design to promote CBS as the 'prestige' TV network (Stanton 1962, 9). This connection of prestige to Modernism explains the design choice for Saul Bass' poster and title sequence designs for *The Man With The Golden Arm*. Unlike TV, feature films were already being accorded a high degree of respect and significance. The simple, graphic imagery of this design led to an association of the white line as a *signifier* of modernity embraced by broadcasting in particular: The titles for TV shows such as *The Twilight Zone* (1959), *Boris Karloff's Thriller* (1959), *Bus Stop* (1961) *The Outer Limits* (1961), *Mission Impossible* (1964), *The Time Tunnel* (1967), and *The Brady Bunch* (1969) repeat this singular element in spite of their otherwise divergent contents. Across all these cultural shifts and aesthetic changes, the role of title sequences as signifiers of prestige that orchestrate audio-visual materials in counterpoint to their credit-texts is consistent.

The reappearance of these white lines in TV title sequences is a reflection of the prestige function of Modernism that Walt Disney described in 1961. It is also an ongoing reassertion of motion graphic's foundations in experimental animation. Throughout the 1960s, the 'designer' (i.e., Modernist) title sequence remained a signifier for serious, important cultural production. The presence of this graphic element in these TV title designs is almost illogical – it has only a limited role in their construction (it is not integral to them so much as precisely a transitional element deployed within them) – and its function shifts, depending on the sequence that employs it: As a door edge seen in *The Twilight Zone*, or the 'fuse' of *Mission Impossible* that runs through the entire montage sequence, or as a visual pause before becoming typography (*Time Tunnel*) or boxed portraits (*The Brady Bunch*) – transforming its role for each specific design. Its reappearance throughout this period as a graphic quotation-reference signifies the Modernity of the programme that follows. These references create a succession of attribution and borrowed significance that began with Bass's quotation of Richter's film in *The Man With The Golden Arm*. The appearance of the white line as an icon of Modernity in television programs during the 1950s and 1960s reveals their *aspirational* character: That TV aspires to the cultural significance and respect accorded to serious art – thus the adoption and use of avant-garde techniques in 'avant-pop' not only makes sense, it shows these aspirations in action.

Contemporary quotations

Within contemporary motion graphic design, these quotations of earlier animation and visual music films have remained an implicit dimension of their sound-image synchronisation. This emergence of an intertextual and explicitly quotational commercial/popular media coincides with the same trends of convergence between popular culture and the avant-garde apparent in McCafferty's term 'avant-pop' itself. Semiotician Umberto Eco recognised that those approaches to repetition and quotation that once were almost exclusively the domain of the avant-garde have become a commonplace part of media (Eco 1994, 96). The relationship between immanence and memory – or novelty and schema (Eco 1994, 96) – is a domain of concern specific to semiotics and how it has been applied to the analysis of storytelling. However, some contemporary designs engage with this history of visual music and experimental animation more-or-less explicitly, producing designs that invite contemporary audiences to draw on their encyclopedic knowledge of both motion graphics and abstract film. These designs engage with their historical sources in ways that recall Eco's comments in 'Interpreting Serials' about the role of quotation in contemporary media:

> Aware of the quotation, the spectator is brought to elaborate ironically on the nature of such a device and to acknowledge the fact that one has been invited to play upon one's encyclopedic competence.
>
> *(Eco 1994, 89)*

Unlike 'independent' design, this type of intertextual work anticipates the audience's recognition of its quotational basis. This 'post-modern aesthetic solution' depends on the audience being aware of both the source of the quotation and how the new context transforms it. These intertextual works necessarily divide the audience into those members who recognise and understand the references and those who do not. Only the audience members who identify the source engage with the serial aspects of the design. The role of quotation in Eco's 'serial form' is an inherent part of his theory: All serials by nature must be quotational to be serial, but it must also be identified – recognised – by the audience. His theory of 'serial form' directs attention to how the audience apprehends the work, for instance *which* intertextual references and quotations they identify and understand. His conception of the audience is as an actively engaged interrogator of what it encounters, anticipating and evaluating the 'serial' work as it progresses. Starting with *The Man With The Golden Arm* and continuing into contemporary title designs, this intertextual dimension unites the commercial and non-commercial aspects of the visual music tradition. For knowing audiences, the explicit quotation in the design is precisely what makes the work interesting. It is also in these designs that the relationship to both experimental animation and the abstract, visual music film becomes evident. In making their quotational references apparent, such designs reveal the formative role that avant-garde animations have played in the formulation of motion graphics as a discipline.

The intertextual references to historical visual music films in title sequences such as *Ça Ce Soigne? (Is It Treatable?* 2008) and *Scott Pilgrim vs. The World* (2010) complicate interpretations of their counterpoint synchronisations, transforming the focus of these designs from immanent perception to memory. They challenge the subordinate role of title sequences by shifting meaning from the immediacy of both paratext and the audiovisual connection to other, parallel meanings evoked through the recognition of historical references via quotation that directs the audience to consider influences and content from their established knowledge. The audience's recognition of earlier films being reiterated or otherwise evoked by contemporary designs directs their attention away from the immanent work to a consideration of its place within this larger history; this historical mediation is explicit for some artist-designers such as Ron Hays. It is worth remembering that some of these historical films, notably those of Walter Ruttmann and Oskar Fischinger in Germany, Len Lye in Britain and Mary Ellen Bute in the United States were produced for and exhibited in commercial movie theatres either as short subjects in their own right, or as hybrid entertainment-advertisements. Their avant-garde and experimental aspects do not circumscribe their equally important connections to the commercial enterprise of motion pictures, a relationship that continues with contemporary motion graphics.

The one minute, forty-five second title sequence of the French comedy *Ça Ce Soigne?* was designed by Julien Baret at Deubal, the French motion graphics studio founded by Stéphanie Lelong and Olivier Marquézy. It begins with the sound of an orchestra 'tuning up' paired with an animation of red squares arranged in a semi-circle. Their motion suggests they represent people finding their seats before a performance. As the music starts, a series of white lines appear on-screen. This initial opening is *not* an example of counterpoint: For each note played, a white line appears in an arc on-screen – an instance of direct synchronisation: for each note played, a line moves in unison. This opening presents an immediate assertion of 'visual music'. These white lines are a visual quotation from the start of the Bach sequence in Walt Disney's 1940 feature *Fantasia*, rather than a reference to *The Man With The Golden Arm*. This intertextual quotation from the Disney film gives *Ça Ce Soigne?* a second level of meaning parallel to its use of the traditions of visual music. The shift this recognition entails challenges the directness of its audio-visual synchronisation by drawing attention away from the immanent work and into a reverie prompted by identifying the quotations. Because the intertextual relationship is explicit (i.e., audience recognition of quotations that blatantly play on intertextuality can be anticipated), the result draws attention to itself, rendering the title sequence for *Ça Ce Soigne?* as a work of visual music *about* visual music. This quotational intertextuality redoubles the already referential dimensions of title design generally, a link that brings the aesthetics of the design itself into consideration quite apart from whatever narrative connections it might have to the story that follows.

Intertextuality in both designs depends on its audience specifically recognising and understanding an alternative, counter-interpretation submerged within the design – its interpretation proceeds through memory, necessitating a distancing from the immanent event to apprehend its organisation as not an original invention, but a novel transformation of an established and already-known form. This role for memory and past experience in recognising counterpoint synchronisation in *Ça Ce Soigne?* explicitly becomes a part of its design and formal organisation as visual music. Intertextual references are an excess in the literal sense; it is an addition that directs attention outwards, away from the narrative linkages that define titles as a paratext, challenging this subordination by drawing audience attention towards the (absent) sources. This title sequence begins with simple geometric shapes – red squares – arranged in a semi-circle; however the movement of these shapes suggests an audience taking their seats, awaiting a performance. Meanwhile an orchestra 'tunes up' on the soundtrack. When the music begins with white lines synchronised to notes and progresses into geometric patterns and jagged, rhythmic lines, these abstract forms become progressively more representational – pills, crying eyes, a heart monitor and skull formed from abstracted tears – while retaining their abstract appearance. The film's narrative about a hypochondriac determines the representational character of the animated elements synchronised with the music. An entirely graphic animation, the 'graphics' shift between recognition – as pills, drops of blood the jagged plot of a heart monitor – and kinetic abstraction as the visual counterpoint to Camille Saint-Saëns' composition *Danse Macabre* (1874). In visualising this relationship to the narrative, the various 'abstract' forms in the title sequence become representational. These images move between abstraction and representation, all evoking the film's title – 'is it treatable?' – through their connection to medicine and medical treatment. The doubling that intertextuality poses within the title sequence expands the recognitions specific to counterpoint synchronisation beyond the typical dynamic that arises between the title sequence and the narrative that follows it. The intertextual references to *Fantasia* link this opening to visual music, but these references are not limited to the opening of the sequence. As it progresses, other quotations to the jagged and angular animations in Bute's film *Tarantella* (1940) – music that makes its own reference to the dance that supposedly could cure the 'deadly bite of the tarantula' – provide an additional level of commentary that suggests the entire narrative about a depressed symphony conductor who may merely be suffering from hypochondria.

A similar play of quotation and design informs Richard Kenworthy's title sequence design for *Scott Pilgrim vs. The World* (2010). It contains the same play of intertextual quotation from the history of experimental animation that appears in *Ça Ce Soigne?*. As Eco notes, the audience's past experience determines meaning. This division of audiences into witting and unwitting enables the title sequence to become an indicator of the film's importance (prestige), not simply through *who* the designer is, but as a formal part of the design itself. This intertextual approach is particular to title designs produced since the 1990s, a reflection of Eco's recognition that as serial form becomes the dominant approach to intertextuality and design, it challenges the paratextual relationship of title sequence to narrative by rendering the titles formally and conceptually distinct from their attachment to the primary text. The history of abstract, avant-garde and experimental animation is crucial to the consideration and interpretation-recognition of these title sequences.

Because *Scott Pilgrim vs. The World* imitates the appearance of traditional 'direct animation' – painting, scratching and drawing directly onto celluloid to create imagery on the filmstrip without using photography – its intertextuality is both formal and visual. This technique, (in use since the Futurists Bruno Corra and his brother Arnaldo Ginna (2001, 66–67) created their first films in 1909, discussing them in the manifesto 'Abstract Cinema—Chromatic Music') has a close association with the historical avant-garde. Both Len Lye and Norman McLaren worked extensively with this technique, and their films provide a referent for the digital animation in Kenworthy's design. The aesthetics of 'direct animation' strikingly contrasts with the sharp vector graphics embedded throughout *Scott Pilgrim vs. The World*. Even though the film's visual design exhibits a wide range of animated typographies and graphics resembling comic books and video games, the title sequence retains a distinct character that is not repeated elsewhere. Its organisation evokes a kinetic play of graffiti and urban scrawls rather than the kinetic abstraction it quotes. Counterpoint synchronisation separates these animated graphics from the other narrative graphics. Flat and highly saturated, they are also gritty and scratched – their irregularity betrays their origins in handwork done directly on physical material.

This second level of meaning – in excess to those references in the design that are proximately concerned with the narrative (the paratextual functions of the title sequence) – opens its interpretation beyond the confines of its pseudo-independence. No longer a subordinate design, the interpretation of these openings proceeds without concern for linkages between title design and the film it 'opens'. The 'reward' for doing so is the establishment of the title as an *independent* entity, effectively separate from the narrative that follows, which is the *raison d'être* for the titles as such.

In being appended to the narrative, the title sequence functions as a synecdoche that requires the decoding made possible only through the narrative as such. The intertextual quotation adds to this displacement a second level hidden from the narrative interpretation that changes the title sequence into a mediator between the proximate encounter with the motion picture and the cultural foundations of its production. By introducing this anteriority into the design, the quotations that organise and inform both *Ça Ce Soigne?* and *Scott Pilgrim vs. The World* demand that the ideological content manifested through synchronisation no longer remain invisible. The same artifact character provided by using known, already-established music (Camille Saint-Saëns' *Danse Macabre*) must be extended to the animation, and potentially even the narrative itself. The audience's recognition of familiar music (even when the composer and title remain unknown) always has this intertextual quality – *déjà entendu* – that finds its analogue in *visual* intertextuality.

Commercialisation: Synaesthesia and realism

The same process of rendering visible an unseen, transcendent 'reality' that is particular to the visual music tradition organises the synchronisation of motion graphics even when they are not immediately or obviously abstract: Synchronisation that illustrates sound creates the same analogy of sound-to-image as the realist approach of naturalistic 'lip-sync' in motion pictures. As historian Christopher Williams notes in the introduction to his study of realist theories in cinema, *realism* tends to disappear into arguments about what is 'real' rather than remain concerned with the aesthetic form – *mimesis* – it describes, creating an explicit parallel between a realism of surface appearance and a 'deeper realism' normally obscured. He writes:

> The debate about realism can perhaps best be grasped through the opposition between 'mere appearances,' meaning the reality of things as we perceive them in daily life and experience, and 'true reality,' meaning an essential truth, one which we cannot normally see or perceive, but which, in Hegel's phrase is 'born of the mind.'
>
> *(Williams 1980, 11)*

Cinema has the capacity to efface the distinctions Williams describes. Visual music may not resemble the world of visible objects and events at all. Their interpretation as exemplars of a 'mental reality' brings even the most abstract animations within the domain of a realism 'born of the mind' – visual music makes the same metaphysical claims as abstract art generally. This audio-visual organisation is definitional for visual music and remains common in motion graphics. It is a 'more true' depiction than those dependent on 'natural' linkages such as 'lip-sync' to create an appearance of the everyday phenomenal world. In place of reproducing the audience's everyday phenomenal encounter, visual music uses synchronisation to demonstrate the 'reality' of an unseen, spiritual world otherwise invisible to our senses. This excess of metaphysical meaning is the visual music heritage in both *Ça Ce Soigne?* and *Scott Pilgrim vs. The World*. The shift from the invocation of a phenomenal encounter to one constructed from ideological belief can be subtle: The fundamental links between synchronisation and realism are constants for commercial production, even when these connections are as simple as the alignment of spoken and written language. This transformation, an equally direct and automatic linkage as naturalistic synchronisation, returns the audible to the realm of signs, assigning particular meaning otherwise absent *outside* the motion picture.

From the very start of Kyle Cooper's title sequence for *Wimbledon* (2004), synchronisation connects sound to typography, evoking naturalistic connection of sound to image comparable to 'lip-sync'. However, although the sound of a tennis ball being hit with a racket has been synchronised to each credit's appearance, it is an artificial relationship that creates a prosaic example of *synaesthetic* form: Typography does not make noise. The addition of live action shots later in the sequence depend on audience expectations to integrate this sound into the narrative space – to become a 'diegetic' element requires a recognition of what the sound in the visible space might be – the title sequence doesn't show a tennis match being played. The shots focus on the spectators, judge and press – but the *sound of playing the game* is clearly heard. The editing and motion in each shot replaces the game with the text of the titles, a substitution that associates the subject of the film (the tennis Championships at Wimbledon) with the formal design of the credits.

Only the audience's past experiences and knowledge can make this arrangement of typography-sound presented in the design coherent: This 'more true' depiction is the audience and other spectacle surrounding the tennis matches at the Wimbledon competition. It is an example of a realism 'born of the mind', shown by the association of hit ball with credit where the text on screen replaces the tennis match as the audience's focus. *What is going on* – a 'simple' question – requires a complex answer that originates with established knowledge of the world that is invoked in the statement through the film title, 'WIMBLEDON', the distinctive sound of the tennis ball being hit in the tennis match itself and the various views of the surroundings of those games. This apparent 'realism' is an illusion, one that is assembled from fragments that are themselves partial, requiring established knowledge to interpret. That the audience makes these connections fluidly and without pause is what renders them 'natural'. In the live action footage in the *Wimbledon* title sequence, connecting the sound to image is superficially direct – understanding the tennis match as a public spectacle requires a recognition of what is happening; it uses the mimetic identification of the sound to link the actions that are shown in the titles to the tennis match that is *not* shown. This convergence of abstract form with a realist meaning is a recurring aspect of how experimental animation has been transformed (Betancourt 2016) by the 'avant-pop' approach to become commercial entertainment. Motion graphics especially reveal this heritage in its consistent assertion of representational meanings for abstract graphics, as in the various needles in *The Man With The Golden Arm*, genetics in *X-Men: First Class*, orchestra and medical imagery of *Ça Ce Soigne?* and the transformation of direct animation into kinetic graffiti in *Scott Pilgrim vs. The World*.

Conclusion

Like experimental animation, motion graphics occupy a marginal position in relation to other histories of motion pictures – the important designers such as Saul Bass are rarely mentioned except in passing. Experimental animation and avant-garde film provide the historical sources for contemporary motion graphics, both in terms of morphology and as structural guides for the synchronisation of sound and image. At the same time, this commercialisation asserts the familiar dimensions of what was challenging – avant-garde images and techniques – making them familiar, mundane. This transformation of difficult, alienated Modernist imagery is as true of the white line-needles of Bass' *The Man With The Golden Arm* as of the spirals in Clowes' *X-Men: First Class*. It is a fundamental shift of meaning that unites these changes from experimental into commercial across the history of motion graphics as a field. This 'normalisation' is a distinguishing feature of McCafferty's 'avant-pop', separating motion graphics from the historical avant-garde. The changed meaning of abstraction as a diagrammatic representation is thus a typical effect of the convergence with commercial production that neutralises the disruptive aspects of its experimental sources by subordinating their effect to the narrative demands of the film to which these otherwise potentially challenging designs are appended.

The pseudo-independence that intertextuality offers the title sequence enables the design to be simultaneously *of* the main narrative *and* distinct from it, a parallel construction with its own internal structure, themes and formal appearance. The acknowledgement of the visual music tradition in these designs brings their formal origins into consideration. By directing attention to the title design as a self-contained entity, this shift insists on an additional level of autonomous signification for both the title sequence and motion graphics more generally. The metaphorical connection of title design to the film it introduces rhetorically masks this pseudo-independence, while for instance the context of Kenworthy's design announces it as belonging to a separate realm than the narrative. Music anticipates narrative. As with Saul Bass's quotation-reference to Richter's film *Rhythmus 21 (Film ist Rhythmus)* in *The Man with the Golden Arm*, the quotations apparent in *Ça Ce Soigne?* or *Scott Pilgrim vs. The World* provide intertextual associations that inform the interpretation of the film/title through these historical references, thus demonstrating the crucial (formative) mediation of experimental animation.

Notes

1 The designation of the German abstract and visual music animations as 'absolute films' began with the filmmakers themselves. The Novembergruppe exhibition of May 3, 1925 (a program which included Ruttmann, Richter and Eggeling's films) was titled 'Der Absolute Film'.

2 There are multiple sources for this history. See Tuchman, M. *The Spiritual in Art: Abstract Painting 1890–1985* (New York: Abbeville Press, 1985) or Brougher, K. *Visual Music: Synaesthesia in Art and Music Since 1900* (New York: Thames & Hudson, 2005).

References

Allen, Irwin. *The Time Tunnel*. US, 1966–1967. Television series

Armstrong, Samuel, James Algar, Bill Roberts, Paul Satterfield, Ben Sharpsteen, David D. Hand, Hamilton Luske, Jim Handley, Ford Beebe, T. Hee, Norman Ferguson, Wilfred Jackson. *Fantasia*. US, 1940. Film.

Betancourt, M. *Beyond Spatial Montage: Windowing, or the Cinematic Displacement of Time, Motion, and Space*. New York: Routledge, 2016.

Betancourt, M. *The History of Motion Graphics: From Avant-Garde to Industry in the United States*. Rockville: Wildside Press, 2013.

Betancourt, M. *Title Sequences as Paratexts: Narrative Anticipation and Recapitulation*. New York: Routledge, 2018, 57–58.

Brougher, K. *Visual Music: Synaesthesia in Art and Music Since 1900* .New York: Thames & Hudson, 2005.

Bute, Mary Ellen. *Tarantella*. US, 1940. Film

_____. *Abstronic*. US, 1952. Film.

Chouchan, Laurent. *Ça Ce Soigne? (Is It Treatable?)*. France, 2008. Film.

Corra, B. 'Abstract Cinema – Chromatic Music.' In *Futurist manifestos*. New York: Art works, 2001.

Currie, H. and Porte, M., eds. *Cinema Now*. Cincinnati: University of Cincinnati Perspectives on American Underground Film, 1967.

Disney, W. 'Adventure Land: The Title Makers.' *Walt Disney Presents*, broadcast on ABC, 11 June, 1961.

Eco, U. 'Interpreting Serials'. In *The Limits of Interpretation*. Bloomington: University of Indiana Press, 1994.

Elsaesser, Thomas. 'Dada Cinema?' In *Dada and Surrealist Film*. Edited by Rudolf E. Kuenzli, Cambridge: MIT Press, 1996.

Folkart, B. 'Ron Hays; Multimedia Conceptualist.' *LA Times*, 19 April 1991.

Geller, Bruce. *Mission Impossible*. US, 1966–1973. Television series.

Golden, William. *The Visual Craft of William Golden*. New York: George Braziller, 1962.

Hays, R. *Report of Activities: June 1972 through January 1974*, grant report to the Rockefeller Foundation and National Endowment for the Arts, 1974.

Hays, Ron. *Space for Head and Hands*. US, 1975. Film.

Hitchcock, Alfred. *Vertigo*. US, 1958. Film.

Huggins, Roy. *Bus Stop*. US, 1961–1962. Television series.

Jacobs, L. 'Experimental Cinema in America 1921–1947.' In *The Rise of the American Film*. New York: Teacher's College Press, 1975.

Loncraine, Richard. *Wimbledon*. UK/US, 2004. Film.

Lukach, J. *Hilla Rebay: In Search of the Spirit in Art*. New York: George Braziller, 1983.

MacDonald, S. *Art in Cinema: Documents Towards a History of the Film Society*. Philadelphia: Temple University Press, 2010.

McCafferty, L. *After Yesterday's Crash: The Avant-Pop Anthology*. New York: Penguin, 1995.

Moritz, W. 'Jordan Belson: Last of the Great Masters.' *Animation Journal* 7, no. 2 (1999): 4–16.

'Pacific Title & Art Studio to be liquidated.' *Variety*, 8 June, 2009, accessed 7 July, 2017. http://variety.com/2009/digital/markets-festivals/pacific-title-art-studio-to-be-liquidated-1118004696/

Potter, R. 'New Scientific Tools for the Arts.' *The Journal of Aesthetics and Art Criticism 10*, no. 2 (December 1951): 121–134.

Potter, R. 'Sources of Stimulus: TV Commercials Often Draw on Avant-Garde Films.' *Art Direction 13*, no. 9 (December 1961): 63.

Preminger, Otto. *The Man With The Golden Arm*. US, 1955. Film.

Richter, Hans. *Rhythmus 21* (aka *Film ist Rhythmus*). Germany, 1921. Film.

_____. *Film Ist Rhythmus*. Germany, 1923. Film.

Robinson, Hubbell. *Thriller*. US, 1960–1962. Television series.

Sandhaus, L. *Earthquakes, Mudslides, Fires & Riots: California & Graphic Design 1936–1986*. New York: Metropolis Books, 2014, 158.

Saint-Saëns, Camille. *Danse Macabre*. 1874.

Schwartz, Sherwood. *The Brady Bunch*. US, 1969–1975. Television series.

Serling, Rod. *The Twilight Zone*. US, 1959–1964. Television series.

Spigel, L. 'Back to the Drawing Board: Graphic design and the Visual Environment of Television at Midcentury. *Cinema Journal 55*, no. 4 (Summer 2016): 28–54.

Spigel, L., *TV by Design: Modern Art and the Rise of Network Television*. (Chicago: University of Chicago Press, 2008.

Stanton, F. 'Introduction.' In *The Visual Craft of William Golden*. New York: George Braziller, 1962, 9.

Sutton, G. 'Stan VanDerBeek: Collage Experience.' In *Stan VanDerBeek The Culture Intercom*. Houston: Contemporary Arts Museum Houston/MIT List Visual Arts Center, 2011, 78–87.

Stevens, Leslie. *The Outer Limits*. US, 1963–1965. Television series.

Tuchman, M. *The Spiritual in Art: Abstract Painting 1890–1985*. New York: Abbeville Press, 1985.

Vaughn, Matthew. *X-Men: First Class*. US/UK, 2011. Film

Weinberg, H. '30 Years of Experimental Film: Hans Richter Has Never Doubted the Validity of Pure Experiment.' *Films in Review 11*, no. 10 (December 1951).

White, Maurice and Wayne Vaughn. 'Let's Groove'. New York: Columbia Records, 1981. Song.

Whitney, J. *Digital Harmony: On the Complementarity of Music and Visual Art*. Peterborough: Byte Books, 1980.

Wilder, Billy. *The Seven Year Itch*. US, 1955. Film.

Williams, C. *Realism and the Cinema: A Reader*. London: Routledge, 1980.

Wright, Edgar. *Scott Pilgrim vs. the World*. US/UK/Canada/Japan, 2010. Film.

PART II
Interviews A

A1

GEORGES SCHWIZGEBEL

Switzerland

Please give us a brief summary of your work, including, if possible, a description of your creative process (e.g., how your creative ideas first appear and take shape).

I live in Geneva, not far from Annecy and its festival where early on I had the opportunity to see inventive short films that could not be found anywhere else. After a year at the School of Fine Arts and four years at the School of Decorative Arts in Geneva, I finished my training as a graphic designer, a trade that I practiced for five years in an advertising agency. Claude Luyet, Daniel Suter and I founded GDS Studio in 1970 with the intention of becoming independent directors of short animated films. I have been practicing this trade full time since the eighties. Like most people of my generation, I am self-taught because there was no animation school at that time. I always liked drawing and also mathematics, that's probably why I chose to make animated films, as it allows me both to draw and to solve technical problems.

I am also very interested in the relationship between rhythm in music (tempo, number of beats per minute) and the rhythm of movements in the animation depending on the number 24 (frames per second), a number that divides in many ways. Movement is primordial in the cartoon. Among my sources of inspiration, it is often music that makes me want to make a film or develop a visual idea and sometimes to tell a story. In an ideal film there should be these three motives combined.

The ideas come while I'm working, and it's difficult at the beginning, then a certain logic is established and, slowly, it is almost the film that indicates the procedure to follow. It is for this reason that I work alone and thus can have the freedom to more easily transform the film as I go along. I spend a lot of time developing line-tests, not just to test a movement but especially to have an overview of the film. In fact, all the editing of the film takes place at this stage, and then I start animating, making the drawings or, most often, paintings. So, the assembly is done before the drawings and shooting. Then there is no longer a lot of modification possible; the camera movements (drawn movements) or the metamorphoses must be planned in advance and form a whole that will become the film.

How would you define your animation practice in terms of its relation to fine art traditions, experimental animation or the (historical) avant-garde? Its relation to commercial industry?

I try to follow the logic of a dream, that is, avoiding interruptions, moving from one plane to another without cutting. My films are often a long (or short) planned sequence. One can define my films as animated painting that deals with poetry. I have not yet used dialogue in my films so as to not make the audience read subtitles and lose part of what happens in the image, and so that it remains a means of international communication.

Who/what are your strongest influences?

I very much admire Norman McLaren who searched in all directions and produced a considerable number of masterpieces, and I also love Jerzy Kucia's films. I should also mention Walerian Borowczyk, Yoji Kuri, Yuri Norstein, Zbigniew Rybczynski and Caroline Leaf. Among recent artists, Igor Kovalyov is my favorite.

Why animation?

The animation short allows us to say a lot in a short time, and for my part I seek to make spectators' imaginations work rather than to deliver a message to them.

Is material or media a particularly important component of your practice? How does it operate in your work?

I work in a traditional way with endangered material, and I need assistance for post-production because I have very poor computer skills.

Is there something you want to articulate with your work that can't be expressed through conventional narrative means?

It seems to me that I use a very classic technique, the cartoon and what maybe is not conventional is that there are no 'characters' and sometimes 'no story'. The aim is to express myself with drawing, movement and sound only. These are constraints that I like to fix while trying to overcome them. In addition to the relationship between image and music, I am particularly interested in metamorphoses, loops (cycles) and movements in space. I continue to be interested in these forms that were specific to the animated film before the arrival of the digital and all its possibilities.

A2
ROSE BOND

Canada/USA

Please give us a brief summary of your work, including, if possible, a description of your creative process (e.g., how your creative ideas first appear and take shape).

My roots are in frame-by-frame, hand drawn and direct animation, while my current work focuses on large scale, site-based animated installations. The installations are content driven and rear projected in windows. They effectively emanate from multiple windows and co-exist with architecture. Drawing themes from the site – the works often exist as monuments to the unremembered. This work is a form of expanded cinema, viewed from the streets, that breaks from the traditional screen and blurs distinctions between public and private.

How would you define your animation practice in terms of its relation to fine art traditions, experimental animation or the (historical) avant-garde? Its relation to commercial industry?

My work falls within a fine art practice, and the projects are grant funded. The form and structure of a project emerges after a period of research and collection. I believe the sketchy storyboards I dash off are my most creative act. The design of my storyboard changes to fit the configuration of windows in my architectural projections. In a way, the installations seem like public processions staged to engage the strata of community. Through timed evocations I orchestrate and reveal layers of story and accretions of memory tied to a place.

Who/what are your strongest influences?

My early films (*Gaia's Dream* (1982) and *Nexus* (1984)) were influenced by Caroline Leaf and Norman McLaren – full of morphing and a black line that streams along consciousness. The Celtic films (*Macha's Curse* (1990) and *Deirdre's Choice* (1995)) were shaped by a study of Sergei Eisenstein.

My installations find inspiration in the projections of Krzysztof Wodiczko and Shimon Attie. They are also heavily influenced by my riding the bus as a kid.

Why animation?

I have a drawing background, and though I didn't really care for cartoons as a child, once I'd seen Caroline Leaf's *The Owl Who Married a Goose* (1974) – literally a moving sand painting – I realised all my drawings were part of sequence. I have a mind that visualises sequences and have developed an ability to place frames around daydreams and transcribe them to paper. Animation gives one the latitude to colour events, to add layers of meaning and to approach the unrepresentable in the gaps.

Is material or media a particularly important component of your practice? How does it operate in your work?

A sense of touch – and the presence of a hand are important to my work. I liked the dynamism of my direct cameraless animation where every pixel is different – alive. They seem like handwritten letters in an age of email. Now, I continue to gladly forsake the index of live action for the haptic imprint of my Blackwing pencil on Canson tracing paper.

For projection – lumens, contrast radio, lenses – all the tech considerations for conditions outside the traditional cinema screening – ambient light, the time of dusk, street noise, dirty windows – all have importance. After Effects is the workhorse – the place where it all comes together.

How do you see your work operating culturally and politically?

For the past 15 years my artistic practice, and its accompanying research, has explored multi-screen animated projections that cohabit with architecture and function as street-viewed cinema. This work is content driven yet fragmentary. I'm particularly interested in picturing voices that have been missing or poorly represented by cliché. I'm also interested in complicating my relationship with the material.

In 1970 Gene Youngblood published his seminal text *Expanded Cinema* where he contends that expanded cinema 'challenged the existing notions of cinema as a commercialised regime of passive consumption and entertainment' (quoted in Rees 2011, 13). In that book's chapter entitled 'The Artist as Ecologist' (1970, 348), Youngblood writes of artists trending towards the role of ecologist: One who deals with relationships among organisms and the environment – 'the act of creation for the new artist is not so much the invention of new objects as the revelation of previously unrecognised relationships between existing phenomena, both physical and metaphysical' (ibid., 346).

My work seems political in a neighbourhood way. Many of the installations are tied to a place. *Illumination No 1* (2002) was sited in Portland's Old Town – the name itself a euphemistic attempt to rebrand what was long called the city's Skid Row and, prior to that, the unnamed zone where people of colour could live in Portland. The woman who headed the non-profit Old Town History project contacted me about creating a piece for her organisation and the neighbourhood. She was concerned that the political/economic powers were intent on 'Disneyfying' Old Town into a scripted narrative centred on white shanghaied sailors and would erase its multicultural past and the working-class men and later the families who made the neighbourhood home.

The Aids Quilt was a major inspiration for me. When I saw the t-shirt that my co-worker and friend Jerry had worn almost every day, I felt its authenticity – the stuff of a gay man's life affixed on fabric – and was deeply moved by the feeling of presence. For the *Illumination No 1* project, I was provided with a foundational piece of research, a student paper citing the city's recorded history of the building and its tenants. With a listing of the names of various businesses and census info, I folded in stories from oral history walks with elders, signatures of the original founders and silhouettes animated from archived newspaper photos – layering, naming and bringing to light the unremembered.

In August 2009 I was invited to explore potential sites for an animated installation that would open the Animated Exeter film festival. Every site-based project takes me out of my familiar zone. Realising that I don't know what is going on – don't know what is important, what is hidden – opens me to an ecological approach in my research. What results is a gathering process – a gleaning of fragments, bits that stick and are interwoven, layered – suggestive of several points of view but, lacking dialogue or linear storytelling, remaining dependent on a viewer for interpretation. The theme for what became *Broadsided!* (2010) was justice – in particular British justice. On one hand the power and promise of a law of precedent and representation, and on the other, roll sheets of the hanged that tipped inexorably towards the incarceration and execution of people from the lower class.

A note on *IntraMuros* (2011) and queering

IntraMuros was commissioned for the Platform International Animation Festival in 2007. I modelled the iconic and primarily faceless character on myself, my movements and relationship with animating. I haven't given this much thought – but gender breaking was a part of that.

References

Bond, Rose. *Gaia's Dream*. US, 1982. Film.
_____. *Nexus*. US, 1984. Film.
_____. *Macha's Curse*. US, 1990. Film.
_____. *Deirdre's Choice*. US, 1995. Film.
_____. *Illumination No 1*. US, 2002. Installation.
_____. *Broadsided!* UK, 2010. Installation.

_____. *IntraMuros*. US, 2011. Installation.

Leaf, Caroline. *The Owl Who Married a Goose*. Canada, 1974. Film.

Rees, A.L. 'Expanded Cinema and Narrative: A Troubled History.' In *Expanded Cinema: Art, Performance, Film*. Tate: London, 2011, 13.

Youngblood, Gene. Introduction to *Expanded Cinema*. Written by R. Buckminster Fuller. London: Studio Vista, 1970.

A3

WILLIAM KENTRIDGE

South Africa

Please give us a brief summary of your work, including, if possible, a description of your creative process (e.g., how your creative ideas first appear and take shape).

I work as an artist making drawings. Sometimes those drawings are erased and continued in front of the camera and become an animated film, sometimes these animated films are used as backdrops in theatrical performances and become a kind of animated scenography.

I never ever make a script or a storyboard. The day I decide I want to start making a film, the first footage will go through the camera. The main series of charcoal animated films I made were first shot in 16mm film. Up until now they have been shot on 35mm film, but since there is no longer film to be bought in South Africa, nor a laboratory to process them, I suspect the next one will be shot digitally.

I start with one or two images or ideas, and because the filmmaking with the animation obviously takes many months, there's a lot of time during the drawing of the first sequences to think about associated images that could come in front or behind them, and the story gradually constructs itself, both in the drawing process and as the process continues with the editing. So, from the second month, say, after eight months, I'd be working both with an editor and a composer, trying to tease out what the film could become.

How would you define your animation practice in terms of its relation to fine art traditions, experimental animation or the (historical) avant-garde? Its relation to commercial industry?

I came to animation as an artist, although if I look back, the first animated films I made were when I was 13 or 14 just with a Super 8mm camera. The success of drawings on thin tracing paper photographed, and working with pixillation of people moving in front of the camera in the studio. But the essential work I've done which is the charcoal animation, came out of the fine art work which was coming out of the charcoal drawings. It was not a technique I developed for animation, the animation simply became an extension of the recording of the process of making a drawing.

Seeing [Norman] McLaren's animation when I was about 15 years old was for me a huge revelation. It showed that one could make animated films not only in the style of Disney or Tex Avery with traditional cel animation.

Who/what are your strongest influences?

Well, McLaren opened the door. But then I suppose Dziga Vertov and *Man with a Movie Camera* (1929) would be the single most important film.

Why animation?

I think that temperamentally, I'm bad at commitment. And there is with animation a provisionality built in. Every frame is only there for the 25th of a second. Any mistake can be rectified, everything can always be rescued, there's always a possibility of redemption. But it's also a question of either seeing the world as a fact or seeing the world as a process.

Is material or media a particularly important component of your practice? How does it operate in your work?

The material and medium are obviously vital. I've done a lot of animation with charcoal, and a lot of animation with torn bits of paper, simple jointed paper puppets and some work with pixillation.

Is there something you want to articulate with your work that can't be expressed through conventional narrative means?

Well I think it's not so much there's stuff I want to express which can't be done with narrative means, it's just that I'm not able to write a narrative film – to write a script or storyboard and work from there. The ideas that I have to write in advance are always much less interesting than the ideas that emerge in the process of making the film.

How do you see your work operating culturally and politically?

I think the way I see all art operating is a demonstration of how we make sense of the world. And that processes that are very obvious in the studio, the artificiality of the meanings that we make, the invitation of the audience to be agents in the construction of meaning are things which are normally invisible in the world, but the same processes apply. Taking fragments from the world, rearranging it and emerging with a possible constructed sense of it.

Reference

Vertov, Dziga. *Man with a Movie Camera*. Russia, 1929. Film.

A4

ROBERT SOWA

Poland

Please give us a brief summary of your work, including, if possible, a description of your creative process (e.g., how your creative ideas first appear and take shape).

I make a lot of notes and sketches. Notes are a quick means for capturing my stream of consciousness. I feel a bit like a 'thought collector'. This is the starting point in the process of creating a film, and then I try to find a film form – I always like to start with music from the very beginning. Through working rapidly on a painting I imagine music or sound that might work well in tandem, and I try to compose the imagery so that it has a musical rhythm. The work becomes tangible through not only its inner structure, but also montage, which is particularly important to me. I view montage as having a holistic role – it infuses order, rhythm, and creates a 'melody' of visual narration.

Sometimes I change the images a lot as a result of the music's rhythm and flow. Music and images can give a third meaning to the work. The relationship between sound and image can alter the sense of a scene, shot or the whole film. While watching a film we often do not realise this, but it is worth paying attention to how music and sound can change the sense of a watched scene.

How would you define your animation practice in terms of its relation to fine art traditions, experimental animation or the (historical) avant-garde? Its relation to commercial industry? Who/what are your strongest influences?

I studied graphic design, painting and drawing. I learned sculpture and ceramics as well. So my background is in fine arts. Our animation tradition in Poland has a very close relationship with the fine arts, literature and philosophy.

The manifestation of such a vision was called the 'Polish school of animation'. The vanguard of Polish avant-garde animation – during the early and difficult period when animation was fighting for its place as a film genre and an art form – includes Władysław Starewicz, Walerian Borowczyk, Jan Lenica, Piotr Kamler, Kazimierz Urbański, and Franciszka and Stefan Themerson.

Of course later artists appeared who have had an immense influence on me, and who I was able to meet in person, namely Mirosław Kijowicz, Daniel Szczechura, Piotr Dumała and my teacher and mentor Jerzy Kucia. These names offer proof of animation's diversity and creative variety, and these are features that have attracted and fascinated me. On the one hand, there are the hard rules of film narration, and on the other, a very open form with a variety of approaches to movement and themes. I also remember the profound impression made upon me by the film 'Vincent' by Australian director Paul Cox. A hypnotic flow of images that gave a strong sense of this artist's creativity.

I remember selected artists who have succeeded, in my opinion, in creating ideal film experiments. They are not afraid to try things out, explore, overstep boundaries. They take risks both thematically and formally. These are the characteristics I associate with experimental film – the courage to play with content and form, which always comes at the personal risk of the author.

I perceive experimental animation as being a form which can be tremendously varied at its very foundation. Having studied fine arts, I saw the potential to infuse such media with a different dimension, namely movement. That's why I like to mix different styles and forms within my films. I think that is what can be called experimental – feeling free to find an original language. I like Tadeusz Kantor, William Kentridge and Len Lye; artists who are thinking and taking a problem as a starting point.

Why animation?

By coincidence! I was planning to study film directing but had to initially finish some other studies. I chose to study at the Academy of Fine Arts, and there I met Professor Jerzy Kucia. He introduced me to animation, and I decided to stay with it. Animation is the best medium for experiments. And experimentation has been integral to animation history, right from the beginning!

Is material or media a particularly important component of your practice? How does it operate in your work?

Because of my skill set, I started with stop motion and object animation. I like to physically feel my objects and characters. I like to feel through touch how they move. It is an organic feeling that one finds out through animation. Some of my recent works are partly 3D but in a very simple graphic way. In 3D, I like even the imperfections and mistakes, which can sometimes make the art much more interesting.

At present we are accustomed to animation in 2D and 3D, and these are the most common forms of animation. There is Japanese manga or the productions of large studies such as Pixar. But animation is so much richer than this in a formal sense, and offers many more types of expression. There is spatial animation, and the animation of light, objects and actors. Originally animation was an art that bordered on magic. And this film genre continues to possess such connotations of mystery, liberation and magic.

What is your work's relation to experimental form and technique? Is there something you want to articulate with your work that can't be expressed through conventional narrative means?

Animation is able to show us different worlds and feelings. I like to create images that are unconventional in terms of form. I prefer conveying emotions rather than telling common stories. I locate animation on a spectrum between poetry and music.

I have worked on animation for documentary films and have collaborated with contemporary music composer Ewa Trębacz on the multimedia project *Errai*.

These are very complicated projects because they combine different art genres. When making animations for documentary films, I have learned to embed animated elements in the context of live footage. It is necessary to carefully study the plot and the characters, considering the role of animation and why it will complement this movie well. It has formulated a new genre that is either an animated document or documentary animation. It has become a common phenomenon, but was once completely new – hence the success of such films as *Waltz with Bashir*.

Errai was a huge spatial and architectural 'site specific' project, that from the outset combined music by Ewa Trębacz with elements of light and object animation, and 3D stereoscopic animation. It experimented with the viewers' cognition and perception, exploring whether they would withstand such a perceptual overload, and how they would react to a large number of visual and auditory stimuli at the same time. Observations and reactions were very positive and diverse, ranging from complete 'reloading' to 'insatiability'. It was an interesting project in relation to film frontiers, installations and psychosomatic responses, and it seems to me that the project in some sense foreshadowed today's VR technology.

How do you see your work operating culturally? Politically?

I am a part of a generation of Polish animators. I feel connected to the tradition of Polish animation and to a large extent have forged my own way of creating. Symbolism, metaphors, acronyms and analysis are features of the Polish school of animation and I feel a part of it. Of course, this is a continuous process and today I am more critical both of the traditional context and myself. Anyway my works are screened at many places and are a part of Polish filmmaking culture. Now I am the Head of the Animation Film Studio at the Academy of Fine Arts, and so I am responsible for the next generation of animation artists.

References

Cox, Paul. *Vincent*. Australia, 1987. Film.
Folman, Ari. *Waltz With Bashir*. Israel, 2008. Film.
Sowa, Robert and Ewa Trębacz. *Errai*. Poland/US, 2009. Multimedia installation.

PART III

From analogue to digital

4

MATERIALITY, EXPERIMENTAL PROCESS AND ANIMATED IDENTITY

Dan and Lienors Torre

In a general analysis of experimental animation, three important (but frequently overlapping) concepts, *materiality*, *process* and *identity*, will be examined in this chapter.

As the term suggests, 'experimental animation' normally involves some form of experimentation – of testing and trying out new or alternative ways of animating. But traditionally the term 'experimental animation' has been somewhat difficult to pin down, probably due to its decidedly multifaceted nature. A particular animated work might be considered to be 'experimental' for a variety of discrete but often overlapping reasons: Its lack of traditional narrative; its lack of traditionally identifiable visual formations; its unconventional production techniques or use of materials; or even the manner in which it is presented to the viewer. Although many of these overlapping approaches to experimentation will be discussed, a primary focus of this chapter will be on experimental animation's engagement with unconventional production techniques and its frequent (and unconventional) use of physical materials.

Frequently, but not always, it is the independent animator who most often engages in these experimental practices. Quite often this experimentation becomes unmistakably entwined with the animator's own unique artistic vision. It is worth noting, however, that not all instances of experimental animation fall neatly into the realm of independent or auteur animation; examples can be found embedded within even the most large-scale commercial animated productions where innovation and experimentation will certainly occur.

As the authors Robert Russett and Cecile Starr have claimed, many experimental animators have also worked in the commercial animation industry, which they note

> did not bring an end to experimental animation. New and exciting films have continued being made by the old and the young, in new styles, lengths, techniques and combinations of techniques.
>
> *(Russett and Starr 1988, 16)*

An essential aspect of an experimental animation is the process by which it becomes animation, and how this becoming process can affect both the content and the aesthetics of the final animation.

Historically, many experimental animations have given prominence to the use of material substances, including: found-objects, three-dimensional puppets, paper cut-outs, sand, clay and oil paint. It is the use of such materials that have often helped to characterise experimental animation, differentiating it from the dominant cel animation productions. Compared to cel animation, these techniques usually afforded the individual artist a more immediate and considerably less expensive means of production. But it is from the use of these unique materials that a number of intriguing significations and interpretations have arisen, from which viewers have tended to interpret this imagery in rather diverse and, ultimately, quite extraordinary ways.

Although technologies have evolved dramatically in recent years, these concepts continue to be indispensable in the practice and the examination of experimental animation. This is particularly relevant when we consider both the inherent configurations of digital animation, as well as its ability to simulate many forms of traditional experimental animations.

Ultimately this chapter will consider concepts of materiality, process and identity which can be described as essential aspects of many experimental animations. It will argue that both the materials used and the processes employed in experimental animation are inherently complex and multilayered, and thus can have a simultaneously profound effect upon the form and reception of the final animation. These facets will be articulated through the application of relevant philosophical concepts that explore process and the complexity of material objects, as well as through a number of pertinent experimental animation examples.

Process and materiality

Although traditional cel animation is a material-based construct (being composed of layers of plastic sheets, ink and paint), historically it has generally sought to disguise its materiality and to project a very graphical and decidedly intangible image.[1] By contrast, many forms of experimental animation have tended to celebrate their material basis, highlighting both how they were made and what they were made of. There are many different materials that can be used – in fact, just about any 'thing' can be animated. This section will survey some of the more common materials that have been explored in traditional experimental animation, including: pencil on paper animation, cut-out animation, found-object animation, abstract stop-motion animation and landscape animation. As will be described, distinct materials can also affect the aesthetics of the final film in unique ways. For example, if an animator chooses to work with predominantly malleable materials (such as clay, oil paint or sand) the resulting animation will be likely to contain a good deal of transformative movement and metamorphosis. From this brief survey of traditional techniques, there will be a further consideration of how some of these material-based techniques have been digitally simulated; and what relevance materiality might continue to have in contemporary experimental animation practice.

Cut-out animation is essentially a two-dimensional form of stop-motion animation involving the manipulation of characters and forms that have been constructed from 'cut-out' pieces of paper. This technique was strongly embraced by a number of experimental animators, independent animators and small studios (Lotte Reiniger, Jiří Trnka, Yuri Norstein) that found the technique to be both an accessible and a creative alternative medium with many advantages. Work that displayed highly detailed graphical imagery that was very expensive to achieve with traditional cel-animation, could be produced economically. Once the cut-out puppets were made, the actual animation could normally be produced in a matter of hours or days (rather than weeks or months). The characters, although somewhat limited in movement, would always 'stay on model' – something that was also challenging to achieve with the cel-animation technique. Plus, by using certain additional strategies, such as replacement animation in tandem with the manipulated cut-out puppet technique, a relatively fluid style of animation could be achieved.[2] Although only marginally more dimensional than the materiality of cel-animation, cut-out animation does not normally attempt to hide its material nature, often appearing to showcase a greater amount of physicality than might actually be present.

Cut-out animation occupies a unique space between the graphical qualities of cel animation and the typical rigidity of puppet animation. Its super-flat two-dimensionality often makes changes in perspective and transformative movements difficult to achieve. But rather than a hindrance, this has often proved to be a remarkable area of experimentation. Whereas drawn animation can freely utilise the apparently limitless conventions of illustrative perspective and depth, cut-outs often have to employ alternative approaches and various deceits in order to achieve such shifting perspectives.

A number of animators have produced some intriguing films that have tested these boundaries of cut-out animation's materiality, finding alternative movement-strategies within the limitations of the medium's super-flatness. For example, Michel Ocelot has utilised intricate cut-out forms and characters that will occasionally break through into the third-dimension in unexpected ways. In *Les Trois Inventeurs* (1980) we see a 2D cut-out character rowing a craft through the air; in the midst of a rowing cycle, the oar can be seen physically to protrude outwards (towards the camera), producing an unexpected dimensional shadow effect that traverses the rest of the imagery. Another noteworthy cut-out animation is Amy Lockhart's *The Collagist* (2009). This animation features both traditional hinged puppet forms (in the shape of human hands), as well as a great deal of very free-flowing animation that was made by sequentially replacing gradually evolving cut-out forms. Thus, the rigidity of the traditionally jointed cut-out 'human' hands contrasts with the refreshingly fluid and amorphous formations of pouring coffee, billowing smoke and blazing flames (see Figure 4.1).

Pencil on paper animation has been a traditional technique generally used by many independent animators. For example, the work of Raimund Krumme, Joanna Priestley, Stuart Hilton and Robert Breer, have all expressly featured graphite lines of either grey or coloured pencils on paper. The initial advantage of this technique was that it did not require the extremely costly and time-consuming use of cels; yet it still provided a strong graphical aesthetic. However, most pencil on paper animations have also featured rather frenetic animated line-work which stems from the inevitable variations of line quality, the texture of the paper, and even the occasional smudge marks of the graphite. Quite often this technique will intentionally feature 'boiling' lines – an animated effect derived from tracing the lines of previous drawings. Normally this process is used as an economical means of adding 'life' to a pencil-drawn animation. Therefore, instead of having to actually animate the character into moving (that is, to redraw it in a substantially different pose each time) the animator can simply make an almost (but not quite) exact copy of it. The resulting boiling image presents a form that is ceaselessly in flux, but at the same time, its movement is limited to the quivering outlines and shaded textures so that it invariably foregrounds the graphite materiality of the image (Torre, D. 2015a, 149–51).

Found-object animation normally involves the animation of objects that are employed as they are: They have not been modified for their role in the animated

FIGURE 4.1 *The Collagist,* Amy Lockhart 2009.

film. They have been selected (rather than constructed), their selection being based upon their intrinsic form, colour and texture. Found-object animation has in recent years enjoyed a surge in popularity amongst animators such as PES, Kirsten Lepore and Max Hattler. This is probably due to the fact that it can be a very immediate form of animation (you don't really need to draw or build anything). Also, there is an inherent authenticity to it that often testifies to the fact that it unquestionably involves the animation of real things without a lot of unnecessary digital intervention. Found-objects can be practically anything – from a rusty nail, to a teacup, to a child's toy doll. According to Maureen Furniss, 'Found materials include everyday items that create a sense of ordinary spaces, which can become extraordinary through the powers of animated motion' (Furniss 2008, 258). Paul Wells describes object animation as embodying the idea of 'fabrication', which includes the 'taken-for-granted constituent elements of the everyday world', which is 'in a certain sense [...] the reanimation of materiality for narrative purposes' (Wells 1998, 91). So, for example, in the Quay Brothers' animation *Street of Crocodiles* (1986) we see commonplace objects – screws, tools, glasses and wire – moving about within the construct of elaborately crafted sets. Here the objects are clearly 'on stage' and although they are ordinary, everyday items, they are engaged in a definite performance. According to Wells:

> the Quay Brothers essentially animate apparently still and enigmatic environments which are provoked into life by the revelation of their conditions of existence as they have been determined by their evolution and past use. This gives such environments a supernatural quality, where orthodox codes of narration are negated and emerge from the viewer's personal reclamation of meaning.
>
> *(Wells 1998, 91)*

It is this animated performance by ordinary objects, set against an extraordinary background, that conveys the Quay Brothers' celebrated surreal and supernatural effect.

There is a sequence in Jan Švankmajer's stop-motion film, *Dimensions of Dialogue* (1982), that uses a number of found-objects. The sequence involves two large, human shaped, clay heads that sit on a table-top. These animated heads are engaged in a sort of confrontation as they glare at each other and project from their mouths a series of increasingly ridiculous 'found-objects'. We know that the human-shaped heads are not real (and are merely constructed out of clay), but we do seem to empathise with them as being human. Yet, part of the strangeness and the humour of this sequence relies upon our clearly recognising the objects which protrude from the figures' mouths as being everyday real objects. When each of the 'real objects' with a specific identity (the knife, the shoe and the pencil) protrudes, we identify in part with how these objects might feel in our own mouths. So, just as we might commonly empathize with a human character, we also identify with recognisable real-life objects when they are made to interact with 'us' in extraordinary ways. Ultimately, there is often a very visceral reaction to the witnessing of real (and what we perceive to be real-life) objects, animated and moving about.

Landscape animation (or environmental animation) is a large-scale form of animation, often set within a real-world landscape (or cityscape), in which the animator will normally work with both found-objects and with *found-spaces* to create site-specific animations. In landscape animation, rather than relying on a more allegorical definition of place (such as a small-scale stop-motion set or a painted background to reference a particular place), the animation is produced directly within the real world. This particular approach to animation is greatly influenced by the location and by the natural materials found at the site. Some notable examples of experimental landscape animation include: *Rippled* (Darcy Prendergast 2011), *Earth Shiver* (John 'Hobart' Hughes 2006), *Bottle* (Kirsten Lepore 2011) and *Land* (Eric Leiser 2012).

Much of the work of landscape animator Eric Leiser involves a controlled manipulation of his natural surroundings. There are extensive sections in his film, *Land*, that involve simply the reconfiguration of found-leaves and sticks into choreographed patterns and evolving geometric forms. In other portions of the film Leiser highlights the various forms within the landscape through the introduction and manipulation of brightly coloured animated ribbons. Later, snow is trampled upon over large hillsides, and on large empty beaches lines appear and large abstract designs are drawn into the sand.

Because of the open spaces of landscape animation, the process of animating will often be made highly visible. For example, animations that are created on sand, grass or snow might highlight the unintentional footprints of the animators as they engage with the elements 'frame-by-frame'. These 'accidents' become an important part of the aesthetic of the animation. Furthermore, these also serve to authenticate the animation – proving to the viewer that it was indeed shot on a grand scale, and in the real world without any digital interventions (Torre, D. 2017, 220–230).

Digital simulations of materiality

Although many animators continue to work with material objects in their animation practice, there is also the capacity for digital animation to reference – and simulate – many of these traditionally material-based forms of experimental animation. Quite often, however, the digital simulation of a particular animation technique, rather than simplifying the process, can actually involve a series of very complex procedures. What might have been an incredibly easy and low-cost approach in traditional filmmaking, can become quite the opposite in the digital realm. This translation of materials and techniques might further complicate the definition of experimental animation, and while on one hand it might merely exhibit an experimental aesthetic, it also potentially allows for a type of *technical* experimentation within the animated form.

One notable early example of a simulated pencil on paper animation technique can be found in Eric Darnell's *Gas Planet* (1991). It is actually a 3D digital animation that employs a simulated pencil texture which is overlaid onto the dimensional digital forms. In contrast to the rather simple intuitive process of shading a drawing with a coloured pencil, this production involved a rather complex and multi-staged process of applying an animated texture map to the 3D forms.

Stop-motion clay animation is another technique that has been digitally simulated. One particularly striking example can be found in a series of promotional advertisements that were produced for the Nickelodeon television network (Plenty Studio, 2013). These ads, made entirely with 3D digital techniques, feature very fluid formations (and transformations) of figures that were made to look as if they were constructed from plasticine, and then animated using a traditional stop-motion technique. They showcase an array of brightly coloured orange 'plasticine' forms which were made to continually transform from one outlandish character to another (such as from a guitar-playing-chicken to a cheerleading-zebra) and then finally culminate into the 'Nick' logo. Although plasticine generally lends itself towards very fluid types of metamorphosis, a modelled and rigged 3D form would strongly resist such manipulations. In fact, an animator would probably end up 'breaking' the digital model if he or she tried to manipulate it in this way. Thus, in order to create the very fluid metamorphic effect of animated plasticine the production team at Plenty Studios constructed hundreds of individual digital models, each slightly different from the previous. These were then sequentially replaced, one at a time and frame-by-frame, within the digital scene. Instead of gradually manipulating a single plasticine form, a digital version of the replacement animation technique was used. In addition, each model was digitally coated with a 'plasticine texture', complete with 'fingerprints', in order to further simulate the hand-made quality of traditional clay animation.

Perhaps the most prominent (and arguably the most expensive) simulation of a traditional material-based animation technique can be found in the commercial animated series, *South Park* (1997–present). The original pilot for the series was created in the traditional manner using characters made from cut-out pieces of paper and animated frame-by-frame under the camera. However, the subsequent long running series (1997–present), as well as the feature film, *South Park: Bigger, Longer and Uncut* (Trey Parker, 1999), were made using state-of-the-art computers and 3D software. Traditionally, cut-out animation has been regarded as one of the most inexpensive ways to make an animated film; yet with the initial set up of the South Park studios, large sums of money were spent on computers and software simply in order to commence production on a simulated cut-out animated series (Dan Torre, one of the authors of this chapter, worked as an animator on the South Park feature, *South Park: Bigger, Longer and Uncut* (Trey Parker 1999)).[3] In the mid-1990s, a meticulous simulated version of the cut-out technique was still a rather untried concept, and the translating of this technique into the digital realm did represent a form of technical experimentation. In those early days of digital animation, the most intuitive way of working within 3D was to exploit the technique's highly dimensional and super-smooth motion qualities, which was in strong contrast to the fundamental aesthetics of cut-out animation. However, as the *South Park* series has continued, it has progressively embraced its digital materiality (using more and more overtly digital-produced effects) in parallel with its simulation of paper cut-outs – creating a hybrid animation aesthetic.

Arguably, these digital simulations of what would normally have been considered a hallmark of experimental animation can represent an intriguing and dichotomous process. On one hand, when animators employ digital tools to simulate the experimental manipulation of materiality they might be engaged in a simple *mimicry of experimental materiality*, but on the other hand they also might be engaged in an *experimental manipulation of digitality*. Depending upon processes used and the context of the animation, either mimicry or an experimental nature might be underscored.

Ephemeral materiality

All animation is, at least to some degree, ephemeral; it is only visible for the fleeting moments that it is presented to us. Yet, to the experimental animator, who may be deeply involved in the overt manipulation of real-world materials, this can be seen as an intriguingly dialectical space for experimentation. And a number of animators have experimented with these alternating concepts of materiality and of ephemerality in quite innovative ways.

For example, Alexandre Alexeieff and Claire Parker (who are best known for their pin-screen animations) also made animated films that featured a distinctive technique, which they referred to as a 'totalization of illusory solids', which was 'a sort of metamorphosis of a movement into an object' (Russett and Starr 1988, 95–96). They made a number of experimental tests of this technique; one of which became the logo for the French film studio, Cocinore. These animated films were made by moving an object (such as a handful of sticks) quickly back and forth in front of a camera while a photo was taken. Because the camera would be set to a very slow shutter speed, the resulting image would be of a large streak or blur. When sequentially shot, frame-by-frame as animation, these ephemeral streaks would appear as an animated 'solid' (yet amorphous) form.

An inverted variant of this concept can be found in the technique known as light-drawn animation, which involves the 'solidifying' of light into apparently material forms. Some of the most intriguing results can be found in Darcy Prendergast's films, *Lucky* (2009) and *Rippled* (2011). Similar to the 'illusory solids' technique, these animations require long-exposure photographs in order to create forms that are composed of streaks and blurs. However, whereas the previous technique by Alexeieff and Parker essentially involved the multi-stage conversion of solid objects into ephemeral streaks and finally manifesting as amorphous solids; light-drawn animation condenses ephemeral light into apparently material forms (see Figure 4.2). One of the unique strategies that Prendergast used in order to 'register' his light-drawings from one frame to the next was the construction of a thin wire 'stencil' that the animators would trace around with their light-torch. If the light-character was required to move, the wire stencil would be bent, adjusted and moved into the next required shape. This new wire form would then be traced with the light in order to create the next frame of animation. Because of the slow-shutter speed, neither the animator that drew the image, nor the guiding wire stencil are visible in the final animation – only the 'materialised' streaks of light (and the extant background settings) will be observable (Torre, D. 2017, 53).

Raimund Krumme has utilized the extensive 'empty white-space' of pencil-on-paper animation to his creative advantage. His films generally feature rather anonymous-looking characters, that seem to be forever walking around and exploring his ever-shifting spaces. Although the white space surrounding his line-work drawings appear devoid of all imagery, he is able to imbue it with alternating connotations of materiality and context. And though there has been a long tradition of subverting form and space in animation, Krumme is able to do this most effectively through his determined use of very simple lines drawn upon white paper. Thus, he is able to creatively explore not only a fluidity of the visible forms, but also of the entirety of the surrounding white spaces. For example, in both *Crossroads* (1991) and *Rope Dance* (1986) we see characters that are continually being flummoxed by the ever-shifting material connotations of simple line-work shapes. At one moment, a rectangle might act as a passageway into another space, but then suddenly become a solid wall, then suddenly gravity

FIGURE 4.2 *Rippled*, Darcy Prendergast 2011.

might be reversed, and it will become a pitfall trap, sucking the character downwards. And although the actual form (the simple line-work rectangle) will not change in physical appearance, its changing impact upon the animated characters will be extreme. The limiting of the mise-en-scène to the simplicity of the white paper, instead of inflicting any actual limitation, in fact provides an infinite space in which to experiment with the material (and immaterial) nature of animation.

Dana Sink's short animation, *Power* (2016), is a particularly interesting digital animation that also involves a sparsely drawn line-work image that is set within a surrounding white space. This animation also experiments with the idea of ephemeral white space, but in addition it experiments with the fundamental nature of the animation effect. The animation consists of approximately 20 different cyclical scenes, each featuring a different mechanical apparatus. Initially each scene is shown for several seconds, allowing for the cycle of the mechanical device 'in action' to play out a few times before the next cyclical scene is presented. After each of the 20 unique cyclical scenes are shown, all 20 scenes are presented again, but this time each of the scenes is displayed for a shorter duration. This strategy is repeated several times, until ultimately each scene is visible for only a single frame (1/24th of a second). The final result, then, is a twenty-frame meta-cycle that is composed of a single-frame from each of the original cyclical scenes. Remarkably, this cumulative aggregate (or 'meta-cycle') manifests itself not as a machine, but instead as a cyclical Muybridge-style representation of a running horse.

Thus, out of 20 rather nonsensical sequences, arises a new cohesive (yet quite ephemeral) entity of a running horse. However, each individual frame of this meta-cycle, in and of itself, does not portray a fully visible single frame of a running horse. In fact, each individual frame continues to look like a nonsensical mechanical device. It is only when we watch it in motion that it suggests a 'running horse'. It actually requires at least three consecutive frames of this 'meta-cycle' to provide the viewer with a substantial enough 'persistence of vision' effect to be read as a horse form. In other words, if one were to take at least three of these frames and overlay them on top of each other (with their opacity reduced) only then would they produce a clearly identifiable image of a horse in mid-stride (see Figure 4.3).

A   B

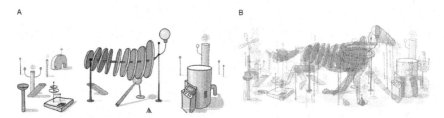

FIGURE 4.3 Frame grabs from *Power*, Dana Sink 2016. Image A depicts a single-frame from the animation, image B is an overlay composite of several consecutive frames from the animation, which simulates the 'animation effect' that is generated when one watches the animation.

Some 45 years earlier, experimental animator Jules Engel created an animation entitled, *Accident* (1973). It also featured a simple, pencil on paper, animated cycle (that was also derived from Muybridge). Engel's animation featured a cycle of a running dog, which was made to repeat dozens of times. However, when filming the animation under the camera, Engel progressively erased his animated image (frame-by-frame) throughout each iteration of the filmed cycle. Thus, the film begins with a very distinct animated visual of a running dog, and progressively becomes more and more ephemeral, until there is virtually nothing left but a slight flickering smudge. But what does remain, is our memory of the iconic Muybridge-styled dog running. And it is this memory, which provides us with an ostensibly persistent form of an illusionary solid.

An animation technique that seems to be growing widely in popularity involves the use of 3D printed characters. These 3D printed figures are then used as elements in stop-motion animations. Conceptually, this technique involves a similar idea to light-stick animation – in that it necessitates the concretising of an ephemeral form – however, rather than a streak of light, it involves the concretizing of a digital animation. One notable example can be found in the animated short, *Bears on Stairs* (DBLG 2014). This animation was created by printing out each frame of a 50-frame walk cycle of a bear climbing a flight of stairs. These printed objects were then placed (and replaced) one by one in front of a camera to create a material-based stop-motion animation. The result is a 3D digital walk cycle which has been concretised into real world spaces – effectively creating a materialistic simulation of a 3D digital animation. And because each and every frame of the digital animation was made into a stop-motion object, the resulting stop-motion animation displays an extremely fluid motion. However, not only do we see an incredibly fluid movement, we also are able to see the rather spline-y 'material' aesthetic of the 3D animation.

Material identity

As discussed earlier, many experimental animations have highlighted the use of materials, and this is perhaps most evident in animations that employ found-objects. Found-object animation tends to feature immediately recognizable forms, such as toothbrushes, teacups or shoes. Yet, when these objects are recontextualised and made to move in novel ways, then we might begin to question their identity. In *The Social Life of Things*, Arjun Appadurai argues that things assume meaning primarily according to how they are used, 'from a methodological point of view it is the things-in-motion that illuminate their human and social context' (Appadurai 1986, 5). Therefore, it makes sense that we might be able to alter an object's projected identity through the use of animation.

The animator known as PES quite often uses found-objects in decidedly metaphorical ways. In his short, *Western Spaghetti* (2009), a number of household items are used in lieu of food ingredients to animate the creation of an Italian dinner. Pincushions are used as tomatoes, and are made to mash down just as a real tomato would. Pads of yellow paper are sliced as a stick of butter might be, and little sugar candies (candy corns) are used to create the flickering flames on the stovetop. The manner in which these objects move is very convincing – and although all the while we know that the pieces of string are not really grated cheese, and that the rubber bands are not pasta noodles – we still can delight in their remarkable embodiment and visual punnery. Similarly, in the animated short, *The Deep* (2010), we see a number of ordinary tools and kitchen utensils made to behave exactly like fish and other underwater creatures. Lengths of chain become waving strands of seaweed, and old keys become darting schools of fish. And in one scene we see multiple measuring devices (calipers) that are, through the process of replacement animation, made to move and swell up just like jellyfish. And although these objects simulate these new roles convincingly (and these roles are further amplified by an underwater themed audio track), we are still very aware that these are found-objects, and their original identity implicitly remains.

Material objects in an animation production are well placed to provide the viewer with a deep complexity of phenomenological meanings. And, as noted above, a good deal of this complexity will stem from the addition of animated movement and context; however, much of it can also be seen to originate from the actual physical objects. According to Graham Harman, objects are inherently very complex entities:

> objects themselves, far from the insipid physical bulks that one imagines, are already aflame with ambiguity, torn by vibrations and insurgencies equaling those found in the most tortured human moods.
>
> *(Harman 2002, 19)*

Although the viewer will likely project their own cognitive complexities, the phenomenological experience of the object is ultimately dependent upon its physical existence. Similar to human actors, objects are fundamentally full of complexities and uncertainties – and it is because of this pre-existing condition that objects are capable of presenting and assuming a wide-range of alternate personas. And it is because of this surprising complexity that we are so readily able to accept new meanings and new identities when we watch animated found-objects (Torre, L. 2017, 4).

According to Martin Heidegger, when an object contains multiple identifiable states, it can be classified as a 'ready-to-hand' object (as opposed to the more diminutive, 'present-at-hand' object). A 'ready-to-hand' object is one possessing an identity familiar to us on account of its usefulness and its complex interconnectedness to the rest of our worldly experience. In relation to an object such as a hammer, Heidegger proposes:

> the more actively we use it, the more original our relation to it becomes and the more undisguisedly it is encountered as what it is, as a useful

thing. The act of hammering itself discovers the specific 'handiness' of the hammer.

(Heidegger 1962, 70)

Thus, a teacup is known and understood by us because we can pour tea into it: It holds tea, we can drink from it and we can hold it in our hands when we take a drink. However, 'present-at-hand' objects would be things that we generally have no need to consider for their individual identity – the anonymous clutter on a shelf for example: it is 'present', but not really of ready use to us.

Heidegger argues that it is quite possible to imbue this apparently useless bric-a-brac with greater context and usefulness; however, if we try to do so, it will usually require us conceptually to distort the objects in a rather artificial manner (Heidegger 1962, 70–72). Perhaps, for example, it would require us to take the anonymous pile of bricks in the corner and use them to build something useful – like a bench to sit on. Similarly, we could argue that the act of animating a found-object can immediately elevate it to a resemblance of a 'ready-to-hand' object. Its resulting 'life-like' movement and context will imbue it with a good deal more than just a 'present-at-hand' understanding. However, even though this might be quite an effective method by which to elevate objects to a higher level of meaning – stop-motion animation does represent a rather artificial means of doing so. Paul Wells seems to echo this when he states that animated found-objects are 'Simultaneously [...] both alien and familiar; familiarity is a mark of associational security while alienation emerges from the displacement of use and context' (Wells 1998, 91).

Heidegger asserts that the opposite is also conceivable, that is, it is possible to strip or reduce a ready-at-hand object (such as a useful teacup) into the realm of present-at-hand objects (for example, the anonymous clutter on a shelf). His reasoning for doing this is so that we might gain a better understanding of the materials of our world that we generally ignore (a sort of vicarious means by which to empathise with that which we do not understand). Thus, if we look at a hammer, we can at least momentarily disregard the fact that it is a useful tool for hammering in nails, and instead focus solely upon its colour, shape and material construction (wood, metal or other material). As a result, we might discover that many of the things that surround us, which we take for granted, are actually of a similar fundamental nature (they are also all composed of wood and metal, etc.).

This is exactly what is required of us when we look at an abstract image or animation; we are compelled to focus upon, not merely the form's real-world context, but instead upon its more elementary qualities. Lambert Wiesing has defined the general idea of abstraction as being primarily about the reduction of associations and context:

Something is abstract if it does not bear any relation to visible, concrete objects. Abstraction, then, is a disregard of a discernible association to an object.

(Wiesing 2010, 63)

A number of other philosophers (including Alfred North Whitehead, Nicholas Rescher and Gilles Deleuze) have also suggested that decontextualisation is one of the integral aspects to the idea of abstraction. That is, if something or some process can be stripped of its context, then it is no longer bound to any particular place or time and can then be infinitely repeated. Whitehead (and later Rescher) referred to colours and shapes as being 'eternal objects', in that they could quite easily be stripped of their context and could then be infinitely repeated without any regard to historical time or place (Rescher 2006, 52).

In recent years, there have been a number of experimental animations that could best be described as 'abstract stop-motion'. These films tend to utilise real-world objects to create non-representational sequences that are much more similar to abstract motion graphics than to traditional forms of stop-motion (Wallace and Gromit, Gumby). Initially, the concepts of abstraction and stop-motion can seem quite divergent and are not intuitively linked in most people's minds. We tend to think of abstraction as being primarily about shape, line and colour, while we think of stop-motion as being primarily about the movement of puppets and other recognisable *things* that have clearly identifiable features.

Yet, it is possible to 'reduce' any identifiable object to one that is much less identifiable (and therefore much more abstract). Abstract stop-motion animation essentially seeks to do this, to strip identifiable 'things' of their associated 'identities' and thereby transform them into components of abstraction. There are some fundamental animation strategies that one can use in order to transform 'things' into the realm of the abstract. These strategies usually involve the:

1. destabilisation of forms, and the
2. repetition of forms.

As a result, the viewer will be encouraged to focus primarily on the indeterminate qualities of shape, colour and movement. The first approach (destabilisation of forms) can comprise such things as flickering, metamorphosis, the splintering of forms or the coalescing of smaller objects into larger forms. Such disrupting movement will tend to shift the emphasis away from a particular form or a recognisable character and instead highlight its constituent abstract qualities. The second approach (repetition of forms) might involve a choreographed manipulation and repetitions of similar objects. Thus, these repetitive forms will no longer represent the specific identity of an object, but rather a larger amorphous collective. In this way, even the most recognisable forms can be transformed into apparently abstract animations.

One recent experimental film that employs these approaches in the animation of real world found-objects is Max Hattler's *AANAATT* (2008). This animation was shot on a mirrored coffee table in a lounge room using natural light and it features all manner of objects, mostly old mechanical spare parts and building materials. Because of his use of replacement animation (in this instance, the subsequent 'replacing' of marginally different paper cut-out forms, one after the other, in a frame-by-frame manner, in order to create a more fluid animation aesthetic), the forms all appear very unstable. They seem to grow and transform, sometimes to break apart into many constituent parts and sometimes reform into larger structures. Hattler also employs the use of flicker where he placed an object in frame for one exposure, then removed it from the frame for the next exposure and placed it back into the frame for the next – effectively destabilising the identifiable form into a flickering transience. Additionally, many of these elements were choreographed into a continuous patterned array. Thus, rather than one single cone shape, dozens of them were made to move about together – creating an ambiguous congregating mass (Torre, D. 2015b). Similarly, Jonathan Chong's animated music video *Against the Grain* (2012) is a stop-motion animation made almost entirely from office supplies and wooden pencils. But because of his heavy use of the repetition of forms, the film becomes not really about a wooden pencil object, but primarily about the shapes, colours and motion-patterns of the moving imagery. As these pencil forms are subsequently duplicated, they lose their individual identity and become complex patterns of repetitive imagery and movement.

By deliberately stripping objects of their identity, the animator can express an intriguing dialectical aesthetic of identity and abstract anonymity. Of course, the viewer can still identify that an abstract stop-motion film might be composed of recognisable real-world objects; but its primary identity will be one of abstraction. Similarly, when the animator PES imbues his found-objects with a staunchly alternate identity of, for example, a jellyfish, we are still able to comprehend the underlying tool-object as well.

Conclusion

Nearly all animation is arguably 'an experimentation of movement', in which the animator attempts, through numerous means, to make inanimate forms *move*. Until recent decades, animation was, for the most part, inescapably a very expensive and time-consuming process – thus, individual artists would often turn to unconventional materials and processes in order to make animation into a more accessible practice. Others, already steeped in the material arts of, for example, painting and sculpture, would seek to extend their work into the animated realm. Still others, perhaps in the midst of industry, would seek to discover new production processes and new kinds of imagery that they might utilize. Whatever the motivation, it was from these pivots towards new materials and new processes that a great deal of uniquely experimental animated films have emerged.

This chapter has explored what are arguably three of the most essential concepts that stem from these animated experimentations: The overlapping ideas of *materiality*, *process* and *identity*. It is from these experimentations with materiality (both actual and simulated), and the many diverse processes that can be employed in the production of animation, that we are able to experience some profoundly distinctive visuals. As technology evolves there will likely be progressive changes in the way we go about animating, yet, the underlying concepts of *materiality*, *process* and *identity* are likely to persist, and continue to provide us with vibrant spaces for experimentation.

Notes

1 For more on the materiality of cel animation see Hannah Frank's essay 'Traces of the World: Cel Animation and Photography' (2016, 23–39).
2 In this instance, the subsequent 'replacing' of marginally different paper cut-out forms, one after the other, in a frame-by-frame manner, in order to create a more fluid animation aesthetic.
3 Dan Torre, one of the authors of this chapter, worked as an animator on the South Park feature, *South Park: Bigger, Longer and Uncut* (Trey Parker 1999).

References

Appadurai, Arjun. *The Social Life of Things: Commodities in Cultural Perspectives*. Cambridge: Cambridge University Press, 1986.
Darnell, Eric. *Gas Planet*. US, 1991. Film.
DBLG. *Bears on Stairs*. UK, 2014. Film.
Engel, Jules. *Accident*. US, 1973. Film.
Frank, Hannah. 'Traces of the World: Cel Animation and Photography.' *Animation: An Interdisciplinary Journal 11* no.1 (2016): 23–39.
Furniss, Maureen. *The Animation Bible*. New York: Abrams, 2008.
Harman, Graham. *Tool-Being: Heidegger and the Metaphysics of Objects*. Chicago: Open Court, 2002.
Hattler, Max. *AANAATT*. Germany, 2008. Film.
Heidegger, Martin. *Being and Time*. New York: Blackwell Publishing, 1962.
Hughes, John. *Earth Shiver*. Australia, 2006. Film.
Krumme, Raimund. *Rope Dance*. Germany, 1986. Film.
Krumme, Raimund. *Crossroads*. Germany, 1991. Film.
Leiser, Eric. *Land*. US, 2012. Film.
Lepore, Kirsten. *Bottle*. US, 2011. Film.
Lockhart, Amy. *The Collagist*. Canada, 2009. Film.
Ocelot, Michel. *Les Trois Inventeurs*. France, 1980. Film.
Parker, Trey and Matt Stone. *South Park*. US, 1997–present. TV series.
Parker, Trey and Matt Stone. *South Park: Bigger, Longer and Uncut*. US, 1999. Film.
PES. *Western Spaghetti*. US, 2009. Film.
PES. *The Deep*. US, 2010. Film.
Prendergast, Darcy. *Lucky*. Australia, 2009. Film.
Prendergast, Darcy. *Rippled*. Australia, 2011. Film.
Quay, Stephen and Timothy. *Street of Crocodiles*. UK, 1996. Film.
Rescher, Nicholas. *Process Philosophical Deliberations*. Frankfurt: Ontos Verlag, , 2006.
Russett, Robert and Cecile Starr. *Experimental Animation – Origins of a New Art, Revised edition*. New York: A Da Capo Paperback, 1988.
Sink, Dana. *Power*. US, 2016. Film.
Švankmajer, Jan. *Dimensions of Dialogue*. Czechoslovakia, 1982. Film.
Torre, Dan. 'Boiling Lines and Lightning Sketches: Process and the Animated Drawing.' *Animation: An Interdisciplinary Journal 10*, no. 2 (2015a): 141–53.

Torre, Dan. 'Persistent Abstraction: The Animated Works of Max Hattler.' *Senses of Cinema*, no. 76, 2015b.

Torre, Dan. *Animation – Process, Cognition and Actuality*. New York: Bloomsbury Academic, 2017.

Torre, Lienors. 'Persona, Celebrity, and the Animated Object.' *Animation Studies Online Journal 12*, (2017): 1–6.

Wells, Paul. *Understanding Animation*. London: Routledge, 1998.

Wiesing, Lambert. *Artificial Presence: Philosophical Studies in Image Theory*. Stanford, CA: Stanford University Press, 2010.

5

'METICULOUSLY, RECKLESSLY, WORKED UPON'

Direct animation, the auratic and the index

Tess Takahashi

In the last decade, direct animation, along with other practices that emphasise the physical presence of the artist, has emerged as one response to the ubiquity of easily produced digital effects. Since the early 1990s, an increasing number of contemporary filmmakers have produced films without cameras. They work directly on the body of the celluloid, using drawing, painting, scratching, contact printing, and the application of materials, in what often is called 'direct' animation. The films considered here are not all animations in the narrow sense that they produce the illusion of coherent movement (or gradual change within a stable pictorial field, as in Norman McLaren's *La Poulette Grise* (1947) or the animations of William Kentridge). For the most part there are no running animals or human figures; most of these films present moving abstract shapes and colours in sometimes unpredictable sequence. Likeness is unimportant. Rather, as an artisanal approach taken up by filmmakers who associate themselves with the tradition of avant-garde production, direct animation emphasises the contact between the artist's hand and the film's surface. In a move that harkens back to the materialist investigations of the so-called 'structural' films of the 1960s and 1970s, these films investigate film's celluloid base: Not just its emulsion, but its capacity to take colour, to be glued, cut, scraped, xeroxed. At first glance, direct animation processes seem to promise a closer relationship to the image's origin and a guarantee of artistic value.

Within discussions of avant-garde film, the digital has been articulated as a threat not only to the medium of film, but to the filmic 'avant-garde'. For example, in the 2001 *October* roundtable, film was said to be threatened with obsolescence, even 'death,' by the proliferation of the digital (Turvey et al. 2002). In this roundtable, the digital was seen as a potential hazard to artistic innovation, the tradition of American avant-garde film, and to avant-garde community. In more practical terms, the ubiquity of digital consumer goods has coincided with the rising cost and outright discontinuation of a variety of film stocks, chemical developing agents, cameras, screening equipment and related services such as professional film processing. The ongoing disintegration of older films and the loss of 16mm classroom rentals to the newer (and ironically less stable) media formats of VHS and DVD has also been cause for concern. At the same time, as noted by the *October* roundtable participants, the filmic avant-garde also seems to be undergoing a revival; it has not been this vital since the 1960s and 1970s. Over the past ten years there has been an explosion of avant-garde film and media exhibition, increased scholarly work,[1] and the revitalisation of long-abandoned avant-garde filmmaking practices. Avant-garde filmmaking seems to have enjoyed a resurgence of activity and popularity just at the point at which the medium of film seems most threatened with obsolescence, both figuratively and literally.

While contemporary avant-garde 'film' is now regularly produced and screened in a variety of combinations of media, including digital, video, slides and various film stocks and gauges (such as 8mm, super 8mm, 16mm, 35mm and 70mm), a significant portion of this work can be described as devoted to the medium of film in its specificity.[2] Generally speaking, the most prominent characteristic of avant-garde work produced on film in the last decade is its attention to the specificity of the filmic medium, its processes of production and film's indexical status. Current discourse on medium-specificity within the contemporary filmic avant-garde reopens questions about the status of authorship, of film as a 'work of art' and of the very possibility of a filmic avant-garde capable of influence within both the art world and the larger culture.

On one level contemporary avant-garde film seems to respond to the encroachment of the digital through a reclaiming of the auratic qualities of the work of art for film and a re-establishing of the centrality of the filmmaker as artist. This movement appears to reclaim aura through a construction of film's specificity as singular, old-fashioned and one-of-a-kind in its attention to the 'craft' of filmmaking. However, this trend does not simply point to a longing for a set of historical conditions set in the past (pre-1960s), when the status of artist and work of art were ostensibly unproblematic. Rather, I believe that appeals to film's aura can be read as symptomatic of the ways in which the proliferation of the digital image is forcing artists and laymen alike to renegotiate the status of all images.

At stake are questions of what constitutes the grounds or guarantee of artistic value when the author has long been dead, the work of art has lost its aura, the filmic medium has lost its specificity and the individual 'work of art' has extended into a textual system in which personal vision is put to the side. However, the emphasis currently placed on the presence of the artist's hand in discourse surrounding contemporary avant-garde film (in programme notes, artist's descriptions and film reviews) obscures other issues that have been crucial to the rise of films concerned with various aspects of film's medium specificity. More than recentring the author and reclaiming the nostalgic work of art, contemporary avant-garde film made on the medium of film can be read as a product of the current crisis of the image. As Mitchell (2005) and others have noted, such crises occur at historical points in which an 'old' medium is being encroached upon by a 'new' representational technology (Williams 1980). The implication of the filmmaker's bodily contact with the image thus emerges as the most important point of reference in its guarantee of authenticity and claims for auratic presence in contemporary avant-garde filmmaking.

Within discourse on avant-garde film, the capacity of digital media for editing within the frame (as opposed to between frames), along with its capacity to alter an image seamlessly, seems most threatening to artistic intention. The work produced by the digital apparatus is considered too 'automatic,' the options it provides too 'cookie-cutter'.[3] As Lev Manovich (2001) observes in *The Language of New Media*, the computer's capacity for 'automaticity' (32), its ability to perform previously time-consuming operations such as collaging, animation and the repeating or looping of images at the click of a button, seems to remove human intentionality from the creative process. Such so-called 'avant-garde strategies', Manovich continues, now 'have become the normal, intended techniques of digital filmmaking, embedded in technology design itself' (307). While Manovich sees these innovations as cause for celebration, for the avant-garde filmmaker they constitute an implicit threat both to his or her place as artist and to the definition of what constitutes a so-called avant-garde film (ibid., 32).[4] Little wonder that a recently reclaimed and increasingly preferred term, 'artists' film,' has achieved currency in avant-garde film discourse.

Within the traditional fine arts at both the turn of the last century and the turn of this one, the uniqueness and contingencies involved in human production have been opposed to, and valued over, what is produced by the machine.[5] Many programmers' and filmmakers' protests against work that utilises the computer's automatic functions reveal a continuing anxiety about the relationship between human being and machine. It is in this context that the digital is figured discursively as unavailable to physical manipulation. One cannot go into the machine and rearrange pixels by picking them up with one's fingers. By contrast, film, figured as a material medium, is constructed as having the capacity to 'index' artistic intervention through its celluloid, its chemistry, its ability to be cut physically and even in its mechanical projection. The physical variability and irregularity of film have become newly important aspects of its ontology. Thus, the medium of film has been reconceived in recent years according to its ability to bear the artist's physical intervention, as well as the indexical touch of light.

Direct animation's emphasis on artisanal processes and homemade qualities is reinforced by textual support that exploits the artist's retreat from not only digital techniques but the traditional mechanical technologies of filmmaking, such as professional chemical processing labs, lenses and even the camera. In turn, much of this writing celebrates the turn toward film as hand-made object. For example, filmmaker Sandra Gibson's process is described in terms of its intricacy and craft. As one programmer writes, Gibson's films are comprised of 'painted, scratched upon and braided strips of film-surfaces meticulously and recklessly worked-upon, until blistering and flowering with the maker's material mark, [they are] further reworked and rephotographed through optical-printing' (Gibson and Recoder 2004). In this description of Gibson's work, her use of an optical printer is carefully downgraded in its importance to the film's production. 'Setting aside the stop-action-of-frames characteristic of the optical printer', the note continues, Gibson's *Tablecloth* (US, 2002) and *Precarious Path* (US, 2003) 'were made without the optical aids of camera, projector and sometimes even circumventing a trip to the lab'. Such descriptions produce the impression of a complicated, but highly personal, artisanal process that takes place in a space set apart from the industrial world of the 'camera,' 'projector' and 'lab.'

Many films that use direct animation techniques suggest a desire for the pure communication of an image through techniques based on the impression of an implement held in the filmmaker's hand. This can be seen in films in which the filmmaker draws on the surface of the celluloid by hand: For example, the films of Goh Harada, Nina Paley, Richard Reeves and Carol Beecher.[6] Much of this work is highly abstract, presents simple geometric or organic shapes and recalls animations from the early twentieth century, like those of Walter Ruttman, Hans Richter, Viking Eggeling and Oskar Fischinger.[7] The framing of these contemporary animations suggests that they do not want to be an 'illustration' of music but rather seek to be a 'presentation' of processes. Reeves's *1:1* (2001), which was drawn and painted directly on the surface of the celluloid, proudly announces that its colourful, geometrically expanding animations were hand drawn on the film stock itself. Not only were no computers used, but the film's caption claims that no cameras were employed in the film's creation. There is, the film announces, a literal 'one to one' correspondence between the mark of the implement and the image produced. Here, Reeves claims a direct, existential link between artist's pen and the strip of celluloid, a link that seemingly avoids the machine altogether, despite the fact that what is screened is surely a print.[8]

Likewise, hand-painted films such as those by Robert Ascher (*Cycle*, 1986), Jeremy Coleman (*I, Zupt 49*, US, 1994; *Ecclesiastic Vibrance,* US, 1995–96), Bärbel Neubauer (*Passage*, Austria, 2001), Zoran Dragelj (*Simulacra*, Canada, 2000), Rena Del Pieve Gobbi (*Insurrection*, Canada, 2000), Courtney Hoskins (*Munkphilm*, US, 2001) and Stan Brakhage emphasize the presence of the artist's body in the production of its image through allusions to the tradition of abstract expressionism. The work of Stan Brakhage, who produced hand-painted and scratched film for three decades before his death in 2003, has been aligned with the abstract expressionist tradition, and his written descriptions of this work would seem to confirm that observation.[9]

Descriptions of these pure colour abstractions tend to suggest that they function as direct presentations of the experience of human emotion or of physical encounter with the natural world. They imply a desire for a prelinguistic, primal form of communication based on texture, color, form and rhythm. Programme notes and artists' statements draw connections between the colours presented

and the embodied experience of the movement and hues of nature such as veg-
etable and animal life, rocks, lava flows, the ocean, stars and branching of roots.
There is also the implication that the films communicate human emotion in a
visceral, unmediated way. For example, *Numerical Engagements* (US, 2004) by
Chelsea Walton is described as a 'lush' and 'colorful ... love poem' in which colour, through 'the film's rhythm of editing is like a heartbeat' (Mad Cat Women's
International Film Festival Notes, 2006). Similarly, Brakhage's *Sexual Saga* (US,
1996) is a hand-painted, step-printed film whose form is said to express the
movement of sexual arousal, beginning with '"explosions" of white, yellow,
orange (deepening into reds), vermillion and darker red flame shapes' (Canyon
Cinema Catalogue). Communicating a very different mood, Brakhage's *Self
Song/Death Song* (US, 1997) produces the struggles between 'glowing ambers'
and blacks that threaten to take over the image in order to 'document a body
besieged by cancer' (ibid.). Films such as these imply a desire for unmediated communication and a distrust of both the indexical image and the written sign's capacity to translate adequately the natural world, human emotion or
individual experience.

These abstract animated films produce their 'guarantee' through a building
of extra-textual evidence that draws on the idea of the pure presentation of colour (as opposed to the presentation of the inadequate sign), the visible material
properties of paint, the implied physical presence of the painter/filmmaker and
the communication of an experience. Their presence and veracity are figured
as abstract and therefore potentially more immediate for a potential spectator.
Many films produced in this mode are described in ways that exhibit a desire to
achieve a basic, universal communication attainable through the medium of film
that depends on its figuration as *material* and *present*, unlike the digital image,
which is figured as ephemeral and always somehow mediated. In some ways,
the process of painting on film seems to promise a prelinguistic fullness, in the
sense that it is figured as able to communicate on the level of the emotional, the
universal and the natural.[10]

Some contemporary avant-garde filmmakers reference the tradition of direct
animation in the work of Len Lye and Norman McLaren, who began working in
the 1920s and 1930s, and the mid-century 'early abstractions' of Harry Smith.[11]
However, many contemporary filmmakers' interpretations of the relationship
between film and image have shifted from Lye's suggestion that direct animation
was a way for the artist to imbue the film with the imprint of the filmmaker's
essential self and suggest that it is physical human contact with the materials of
filmmaking that emerges as most important today. As Arthur Cantrill (2002)
writes for *Senses of Cinema*, Lye asserted that 'his "absolute truth" was in "the
gene-pattern which contains the one and only natural truth of our being"'. When
film art draws on this information through direct contact with the artist, Cantrill
continues, paraphrasing Lye, 'it resonates with our sense of essential selfness,
and we experience the aesthetic value as happiness. For Lye, this "selfness" was
anchored to the body and to bodily weight and motion' (ibid.). The filmmaker's

essential self, represented for Lye by the then new discovery of DNA, was transmitted in the process of direct animation.

Stephanie Maxwell, one of a number of young filmmakers inspired by Len Lye, adjusts his theories to suggest that all that is transferred in the process of filmmaking is evidence of physical contact – though that contact is crucial to the individual work of art. Maxwell (2006) describes direct animation as a 'process which reproduces very exactly the individual physical impulses of the artist: The artisanal images reflect the vibration of the fingers, the variations of pressure, the internal rates/rhythms externalized'. There is no claim for the transfer of 'essential selfness' through direct animation. Rather, Maxwell and others point to the importance of the physical proximity of the artist's body to the film. This contact is between the physical human body and the material embodiment of the image on celluloid, not a transmission of the 'self'. However, still present is the idea that working on film 'directly' produces the artist as a guarantee of meaning. More often, direct animators claim the capacity for direct, primal communication via the filmstrip, the communication of bodily 'rates' and 'rhythms externalized' as opposed to the communication of emotion, vision or artistic genius.

While all direct animation film produces a gap between the image projected and the image on the celluloid, these abstractions eliminate the problem of the gap between indexical representation on film and material referent. Hand-drawn and painted films such as those described above index the *process* of their production. Films that use the techniques of the photogram, layering objects onto the celluloid, or using bodily fluids to produce an image, introduce the problem of indexical *representation*. They point to the direct, unmediated experience of an object (often taken from the natural world) and to the necessary gaps between the image's point of capture, its index on celluloid and screened projection.[12] However, the desire for the immediacy of presentation rather than the gap in time and space associated with representation can be observed in the discourse surrounding contemporary photogram films such as Izabella Pruska-Oldenhof's *Light Magic* (Canada, 2001) and Jeanne Liotta's *Loretta* (US, 2003). This suggests a desire to align film with nature rather than with the world of machines and computers. In reference to *Light Magic*, Marcus Robinson (2001) writes that Pruska-Oldenhof's images are 'created through this technique are traces of light that passes through each object leaving its mark on the film surface'. He continues, 'Photograms bring both the maker and the viewer closer to the object, thus revealing the *essence*, that neither the naked eye could see, nor the camera lens could capture' (my emphasis).

Something similar occurs with films that not only eliminate cameras but incorporate actual objects and transparent materials into the celluloid itself. For example, Jon Behrens's *Anomalies of the Unconscious* (US, 2003) uses bleaching, baking, painting, inking and chemical hand processing in conjunction with the inclusion of leaves, flowers, hair and insects. San Francisco collective silt's *Ouroboros* (US, 2000) incorporates cast-off snakeskin, and Rena Del Pieve Gobbi's *Interception* (Canada, 2003) uses dried fruit as negative. Johanna Dery's

The Natural History of Harris Ave, Olneyville (RI) (US, 2002) utilizes actual plant life found during her walks along this avenue and attaches it to the celluloid in a way reminiscent of Brakhage's *Mothlight* (1963) and *Garden of Earthly Delights* (1981). In ironic contrast to the natural objects incorporated into most films in this genre, Rock Ross's *Baglight* (US, 1998) was made by ironing plastic bags onto film stock. Here, it is the filmmaker's engagement in the process of selection and application of materials that is narrativised. Films in this mode rely on the assertion that artist, worldly referent and medium were present together at the site of the film's production for their claims to immediacy, presence and singularity. Although the spectator cannot touch the film, the material body and testimony of the filmmaker can serve as a guarantee of authenticity. 'I saw' is supplemented by 'I found', 'I touched', 'I made' and 'I bring to you'.

Like films that incorporate material objects, films that incorporate the artist's own body seem to want to present those bodies as physically present in the film, rather than represented. Filmmaker Thorsten Fleisch's films are striking in that they present the filmmaker's bodily fluids and oils directly on the celluloid and on the audio track. *Blutrausch* (Germany, 1999), translated as 'bloodlust', was made through the application of the filmmaker's own blood to both the optical audio track and the picture area in order to produce a 'dizzying variety of splotches, drips, and cracks in dried blood which fleetingly resemble butterfly wings and stained glass windows' (Finkelstein 2002). Fleisch's *Hautnah* (Germany, 2002) begins with sounds 'produced by running a finger on a phono cartridge' (Finkelstein 2002) and images produced by the filmmaker's fingerprints where they made contact 'directly' with the celluloid. In a film that points to its status as a direct index of the filmmaker's body, Emma Hart's *Skin Film* (UK, 2004) uses cellophane tape to produce a map of the artist's body from head to toe as the tape picks up pieces of her hair, body oils and skin (Rees, personal communication to author, September 2004). This film fluctuates between presenting bits of hair and skin as objects for the eye and producing a readable map of a woman's body that must be mentally reassembled. In their use of materials from the filmmaker's own body, films like this literalise the filmmaker's physical role in their production. However, their implicit reference to the traditions of conceptual, performance and body art draws attention to the gap between image and the presence (or absence) of the filmmaker's body in the exhibition space. Despite the desire for presence implied, such films inevitably draw attention to the spectatorial experience as an act of reading rather than of immediacy.

Many contemporary hand-scratched films, in which filmmakers scratch directly into black leader, tie the specificity of celluloid and its emulsion to the idea of an originary language, making reference to ancient, hieroglyphic, cuneiform and non-Western alphabets. However, they also invoke problems of translation, between written language, image and worldly referent. Donna Cameron's *World Trade Alphabet* (US, 2001) utilizes oil, charcoal and ink on paper emulsion to combine drawing and scratching in the production of cuneiform symbols. Bärbel Neubauer's *Passage* and *Moonlight* (Germany, 1997) utilise basic, geometric shapes meditating on the evolution of the alphabet. Brakhage's *Chinese Series* (Canada, 2003), made while bedridden in the last months of his life, was produced by 'scratching on spit-softened emulsion with bare fingernails' (NYFF programme note 2003). It is the last of a series of major works based on ancient languages undertaken by Brakhage in the last two decades of his life. Such practices, and their framing discourse, suggest a desire to get back to an original, primal language of film, made through direct contact with the most basic of materials – fingernails, spit, wood (celluloid). In the *Chinese Series*, there is no tool mediating between the filmmaker's hand and the film in the creation of such an image. Scratched films suggest that the filmmaker's body is essential to the representation of the basic forms they image, and yet point to the problems and gaps inherent in the process of translation and the need for the caption in order to be understood.

Likewise, David Gatten's *Fragrant Portals, Bright Particulars and the Edge of Space* (US, 2003) presents stick-like forms, scratched individually into the emulsion, based on the Ogham alphabet. Most spectators would not guess that these are the letters of an ancient writing system until reading the programme note, in which Gatten (2004) describes the film as spelling out one 'early' and one 'late' Wallace Stevens poem, 'both about making sense/language from the natural world – the palm tree and the ocean'. These were then 'translated into Ogham, the 5th century "tree alphabet" derived from a notational system used by shepherds to record notes on their wooden staffs', Gatten's note continues, 'and carved a letter at a time into a piece of semi-transparent flexible wood (black leader)'. As such, *Fragrant Portals*, like much of Gatten's work on film, invokes the relationship between written text, image and the material world through the use of an early alphabet, whose letters bear a striking, if abstract, relationship to the trees on which their form is based.

The problem of translation between spoken text and image can be seen in Québecois avant-garde animator Pierre Hébert's live enactment of the process of hand-scratched animation. Sitting at a light table in front of an audience, Hébert progressively adds scratches and shapes to a loop of black leader as it repeats its lengthened path around the room and back through the projector (Chris Gehman and Elizabeth Czach, personal communication to author, January 2005). In one Montréal performance, Hébert collaborates with his partner by animating a poem she wrote about a homeless woman falling on the street. Hébert animates the poem using simple, gestural figures as it is read aloud, a few lines at a time, in French by his partner. There is a gradual accumulation of both markings and language over the period of time in which the poem is read and the marks are scratched. As the performance progresses, the image is transformed from a series of unreadable marks to a legible animation of a stick-figure woman falling on the sidewalk. In this piece, the filmmaker's presence before the audience anchors the image to his readily observable handiwork, while the poem/ narration directs the reading of the images. However, the gaps between written language and spoken language, French and English, still images and moving images, dark and light, one person and another (whether an intimate like his partner, or a stranger like the homeless woman) resonate with one another in their various translated versions.

While most of the filmmakers discussed do not incorporate indexical filmic images within their texts, quite a few do, including Naomi Uman (*Removed*, Mexico/US, 1999), Lawrence Brose (*De Profundis*, US, 1997), Christophe Janetzko (*Axe*, Germany, 2004) and Steven Woloshen (*The Babble on Palms*, Canada, 2001 and *Two Eastern Hairlines*, Canada, 2004). Hébert himself has produced a large body of work over the course of his career that deals with the relationship between image and text, world and representation and the aesthetic in relation to the political. Steven Woloshen has produced films that combine filmed images with scratched and painted animations. In *The Babble on Palms*, Woloshen paints over a filmed 35mm colour image of a hand and forearm blocking the camera's unobstructed view of a sequence of seemingly unrelated scenes. The painted hand pulsates and transforms itself in bluish purples, drawing attention to its status as an intruder within the frame of the camera's indexical view. However, the painted hand transforms quickly into the film's point of interest, contrasting with the film camera's stasis. The paint, messy and throbbing, draws attention to its own 'life', to the celluloid as a surface and to the indexical scenes' illusory impression of depth. It produces the celluloid as a material, embodied medium, rather than a window onto the world. *The Babble on Palms* thus thematises the role of the filmmaker/animator as having a direct 'hand' in the production of the image in an explicit way that emphasizes the physicality of the animation process.

The body of films discussed here, in their attention to the material aspects of film, can be read as commenting on the problems of representation, translation and experience in the age of the digital. Unfortunately, many contemporary avant-garde animations have been categorised as purely formal, decorative or conservative in their preference for film over the digital. As such, some see these films as hermetic and inward-looking, a charge levelled at many of the medium-specific investigations of so-called structural films of the 1960s and 1970s, a period also marked by the introduction and convergence of new and old media forms. However, there is a complicated politics at work in the aesthetic choices made in these films that evokes contemporary problems of relationship and communication over both distance and difference.

Notes

1 There has also been a remarkable development of individually or collectively run microcinemas devoted to the avant-garde, such as The Robert Beck Memorial Cinema (NYC), Movies With Live Soundtrax (Providence) and Pleasure Dome (Toronto). There has also been increased activity among avant-garde film festivals and organizations such as Black Maria (Jersey City), Ann Arbor (Ann Arbor), Images (Toronto), Views from the Avant-Garde (New York), Wavelengths (Toronto), Anthology Film Archives (New York), Northwest Film Forum (Seattle), Pacific Film Archive (Berkeley), the Iota Center (Los Angeles) through its touring programs,

Cinematheque Ontario (Toronto), Harvard Film Archive (Cambridge, MA), Bangkok Experimental Film Festival (Thailand), Seoul Experimental Film Festival (Korea), Image Forum Festival (Tokyo), Oberhausen Film Festival (Germany), London International Film Festival (UK), Rotterdam International Film Festival (Netherlands) and the Videoex Festival (Switzerland).

2 Some of the most prestigious festivals, like Views from the Avant-Garde (called Projections since 2014, a part of the New York Film Festival) privilege work made almost exclusively on film, although this is a practice that has been criticized by some.

3 In terms of its threat to artistry and singularity, the threat of digital technology to analogue media closely resembles nineteenth century disputes about the artistic value of photography in relation to painting. According to popular nineteenth century claims, photography was not an 'art' due to its mechanical nature. Now, film and photography have taken on the status of 'art' and it is the digital that is too automatic.

4 This is despite the claims of Manovich and others who see the artist's ability to manipulate pixels as more akin to painting (and thus more easily under the control of the artist). Paul Arthur (2001, 35) also found this formulation troubling in his review of Manovich's book.

5 As has been discussed by theorists from Walter Benjamin to Peter Bürger, the historical avant-gardes in the form of the dada and surrealism embraced mechanical reproduction, looking to the machine (and to film) as a way to escape the hold of the bourgeois museum and the traditional fine arts.

6 Goh Harada's *Lampenschwartz* (Japan/Germany, 2001), Nina Paley's *Pandorama* (US, 2000), Rick Raxlen's hand-drawn *Rude Roll (or how to dance ska)* (Canada, 2001); Richard Reeves's *Linear Dreams* (Canada, 1997) and *1:1* (Canada, 2001), Carol Beecher's *Ask Me* (Canada, 1994) and Sandra Gibson's colourful *Edgeways* (US, 1999), *Soundings* (US, 2001) and *Outline* (US, 2003).

7 Walter Ruttmann (*Lichtspiel Opus I*, 1921), Hans Richter (*Rhythmus 21*, 1921) and Viking Eggeling (*Diagonal Symphony*, 1925), Oskar Fischinger (Study No. 7, Germany, 1930–31), etc. Such techniques can also be seen in avant-garde films from the 1960s and 1970s, such as Michael Mideke's *Twig* (US, 1967), Storm De Hirsch's *Peyote Queen* (USA, 1965) and Margaret Tait's *Color Poems* (UK, 1974).

8 Reeves is a founding member of the Calgary-based Quickdraw Animation Society, founded in 1989, which works to support artists engaging in direct animation and to spread the practice.

9 Brakhage explains that he was 'strongly drawn to the Abstract Expressionists – Pollock, Rothko, Kline – because of their inner vision ... To me, they were all engaged in making icons of inner picturisation, literally mapping modes of non-verbal, non-symbolic, non-numerical thought. So, I got interested in consciously and unconsciously attempting to represent this' (quoted in Ganguly 1993, 21). Sam Bush, Courtney Hoskins and Phil Solomon, among others, have optically printed Stan Brakhage's hand-painted films, which he has been producing since the mid-1980s. Brakhage describes these films as collaborations with the printer. Among the most recent of which are the hand-painted, step-printed shorts *Autumnal* (US, 1993), *First Hymn to the Night – Novalis* (1994), *The Preludes 1-24* (1996), *Shockingly Hot* (1996, made with his young sons), *The Birds of Paradise* (1999) and *Lovesong* (2001).

10 In this way, contemporary avant-garde filmmaking practice recalls one of the fundamental questions of film theory – the tension between film's status as language (Eisenstein) and its capacity to represent the world (Bazin).

11 For example, Len Lye's hand-painted and scratched *A Colour Box* (UK, 1935), *Free Radicals* (UK, 1948) and *Color Cry* (US, 1952); Norman McLaren's *Hen Hop* (Canada, 1942) and *Begone Dull Care* (Canada, 1949); Harry Smith's *Early Abstractions #1–5, 7, and 10* (US, 1939–1956).

12 If early uses of photogram techniques, such as those of Man Ray, imaged man-made objects (like nails), today the objects imaged are overwhelmingly taken from the natural world.

References

Arthur, Paul. 'What Makes the Digital Tick?'. *Film Comment* 37, no. 6 (November/December 2001): 35.

Ascher, Robert. *Cycle,* 1986. Film.

Beecher, Carol. *Ask Me.* Canada, 1994. Film.

Behrens, Jon. *Anomalies of the Unconscious.* US, 2003. Film.

Brakhage, Stan. *Mothlight.* US, 1963. Film.

_____. *Garden of Earthly* Delights. US, 1981. Film.

_____. *Autumnal.* US, 1993. Film.

_____. *First Hymn to the Night – Novalis.* US, 1994. Film.

_____. *The Preludes 1-24.* US, 1996. Film.

_____. *Shockingly Hot.* US, 1996. Film.

_____. *Sexual Saga.* US, 1996. Film.

_____. *Self Song/Death Song.* US, 1997. Film.

_____. *The Birds of Paradise.* US, 1999. Film.

_____. *Lovesong.* US, 2001. Film.

_____. *Chinese Series.* Canada, 2003. Film.

Brose, Lawrence. *De Profundis,* US, 1997. Film.

Cameron, Donna. *World Trade Alphabet.* US, 2001. Film.

Cantrill, Arthur. 'The Absolute Truth of the Happiness Acid.' 2002, http://sensesofcinema.com/2002/feature-articles/lye-2/

'Chinese Series.' 'New York Film Festival Views From the Avant-Garde' programme notes. October 18–19, 2003, accessed June 20, 2018. http://archive.li/XXvMY

Coleman, Jeremy. *I, Zupt 49.* US, 1994. Film.

_____. *Ecclesiastic Vibrance.* US, 1995–96. Film.

De Hirsch, Storm. *Peyote Queen.* USA, 1965. Film.

Del Pieve Gobbi, Rena. *Insurrection.* Canada, 2000. Film.

_____. *Interception.* Canada, 2003. Film.

Dery, Johanna. *The Natural History of Harris Ave, Olneyville (RI).* US, 2002. Film.

Dragelj, Zoran. *Simulacra.* Canada, 2000. Film.

Eggeling, Viking. *Diagonal Symphony.* Germany, 1925. Film.

Finkelstein, David. 'Blutrausch (Bloodlust).' *Film Threat.* May 13, 2002, accessed June 20, 2018. http://filmthreat.com/uncategorized/blutrausch-bloodlust/

Finkelstein, David. 'Hautnah (Skinflick).' *Film Threat.* May 13, 2002, accessed June 20, 2018. http://filmthreat.com/uncategorized/blutrausch-bloodlust/

Fischinger, Oskar. *Study No. 7.* Germany, 1930–31. Film.

Fleisch, Thorsten. *Blutrausch.* Germany, 1999. Film.

_____. *Hautnah.* Germany, 2002. Film.

Ganguly, Suranjan. 'All that is Light: Brakhage at 60.' *Sight and Sound* 3, no 10 (1993).

Gatten, David. *Fragrant Portals, Bright Particulars and the Edge of Space.* US, 2003. Film.

Gatten, David. 'Fragrant Portals, Bright Particulars and the Edge of Space.' Programme notes for 2004 Onion City Festival. Chicago. September 23–26, 2004.

Gibson, Sandra. *Edgeways.* US, 1999. Film.

_____. *Soundings.* US, 2001. Film.

_____. *Tablecloth.* US, 2002. Film.

_____. *Outline.* US, 2003. Film.

_____. *Precarious Path.* US, 2003. Film.

Gibson, Sandra and Luis Recoder. 21st Annual Olympia Film Festival Programme. November 2004.

Harada, Goh. *Lampenschwartz*. Japan/Germany, 2001. Film.

Hart, Emma. *Skin Film*. UK, 2004. Film.

Hoskins, Courtney. *Munkphilm,* US, 2001. Film.

Janetzko, Christophe. *Axe,* Germany, 2004. Film.

Liotta, Jeanne. *Loretta*. US, 2003. Film.

Lye, Len. *A Colour Box*. UK, 1935. Film.

_____. *Free Radicals*. UK, 1948. Film.

_____. *Color Cry*. US, 1952. Film.

'Mad Cat International Women's Film Festival 2006.' Accessed July 2, 2018. http://hcl.harvard.edu/hfa/films/2005spring/madcat.html

Manovich, Lev. *The Language of the New Media*. Cambridge: MIT Press, 2001.

Maxwell, Stephanie. 'Stephanie Maxwell Homepage.' August 8, 2006, accessed 20 June 2018. https://people.rit.edu/sampph/

McLaren, Norman. *Hen Hop*. Canada, 1942. Film.

_____. *La Poulette Grise*. Canada, 1947. Film.

_____. *Begone Dull Care*. Canada, 1949. Film.

Mideke, Michael. *Twig*. US, 1967. Film.

Mitchell, W.J.T. 'Cloning Terror: The War of Images, 2001–Present.' Lecture at Urban Interventions: A Symposium on Art and the City. April 9, 2005, Toronto.

Neubauer, Bärbel. *Moonlight*. Germany, 1997. Film.

_____. *Passage*. Austria, 2002. Film.

Paley, Nina. *Pandorama*. US, 2000.

Pruska-Oldenhof, Izabella. *Light Magic*. Canada, 2001. Film.

Raxlen, Rick. *Rude Roll (or how to dance ska)*. Canada, 2001. Film.

Reeves, Richard. *Linear Dreams*. Canada, 1997. Film.

_____-. *1:1*. Canada, 2001. Film.

Richter, Hans. *Rhythmus 21*. Germany, 1921. Film.

Robinson, Marcus. LIFT Newsletter. March/April 2001, accessed June 20, 2018. www.balaganfilms.com/ARCHIVE/devon_spring2003.html

Ross, Rock. *Baglight*. US, 1998. Film.

Ruttmann, Walter. *Lichtspiel Opus I*. Germany, 1921. Film.

'Sexual Saga.' (n.d.). Canyon Cinema Catalogue. Accessed June 20, 2018. http://canyoncinema.com/catalog/film/?i=448

'silt', *Ouroboros*. US, 2000. Film.

Smith, Harry. *Early Abstractions #1–5, 7, and 10*. US, 1939–1956. Film.

Tait, Margaret. *Color Poems*. UK, 1974. Film.

Turvey, Malcolm, Ken Jacobs, Annette Michelson, Paul Arthur, Brian Frye and Chrissie Iles. 'Round Table: Obsolescence and American Avant-Garde Film.' *October* 100 (2002): 115–32.

Uman, Naomi. *Removed*. Mexico/ US, 1999. Film.

Walton, Chelsea. *Numerical Engagements*. US, 2004. Film.

Williams, Raymond. 'Base and Superstructure in Marxist Cultural Theory.' In *Problems of Materialism and Culture*. London: Verso, 1980.

Woloshen, Steven. *The Babble on Palms*. Canada, 2001. Film.

_____. *Two Eastern Hairlines*. Canada, 2004. Film.

'World Trade Alphabet.' (n.d.). Canyon Cinema Catalogue. Accessed June 20, 2018. http://canyoncinema.com/catalog/film/?i=3743

6

DIGITAL EXPERIMENTATION

Extending animation's expressive vocabulary

Miriam Harris

In their book *Remediation: Understanding New Media* (1999), Jay Bolter and Richard Grusin locate overlaps between media, culture and society that run counter to the modernist bid – in numerous sectors – for clear compartmentalisation. They write that 'No medium today, and certainly no single media event, seems to do its cultural work in isolation from other media, any more than it works in isolation from other social and economic forces' (15). Although the text was published almost 20 years ago – a span that in digital terms seems to verge on the Jurassic period, given the lightning-pace changes that continue to shape digital technology – Bolter and Grusin's observation about intermediality is one that still holds significant currency. Examined through the lens of hybridity, rather than specificity, the medium of digital animation is rhizomatous; one that unfurls in a variety of directions, closely linked with its cultural and economic environment, with roots formed in the analogue era, rather than an abrupt severance with the past. When such a metaphor is applied to the realm of experimental digital animation, with its extended vocabulary and licence to explore beyond commercial constraints, the branches and offshoots become manifold. This kind of creative fecundity has the potential to enlarge our understanding of digital animation's ontology, to review some knee-jerk dismissals and to consider examples that reveal its capacity as an expressive, richly communicative medium.

Such a perspective challenges the outlook that has predominated in some circles, where digital animation is associated with technological spectacle rather than creative innovation. This is a view that has been spawned to some degree by the correlation of digital animation solely with blockbuster productions. It has been maligned for supposedly displaying qualities that are diametrically opposed to emotional engagement, such as being mechanical, ephemeral, cold, lacking a human touch and non-indexical. In this chapter I will seek to counter some of the latter criticisms by investigating examples of experimental digital animation that generate emotional resonance, reflect conceptual depth and also manifest considerable imagination, innovation and experimentation in their creative communication. Such a level of expression may draw upon strategies utilised by their analogue counterparts, but it also ventures into new modes of perception and technology. I will consider some of the factors contributing to such resonance – formalist, semiotic, cognitive, phenomenological – and will contemplate the ways in which our responses to digital animation overlap with responses to analogue media, together with their points of difference. While acknowledging valid criticisms that have been levelled at the digital animation domain, I propose that the experimental arm of digital animation extends the medium's vocabulary and expressive power, and that the commercial sector also initiates examples of experimentation; a permeability exists between the two spheres. Such porousness can be explored in the light of experimental animation's history in the early decades of the twentieth century, when art movements and society wrestled with the implications of another monumental technological shift – the rise of photography and film.

Digital animation has the capacity, when viewed through Bolter and Grusin's concept of 'remediation', to reflect qualities commensurate with analogue avant-garde and experimental artistic expression: A materiality that engages the senses, reflexivity, aesthetics that range beyond seamless photorealism and literal representation, and a questioning of formal and narrative conventions. These are qualities that Paul Wells (1998) and Maureen Furniss (1998) both identify as being characteristic of experimental animation. Yet in achieving emotional resonance, digital experimental animation also draws upon less tangible features that are particular to its medium – light, code, spatial gymnastics, infinitude and virtuality – and diverges from the realm of haptic media. In exploring the overlaps and differences between analogue and digital expressivity, I will refer to the observations of several theorists who have illuminated the ways in which we think about digital media, such as Lev Manovich, Vivian Sobchack, Thomas Elsaesser, Sean Cubitt, Aylish Wood and Meredith Hoy, while also turning to digital media practitioners whose writings draw upon theory, such as Patrick Power, Claudia Hart, Birgitta Hosea, Adam Nash and David O'Reilly. In addition, I will draw upon some of my own experiences gathered as an experimental digital animation practitioner.

Digital animation and its theoretical context

Both Lev Manovich and Vivian Sobchack have been critical of digital animation's seemingly limited capacity for emotional and creative expression. In his essay 'The Aesthetics of Virtual Worlds: Report from Los Angeles', Manovich perceives *Toy Story* (1995), the first feature length computer animated film, as: 'Frighteningly sterile, this is the world in which the toys and the humans look absolutely alike, the latter appearing as macabre automatons' (Manovich 1995). Manovich's 2006 essay 'Understanding Hybrid Media' however, reveals a change of heart, an exponentially increased enthusiasm for digital animation's creative capabilities. He asserts that in 'the second part of the 1990s, moving-image culture went through a fundamental transformation', and that the interdisciplinary mixing of video, typography, 2D and 3D animation – facilitated by digital media's code-driven hybridisation – represents 'a new "species" – a new kind of visual aesthetics that did not exist previously' (2006). Rather than simply chase the holy grail of photorealism, Manovich notes examples in which digital media integrates more painterly and illustrative strategies, as seen in motion graphics and music videos by MK12, the feature film *Sin City* and the experimental animation work of artists Jeremy Blake, Ann Lislegaard and Takeshi Murata. Moreover, in coining the term 'deep remixability', Manovich embraces digital animation's power to affect a viewer by doing things outside the realm of analogue media's capabilities, through the extracting of media 'from their particular physical medium of origin and turning them into algorithms':

> Here are a few examples of this "crossover" logic: typography is choreographed to move in 3D space; motion blur is applied to CGI; algorithmically generated fields of particles are blended with live-action footage to give it an enhanced look; a virtual camera is made to move around a virtual space filled with 2D drawings. In each of these examples, the technique that was originally associated with a particular medium – cinema, cel animation, photorealistic computer graphics, typography, graphic design – is now applied to a different media.
>
> *(Manovich 2006)*

Sobchack continues to yoke the digital with images of barrenness and soulless mechanisation in her 2009 essay 'Animation and automation, or, the incredible effortfulness of being' (Sobchack 2009). Unlike Manovich, her survey of examples stems purely from the blockbuster zone, rather than delving into the innovative potential afforded by music videos, motion graphics and experimental animation. She focuses on two special effects movies, comparing the 1933 version of *King Kong* with Peter Jackson's 2005 digital blockbuster. Sobchack builds a strong case for the superior qualities of the earlier interpretation, arguing that the stop-motion animation of King Kong, the gorilla, contains features such as an analogue tactility and a temporal protractedness that make for a more poignant and deeply affecting experience for the viewer than the elaborately constructed CGI. Sobchack concludes the essay by acknowledging that Pixar's *WALL-E* (2008) has broadened digital animation's scope for engaging and emotionally transporting its audiences, but that such achievements are still surpassed, in her opinion, by the analogue, haptic films of experimental animators Jan Švankmajer and the Brothers Quay:

> And I much prefer the effortful animations of Jan Švankmajer or the Brothers Quay in which puppets are chipped and broken and always in

a visible, intermittent, intervallic movement that stutters and starts anew, reminding one (at least on the far side of fifty) how difficult it is to be animate, to be alive, to struggle against entropy and inertia.

(Sobchack 2009, 389)

In her earlier essay 'Final Fantasies: Computer Animation and the [Dis]Illusion of Life' (Sobchack 2006), Sobchack is more condemnatory of digital animation's capacity for depicting human warmth and fragility, and its ability to venture into conceptual territory such as the posing of existential quandaries. In fact, in the relentless quest of *Final Fantasy* (2001) to capture a lifelike photorealism, the film endows digital human figures conversely with corpse-like attributes, and thereby ushers in the psychoanalytical phenomenon of the uncanny. I find that Sobchack's observations have considerable validity in the context of early twenty-first century digital outputs, but that subsequent technological developments have created numerous shifts in the digital landscape.

In 2001, I watched *Final Fantasy* in a Toronto movie theatre while studying Digital Animation and VFX at Sheridan College; the audience vocally expressed their discomfort when the film's cadaverous protagonists kissed. Seventeen years later, however, digitally locked-lips and embraces contain greater passion and pathos. Theorists who have explored the trajectory of this shift, through complex, dimensional analyses of commercial digital outputs, include Aylish Wood, Lisa Bode, Misha Mihailova and Leon Gurevitch. A younger generation of academics has grown up enjoying digital technology; familiarity, and not only advances in software, has helped establish a sense of connection. In her essay 'Animation and Automation', Sobchack herself recognises that our responses to different media partly stem from generational difference – 'Our encounters with the dominant technologies of our respective generations have each differently informed – and transformed – us as embodied and self-reflexive subjects' (Sobchack 2009, 377).

In spite of these generational divides, the question arises as to whether experimental digital animation – in the subversive spirit of previous avantgarde movements – might also critique political and cultural systems that are unreservedly accepted as normative. In the next sections of this essay I will refer to the work of several experimental digital animation artists who challenge the status quo and offer a diverse take on culture and aesthetics. In addition, the role of current pedagogical approaches to digital animation needs to be taken into account and contrasted with experimental digital animation courses that expressly seek to foster a divergent approach to process and creativity, such as Claudia Hart's programme at the Art Institute of Chicago. Hart has observed that digital animation education has been heavily influenced by its ties with military and Hollywood industrial pipelines, rather than geared towards fostering conceptual investigation and experimentation in the style of creative studio practice.

In 'Beginning and Endgames: A Parable in 3D', Hart explores the larger implications of this approach to teaching:

> Students are taught to resist 'big picture' thinking, which also means to resist thinking that is conceptual, holistic, lateral, or creative. Indicative of this trend are course titles that are typically named after technical terms. Modelling, Rigging, Character Animation, Rendering, Texturing, and so on.
>
> *(Hart 2013)*

In contrast with this regimented approach to digital animation education, analogue media practice has typically been accorded a much wider vista for exploration. In the field of experimental film and animation studies, haptic media has been linked with a visceral propensity to move the spectator. Phenomenological theory – which Sobchack draws upon – has provided an effective lens for understanding a spectator's response, referencing theorists such as Henri Bergson, Maurice Merleau-Ponty, Gilles Deleuze and Stanley Cavell. Laura Marks has written about the multi-sensory stirrings triggered in the film *Institute Benjamina* by the Brothers Quay (Marks 2006), and Suzanne Buchan has explored the haunting, uncanny attributes possessed by animated tactile objects in a range of Brothers Quay animations (Buchan 2006). Rosalind Krauss has investigated the poignancy and potency of the animated dusty, charcoal mark – accompanied by its palimpsestic erasure – in William Kentridge's films (Krauss 2000). Experimental animator Dirk de Bruyn, in his essay 'Materialist Performance in the Digital Age', draws upon Vilém Flusser's concept of the 'technical image' to make the convincing point that computers, in contrast with photographic chemical processes, render invisible 'the means of constructing these meaningful surfaces', and this leads to 'a form of amnesia in its audience' (de Bruyn 2013). These texts all make insightful observations about the ways in which experimental analogue animation reverberates with the spectator's body and senses. My aim in this essay is not to argue for the privileging of digital over analogue media – or vice versa – but to move beyond exclusive declarations of preference and consider the ways in which certain experimental digital examples are imbued with an expressive power that is on a level with that of their analogue counterparts.

Furthermore, it can be claimed that an essentialist notion of digital media is problematic, and that so-called digital and analogue characteristics increasingly overlap within a digital context. Birgitta Hosea's experience as a practitioner strongly informs her writing, and she puts forward a term – the 'post-digital' – that can be linked with Manovich's assertion that all cinema is animation. Such a term is helpful in extending our understanding of current digital practice: 'As computer technology increasingly becomes an essential part of the production and dissemination of all media, the notion of a binary opposition between the digital and the handmade becomes meaningless and a new synthetic paradigm – the *post-digital* – emerges' (Hosea 2010). A variety of texts, amalgamating conceptual concerns with case studies of digital creative practitioners' work, intriguingly explore the fluid nature of this paradigm, such as experimental animator Steven Subotnick's how-to manual *Animation in the Home Digital Studio* (2002), Betti-Sue Hertz's 2007 compilation 'Animated Painting', Paul Wells and Johnny Hardstaff's book *Re-Imagining Animation: The Changing Face of the Moving Image* (2008), Patrick Power's essay 'Animated Expressions: Expressive Style in 3D Computer Graphic Narrative Animation' (2009) and Sara Álvarez Sarrat and María Lorenzo Hernández's essay 'How Computers Re-Animated Hand-Made Processes and Aesthetics for Artistic Animation' (2013).

The length of this chapter does not permit me to explore all of the features that Wells and Furniss associate with analogue experimental animation. Rather, in the next sections of this essay I will focus upon three items from their list – materiality, aesthetic and formal diversity and reflexivity – and will refer to a range of experimental digital animations that enlist strategies that are comparable, in their communicative power, with their experimental analogue counterparts, as well as consider their points of difference. I have included issues surrounding form and space alongside materiality, as I believe these items are closely interlinked and play a significant part in a spectator's sensory and emotional response. In the exploration of reflexivity, the spectator is afforded the opportunity to 'look under the hood', as Dirk de Bruyn comments, and this in turn extends the works' creative and expressive repertoire.

Materiality, form and space

In her book *Hollywood Flatlands*, Esther Leslie views the cultural, political and economic context of a particular era as being indivisible from concurrent developments in animation. At the beginning of the twentieth century for instance, Marxist philosophy, utopian ideals of collectivity and the Dadaist subversion of old orders of hierarchy all had a profound impact upon German experimental animators such as Hans Richter and Walter Ruttmann (Leslie 2004). In the area of pedagogy and materiality, this zeitgeist was reflected in Bauhaus teachers and artists intertwining modernist experiment and innovation with a commercial functionalism; formal inventiveness was applied to items that could be touched and used. Thomas Elsaesser and Malte Hagener, in their chapter 'The Body Digital', draw similarly useful parallels between digital media and our contemporary twenty-first century landscape, and note that a current economic and social logic of the cinema has to do with 'a tendency towards dematerialisation (Marx's "all that is solid melts into air"), towards equivalence and exchange, but also enabling calculability and measurement – all of which the digital both fosters and facilitates' (2015). Dematerialisation makes sense when we think of the recent fallout generated by housing market bubbles inflated with non-existent credit and the more altruistic Bitcoin phenomenon. Paradoxically, in contrast with some theorists who regard digital materiality as lamentably ephemeral, Elsaesser also notes digital media's strong alignment with things corporeal and sensory:

> Digital cinema's chameleonlike mutations, its morphing of shapes, scaling of sizes, and uncanny rendering of textures – in short, its re-embodied

manifestations of everything visible, tactile, and sensory – allow the digital to become much more closely aligned and attuned to the body and the senses.

(2015)

Digital media's evanescence, Elsaesser observes, exists at the level of the 'recording and storage' of data; on the other hand, in terms of 'presentation and display', it can have 'a point of view, with feelings and affects' (2015). He cites Woody from *Toy Story* as being such an example, but also refers to Spike Jonze's film *Her* (2013), which features an animated sequence by experimental digital animator David O'Reilly. Set in the near future, we witness the central protagonist Theodore, playing an immersive computer game in the privacy of his apartment, and being startled by a glowing, potty-mouthed hologram who steps out of the game and confronts him with a series of expletives. Their interchange is filled with heightened passion, and serves to jolt Theodore out of his state of affectless lethargy. Elsaesser notes that in this world, enveloped in dimensional sound and light, the body is a 'sensuous surface' granting a 'remarkable array of sense experiences', but that 'such exposure of the senses makes humans also more vulnerable and emotionally volatile' (2015).

In *Her*, the hologram character's materiality is incandescent and ethereal, but irreverently brought down to earth by its Doughboy proportions and the unexpected crassness of its human speech. Similarly, other experimental digital animation works enlist a variety of materials and media combinations in generating communicative resonance. In order to explore the characteristics of a range of approaches, I have divided examples of work roughly into three categories: Experimental digital animations exploring materiality in a fashion that evokes the analogue and handmade, works – like David O'Reilly's *Her* sequence – that focus on sound and light, and those exploring facets of photorealism. These categories are each surrounded by concomitant cultural and political associations. For instance, the incorporation – or simulation – of analogue elements can be linked with a backlash against the smooth slickness predominantly associated with commercial digital aesthetics. Variations upon the photoreal – such as Faiyaz Jafri's concept of 'Hyper-Unrealism' (http://faiyazjafri.com/aboutfaiyazjafri) – afford the potential to comment upon Hollywood and corporate-based aesthetics and narratives. And certain experimental digital works that resolutely embrace sound and light may also be interpreted as a political comment, in their acknowledgement of the social and ecological fragility of our gleaming blue orb.

Film, music videos, motion graphics, art installations, gaming and even virtual reality experiences may fall within the category of experimental digital animation works that incorporate analogue references. Such references might involve gestural mark-making, painting, claymation, puppetry, objects and collage. A roll call of practitioners – not intended to be exhaustive – located throughout the globe who explore this zone include Evert de Beijer, Steven Subotnick, Jonas Odell, Annapurna Kumar, Robert Sowa, Diego Akel, Rose Bond, Joshua

Mosley, Sasha Svirsky, Mirai Mizue, Amanita Studio, Michel Gondry, Mehdi Shiri, Gina Thorstensen, Joel Kefali and Damian Gascoigne. These creators all combine experimental analogue and digital processes in a way that alludes to both the past and present. For instance, in 2004, Swedish animator Jonas Odell and the Filmtecknarna studio released the music video *Take Me Out* for the band Franz Ferdinand. Created in Adobe After Effects, the animated video draws upon experimental semiotics of the past – a re-embodied manifestation of Bauhaus and Dada-inspired graphics and cut-out animation – together with a host of features that Elsaesser ascribes to the digital. At the time of its release, this kind of aesthetic blend connoted a playful edginess appropriate for an indie band composed of art school graduates. Grafted onto live action footage of the band members, with surreal, mutant-like results, the graphics in the animation bear traces of age and tactility. Presumably taken from analogue samples, converted into data and manipulated, they impart the same haptic charge that phenomenological theory bestows upon dusty charcoal or thumb-printed clay. This knowing recourse to art history defies claims that digital media represents an abrupt break with the past; instead of printing being dragged from books onto the streets – 'forced to leave its supine position in books' (cited in Leslie 2004), as Walter Benjamin had written in 1917 of graphic signs found in urban locales – Dadaist collage is now set in motion within a digitally simulated space.

From both a practitioner and a viewer's perspective, such experimentation is hugely liberating, declaring that fine art, graphic design and experimental media are all suitable provinces for digital aesthetic inspiration, and that the visual vocabulary of 'perceptual realism' dominating blockbuster films – as detailed by Stephen Prince – is but a sub-section of existing creative possibilities (Prince 2002). Manovich's essay on hybrid digital media welcomes the increased integration of painterly and illustrative approaches, and Patrick Power similarly notes that technological advances and user-friendly interfaces have made digital software more accessible to fine artists; another factor in the growth of a vibrant body of experimental works reflecting a diverse approach (Power 2009). One of the problems that is faced by viewers in connecting 3D digital animation with all the trappings that we associate with analogue creative expression – the gestural flourish, accidental spillage, poetic symbol or metaphor – is that peering over the shoulders of practitioners, viewers can be faced with a seemingly impenetrable interface of numbers, graphs and sliders. Yet, when you are actually in the driving seat of a programme such as Maya – even if you are only furnished with the basics – it is possible to experiment in a tactile and intuitive fashion. In my experience, human agency and artistic input are there from the outset when working in Maya, and may be experienced in quite a visceral fashion – rotating in space, one negotiates an object in three dimensions, pulling points and moulding, creating a rhythm with increased proficiency, and receiving instant visual feedback through renderings in real-time. In an interview with Sabin Bors, Claudia Hart very usefully compares such a process to working with a prosthesis (Hart 2011). I have watched students at the beginning of a Maya course sculpt objects that are each indelibly stamped with the personal predilections of their creator, ranging from abstract futuristic funk to characters with Lisa Simpson hairdos.

Several digital experimental animators have written about this connection between computers and human subjectivity. Birgitta Hosea quotes the visual effects artist Gareth Edwards: 'CGI is an unhelpful term implying that the computer autonomously generates imagery without the involvement of human agency or artistic input (Edwards 2009)' (Hosea 2010, 356). The traffic between analogue imagery, algorithmic data and tangible, albeit prosthetic, agency also challenges notions that the digital has severed connections with the indexical. For instance, photographs and hand-drawn scribblings may be scanned (or drawn with a tablet), converted into data, and then projected upon geometry within a 3D software programme. This mode of representation can be seen in the work of Dutch experimental animator Evert de Beijer, who incorporates analogue marks and gestural drawing within Maya 3D sets and projections upon animated rigs. In a stylistic departure from cinematic photorealism, de Beijer constructs worlds that delight in wonky line work, spattered textures and absurd characters resembling volumetric abstractions by Picasso. Yet the aesthetics are not completely derived from the analogue past – in his short experimental animations *Car Craze* (2003), *Get Real!* (2010) and *Lucy* (2015), de Beijer references the current digital age not only in terms of its accessories and phenomena such as computer gaming, mobile phones and ecological disaster, but also in sensory effects that include faint traces of pixellation, Paint Effects outlines simulating crayon and pen, vertiginous digital camera moves and garbled electronic voices.

The effect is the construction of a universe that reflects life's materiality at this particular juncture in time, in which our relationship to elements is informed by both the analogue and digital. Viewing de Beijer's animations, I find myself responding viscerally to the hand-drawn markings and the gleefully contorted shapes and figures, but also experiencing the thrill of seeing things anew. Just as Manovich points out that digital technology enables a 'deep remixing', where creative media acquires unprecedented properties – for instance, 'typography is choreographed to move in 3D space' (Manovich 2006) – so do the components in de Beijer's films undergo shifts that would not be possible in an analogue dimension. Cameras spin around spaces replete with signatures of the hand-made, crayon-smeared figures bend and mutate. Artists such as de Beijer push the potentialities of Maya into unexpected places, away from its intended engineering as 3D software with a powerful capacity to simulate the photoreal. Manovich observes how architectural studios such as that of Zahar Hadid, experiment with Maya in a similar vein, utilising the physics of animated splines to bend geometry and emerge with organic-shaped buildings that would be difficult to visualise through pencil-based drafts.

These kinds of spatial acrobatics and distortions have also been merged with photoreal aesthetics in mainstream films, in a fashion that may be considered experimental. For instance, a memorable sequence in David Fincher's *Panic Room* (2002) employs a virtual camera and CGI to pass through a lock in the door and both literally and figuratively explore the hidden levels in a storeyed house. Jonathan Romney, in his 2014 essay for the online Aeon website, bemoans the fact that digital animation – as reflected by blockbusters – has become 'wearingly dull and clichéd', but he does write enthusiastically about the creative opportunities that are unique to the capacities of digital media: 'With CGI, we've seen a shift in the imagination and representation of three-dimensional space, a kind of mind-bending geometric ingenuity' (Romney 2014). Romney refers to Christopher Nolan's *Inception* (2010) as an example of such inventiveness, and Alfonso Cuarón's *Gravity* (2013) as being 'a \$100-million special-effects production that is nonetheless genuinely experimental', which 'makes us feel as dizzily untethered as its heroine' through the use of its virtual camera and 'unusually long takes that weave intricate trajectories in space' (2014).

Virtual and digital cameras, when integrated within an experimental animation environment, have the potential to capture more than an untethered Sandra Bullock, and can offer startlingly fresh and profound perspectives in a range of media. For instance, Joshua Mosley's *Jeu de Paume* (2014), which was exhibited at the 2014 Whitney Biennale, inhabits the subjective awareness of two analogue puppets, who are playing a game of tennis at the Château de Fontainebleau, in 1907. Ingeniously orchestrated through a combination of virtual camera moves, a physical digital camera on a robotic arm that captures the analogue set and puppets, and digital compositing, the sequence quietly and poetically fastens on atmospheric nuances that tantalise the senses of the distracted player – and in turn immerse the spectator within both the tactile present and a state of sublimity – alongside athletic action. These impressions include changes in light across the stadium's wall, glimpsed as the eye moves heavenward; the digital camera also enables ground-level, slow-moving passages as the ball comes to a standstill, that are cut with shots of the heightened action and dance of the players.

Ann Lislegaard's installation *Bellona (after Samuel R. Delany)* (2005) similarly captures a point of view that leads an audience through a space both psychological and physical. Using 3D software in a fashion that eschews photorealism and textural complexity, the work instead pares down architectural space into gleaming geometries of colour and tone, set in a painterly state of flux as lights hauntingly turn on and off, and doors open and close. In resurrecting the past, Mosley's puppets and set evince the same kind of exquisite attention to miniaturist physical detail found in features by the LAIKA stop-motion studio; Lislegaard however is conjuring the futuristic world of Samuel Delany's 1974 science fiction novel *Dhalgren* and it seems apt that the work's materiality appears as more ephemeral, with algorithms and electricity at its core.

Digital ephemerality

The nature of digital ephemerality is explored in Aylish Wood's writing, which constitutes an integral contribution to understanding digital materiality; her layered deconstruction ranges from the surface manifestation of the digital to its most fundamental ingredients and operations. Wood's observations derive from numerous interviews with Maya practitioners, as well as theoretical interpretations, and she notes that digital information 'is inaccessible to direct experience by humans, as we are not hard wired, unless perhaps we have some kind of implant directly stimulating our muscles' (Wood 2007). Instead, we encounter such information as 'text, sound or visual elements; in other words, we encounter it through a range of interfaces' (2014). Such interfaces I believe, can be analysed in terms of their materiality – propelled by electricity and code, they manifest an RGB luminance that carries a variety of connotations. Sean Cubitt's book *The Practice of Light: A Genealogy of Visual Technologies from Prints to Pixels* (2014) forges invaluable links between analogue and digital art practices, as does Meredith Hoy's book *From Point to Pixel: A Genealogy of Digital Aesthetics* (2017). Cubitt regards the gleaming monitor as a contemporary successor to light's historical association with the celestial, as found in examples such as Rembrandt's paintings and Goethe's writings: 'Because it is itself forever unstill and forever unnameable, light was for Goethe as it was for Grosseteste and the neo-Platonists: the crucial channel between human and divine' (Cubitt 2014, 128). A category of digital experimental animations exists that foregrounds properties of light, space and sound, and their glowing interfaces encompass monitors, handheld devices and projections. When a reductive aesthetic is employed, these screens become incandescent portals, evoking alternate worlds, the future and transcendent states. Ann Lislegaard's installations *Bellona* (2005), and *Time Machine* (2011) are examples, as are David O'Reilly's groundbreaking games *Mountain* (2014) and *Everything* (2017), as well as *Monument Valley* (2014) created by Ustwo Games.

David O'Reilly's experimental digital animation *Please Say Something* (2008), in the fashion of Lislegaard's *Bellona*, intentionally pares 3D CGI down to its non-ornamental fundamentals. Futurity and sublimity are in turn evoked, but also a very contemporary space that reverberates with familiarity for those who have grown up with screens beaming video games, animated vector graphics and the loneliness and interconnectedness of the Internet. Lislegaard's installation contains rich layers of reference to Modernist painting and architecture, and O'Reilly also draws upon a referential cornucopia, that includes digital media history, the cat and mouse trope in animation, Disney, Tarkovsky and Michael Haneke. In his essay 'Basic Animation Aesthetics' (2009), which can be downloaded from his website, O'Reilly offers an intriguing analysis of the importance of aesthetics in creating *Please Say Something*: 'My central idea in constructing the world of the film was to prove that something totally artificial and unreal could still communicate emotion and hold cinematic truth' (2009). His essay can be read as an essential animation and film primer; he prioritises coherence and a clear set of laws and parameters in creating an emotionally resonant world:

> If something in a world seems too out of place, if it breaks or overextends these rules, believability evaporates. For this reason we can look at a very simple, basic animation style and find it just as absorbing as if it was filmed

(sic) world-class actors in an elaborate set. Even if animation is technically bad, but *consistently* bad, it will be coherent and thus potentially believable.

(2009)

Through non-linear sequences, and an aesthetic that 'makes no effort to cover up the fact that it is a computer animation', *Please Say Something* moves viewers with its depiction of a troubled relationship between a cat and mouse. It is illuminating to ponder the aesthetic rules laid down by O'Reilly; he describes them as being 'centered around the idea of economy', because one of the main problems in working artistically with 3D is 'that it takes so long to learn and then to use, from constructing a world to rendering it' (2009). Accordingly he employs preview renders, simple geometry, flat shading, aliasing (which makes edges seem jagged), animation on 2s and the synthetic voice of the computer, while shunning more complex operations such as blur, transparency and fade-outs. These simple elements nevertheless conjure a world with wintry streaks of sleet, polygonal cubes describing office cubicles and a hospital room, wireframe models suggesting departed souls and even a recreation of the rewind section in Michael Haneke's *Funny Games* (1997). A viewer's senses become more involved, due to the aesthetic economy requiring them to create connections and meaning. Here too, O'Reilly shares Lislegaard's concern with Modernism's quest to reduce materiality and form to its basic essence; it is through layers of association, together with a spatiality and temporality activated by audio and the animated image, that a deep resonance is achieved.

Some experimental digital animators pare imagery down still further to a state of abstracted light and geometry. Eastern mandalas, stained glass windows, Islamic geometric designs and the sublime evocations of Mark Rothko paintings, together with light installations by James Turrell and Dan Flavin, are all invoked by association. These works, although evanescent, nevertheless arouse a primal sense of wonder and cosmic infinitude. Certain works by Max Hattler and Vibeke Sorensen embody this approach, as do installations and animations by Jennifer Steinkamp, Larry Cuba, Robert Seidel, Stephanie Maxwell, Ryoichi Kurokawa, Janine Randerson, Jonathan Gillie, Paul Prudence and Shannon Novak. The interactive iPad experience *Biophilia*, produced by Bjork, and designed by Scott Snibbe, summons through sound and animated abstract imagery, light-filled visions of stars, planets and the endless expanse of the universe. By drawing upon the 'z' axis, as well as 'x and y' (the z axis represents depth, whereas x and y represent horizontal and vertical coordinates), the viewer interactively navigates both the space of the computer and that of the galaxy. Interestingly, Snibbe is a graduate of both computer science and Amy Kravitz's Experimental Animation programme at RISD, and *Biophilia* can be perceived as belonging to that category of artworks exploring primordial origins, such as experimental animated films by Len Lye and Jordan Belson.

Len Lye observed that 'We might say, speaking in terms of light, color, sounds, atoms, that nothing physical exists in a static state' (www.govettbrewster.

com/exhibitions/set-in-motion-len-lye-rebecca-baumann-dale-frank-z). In an explanation of the expressivity inherent in such elements, which stir the emotions but lack tangible heft, experimental digital media artist Adam Nash refers to Deleuze and Spinoza's analysis of the physical and virtual's affective power. He writes that 'if we take a Spinozan view of affect, then we do not need to be concerned with the difference between nature and artifice' (2012, 18). Nash quotes Deleuze: 'a body can be anything; it can be an animal, a body of sounds, a mind or an idea' (2012, 18). He thereby makes the legitimate assertion – as does Thomas Elsaesser in his analysis of *Her* – that the non-physical can manifest as a sensuous body that impacts a viewer's senses in a deep and resonant fashion.

The trifecta body of light, colour and sound can conjure metaphysical associations, but also signifiers connoting more vernacular intersections with popular and urban culture, such as animated billboards, glossy advertisements, gaming consoles, Disney and an inventory of films. Experimental animators who have drawn upon this kind of repertoire include Katie Torn, Faiyaz Jafri, Eva Papamargariti, Geoffrey Lillemon, Peter Burr, Jeremy Couillard, Rachel Rossin, LuYang, Marina Zurkow and Takeshi Murata. In terms of content, a number of these works refer to issues of urgent social and political currency – searing warnings about ecological disaster, an ambivalence concerning capitalism and consumerism, multifaceted explorations of gender and sexual identity, and the envisioning of dystopian/utopian futures. Artists such as Torn, Lillemon, Jafri and Couillard, draw upon a comedic absurdity, with gloriously unhinged juxtapositions echoing contemporary society's digital cacophony. In several of these animations, the body is distorted, hacked into and rearranged, to deliberately foster a sense of corporeal unease. Couillard's *The Bob Monroe 24/7 Out of Body News Network* (2015), for instance, taps into the visceral grotesque, while hilariously echoing CNN newscasts. Diverse modes of display further enhance these works' relationship with the surrounding cultural context, and strongly influence the degree of affect and emotional valence for a spectator. These modes of display include MTV idents, art galleries, architectural projections, Vimeo, the Internet, large urban outdoor screens, film festivals, virtual reality installations and the stirring, multi-media live performances of Peter Burr.

Reflexivity

Reflexivity – a medium's acknowledgement of its own inner-workings – is another strategy that Wells and Furniss identify as being a feature of experimental analogue animation. Given that commercial digital animation often strives towards a slick seamlessness, experimental digital animation that exposes what lies beneath a smooth veneer contains the potential to subvert the status quo. A slick, smooth veneer nevertheless can also expose economic and cultural power structures: Jonathan Monaghan's harnessing of the metaphoric powers of digital shaders creates a crass, gold surface, that in its context conjures associations with the interior decoration favoured by the Versailles palace and Trump. Experimental digital animator Alan Warburton identifies the political nature of peering under the digital hood, observing that CGI as an 'ideological tool' is 'powerful, ubiquitous and (most importantly) it obscures its origins. I'm pretty sure that anything powerful that is designed to be made invisible should be made visible' (Warburton 2014).

In terms of how such a visibility might impact upon our senses and emotions, the revelation of a work's digital guts – much like the Pompidou Centre's innards of plumbing being displayed on its exterior – can possess a raw honesty and vulnerability, in which digital materiality becomes palpable. Experimental animations that draw upon a photoreal aesthetic, while exercising reflexivity, have a particular kind of subversiveness – they adopt the tropes of commercial production, but also question its conventions. A selection of experimental digital animators who employ aspects of photorealism alongside reflexive strategies includes Alan Warburton, David Theobald, Morehshin Allahyrai, Nikita Diakur, Gregory Bennett, Jonathan Monaghan, Chris Landreth, Claudia Hart, Kim Laughton, Mike Pelletier and Esteban Diacono.

In his chapter in this book, Paul Taberham provides a thoughtful analysis of David Theobald's installation *Kebab World* (2014), and Lilly Husbands' perceptive essay, 'Animated Alien Phenomenology in David Theobald's Experimental Animations', applies the theoretical angle of speculative realism to several Theobald short animations. Husbands notes how detailed and labour-intensive photorealism, prolonged camera takes and a lack of anthropomorphic subjectivity decrease the primacy of the human spectator and instead focus our attention upon scenes not usually accorded value by Pixar and blockbuster films (Husbands 2015). Theobald's installation, *Modern Wonder* (2017), also foregrounds extensive digital labour that is not usually noticed – unless one is familiar with the 3D digital animation process, as Jason Kennedy points out (Kennedy 2017) – and depicts a comparatively banal scene. A 3D printer gradually lays down striations of green plastic, to create a volumetric Jesus icon with hands outstretched; a miniature rendition of the famous statue overlooking Rio de Janeiro. A reflexivity exists – this is a digital sequence depicting a digital operation. A virtual animated model is shown fabricating a physical object that is actually virtual itself, thus creating a conundrum for both our mind and senses.

I find that the work of the American/Iranian artist Morehshin Allahyrai also offers an intriguing interrogation of digital materiality in the experimental realm, with her movement between data-driven animation and the physical 3D printing of objects. Her investigation powerfully illustrates the degree to which the political and social context informs our emotional response to an artwork. Seemingly innocuous code has the potential to be sent electronically and metamorphose into 3D printed objects charged with meaning and danger, depending on the code's destination. In Allahyrai's work *Dark Matter* (2014) for instance, the 3D printed configuration of items such as a dog, dildo and satellite dish, all represent things that are banned or made unwelcome by the Iranian government.

Our response to *Dark Matter* would vary depending on our location; if we printed it in Iran, our senses might be filled with fear and alarm.

Russian experimental digital animator Nikita Diakur has spoken about his desire to create an emotionally nuanced, 'silly, unreasonable' (www.youtube.com/watch?v=9UEQAvmZpMM) digital world, in which creative accidents occur, and things even fall apart. He compares such an approach to Yuri Norstein's wife deliberately using her left hand in painting and drawing, to infuse the linework with greater character than images created with her trained right hand. Consequently, in his film *Ugly* (2017), characters' wireframes are reflexively revealed, textures are mapped awkwardly, polygons remain unsmoothed and traditional keyframing is bypassed. The characters are virtual puppets vertically tugged upwards by strings, their movement propelled by physics simulations for wind and cloth. Diakur and his team relished the fact that the characters' movement path could not be predicted; rather, numerous tests were carried out and curious collisions and distortions embraced. The result is a beautiful short animation, that reveals its digital guts and moves us due to its imperfections (see Figure 6.1).

Further examples of experimental digital animations can be cited that acknowledge the qualitative potential of digital software, and not just the quantitative. David O'Reilly, Ann Lislegaard and Peter Burr have incorporated glitch effects to introduce a painterly sketchiness and fragility; digital materiality is revealed as not being immune from upsets, just like humanity. O'Reilly's use of the glitch has even extended into the commercial zone, with his guest direction of a celebrated *Adventure Time* episode, that references Gertrude Stein's experiments with the title *A Glitch is a Glitch*. Gregory Bennett's animated naked male figures draw upon motion capture data to move in ceaseless, oppressive loops, but also acquire a poignant vulnerability due to the fact that they are rendered with default Lambert shaders and therefore exist in a state of digital undress. In David O'Reilly's game *Everything* (2017), the lengthy business of rigging and animating walk cycles is cast aside in favour of hilarious rotations. Watching

FIGURE 6.1 Still: *Ugly,* Nikita Diakur 2017.

standing, revolving bears roll across the landscape can make our bodies feel like we're in a gyroscope, but such disorientation however, also moves us emotionally. We're provided with a strange, sublime and familiar perspective that nonetheless makes total sense, and our perceptual faculties delight in the fresh neural pathways that are activated by such an experience.

Conclusion

In this chapter, through the examination of a number of experimental digital animation examples, and referencing the viewpoints of a variety of animation theorists and practitioners, I have explored the ways in which digital media can prompt a sensory and emotional response, that is equal in its intensity to that of its analogue counterparts. By focusing on the areas of materiality, digital ephemerality and reflexivity, I have investigated overlapping concerns that exist between analogue and digital experimental animation, as well as specific differences. A vital body of expressive, highly creative experimental digital animation continues to develop, that challenges previous narratives maligning digital media as being mechanical, cold and lacking in imaginative innovation.

In addition, an experimental digital animation practitioner can straddle both the analogue and digital, commercial and experimental realms; as Bolter and Grusin point out, media does not do its cultural work in isolation from other media, nor from social and economic forces. Like Grandpa Simpson (in a past episode of the long-running series) dreaming that he is a lithe, frock-wearing female in the Wild old West, with two macho cowboys literally duelling for his affections, such fluidity can be expressed with his intervening exclamation: 'Boys, stop! You can both marry me'. The two arenas do not need to be viewed as mutually exclusive zones stuck in a binary face-off, but rather as spheres in which there is considerable overlap and leakage. Nevertheless, experimental digital animation does enjoy a greater freedom to roam, push boundaries and ignore the entrenched aesthetics and values of corporatist models, and these characteristics help constitute both its expressive charge and its power to challenge embedded systems.

References

Allahyrai, Morehshin. *Dark Matter*. US, 2014. Film.

Bolter, Jay David and Richard Grusin. *Remediation: Understanding New Media*. Cambridge: MIT Press, 1999.

Buchan, Suzanne. 'The Animated Spectator: Watching the Quay Brothers' "Worlds"'. In *Animated Worlds*. Edited by Suzanne Buchan. Eastleigh: John Libbey Publishing, 2006.

Cooper, Merrian C. and Ernest B. Schoedsack. *King Kong*. US, 1933. Film.

Couillard, Jeremy. *The Bob Monroe 24/7 Out of Body News Network*. US, 2015. Film.

Cuarón, Alfonso. *Gravity*. US, 2013. Film.

Cubitt, Sean. *The Practice of Light: A Genealogy of Visual Technologies from Prints to Pixels.* Cambridge, MA: The MIT Press, 2014.

de Beijer, Evert. *Car Craze.* Holland, 2003. Film.

de Beijer, Evert. *Get Real!* Holland, 2010. Film.

de Beijer, Evert. *Lucy.* Holland, 2015. Film.

de Bruyn, Dirk. 'Materialist Performance in the Digital Age.' *Screening the Past* 37, 2013, accessed November 20 2017. www.screeningthepast.com/2013/09/materia list-performance-in-the-digital-age/

Delany, Samuel. *Dhalgren.* New York: Bantam Books, 1975.

Diakur, Nikita. 'Animateka Masterclass – 2017: Nikita Diakur.' 2017, accessed January 10 2018. www.youtube.com/watch?v=9UEQAvmZpMM

Diakur, Nikita. *Ugly.* Germany, 2017. Film.

Edwards, Gareth. Adobe Inspired Media, Curzon Cinema, London, May 2009. Presentation.

Elsaesser, Thomas and Malte Hagener. *Film Theory: An Introduction Through the Senses.* New York: Routledge, 2015.

Fincher, David. *Panic Room.* US, 2002. Film.

Furniss, Maureen. *Art in Motion: Animation Aesthetics.* Barnet: John Libbey Publishing, 1998.

Guðmundsdóttir, Björkand Scott Snibbe. *Biophilia.* UK/US, 2011. Interactive app.

Haneke, Michael. *Funny Games.* Germany, 1997. Film.

Hart, Claudia. 'Swapping Identities. A Conversation with Claudia Hart.' By Sabin Bors. In *Anti-Utopias*, accessed November 10 2017. https://anti-utopias.com/editorial/swapping-identities-a-conversation-with-claudia-hart/

Hart, Claudia. 'Beginning and Endgames: A Parable in 3D.' *Cultural Politics 9.* March 1 2013 accessed November 20 2017. https://read.dukeupress.edu/cultural-politics/article/9/1/86/25923/Beginning-and-End-GamesA-Parable-in-3DBeginning

Hertz, Betti-Sue. *Animated Painting.* San Diego: San Diego Museum of Art, 2007.

Hosea, Birgitta. 'Drawing Animation.' *Animation: An Interdisciplinary Journal 5*, no. 3 (2010): 353–367.

Hoy, Meredith. *From Point to Pixel: A Genealogy of Digital Aesthetics.* Hanover, New Hampshire: Dartmouth College Press, 2017.

Husbands, Lilly. 'Animated Alien Phenomenology in David Theobald's Experimental Animations.' *Frames Cinema Journal* (2015), accessed December 5 2017, http://framescinemajournal.com/article/animated-alien-phenomenology-in-david-theobalds-experimental-animations/

Jackson, Peter. *King Kong.* New Zealand, 2005. Film.

Jafri, Faiyaz. Website faiyazjafri.com, accessed November 20 2017. http://faiyazjafri.com/aboutfaiyazjafri/

Jonze, Spike. *Her.* US, 2013. Film.

Kennedy, Jason. 'The Animator's (Missing) Hand: How Practice Informs Seeing in 3D Animation.' In *CONFIA 2017: International Conference on Illustration & Animation*, Morada: Instituto Politécnico do Cávado e do Ave, 2017.

Krauss, Rosalind. '"The Rock": William Kentridge's Drawings for Projection.' *October*, no. 92 (2000).

Lasseter, John. *Toy Story.* US, 1995. Film.

Leslie, Esther. *Hollywood Flatlands: Animation, Critical Theory and the Avant-Garde.* London: Verso, 2004.

Lislegaard, Ann. *Bellona (after Samuel R Delany).* Denmark, 2005. Film.

Lislegaard, Ann. *Time Machine.* Denmark, 2011. Film.

Lye, Len. *Set in Motion* exhibition, Govett-Brewster Art Gallery, New Plymouth, New Zealand. 2016, accessed November 2017. www.govettbrewster.com/exhibitions/set-in-motion-len-lye-rebecca-baumann-dale-frank-z

Manovich, Lev. 'The Aesthetics of Virtual Worlds: Report from Los Angeles.' 1995, accessed February 19 2018. http://manovich.net/content/04-projects/016-the-aesthetics-of-virtual-worlds/13_article_1996.pdf

Manovich, Lev. 'Understanding Hybrid Media.' 2006, accessed December 15 2017. http://manovich.net/content/04-projects/055-understanding-hybrid-media/52_article_2007.pdf

Marks, Laura. 'The Quays' Institute Benjamina: An Olfactory View'. In *The Sharpest Point: Animation at the End of Cinema.* Edited by Chris Gehman and Steve Reinke. Toronto: Yyz Books, 2006.

Nash, Adam. 'Affect and the Medium of Digital Data.' *The Fibreculture Journal*, Issue 21, 2012, accessed November 10 2017): 1–29. http://twentyone.fibreculturejournal.org/fcj-148-affect-and-the-medium-of-digital-data/#sthash.R14GcF95.dpbs

Nolan, Christopher. *Inception.* US, 2010. Film.

O'Reilly, David. *Take Me Out.* Sweden, 2004. Music video.

O'Reilly, David. *Please Say Something.* US, 2008. Film.

O'Reilly, David. *Adventure Time: A Glitch is a Glitch.* US, 2013. TV episode.

O'Reilly, David. *Mountain.* US, 2014. Video game.

O'Reilly, David. *Everything.* US, 2017. Video game.

O'Reilly, David. 'Basic Animation Aesthetics.' 2009, accessed November 2 2017. www.davidoreilly.com/downloads/

Power, Patrick. 'Animated Expressions: Expressive Style in 3D Computer Graphic Narrative Animation.' In *Animation: An Interdisciplinary Journal 4*, no. 2 (2009).

Prince, Stephen. 'True Lies: Perceptual Realism, Digital Images and Film Theory.' In *The Film Cultures Reader*, edited by Graeme Turner. New York: Routledge, 2002.

Quay, Stephen and Timothy. *Institute Benjamenta.* UK, 1996. Film.

Rodriguez, Robert and Frank Miller. *Sin City.* US, 2005. Film.

Romney, Jonathan. 'Numbing the Imagination.' 2014, accessed November 20 2017. https://aeon.co/essays/can-the-creative-weirdness-of-cgi-be-recovered-from-cliche

Sakaguchi, Hironobu. *Final Fantasy: The Spirits Within.* US, 2001. Film.

Sobchack, Vivian. 'Final Fantasies: Computer Animation and the [Dis]Illusion of Life.' In *Animated Worlds*, edited by Suzanne Buchan. Eastleigh: John Libbey, 2006.

Sobchack, Vivian. 'Animation and Automation, or, the Incredible Effortfulness of Being.' *Screen 50,* no. 4 (Winter 2009): 375–391.

Stanton, Andrew. *WALL-E.* US, 2008. Film.

Theobald, David. *Kebab World.* UK, 2014. Film.

Theobald, David. *Modern Wonder.* UK, 2017. Film.

Ustwo Games. *Monument Valley.* UK, 2014. Video Game.

Warburton, Alan. 'Spherical Harmonics.' *The Photographer's Gallery.* 2014, accessed 20 November 2017. https://thephotographersgalleryblog.org.uk/2014/02/13/spherical-harmonics-alan-warburton-interviewed-by-katrina-sluis/

Wells, Paul. *Understanding Animation.* London: Routledge, 1998.

Wood, Aylish. *Digital Encounters.* London: Routledge, 2007.

Wood, Aylish. 'Behind the Scenes.' *Animation: An Interdisciplinary Journal 9*, no. 3 (2014): 317–332.

7

BEYOND A DIGITAL ÉCRITURE FÉMININE

Cyberfeminism and experimental computer animation

Birgitta Hosea

Where is the feminist experimental computer animation?

With the current resurgence of interest in feminism and growth in the proportion of women choosing to study animation at university (Vankin 2015), this chapter began with a search for examples of innovative, feminist approaches to experimental computer animation. Despite extensive literature review, online searches, calls on social media and academic networks, these proved harder to uncover than anticipated, which led to three further, related questions:

- Where are the women working in computer animation (and animation in general and in Information Technology (IT))?
- How do you define experimental computer animation?
- What might a feminist approach to experimental computer animation be?

As part of this enquiry, women artists who contributed to the earliest emerging forms of computer animation and cyberfeminist[1] discourses from the turn of the millennium will be re-examined. Following the utopian ideas of these early adopters of technology, did women go on to liberate themselves through technology? The chapter will conclude that negotiating the issues of essentialism and intersectionality that follow a re-examination of cyberfeminism has wider implications for the possible futures that our society creates for itself.

Where are the women in computer animation?

To be assigned the female gender at birth is to be subject to a number of gendered assumptions and discourses from day one. From the pressure to wear a pink Disney princess outfit and play with *girls'* toys, to the idea that technology is too complicated for women, we are, to paraphrase Simone de Beauvoir, not born but become women. We may choose to either perform or defy these expectations, but, despite a century of four successive waves of feminism, they still run deeply in the fabric of our society. Although the current, fourth wave of feminism is heavily identified with social networks such as the Vagenda[2] and the Everyday Sexism Project,[3] this familiarity with online technologies has not correlated with equality of employment for women in IT, animation or games and women of colour remain particularly under-represented. There is a shocking lack of diversity amongst the individuals who are employed to make the popular culture that surrounds us and that reinforces all of our ideas about the world.

Rather than considering the mainstream animation industry as a whole, however, this chapter is concerned with digital experimentation: Animations on the cutting edge that have been created with a spirit of creative investigation rather than for the purpose of entertainment. Experimentation and innovation are vital, because if the developers of new technologies and new forms of entertainment continue to be limited to a small section of the population, they will continue to represent their own interests and not the wider concerns of the general population.

How do you define experimental computer animation?

A quick survey of many experimental animation festivals around the world today will reveal that there is a tendency for animation that foregrounds its digital origin to make up the minority of films on offer.[4] Although all animation can now be considered digital, or at least digitised (unless it only exists on film), animation that appears autographic (Foá and Hosea 2019) – handmade or hand-drawn – tends to have a privileged status in the experimental context (Hosea 2019), as opposed to work made through industrial processes, such as CGI or code-driven animation, which may be considered as commercial or overly led by mainstream graphic design trends.[5] This was not always the case. Since the beginning of computer animation, artists, avant-garde filmmakers and creative technologists have been producing new methods of expression through digital processes. However, if all animation now involves the computer at some point in its making, does that mean all experimental animation is experimental computer animation? Further clarification about these terms becomes necessary in order to be more specific about what is under discussion here.

'Experimental' is a slippery concept to pin down and there are many ways to be experimental in and with animation. For the purpose of this chapter, experimental computer animation is considered as being a work of expanded moving image – which could be a linear short film: form part of a spatial experience in an installation or be non-linear and interactive – that experiments with computing itself: Animation in which material and conceptual investigation can be demonstrated to go beyond the realm of aesthetic style or subject matter to examine the very notion of the digital. This is not intended to be a reductive formula for how to be experimental in computer animation, but to define the scope of examples of animation to include in this chapter. Its concern with medium and materiality may be considered Modernist and 'retro', but the intention is to make an argument about the importance of a more diverse group of artists taking control of technology.

'What special capacities can the computer offer the artist?', asked experimental filmmaker, Malcolm Le Grice in 1974 (2016, 219). Le Grice, who first joined the Computer Art Society in 1969, argued that for computing to be considered as an art form, it should explore digital materiality – that which was unique to and could only be created through computers (1974, 162). By necessity, all the animations he produced were programmed directly through code, a process in which visual investigation was analysed and translated into a text-based programming language. Clearly influenced by Conceptual and Systems artists of the era, such as Sol le Witt, for him this new tool had the potential to explore variation: 'systems of incrementation, permutation and random number generation' (Le Grice 2006, 220) as well as the potential to expand the very structure of film language itself (Le Grice 1974, 166–167).

In addition to an exploration of what is specific about the digital, for computer animation to be considered as experimental (in the terms of this chapter) there should be a control over and extension of technical processes, rather than a reliance on the default settings of commercial software programmes. Frieder Nake, who first exhibited his computer art in 1965, argues that to create imagery through code is to work without the clichés of conventional processes that are inherent in mainstream software. To use software is to lack authorship over the results since it means working with the 'ready-made' and appropriating someone else's ideas about how a computer can be used (Hosea 2010, 357). This tendency to 'appropriate' is not restricted to the use of software, however. Traditional techniques and learned assumptions about how to work in a particular discipline that are not critically examined have been termed 'automatisms' in 1974 by the philosopher Stanley Cavell (quoted in Krauss 2000, 4). In this sense, commercial software comes with a set of implicit 'automatisms' that can influence the aesthetic outcome. This can be seen in style trends in computer graphics and animation that follow new developments in software such as gradients, opacity and fur texture (Hosea 2010, 356–357). Nake's early plotter drawings, such as, *Hommage à Paul Klee, 13/9/65 Nr.2* (1965) drew upon mathematics and probability theory to extend what was predictable and introduce the element of chance into his programming through a use of random variables (V&A Museum, 2017). His work illustrates how innovation results from the critical questioning of conventional modes of practice.

Pioneering female innovators in computer animation

Amongst the early developers of computer animation who took an active role in discovering new ways of working were a small number of women, including artist Lillian F. Schwartz, who worked on developing code to produce images and animation. Through her experimentation with kinetics she began to collaborate with computer technologists at Bell Labs in 1968, where she remained artist-in-residence for three decades. Frequently returning to art history for inspiration, she endorsed a consistent exploration of digital tools in terms of colour, form, tone, kinetics, proportion and the representation of movement that underpinned her own pioneering work in computer animation, which continued to push the boundaries of what was possible. Her enthusiasm for this evolving medium is palpable from an article she published on computer animation in 1974:

> To give more variety and interest to a given set of instructions, there is flexibility in programming allowing for surprises and unexpected images. It is this element of excitement, of new, amazing images, shapes and textures that I find so rewarding. These visual surprises coming out of the computer are awesome experiences.
>
> *(159)*

In an industrial society subject to increasing automation, Schwartz argues that artists bring freedom, new approaches and an assertion of the human spirit to computers, instruments with the potential to be 'devastating tools of oppression' (ibid). At times, unexpected outcomes contributed to developments in her work. While creating her film *Trois Visage* in 1977, a bug in the programme caused the image to disintegrate. The code for this was then examined and reproduced as an effect in future work (Schwartz 1992, 218–219). Although her work is not primarily concerned with feminism, her poster commissioned for the opening of the Museum of Modern Art in New York, *Big MOMA* (1984) is considered an icon of digital art (Prince 2003, 6). This single image took over a year to produce. Developing new techniques for analysing visual data, appropriating a database of scanned images, palette matching and simulating perspectival mapping in three-dimensional space, the work features Gaston Lachaise's giant sculpture, *Standing Woman* (1932), covered in a three-dimensional, digital 'skin' of iconic paintings from MOMA's collection. The material that she created in the making of this poster was later used for a thirty-second public service announcement on local TV stations about the new MOMA, for which she won an Emmy (Schwartz 1992, 98–109). Creating a giant woman out of paintings made by male artists was not just a technical challenge. This image draws attention to the lack of work by female artists at the centre of the MOMA's collection.

Although a few women artists were able to get access to the highly specialised facilities needed to develop computer animations in the 1970s, there were significant barriers. Very few research labs were engaged with creative computing at the time, so this kind of investigation was limited to those countries with the economic capacity to invest in such expensive facilities. In an interview from 2003, Rebecca Allen relates how she had to persuade her teachers at RISD to allow her to create her first computer animation in 1974 and subsequently spent a lot of time contacting the few research labs she could find in her native USA before she got taken on as a graduate student by the MIT Architecture Machine Group. The first projects she worked on were for the Defence Department. However, her interest was in subverting the 'antihuman' nature of the computer and bringing sensuality to it. Her first animation, created with graphs and punch cards, featured abstracted rotoscoping of a 1950's erotic film of a woman lifting her dress (Allen and Huhtamo 2003, 226–227). She went on to build a formidable career investigating natural motion and the organic through advanced technologies in three-dimensional scanning, CGI modelling, virtual and augmented reality and interactive experience design. Amongst many other projects, Allen is responsible for milestones in computer animation such as the Kraftwerk's *Musique Non-Stop* video in 1986, for which she developed state-of-the-art facial animation software (Allen 2016).

The barriers to women were not limited to the scarcity of research facilities available. Reflecting in 1990 on her experiences in the 1970s, artist Vibeke Sorensen (1990) describes how the expectations of equality she had inherited from her Danish background were confounded by a number of 'glass ceilings' that she encountered in the United States. After studying architecture in Copenhagen, she was turned down for two Masters course in Architecture for being a woman and also had evidence of direct discrimination when applying for jobs. She also faced assumptions that a woman couldn't be technical or work with complex mathematics. She observes:

> The bottom line is that there is not a conflict between numerical reasoning and women's nature. There is simply no math gene! Numerical ability, scientific observation and artistic expression are basic to women's nature. It seems that this knowledge and confidence has been lost from the general population. Women in computer graphics are reclaiming this territory.

These experiences led her to make one of her first films, *Etyma*, in 1974, which examined

> the relationship between the history of written language and patterns of thought, especially the origins of the word "woman," and I asserted my identity as a woman experimental filmmaker through symbolic visual poetry.
>
> *(Sorensen 1990)*

Sorensen had hopes, however, that there would be more opportunities for women to come and that women working with technology might make a positive contribution to the future. In 1990, she noted:

> while there are quite a few women in computer graphics, they are still a minority and I observe that even fewer women are entering the field from

the next generation of artists. However, because the field is young, there is less of an "old boy's club" rife with harassment, and the field is more open to women than are other fields. Indeed, the democratization of the personal computer has provided women more opportunity for access with dignity. After all, the computer itself does not discriminate on the basis of age, sex, or race. Perhaps it can help to lead us to a more integrated and idealistic society than we currently live in.

Tenaciously continuing with her work in computing, Sorensen has gone on to explore visual music, generative systems, nature, stereoscopy and Asian cosmologies through computer animation, networked performance and interactive architectural installation, such as *Mood of the Planet* (2015). In this installation that takes the shape of an arch or doorway, live data based on keywords is sampled from Twitter to create colour animation that is generated from human emotions around the world at that particular point in time (Sorensen 2015).

Feminist approaches to computing

As access to personal computers became more widespread in the 1990s, techno-utopianists and cyberfeminists made a number of grand claims for the computer age including the potential for the creation of new, virtual worlds and the transformation of gender relationships in society. Inspired by Donna Haraway's *Cyborg Manifesto*, the term cyberfeminism was coined in 1991 in two places at once, both by cultural theorist Sadie Plant in the UK and the feminist art group VNS Matrix in Australia (Sofia 2003, 511).

Although there were many approaches to cyberfeminism, the movement builds on the work of post-structuralist French feminists, such as Hélène Cixous, Monique Wittig and Luce Irigaray, in seeking new forms of female language – *écriture féminine*. These ideas came from the *politique et psychanalyse* group – radical French women who did not actually call themselves feminists as they did not want equality with men, but rather aimed for a revolutionary overthrow of the patriarchal social order. The term, *écriture féminine*, was first presented in Hélène Cixous's 1975 essay 'The Laugh of the Medusa'. In a society in which the mainstream media, literature and institutions were all dominated by the ideas of men, she argues for women – who had never had their turn to speak, to assert their own voices, take control of their own representation – to defy the ways in which they had hitherto been portrayed and overturn the oppressive tongue of patriarchy. She wrote:

> Now, I-woman am going to blow up the Law: an explosion henceforth possible and ineluctable; let it be done, right now, in language [...] If woman has always functioned "within" the discourse of man [...] it is time for her to dislocate this "within," to explode it, turn it around, and seize it; to

make it hers, containing it, taking it in her own mouth, biting that tongue with her very own teeth to invent for herself a language to get inside of.

(1986, 257)

For Cixous, writing is important to the process of liberation because it introduces 'the very possibility of change' and is a 'springboard for subversive thought' that could transform society (ibid., 249). This should be a new kind of writing, not logical or full of reason, but saying the unthinkable, poetic, plural, resisting definition, transgressive, of the body, of pleasure and physical desire, liberated from censorship or guilt about sexuality, erotic, dirty, oozing the abject. A woman should have no fear of her own bodily fluids: 'There is always within her at least a little of that good mother's milk. She writes in white ink' (ibid., 252). Getting in touch with her body would allow woman access to her primordial strength, for so long repressed. Cixous continues:

> A woman's body, with its thousand and one thresholds of ardour – once, by smashing yokes and censors, she lets it articulate the profusion of meanings that run through it in every direction – will make the old single-grooved mother tongue reverberate with more than one language [...] Women must write through their bodies, they must invent the impregnable language that will wreck partitions, classes, and rhetorics, regulations and codes.
>
> *(ibid., 256)*

Other women associated with the group became similarly inspired by the notion of *écriture féminine*. In her text, *Body I*, Madeleine Gagnon (1986) reflects on the frustration of being a woman speaking a language that had been defined by men, 'I am a foreigner to myself in my own language and I translate myself by quoting all the others' (180). For Marguerite Duras (1986), the writing of women is 'translated from the unknown ... like a new way of communicating rather than an already formed language' (174). It bypasses rational thinking. Duras declares:

> I know when I write there is something inside me that stops functioning [...] – the analytical way of thinking inculcated by college, studies, reading, experience [...] It's as if I were returning to a wild country.
>
> *(ibid., 175)*

The issue was not to stop speaking in French, but to find new ways to use that language: To customise it in a manner that reflected female experience since that had not been represented in the mainstream before.

For the cyberfeminists two decades later, developments in personal computing and the spread of the internet represented new frontiers to this 'wild country'. Cyberfeminism did not simply argue for equality of access to digital technology, but for a profound rethinking of how to use it. Women had the opportunity to adopt this new technology to recode the way they had been represented and to create a digital *écriture féminine*, in the words of Faith Wilding (1998), to create 'new languages, programs, platforms, images, fluid identities and multi-subject definitions' (9). Leading the way on these utopian ideas was Sadie Plant's 1998 book *Zeros + Ones*, which made a series of connections between the essential nature of women and the new skills needed for an information society, between the traditionally female craft of weaving and non-linear hypertext. Plant believed in the possibility for an 'unmanned' future through new forms of technology that could be adopted by women and no longer dominated by white men (Sofia 2003, 511). Seeking to reveal the repressed feminine side of technology, Plant (1998) argues that the skills women have always had – such as networking, multi-tasking, the ability to continuously update their skills – makes them ideal for working in a new digital era of interconnected computing. She writes:

> Weaving was already multimedia: singing, chanting, telling stories, danc-ing and playing games as they work, spinsters, weavers, and needle workers were literally networkers as well [...] the textures of woven cloth func-tioned as means of communication and information storage long before anything was written down.
>
> *(65)*

The non-linear structure of the book itself adds to the discourse about multiplic-ity, fluidity and hypertextuality. Refuting Freud's claim that women had made few contributions to the invention of new technologies apart from weaving, the book interlaces many discourses from the history of computing such as the role of women in computing, textiles and the manufacture of electronics. *Zeros + Ones* celebrates the achievements of Ada Lovelace, the Victorian mathematician who is considered as the first computer programmer for her work on extending the theoretical capabilities of Charles Babbage's proposed mechanical computer, the Analytical Engine. In translating the Italian engineer Luigi Menabrea's notes on the Analytical Engine, Lovelace's footnotes contained commentary more sophis-ticated and three times longer than the original text itself, which Plant argues is a precursor of hypertext.

The utopian zeitgeist that the future could be female through new technolo-gies inspired artists in Australia such as VNS Matrix and Linda Dement to create new kinds of female-centred artwork using 'new media'. Australia in the 1990s was a fertile ground for cyberfeminist art due to a supportive environment for art and technology that included the Australian Network for Art and Technology (ANAT) (Barnett 2014). VNS Matrix (pronounced Venus Matrix) was founded in 1991 by four artists: Virginia Barratt, Francesca da Rimini, Julianne Pierce and Josephine Starrs who, in the words of their own myth of origin:

> crawled out of the cyberswamp [...] and via an aesthetics of slime [...] forged an unholy alliance with technology and its machines [...] on a

mission to hijack the toys from technocowboys and remap cyberculture with a feminist bent.

(Barratt et al. 2015)

Declaring a *Cyberfeminist Manifesto for the Twenty-First Century,* they exhibited this text in different arenas, such as on billboards in Sydney, in print form posted around their hometown of Adelaide and at the 1992 SIGGRAPH convention in Chicago (Sofia 2003, 511–512). It reads as follows:

> We are the modern cunt
> positive anti reason
> unbounded unleashed unforgiving
> we see art with our cunt we make art with our cunt
> we believe in jouissance madness holiness and poetry
> we are the virus of the new world disorder
> rupturing the symbolic from within
> saboteurs of big daddy mainframe
> the clitoris is a direct line to the matrix
> VNS MATRIX
> terminators of the moral code
> mercenaries of slime
> go down on the altar of abjection
> probing the visceral temple we speak in tongues
> infiltrating disrupting disseminating
> corrupting the discourse
> we are the future cunt

(Barnett 2014)

With its reference to *jouissance,*[6] making art with the body and the abject, there is a clear link to the earlier French radical feminist ideas of *écriture feminine,* although this is taken into the digital age through the use of multimedia and the adoption of metaphors from hacking, such as corrupting the patriarchal discourse of the military-industrial complex like a virus. *All New Gen* (1994) expresses these ideas in the form of a video game in which play is based around the hacker as virus infecting the patriarchal corporate culture in a quest to sabotage the databanks of Big Daddy Mainframe. At the start of the game, the player is asked to indicate their gender as Male, Female or Neither. However, only a gender fluid position is available – unless Neither is chosen the game will terminate (Evans 2014). Enemies to avoid include the techno-himbo, Circuit Boy (whose penis morphs into a mobile phone) and Big Daddy Mainframe himself, a 'transplanetary military-industrial-imperial data environment' (Barratt et al. n.d.). The players measure their energy in stores of G-slime and can receive assistance from mutant *sheroes,* the DNA sluts (Sofia 2003, 511–512).

These themes of sexually active women, slime and abjection polluting the rational, clean digital world can also be seen in the work of Linda Dement, another Australian artist. In her interactive works for CD-ROM such as *Typhoid Mary* (1991), *Cyberflesh GirlMonster* (1995) and *In My Gash* (1999) clicking without an apparent interface on an on-screen monstrous recombination of wounds, organs and dismembered body parts reveals hyperlinks to stories, animations, sounds, quotes, diary extracts, medical information, statistics and images telling tales of patriarchal violence, addiction, prostitution, suicide and abuse (Davis 2006; Plant 1998, 192; Sofia 2003, 516). In an artist's statement, Dement (2003) describes her preoccupations in these works thusly:

> I work with the disease and detritus of bodily interiors, subcutaneous landscapes, in order to give form to lived experience and its inner disturbances. I am interested in the possibilities for embodiment and technology, particularly where the bodies concerned are those mad, damaged, uncontrolled and perverse ones from the peripheries of mainstream culture. It's in the outpourings of bloody unreason from bent flesh and fast machines that I find a potential for something truthful and real.

Through a multimedia assemblage of animation, digital imaging, hypertext and audio, Dement gives a non-linear voice to the dispossessed – the junky, the suicide, the prostitute.

Essentialism or intersectionality

Despite its radical intentions, cyberfeminism came under fire at the turn of the millennium for its unquestioned fetishisation of new technology and unexamined reliance upon privilege. In 1998, Faith Wilding warned against an uncritical attitude towards new technologies that were not neutral zones, but had resulted from military research projects. She pointed out that new media was inscribed in a social system rooted with sexual and racial prejudice (9). In addition, many developments in online technology, such as video streaming, were led by the economics of investment in pornography.

It was also unrealistic to presume that cyberfeminism would have relevance for all women. Equal access to digital technologies is predicated not only on being able to afford the hardware, but on having stable telecommunications networks and consistent electricity supplies. There are also other access issues – being able to learn how to use and contextualise these tools – more available for speakers of dominant language groups and the simple economic luxury of having the time to creatively engage with technology outside of work, domestic labour or childcare. Adopting a postcolonial position, in 2002 Radhika Gajjala and Annapurna Mamidipudi questioned the reproducibility of cyberfeminist models to the third-world and the 'blindspot' of race, class and location. They noted:

> we are concerned with the issue of whether "the bequeathed" are or are not empowered through the transfer of technologies produced and

designed within socio-cultural environments situated in a Westernized and Masculinized world [...] Thus, our approach to finding solutions emphasizes the re-designing of "new" technological environments, rather than a mere attempt at "transferring" so-called advanced technologies in the name of a notion of Progress that is in itself situated in socio-economic, historical and political contexts not necessarily empowering to all communities of the world.

How could liberation in cyberspace materially improve the lives of women in rural India? Technology, they argued, needed to be rethought for localised contexts.

A backlash against feminism in the popular consciousness of the first decades of the twenty-first century has focussed on its concerns with language, which came to be thought of as policing expression, desire and appearance through 'political correctness', and being 'anti-sex'. However, as the previous section demonstrates, there was never one type of feminism, but many approaches to feminism. Those feminist arguments derived from the post-structuralist French theorists were not about censoring or denying, but were both utopian in conceptualisation, through exploring language or technology as new forms of articulation to express sexuality and subjectivity from a female perspective, and revolutionary in aiming to overthrow the patriarchy. The biggest criticism of all forms of radical feminism, however, came from within the women's movement itself and was that of essentialism: That assumptions were being made about what it is to be 'woman' from a primarily privileged white and Western perspective and subsequently presented as if this were a universal experience and applicable to all women, whatever their circumstances may be.

Addressing accusations of essentialism and exclusivity, new generations of feminism seek to engage with intersectionalism, a more expanded conceptualisation of inequality that grows from Black feminism, cultural studies and the increasing realisation that a feminist analysis on its own is not enough to explain the complex intertwining of social injustice (Collins 2015, 6). Indeed, how can an understanding of violence against women in Iraq result from an analysis of gender alone (ibid.)? Through the study of how different social categories – such as race, gender, sexuality, class, age, location – are complex, interconnected and mutually constitutive, intersectionality aims to unite communities of practice who seek social justice to understand and counter multiple inequalities. This approach enables links to be created between communities and a more nuanced view of power relations.

Post-cyberfeminism: Xenofeminism, Afrofuturism and glitch feminism

A renewed interest in cyberfeminism appears to be emerging that takes into account the critiques of essentialism that tore apart the women's movement in the

1990s. A new open-access peer reviewed journal *Ada: a Journal of Gender, New Media and Technology* was launched by the Fembot collective in 2012.[7] Google launched a Made with Code project in 2014 to encourage school girls to take up coding.[8] Indeed, Helen Hester argues that cyberfeminism should be re-visited and upgraded in order to develop a post-cyberfeminism that aims for social and political activism rather than neo-liberal individual freedoms. For Hester, 1990s feminism was too fragmented and dispersed across networks to form a unified, radical plan for action: Resulting in decentralised micro politics rather than organised, mass political action. For Hester (2017), this is exemplified by Sadie Plant's hypertextual weaving together of different information sources and blurring of conceptual boundaries in *Zeros and Ones*, which has the consequence of 'substantially restricting much of the text's diagnostic capacity and political utility'. To counter this, Hester argues for the collective Laboria Caboniks's proposal for a new xenofeminist movement defined through means of an *n* hypothesis – a theory that is constantly reviewed, iterated, updated like new software patches or open source software and 'awaits and invites revision':

> '**Hypothesis:** Xenofeminism is a gender abolitionist, anti-naturalist, technomaterialist form of posthumanism, building upon the insights of cyberfeminism. Its future is unmanned.'
>
> *(ibid.)*

This manifesto for xenofeminism has the ambition to go beyond the 'excess of modesty in feminist agendas of recent decades' that was 'not proportionate to the monstrous complexity of our reality' (Cuboniks 2015, 3). It stands firmly against essentialism: 'Nothing should be accepted as fixed, permanent, or 'given' – neither material conditions nor social forms' (ibid., 1). Central to this is 'gender abolitionism' or 'the ambition to construct a society where traits currently assembled under the rubric of gender, no longer furnish a grid for the asymmetric operation of power' (ibid., 6). They argue for an intersectional approach that would abolish power relations based on race or class (ibid., 6). They state:

> Gender inequality still characterizes the fields in which our technologies are conceived, built, and legislated for, while female workers in electronics (to name just one industry) perform some of the worst paid, monotonous and debilitating labour. Such injustice demands structural, machinic and ideological correction.
>
> *(ibid., 2)*

Xenofeminism is concerned with who is authoring the technology and whose interests it reproduces:

> XF seeks to strategically deploy existing technologies to re-engineer the world. Serious risks are built into these tools; they are prone to imbalance,

abuse, and exploitation of the weak. [...] Technology isn't inherently progressive. [...] Technoscientific innovation must be linked to a collective theoretical and political thinking in which women, queers, and the gender non-conforming play an unparalleled role.

(ibid., 2)

In animation, these themes of technology and gender fluidity are explored in the work of contemporary Chinese artist, LuYang, whose film *Moving Gods* was included in the Chinese Pavilion at the Venice Biennale in 2015. Her short film, *Delusional Mandala* (2015) shows the artist being 3D-scanned, desexualised and becoming a CGI avatar of indeterminate gender alongside medical imagery, brain surgery and Buddhist iconography. This is accompanied by an automated voice in Chinese drily recounting medical facts with a rock music background. Parodying the pop video, the dancing figure morphs, ages and reveals its internal organs before being entombed in a psychedelic hearse. Although the artist states that her work is a meditation upon neuroscience and consciousness (Pangburn 2015), it can also be read as a comment upon the medical construction of gender. This interpretation is reinforced by her earlier creation, *Uterus Man*, produced in the form of an animation in 2013 and subsequently an arcade game in 2014. Adopting the visual language of manga, this character is an asexual hero enmeshed within powerful armour formed from a uterus (LuYang 2016).

A thread of intersectional cyberfeminist discourse can be seen re-emerging occasionally in Afrofuturism, a movement in music, literature and art that uses the form of science fiction to analyse the injustices of the past and suggest alternative futures. Key figures such as musician Sun Ra and writer Octavia Butler use the form of speculative fiction to examine race and identity through a range of approaches including the utopian, the dystopian and the grotesque. In the collages and animations of artist Wangechi Mutu, such as *The End of Eating Everything* (2012), themes of the monstrous female body re-emerge (Richardson 2012). Mutu's use of collage to re-member and distort disparate body parts into female figures shows a similar approach to the earlier work of Linda Dement, but the result speaks more of the body victimised through colonialism, ecological disaster, hunger and slavery rather than Dement's concern with abjection and the results of sexual violence.

Glitch feminism, a term coined by Legacy Russell in 2012, is another form of post-cyberfeminism that considers gender to be a technology that is fundamentally broken. Russell (2012) regards the 'mechanized micro-seizures' of mechanical failure as deeply significant in our relationship with technology:

The glitch is the digital orgasm, where the machine takes a sigh, a shudder, and with a jerk, spasms. [...] The glitch is the catalyst, not the error. The glitch is the happy accident. When the computer freezes mid-conversation, when the video buffers and refuses to progress.

Thus, the glitch is a revolutionary moment of malfunction when the smooth functioning of a piece of technology comes into question and reveals its mechanics. As a metaphor, it can be extended to an approach to gender:

> Glitch Feminism [ ] embraces the causality of "error", and turns the gloomy implication of *glitch* on its ear by acknowledging that an error in a social system that has already been disturbed by economic, racial, social, sexual, and cultural stratification and the imperialist wrecking-ball of globalization – processes that continue to enact violence on all bodies – may not, in fact, be an *error* at all, but rather a much-needed erratum.
>
> *(ibid.)*

For Jenny Sundén (2015), 'Glitch is a struggle with binaries': This could be binary code or binary approaches to gender. Indeed, perhaps the glitch, the error, the failure to conform to accepted codes is more indicative of the system than the ideal:

> femininity is a technology of failure, and the ideal of smooth, slick, seamless, effortless femininity impossible. There will always be glitches, slippages, slips; too feminine, not feminine enough, not feminine in the right way, a never-ending struggle for everybody with femininity aspirations. There is no such thing as flawless technologies, or bodies, this is the ideal.
>
> *(ibid.)*

This fascination with the glitch and an exploration of the limitations and failures of CGI is apparent in the work of a number of contemporary female experimental computer animators. The glitchy CGI visuals of Kathleen Daniel in films such as *Hillbilly* (2013) demonstrate a deliberate disregard for photorealism and feature strong female characters, oversized body shapes, relationship issues and the experience of being an African American woman in Berlin. In the film, *alteration-de-la-voix* (2015) by Wednesday Kim, which is based on dreams that resulted from traumatic childhood memories, multiple body parts join together to form writhing, mutant bodies (Kim 2015). In Lilli Carré's film *Jill* (2016) a rebellious CGI character refuses to obey the instructions of the narrator and her digital body refuses to obey the rules of a human body.

Conclusion: Whose future?

This chapter began with a search for examples of innovative, feminist approaches to experimental computer animation. Although a few were uncovered, these were not easy to find and more research needs to be done on this subject. Despite a small number of contemporary women animation artists working at a very high level of technical and conceptual sophistication in experimental digital processes, to name but a few – Chunna Yu, Claudia Hart, Katerina Athanasopoulou,

Carol MacGilivray, Hito Steyerl, Oddscene, Jennifer Steinkamp, Zarah Hussein, Bärbel Neubauer, Kim Laughton, Eva Papamargariti, Kathy Smith and this list is not intended to be exhaustive – their work does not show a consistent engagement with an explicitly feminist agenda. Films that engage more overtly with feminism – and a look through the catalogue of films on offer at feminist animation festivals such as Tricky Women in Austria will confirm this – are overwhelmingly created through hand-drawn or handmade processes. It is also the author's experience as an educator in animation, that the majority of female students – whether feminist in outlook or not – prefer to engage with hand-drawn or handmade aesthetics over more technical processes such as CGI or code.

Reading between the lines of existing literature on the history of computer animation, traces of women artist pioneers using technology can be found as potential role models – Schwartz, Allen and Sorensen, but they are few and far between. Is it that it was too hard for women to access the technology, which required an affiliation with big institutions, or have others been written out of history? At the opening of the Electronic Superhighway exhibition of digital arts at London's Whitechapel Gallery in 2016, a protest was staged at the omission of many key female artists and none of the 1990s Australian cyberfeminist artists were included. What is at stake here is not simply about history. Why are equal numbers of women not adopting technology in either experimental practice or the mainstream labour market? It's not just women that are under-represented – experimental practice in computer animation itself is also a minority discourse. However, experimentation is needed for innovation and to imagine new ways of using these technologies. To be in control of technology is to be in control of the future and to not engage with technology is to take no responsibility for the future. It has been argued that inequality is hardwired into the very code of the technologies we take for granted due to the language used and assumptions programmed into them by the people who created them. This has been demonstrated by recent cases documenting how search engines return ALT-right results. A 'bug' in the automatic tagging of photographs in Google Photos, claimed the manufacturers, led to photos of Black people being labelled as gorillas. Tay, Microsoft's experiment in artificial intelligence was 'led astray' on Twitter and ended up pledging allegiance to Hitler (Penny 2017).

This chapter is not intended as a definitive study, but as a call for action. There needs to be more research into why women and BAME groups are under-represented in the tech sector, calls for funding and strategies to counteract this – otherwise a large part of the talent pool is being neglected at a time when economies need skilled workers. This is not just a matter for the labour market. This is about social justice and who creates the fabric of the electronic world we live in. The importance of more diversity is not just because of whose viewpoints are being represented now, but, in an age of increasing disparity between rich and poor, also about whose perspectives shape the future. In order to deal with the complex and challenging future our world faces, we need to be able to draw upon a diverse range of ideas and solutions to the many problems that face us.

The advance of technology is not simply the result of some neutral force of 'progress', but results from political decisions about where research and development funds are invested and what issues have priority. We all need to take collective responsibility to ensure that inclusivity, not division, is at the centre of this. But we also need new ways to work with these tools, not simply learning to be part of the power structure but finding new and surprising strategies in articulating the voices of those whose languages – female, Black, postcolonial, trans, queer, migrant, old, poor – have all been excluded from the mainstream. Radical experimenters need to dismantle and reassemble these technologies, to subvert dominant discourses, imagine and work towards new and more inclusive futures.

Notes

1 Cyberfeminism is a term originating in the 1990s that refers to a feminism that engages critically and conceptually with digital media and networked technologies.
2 'The Vagenda', accessed 20 April 2017, http://vagendamagazine.com/.
3 'Everyday Sexism Project', accessed 20 April 2017, https://everydaysexism.com/.
4 This tendency is less noticeable in animations chosen for exhibition in a gallery context.
5 This observation refers to tendencies rather than absolute selection criteria. Some experimental CGI and algorithmic animations are selected for experimental animation festivals, but they are in the minority.
6 When translated into English this word has multiple meanings – use, pleasure and orgasm.
7 http://adanewmedia.org/about/
8 www.madewithcode.com

References

Allen, Rebecca. *Musique Non-Stop.* US, 1986. Music video.
Allen, Rebecca. 'About.' Artist's website. *Rebecca Allen* (blog), 2016, www.rebecca allen.com.
Allen, Rebecca, and Erkki Huhtamo. 'I Always Like to Go Where I Am Not Supposed to Be.' In *Women, Art and Technology,* edited by Judy Malloy. Cambridge, Mass.; London: MIT Press, 2003.
Barnett, Tully. 'Monstrous Agents: Cyberfeminist Media and Activism.' *Ada: A Journal of Gender, New Media, and Technology,* no. 5, 2014, http://adanewmedia.org/2014/07/issue5-barnett.
Barratt, Virginia. (n.d.). 'All New Gen.' *VNS Matrix: Merchants of Slime* (blog), accessed April 22 2017. http://vnsmatrix.net/all-new-gen/#prev.
Barratt, Virginia, Julianne Pierce, Francesca da Rimini and Josephine Starrs. 'About VNS Matrix.' *VNS Matrix: Merchants of Slime* (blog), 2015, accessed April 22 2017, http://vnsmatrix.net/about/.
Carré, Lilli. *Jill.* US, 2016. Film.
Cixous, Hélène. 'The Laugh of the Medusa.' In *New French Feminisms: An Anthology,* edited by Elaine Marks and Isabelle de Courtivron. Brighton, Sussex: The Harvester Press, 1986.
Collins, Patricia Hill. 'Intersectionality's Definitional Dilemmas.' *Annual Review of Sociology,* no. 41 (2015): 1–20.

Cuboniks, Laboria. 'Xenofeminism: A Politics for Alienation.' *Laboria Cuboniks* (blog), 2015, accessed April 22 2017, 1–10, www.laboriacuboniks.net.

Daniel, Kathleen. *Hillbilly*. US/Germany, 2013. Film.

Davis, Juliet. 'Representing the Body in Cyberfeminist Art.' *Media-N: Journal of the New Media Caucus 2*, no. 1, 2006. http://median.newmediacaucus.org/archives_in_progress/pre_2009_issues/html_only/2006_spring/Sp06_Davis.htm.

Dement, Linda. *Typhoid Mary*. Australia, 1991. Interactive CD-ROM.

Dement, Linda. *Cyberflesh GirlMonster*. Australia, 1995. Interactive CD-ROM.

Dement, Linda. *In My Gash*. Australia, 1999. Interactive CD-ROM.

Dement, Linda. 'Linda Dement: Statement.' *Australia Video Art Archive* (blog), 2003, www.videoartchive.org.au/ldement/index.html.

Duras, Marguerite. 'From an Inteview.' In *New French Feminisms: An Anthology*, edited by Elaine Marks and Isabelle de Courtivron. Brighton, Sussex: The Harvester Press, 1986.

Evans, Claire L. '"We Are the Future Cunt": CyberFeminism in the 90s.' *Motherboard/Vice.com* (blog), 2014, https://motherboard.vice.com/en_us/article/we-are-the-future-cunt-cyberfeminism-in-the-90s.

'Everyday Sexism Project.' 2012, accessed April 20 2017. https://everydaysexism.com/.

Foá, Maryclare, and Birgitta Hosea. 'Chapter 1. Communicating.' In *Performance Drawing: New Practices since the 1960s*, edited by Maryclare Foá, Jane Grisewood, Birgitta Hosea, and Carali McCall. London: I B Tauris, 2019.

Gagnon, Madeleine. 'Body I.' In *New French Feminisms: An Anthology*, edited by Elaine Marks and Isabelle de Courtivron. Brighton, Sussex: The Harvester Press, 1986.

Gajjala, Radhika, and Annapurna Mamidipudi. 'Gendering Processes within Technological Environments: A Cyberfeminist Issue.' *Rhizomes* (blog), 2002, www.rhizomes.net/issue4/gajjala.html.

Haraway, Donna. 'A Cyborg Manifesto: Science, Technology, and Socialist-Feminism in the Late Twentieth Century.' In *Simians, Cyborgs, and Women: The Reinvention of Nature*. New York: Routledge, 1991.

Hester, Helen. 'After the Future: N Hypotheses of Post-Cyber Feminism.' *Res* (blog), 2017. http://beingres.org/2017/06/30/afterthefuture-helenhester/.

Hosea, Birgitta. 'Drawing Animation.' *Animation: An Interdisciplinary Journal 5*, no. 3 (2010): 353–367.

Hosea, Birgitta. 'Made by Hand.' In *The Crafty Animator*, edited by Caroline Ruddell. Basingstoke, Hampshire: Palgrave Macmillan, 2019.

Kim, Wednesday. 'Alteration-de-La-Voix.' *Wednesday Kim* (blog), US, 2015, www.wednesdaykim.com/alteration-de-la-voix.

Krauss, Rosalind. '"The Rock": William Kentridge's Drawings for Projection.' *October*, no. 92 (2000): 3–35.

Lachaise, Gaston. *Standing Woman*. US, 1932. Sculpture.

Le Grice, Malcolm. 'Computer Film as Film Art.' In *Computer Animation*, edited by John Halas. London; New York: Focal Press, 1974.

Le Grice, Malcolm. *Experimental Cinema in the Digital Age*. London: British Film Institute Publishing, 2006.

LuYang. *Uterus Man*. China, 2013. Film.

LuYang. *Uterus Man*. China, 2014. Arcade game.

LuYang. *Delusional Mandala*. China, 2015. Film.

LuYang. *Moving Gods*. China, 2015. Film.

LuYang. 'About'. *LuYang* (blog), 2016, http://luyang.asia/about/.

LuYang. *Gong Tau Kite*. (blog), 2016, http://luyang.asia/2016/12/09/luyang-gong-tau-kite/.

Mutu, Wangechi. *The End of Eating Everything*. Kenya/United States, 2012. Film.

Pangburn, D J. '"Nonsexual" Humanity Takes Form as an Artist's 3D Avatar.' *Creators/Vice.com* (blog), 2015, https://creators.vice.com/en_au/article/nonsexual-humanity-takes-form-as-an-artists-3d-avatar.

Penny, Laurie. 2017. 'Robots Are Racist and Sexist. Just like the People Who Created Them.' *The Guardian Online*, April 20 2017, www.theguardian.com/commentisfree/2017/apr/20/robots-racist-sexist-people-machines-ai-language?CMP=Share_iOSApp_Other.

Plant, Sadie. *Zeros + Ones: Digital Women + The New Technoculture*. London: Fourth Estate, 1998.

Prince, Patric D. 'Women and the Search for Visual Intelligence.' In *Women, Art and Technology*, edited by Judy Malloy. Cambridge, Mass.; London: MIT Press, 2003.

Richardson, Jared. 'Attack of the Boogeywoman: Visualizing Black Women's Grotesquerie in Afrofuturism.' *Art Papers*, 2012, www.artpapers.org/feature_articles/feature1_2012_1112.htm.

Russell, Legacy. 'Digital Dualism and the Glitch Feminism Manifesto.' *The Society Pages* (blog), 2012, https://thesocietypages.org/cyborgology/2012/12/10/digital-dualism-and-the-glitch-feminism-manifesto/.

Schwartz, Lillian F. 'The Artist and Computer Animation.' In *Computer Animation*, edited by John Halas. London; New York: Focal Press, 1974.

Schwartz, Lillian F.. *Trois Visages*. US, 1977. Film.

Schwartz, Lillian F.. *Big Momma*. 1984. Poster.

Schwartz, Lillian F. *The Computer Artists Handbook: Concepts, Techniques and Applications*. New York; London: W. W. Norton, 1992.

Sofia, Zoë. 'Contested Zones: Futurity and Technological Art.' Edited by Judy Malloy. Cambridge, Mass.; London: MIT Press, 2003.

Sorensen, Vibeke. *Etyma*. US, 1974. Film.

Sorensen, Vibeke. 'Panel Session: A Feminine Perspective. Transcript of Talk by Vibeke Sorensen.' *ArtTransition '90 Conference, Massachusetts Institute of Technology, Center for Advanced Visual Studies, Boston, Massachusetts* (blog), 1990, http://visualmusic.org/text/women.html.

Sorensen, Vibeke. 'Mood of the Planet.' Artist's website. *Vibeke Sorensen* (blog), Singapore, 2015. Interactive installation. http://vibeke.info/mood-of-the-planet/.

Sundén, Jenny. 'On Trans-, Glitch-, and Gender as Machinery of Failure.' *First Monday: Peer Reviewed Journal on the Internet 20*, no. 4, 2015. http://dx.doi.org/10.5210/fm.v20i4.5895.

'The Vagenda'. 2012, accessed April 20 2017. http://vagendamagazine.com/.

Vankin, Deborah. 'Animation: At CalArts and Elsewhere, More Women Are Entering the Picture.' *Los Angeles Times*, May 25 2015.

Victoria and Albert Museum. 'Hommage À Paul Klee, 13/9/65 Nr.2.' *V&A Catalogue: Computer Art* (blog), 2017, http://collections.vam.ac.uk/item/0211685/hommage-a-paul-klee-13965-print-nake-frieder/.

VNS Matrix. *All New Gen*. Australia, 1994. Video game.

Wilding, Faith. 'Where Is the Feminism in Cyberfeminism?' *N. paradoxa* 2 (1998): 6–13.

PART IV
Interviews B

B1

JODIE MACK

UK/USA

Please give us a brief summary of your work, including, if possible, a description of your creative process (e.g., how your creative ideas first appear and take shape).

My animations study domestic and recycled materials to illuminate the elements shared between fine-art abstraction and mass-produced graphic design. Extending a long tradition of abstract animation – a history shared between, dance, music, film and art – my handmade films use collage to explore the relationship between graphic cinema and storytelling, the tension between form and meaning. Over the past ten years, I have made over 30 animated shorts spanning focused object studies to epic musicals documenting the pitfalls of modern materiality. My work considers the history of experimental animation's various applications – from pre and early cinema through experimental film, contemporary art, video art and motion graphics – to survey trends of ornamental patterns, cycles of industry and material waste.

Ideas definitely sort of spiral outwardly and differently for different projects. For example: What started out as a temporal record of my mother's inventory from her place of work – a warehouse full of movie, music and celebrity imagery – became *Dusty Stacks of Mom: The Poster Project* (2013), a project that interwove the forms of personal filmmaking, absolute animation, the rock opera and the musical documentary. A simple examination of the rise and fall of a nearly defunct poster and postcard wholesale business unveiled themes surrounding the changing role of physical objects and virtual data in commerce and the division (or lack of) between abstraction in fine art and psychedelic kitsch. Then other themes and materials extended and complicated themes of inventory, merchandise industries, kitsch, light shows, multiples, appropriation, obsolescence – with an additional four films: *Undertone Overture* (2013), *New Fancy Foils* (2013), *Glistening Thrills* (2013) and *Let Your Light Shine* (2013). Together, the five films worked like a feature essay film maturing my interests in the ways found materials and decorative detritus can illuminate truths about economic cycling and cultural value. Something large built out from something very little. This is generally the case.

Is material or media a particularly important component of your practice? How does it operate in your work?

My work always starts with a physical material and extracting as many possibilities from it as possible. My formative experience producing cameraless films made by drawing, painting or adhering objects directly to the 16mm filmstrip – *Two Hundred Feet* (2004), *A Joy* (2005), *All Stars* (2005) – ignited interests in abstraction, materials and patterns. The constraints of the miniature 16mm canvas and the ability to view the animations both as moving images and as sculptural objects – filmstrips depicting the temporal scores of movement – grounded my sensibilities within a trajectory of abstract animation cultivated by the approaches of early experimental pioneers relating to the performing and the plastic arts.

I take pride in activating the cosmos from scraps, pieces of trash, tragedies of the physical world. And my work develops exclusively out of studying materials under the animation camera. My material studies target abstract animation's entanglement with the decorative and the modern, asking the questions: What are the tensions between high and low culture revealed by materials? How can these tensions inform an understanding of cinema's branched connection to art and industry? My current filmography possesses formal rigour alongside a fanciful interrogation of contemporary anxieties responding to social and cultural trials and disappointments.

How would you define your animation practice in terms of its relation to fine art traditions, experimental animation or the (historical) avant-garde? Its relation to commercial industry? Who/what are your strongest influences?

I think I am definitely one of many artists in my generation who find hybrid modes from seemingly disparate worlds: High art and low culture and how their tension remains the same, despite infinite technological upgrades and complications. So, my strongest influences come from both A/G circles and the commercial industry: Len Lye, Frank Mouris, Jules Engel, Scott Stark, Robert Breer, Paul Glabicki, Paul Sharits, Motion Graphics for Channel Four, *Grease, Tommy, The Umbrellas of Cherbourg, The Cantor's Son*, Bob Fosse, etc.

I also have a growing sculpture and installation practice fuelled by my interests in materials and newly antiquated technology: *No Kill Shelter*. This growing collection currently features 25 video sculptures, 'screensavers', born from interests in materials, waste and old technology. Animated loops inspired by mesmerising computer graphics play on discarded monitors and computers hand decoupaged with wrapping paper. Highlighting rapid technological obsolescence and the role of abstract animation in everyday life, the screensavers question the preciousness and fetishisation of antiquated technology and the relationship between fine art, design and craft. I see a lot of possibilities for the expansion of my work into sculptural and installation forms. And, to this end, I admire Nam June Paik, Jennifer Steinkamp, Lee Yong-Baek, etc.

Why animation?

I am constantly inspired by animation's ability to create what is not possible in reality and for its potential for the manipulation of time. I often joke that art has an inferiority complex to nature. Imprisoned by nature's perfection we strove to replicate it by hand; we created systems to describe its size, its components. We then built technologies to replicate what we had just perfected manually. We chugged through mechanical technologies, now into digital and virtual means of again replicating and inventorying reality. By virtue of the fact that environments are so often fabricated in animation, we are freed from those authorial arguments about painting vs. photography; we are freed from a diegetic space. Or, rather, we have the potential for freedom of 'reality' as mandated by flow of religion->literature->theatre->cinema->internet->mobile media->self-reflexive positioning of self. To me, animation foregrounds the role of mimicry not only in cinema but in all of art, which has made it an infinitely exciting field thus far.

What is your work's relation to experimental form and technique? Is there something you want to articulate with your work that can't be expressed through conventional narrative means?

I'm a pseudo-formalist at my core. Very quickly, I began to question pure formalism's ability to move beyond decoration and started to combine the formal techniques and structures of experimental/abstract animation with those of cinematic genres. I had already developed parallel but separate modes of explorations: Short form abstract studies and long form genre interrogations (e.g., *Lilly* (2007) pairs cameraless film techniques and alternative darkroom processes with the goals of the documentary form, using photo-negatives to animate a World War II tragedy). *Yard Work is Hard Work* (2008) borrows from tropes of the Hollywood musical to create a critique of contemporary life from discarded magazine cut-outs. I'm interested in the fertile territory for the combination of abstract animation techniques with different cinematic modes and forms. I'm certainly interested more in documentary than I am in narrative. But, I very well know that documentary *is* essentially narrative anyway. So, I welcome the blurring of any and all lines between genres. I think my work is deceptive. It's colour, speed and humour give notes of cuteness and superficially detract from a sense of rigour. Many people see these films as 'abstract films', but I surely see them more as documentaries, something I'd like to call inventory documentary – the temporal record of incomplete archives. I want my work to demand a new viewing position, not from the position of a spectator who is viewing an 'abstract film' or a 'flicker film' or a 'documentary' or a 'musical' or an 'essay film' but from the position of a spectator who is considering a new mode.

How do you see your work operating culturally? Politically?

I suppose in some ways my work attempts to locate the slippery slope between what is cultural and what is political, this entangled relationship. With my continued questions surrounding the decorative roadblocks plaguing the history of abstract animation as well as my gained knowledge and confidence that material is the message, I re-approached the 'purely' abstract film and focused on the types of objects in question themselves: Ornamental scree. My stroboscopic material studies apply formal principles of abstract cinema while pursuing an interest in found materials, evolving modes of production and forms of labour. Questioning the role of decoration in daily life, my eight fabric studies – *Harlequin* (2009), *Rad Plaid* (2010), *Posthaste Perennial Pattern* (2010), *Point de Gaze* (2012), *Persian Pickles* (2012), *Blanket Statement [s] #1 and #2* (2012 and 2013) and *Razzle Dazzle* (2014) – extend the temporal concerns of the structural film while calling for a critical formalism. These films conceptualise abstraction by reflexively activating the referential properties of objects, foregrounding questions of Romanticism surrounding metaphor and exchanging lyrical and mythopoeic modes for those of economic observation (that examine the commodification of abstraction/the decorative). In my film *Persian Pickles* (2012), a swimming study of paisley patterns traces this motif from its origins in Persian weavings to appearances in Irish quilting and American counterculture. My ongoing *Blanket Statement* series uses quilts to evoke issues of domestic security, citing appearances of quilts in the fine arts from Michelangelo Pistoletto to Beryl Korot. *Point de Gaze* (2012) and *Razzle Dazzle* (2014) feature handmade and machine produced laces, tattings and intricate weavings to meditate upon the industry of desire and the phenomenology of cinema. *Undertone Overture* (2013) uses tie dye – from ancient hand-practiced dyeing techniques to hippie stigma'd gift shop merchandise to amorphous abstract paintings – to locate the tension regarding the aesthetic value of forms of fine art and craft. Most of my work at this point examines the commodification of abstraction, examining it curiously as it pans out through the development of the global economy and the globalised identity.

References

Demy, Jascques. *Les Parapluies de Cherbourg (The Umbrellas of Cherbourg)*. France/West Germany, 1964. Film.

Kleiser, Randal. *Grease*. US, 1978. Film.

Mack, Jodie. *Two Hundred Feet*. US, 2004. Film.

_____. *A Joy*. US, 2005. Film.

_____. *All Stars*. US, 2005. Film.

_____. *Lilly*. US, 2007. Film.

_____. *Yard Work is Hard Work*. US, 2008. Film.

_____. *Harlequin.* US, 2009. Film.

_____. *Posthaste Perennial Pattern.* US, 2010. Film.

_____. *Rad Plaid.* US, 2010. Film.

_____. *Persian Pickles.* US, 2012. Film.

_____. *Point de Gaze.* US, 2012. Film.

_____. *Blanket Statement [s] #1 and #2.* US, 2012 and 2013. Film.

_____. *Dusty Stacks of Mom: The Poster Project.* US, 2013. Film.

_____. *Glistening Thrills.* US, 2013. Film.

_____. *Let Your Light Shine.* US, 2013. Film.

_____. *New Fancy Foils.* US, 2013. Film.

_____. *No Kill Shelter.* US, 2013. Film.

_____. *Undertone Overture.* US, 2013. Film.

_____. *Undertone Overture.* US, 2013. Film.

_____. *Razzle Dazzle.* US, 2014. Film.

Motyleff, Ilya. *The Cantor's Son.* US, 1937. Film.

Russell, Ken. *Tommy.* UK, 1975. Film.

B2

MAYA YONESHO

Japan/Germany

Please give us a brief summary of your work, including, if possible, a description of your creative process (e.g., how your creative ideas first appear and take shape).

My films can basically be divided into two types of projects. The first is 'Lip-Sync', which I learned whilst a student in London. I could not speak nor understand English very well, and one of my first assignments was a lip-sync exercise. It was hard to do because I could not hear English as a comprehensible language. After a while, I realised that these spoken words were not only words that I did not understand, but they were also sounds. I began to write all the English words out in Japanese phonetic characters to count frames. It worked. I began to apply the same technique to other languages. Also, I learned from my international flatmates and new friends in London that people can become friends without knowing each other's languages all that well. The idea suited my situation. This is the backstory of my first film *Introspection* (1998) which featured friends speaking 13 different languages. Since then, I have made several 'Lip- or Music Sync' films.

The second type is the 'Daumenreise Project', which is a mixture of hand-drawings and real backgrounds. When I got a chance to stay in Vienna, Austria, I got this idea to make a film whilst enjoying the view, or food, even out with friends. I made small animated drawings (about business card size), which I held with my left hand and shot with a small digital camera in the city, or places that are connected to the drawings. I believe it is one of the easiest and most fun ways to make a film.

In terms of theme, I try to pick the strongest and the most realistic theme for me at a particular moment. It is not always a new theme but is sometimes drawn from memories too. My pattern for the 'Lip- or Music Sync' films is to collect voices and make music first; then I edit all the sounds before starting to draw. Another pattern of mine is compiling lots of small idea sketches under a certain theme, finding an order for them, creating a storyboard and then drawing the in-betweens.

How would you define your animation practice in terms of its relation to fine art traditions, experimental animation or the (historical) avant-garde? Its relation to commercial industry? Who/what are your strongest influences?

Growing up I always liked animation on TV, but when I was a student there was no course to study animation film-making. So, I began to study Visual Design. After two years of studying art, I became a fine art teacher and worked for six years before deciding to go to Kyoto City University of Arts to study more. Out of the three choices for the first-year students, I took Japanese Painting (the other two choices were Oil Painting and Sculpture). The university had a unique system that allowed students to choose their course after entering. We took one of three courses first, then after that we could continue or enter a new course of two more courses, Printmaking and Conceptual & Media Art. After Japanese Painting, I decided to study Conceptual & Media Art because I thought it was the closest to animation. I felt like a stranger on the course because I was the only one who wanted to make animated TV programmes for children. Although I picked up some ideas about art from my studies, I basically taught myself how to animate. From Japanese Painting, I learned about observing and making lots of sketches to get to the essence of the image, and from Conceptual & Media Art I learned to ask important questions about my work and my role as an artist more broadly.

During my time as a student, I did some work for television. But I decided to continue my master's degree and went to the Hiroshima Animation Festival for the first time. It totally changed my idea about animation. Before, I wanted to make films to make money, but after Hiroshima I began to think that I needed money to make my own films. The following year I enrolled on an animation course at the Royal College of Arts in London as an exchange student. It was there that I began to explore my own style.

My strongest influence has come from puppet animation master, Kihachiro Kawamoto. His words about my films were very strong, severe and full of meaning.

Why animation?

I liked magic and wanted to be a magician when I was little. Animation is a kind of magic. I admire theatre, music and other performance-based art forms, but I like to make things by myself. I can make animation in my own time, and it is also possible to continue to refine it as much as I like. Animation is like a poem. Sometimes I cannot find the right word to express my idea, but I believe I can say something through animation.

Is material or media a particularly important component of your practice? How does it operate in your work?

I like to move, walk and see things as I work, so I like to use handy materials. I like to be able to make animation whenever and wherever I want to. This was the first motivation to use small sketchbooks to draw on and shoot on location. Now I use small papers, they're handier. Maybe an iPad would be even more convenient, but I still really like the texture of Japanese rice paper and inks. I think that they express a more 'human-hand-feeling'.

What is your work's relation to experimental form and technique? Is there something you want to articulate with your work that can't be expressed through conventional narrative means?

In my work I want to crystallise the feeling or thinking at that moment. I want to include the atmosphere also. So, I use peoples' voices around me, or shoot in the city where I am. It is very important for me to use 'live' backgrounds for the 'Daumenreise' project.

I use associative connections instead of conventional narrative. I don't like to offer a complete picture but instead bits of 'structure' or 'content' that people can construct into their own final picture.

How do you see your work operating culturally? Politically?

In my work I show my ideas or ways of thinking, and I see my work as a form of poetry. So, it is culturally relevant; even more so, for example, in the 'Daumenreise' animations, because they are often portraits of cities, people who live there, or how they live.

Reference

Yonesho, Maya. *Introspection*. UK, 1998. Film.

B3

LARRY CUBA

USA

Please give us a brief summary of your work, including, if possible, a description of your creative process (e.g., how your creative ideas first appear and take shape).

In summary, my work should be considered as a single long-term research project into the relationship between algorithm and image and the perception of motion. At its heart is abstraction: Mathematical abstraction and visual abstraction, a (relatively) new art form that has been enabled by a technological development: digital computer graphics. It is characterised by the use of algebraic expression to generate compositions of abstract form and movement much like a computer music composer writes algorithms to produce music compositions.

This project consists of an endless stream of experiments – animation sequences that reveal the relationship between the text that I write and the images that the computer produces by executing that code. This correspondence between text and image has fascinated me since I first encountered it in high school geometry class.

Instead of a traditional animation storyboard, the process begins with an algebraic structure, an idea for a set of mathematical expressions that represents the score of a scene. The score defines the structure of a complex array of forms and their movements through space over time.

The actual results of these expressions are unimaginable – *literally*. In fact, the goal is to produce something that *cannot* be pre-visualised, to go beyond the imagination and into the realm of discovery and surprise, akin to what John Cage once said: 'I don't hear the music I write. I write in order to hear the music I haven't yet heard' (Cage 1990).

In thinking about the creative process as it pertains to a long-term research project in generative animation, one could easily imagine an ideal situation where the artist writes software to perform some experiments and ultimately creates a film from this material. Then by building on the existing software, continually modifying it and experimenting with it, a series of works would emerge and evolve, designed by successive refinement.

With the advanced technology that we enjoy here in the twenty-first century, this could easily be the norm. However, the history of this project begins much earlier, and the actual process was far from this ideal.

The three films I'm known for (*3/78 (Objects and Transformations)* (1978), *Two Space* (1979) and *Calculated Movements* (1985)) were all made in the 1970s and 80s. In the 70s, we were still in the 'mainframe' era of computing when all the machines were giants locked away somewhere in large institutions. A graphics peripheral was a rare bird. So, the first challenge to overcome was obtaining access to a machine to work on. In addition, everything was so new and unknown. I had much to learn about what I was doing and what I wanted to do.

This is the pattern that actually emerged:

First, working on whatever system I could get access to, doing as much experimenting as I could, under those particular technical and logistical circumstances, then constructing a film from that material. And finally going off in search of a better system more oriented to the needs of my particular research. After a sufficient amount of hustling eventually produced the required access to a computer graphics system, I rebuilt the software from scratch, while learning a new programming language and all the idiosyncrasies of this particular system.

My frustration with the current system always led me to hunt for a system more suited to my needs while I was still in the process of figuring out what that would be. It was difficult to evaluate a system's fitness to a purpose without actually trying to apply that system to the problem. What was it capable of, how was it programmed and how do you get your images onto film?

Over the years, this journey led me from NASA's Jet Propulsion Lab in Los Angeles to the chemistry department of the University of Illinois in Chicago and then back to LA to a company in the business of producing computer film plotters, called 'Triple-I' (with lots of knocking on doors and false starts along the way). Finally in the 80s, personal computer technology matured to the point where a machine powerful enough for the demanding work of animation became affordable and I was finally able to have my own system and work in my studio at home.

So, each film was produced on a different system at a different time in the evolution of the technology and my ideas. Each represents the limit of what I could accomplish at that moment in time with those available resources.

The creative process always included a negotiation with the technology as it existed at the time. There were the mathematical ideas I wanted to explore and there were the parameters of the particular computer I had to work with. This effort has been an ongoing dialogue between the two.

How would you define your animation practice in terms of its relation to fine art traditions, experimental animation or the (historical) avant-garde? Its relation to commercial industry?

There has never been any interest in abstraction in the commercial film industry or in the mainstream movie-going public. Abstract animation derives directly from non-narrative filmmaking and the fine arts tradition of abstract painting.

Although the art of animating pure abstract forms (with all its concomitant discussion) can be found in the world of the avant-garde and experimental film, it really bears no more connection with these forms than it does with mainstream commercial filmmaking.

Born as it was with abstraction in the fine arts of painting and sculpture at the dawn of the twentieth century, the abstract film should be considered in the context of painters intent on bringing motion and the dimension of time into their work, that is, actual motion rather than just the suggestion of motion.

Who/what are your strongest influences?

Growing up as I did in the pre-YouTube era, I did not have the opportunity to see films by any abstract artists such as Jordan Belson, Oskar Fischinger or even Norman McLaren until I attended college. Their works were a revelation to me both because of their perceptual impact and the fact that such a profound art form existed completely under the radar of mainstream film and art culture. I thought I'd like to pursue this art myself. When I became aware of John Whitney's animation being based on mathematical structures and generated with computers, there was no question. The course of my life was set.

References

Cage, John. 'Autobiographical Statement'. Johncage.org. 1990. Accessed November 12 2018. http://johncage.org/autobiographical_statement.html

Cuba, Larry. *3/78 (Objects and Transformations)*. US, 1978. Film.

_____. *Two Space*. US, 1979. Film.

_____. *Calculated Movements*. US, 1985. Film.

B4

MAX HATTLER

Germany/Hong Kong

Please give us a brief summary of your work, including, if possible, a description of your creative process (e.g., how your creative ideas first appear and take shape).

The basis of my work is animation, but it has close connections to painting, graphics, computing and music. It manifests itself as short films, video installations, VR works and audiovisual live performances that explore relationships between abstraction and figuration, aesthetics and politics, sound and image and precision and improvisation. The threads that hold my oeuvre together are synaesthetic experience, visual music, the use of temporal and visual loops and symmetries, the exploration of abstraction as a meaning-making device and resulting open-ended narratives. The creation process is similar from one work to the next: I tend to feel my way from a vague starting point to the final version through a discovery-led process of trial and error. I rarely have a clear picture of what I want to achieve, but instead have a combination of conceptual, technical, visual, sonic, kinetic or other cues from which to start, and then let the work lead me through iterations until a finishing point is reached. Since animation is a slow and laborious process, this keeps the making-process interesting and scary.

How would you define your animation practice in terms of its relation to fine art traditions, experimental animation or the (historical) avant-garde? Its relation to commercial industry? Who/what are your strongest influences?

I try to approach the moving image from an angle somewhere between non-objectivism and figurative representation, between narrative and non-narrative structuring, between sculpting in time and visual music. As such, the Absolute

Film movement around Walter Ruttmann, Hans Richter, Viking Eggeling and Oskar Fischinger is an important reference point for me. Their rejection of cinematic conventions in favour of visual forms structured by musical principles is close to my own practice. The more spiritual-psychedelic semi-narrative elements of my work connect to West Coast avant-garde animators like Harry Smith, James Whitney and Jordan Belson. Often, my work aims to negotiate a dialogue between contemporary culture and historical influences ranging from pop to avant-garde, from religious to political: From El Lissitzky to László Moholy-Nagy in my works *AANAATT* (2008) and *Shift* (2012); from Busby Berkeley to Leni Riefenstahl in *Spin* (2010), from Islamic patterns to American quilts in *Collision* (2005) and *Stop the Show* (2013), from Buddhist mandalas in *Sync* (2010) to Augustin Lesage's spiritualist paintings in *Heaven and Hell* (2010).

Why animation?

I came to animation through what for a long time I perceived as diverging interests, in visual arts, music and computing. As a child, I was always drawing and painting. Throughout my teens, I used computers to make electronic music. Animation allowed me to combine these interests into a unified expression. Animation not as cartoons but as an intricate and intimate approach to the spatio-temporal shaping of sound and image. For me, animation is about intensity and precision, and about the compression of time and meaning. About poetry rather than prose; about the creation of audio-visual worlds that take the viewer somewhere else, which can serve as an abstraction from, and critical reflection of, the real world.

Is material or media a particularly important component of your practice? How does it operate in your work?

I'm most comfortable with the notion of animation as a frame-by-frame approach to orchestrating time and movement. Guided by this principle, I work with different media, materials, techniques and technologies, depending on conceptual and budgetary constraints, level of adventurousness and so on. I often switch parameters from one work to the next, but then return to revisit old approaches again after some time, from a new perspective. Some works such as *Nachtmaschine* (2005), *Model Starship: Unclear Proof* (2014) or *Shift* (2012) are photography-based because conceptually they are about an abstraction from the everyday. Therefore, the source material needs to originate in the real world. Other works like *Sync* (2010) or *Divisional Articulations* (2017) are digitally created precisely because this removes every trace from the here and now, placing the work in a virtual space removed from recognisable reality. I am a media artist in the sense that my work investigates media and depends on technological components to function, but not in the materialist-structuralist sense. For me, the medium also always takes on a conceptual-narrative role; the work is never only *about* the medium.

What is your work's relation to experimental form and technique? Is there something you want to articulate with your work that can't be expressed through conventional narrative means? How do you see your work operating culturally? Politically?

In my work, I use audio-visual abstraction to create alternative spaces and experiences that aim to take the viewer outside of the everyday. Some works have a mesmerising, meditative quality, while others are compressed sensory assaults. Some more than others are 'thinking spaces' that offer narrative elements through which the viewer is invited to construct meaning. I would argue that abstraction-in-motion can enable a reflective position from which to comment back on reality. Shapes and textures can suggest meanings through movement, repetition, metamorphosis and juxtaposition, or through their combination with sound or figurative elements. All these aspects can work together to provide pointers in the reading of the work. Animation, employing the aesthetics of abstraction in this sense, exploits ambivalence and ambiguity in the construction of more open-ended narratives that engage the viewer in a different way. Not non-objectivism as a complete negation, but abstraction as a way of undermining, of injecting irony and of removing the viewer from the everyday, to enable a questioning of the perceived realities of human existence. In an environment oversaturated with the same media images, representing things in a more abstract sense, while giving hints of meaning that feed the viewer's imagination, may be more engaging for some people by offering up an alternative view.

References

Hattler, Max. *Collision*. UK, 2005. Film.

_____. *Nachtmaschine*. UK, 2005. Film.

_____. *AANAATT*. Japan/Germany/ UK, 2008. Film.

_____. *Divisional Articulations*. Hong Kong, 2017. Film.

_____. *Heaven and Hell*. UK/Germany/Denmark, 2010. Film.

_____. *Spin*. France/Italy, 2010. Film.

_____. *Shift*. UK/Germany, 2012. Film.

_____. *Sync*. UK/Netherlands/Germany/Denmark, 2010. Film.

_____. *Stop the Show*. UK/Spain, 2013. Film.

_____. *Model Starship: Unclear Proof*. Germany/UK, 2014. Film.

PART V

Close analysis of individual artists

8

A HERMENEUTIC OF POLYVALENCE

Deciphering narrative in Lewis Klahr's *The Pettifogger* (2011)

Lilly Husbands

The historical marginalisation of experimental animation within scholarly discourse has resulted in a lack of examination of the formal and narrative complexities that have manifested in experimental animations, particularly since the last quarter of the twentieth century.[1] Animation as a technical process offers artists extraordinary potential for formal experimentation and expressive freedom, where the conceptual and aesthetic concerns of visual and graphic arts are combined with the duration and motion of cinema. Individual animators' explorations of this freedom in their creative processes have generated works that express many different aesthetic, formal and conceptual agendas (sometimes within a single animation). Experimental animators tend to reject or subvert mainstream storytelling conventions, and their alternative techniques and expressive modes invite us, in the words of Robert Russett and Cecile Starr (1988), to 'develop new standards of judgment and [...] even new aesthetic attitudes' (11). This unconventionality makes it beneficial to engage with them on their own terms. Yet, despite an increased output of scholarly studies of animation and experimental cinema over the last 20 years, experimental animations rarely receive the kind of in-depth analyses that their formal and conceptual intricacies demand.

Examining experimental animations in their specificity is a particularly productive way of approaching the art form, and a rich multitude of insights and interpretations can arise from submitting them to close analysis. This is especially true in terms of understanding the complex ways that experimental animators have engaged with narrative in their works. Experimental animation's historical rootedness in modernist abstraction has attached to it connotations of non-objectivity and non-narrativity which, while not entirely inaccurate as generalisations, fail to acknowledge the wide range of engagements with narrative that can be seen across its long history.[2] Experimental animations such as Harry Smith's *Heaven and Earth Magic* (1957–62), Suzan Pitt's *Asparagus* (1979),

Larry Jordan's *Sophie's Place* (1986), Run Wrake's *Jukebox* (1994), Janie Geiser's *Ghost Algebra* (2009) and James Lowne's *Our Relationships Will Become Radiant* (2011) – to name but a few – exhibit narrative elements such as goal-orientated protagonists and causally linked events unfolding across relatively coherent times and spaces (Bordwell and Thompson 2012, 73). However, the precise significance of these elements (characters' actions and motivations, connections between and identity of locations) often remains opaque, and animation's capacity for fantastical or imaginative visualisation is often used in complex and mystifying ways that complicate any straightforward understanding of a work.

In this chapter, I hope to demonstrate the benefits of giving experimental animations their due attention by offering a close reading of Lewis Klahr's enigmatic and polyvalent feature-length collage animation *The Pettifogger* (2011). Since the beginning of his career in New York in the late 1970s, Klahr's films and collage animations have circulated within the interconnected worlds of avant-garde cinema, experimental animation and, more recently, gallery installation.[3] One of the most prolific and well-known contemporary American collage filmmakers, Klahr's work blends structures and modes of engagement found in classic Hollywood narrative with poetic modes of expression that are germane to avant-garde cinema. As an artist Klahr aligns himself directly with the traditions of experimental filmmaking, citing avant-garde filmmakers such as Kenneth Anger, Bruce Conner, Ken Jacobs and Jack Smith as influences (Klahr 2005, 234). In particular, he shares with these filmmakers an affinity for subversive engagements with classic Hollywood storytelling conventions and an allusive, elliptical approach to structure and composition. As I will demonstrate, understanding Klahr as an avant-garde *filmmaker* provides essential clues for interpreting the complex visual language of his imagery. However, the ways he combines mimetic representation, abstract imagery and actual objects are unique to the graphic characteristics of collage animation. As *animations*, his works expand upon classic Hollywood and avant-garde cinema traditions and techniques in inventive ways.

Narrative as hermeneutic in experimental animation

In general, experimental animations tend to defy univocality and actively resist straightforward interpretation. Their indeterminacy is one of their most stimulating and productive aspects because it invites the viewer to actively participate in their comprehension of the animation. Rather than coming across as vague or confused, indeterminacy in experimental works is often what immediately piques our curiosity, urging us to discover all the various ways of understanding them. One of the most instinctive ways we seek to comprehend a work (particularly when characters are present) is by searching for some semblance of narrative structure. When narrative is understood as an experiential element of spectatorship – as cognitive process, as a means of interpretation, as hermeneutic – the very possibility of 'pure' non-narrativity comes into question.

This way of thinking is aligned with cognitive approaches to avant-garde cinema developed by scholars such as James Peterson, Noël Carroll and Paul Taberham. Taberham (2018) has noted that in a cognitive context narrative can be understood as both a text structure and also a mode of comprehension, where the former informs and activates the latter. Peterson (1996) has argued that avant-garde film viewing is a kind of problem solving. He suggests that over the course of a given film, viewers apply various heuristics in the form of educated guesses, intuitive judgements, categorisation or common sense, noting that viewers often draw more or less explicitly from their knowledge of the world in order to integrate a 'film's details into a coherent, though not necessarily highly unified, whole' (Peterson 1994, 31). With these ideas in mind, my analysis of *The Pettifogger* serves as an illustration of some of the ways that experimental animations invite viewers to exercise their powers of perception, cognition and interpretation.

Collage animation is one of the forms of experimental animation that historically has been discussed in narrative terms.[4] Commonly comprised of a combination of printed and photographic materials, a single image in a collage animation has potentially numerous ways of interconnecting with the images that surround it – both spatially and temporally – and therefore is able to operate on multiple levels of communication (as mimetic representation, metaphor, metonym, symbol, allegorical allusion, extra-textual or historical reference).[5] How a given collage animation is encountered on phenomenological, cognitive and conceptual levels is largely affected by the artist's compositional strategies as well as the images' material, representational, historical and connotative properties.[6] This chapter aims to illuminate the ways in which Klahr's particular approach to collage animation in *The Pettifogger* constructs and conveys narrative meaning. As with many forms of experimental cinema, viewers must learn how to engage with the specific conceptual, formal or narrative logic at work in the animation and decode its image and sound compositions in order to gain access to its narrative. Through its sparse and roughly assembled cut-out images, *The Pettifogger* presents viewers with an elliptical crime film narrative that must be deciphered on the level of form.

Polyvalence in Lewis Klahr's collage animations

In 'Towards a Minor Cinema', Tom Gunning (1989–90) included Klahr in his list of avant-garde filmmakers working in the 1980s whose films re-engaged with narrative after its reputed rejection by the so-called structural filmmakers of the 1970s. One of the distinguishing features of this 'minor' cinema was that its approach to narrative returned to the sort of polyvalent montage that characterised earlier works of the American 'poetic' avant-garde.[7] These forms of cinema exhibited a 'highly meaningful flow of images' – 'rhythmic montages', 'syntagms of images' and 'language of juxtaposition' (Gunning 1989–90, 4) – whose meaning nevertheless evaded straightforward comprehension. Although Klahr often makes use of the iconography and music associated with classic Hollywood genres like film noir and melodrama, his works also share with the poetic traditions of avant-garde cinema an emphasis on atmosphere, lyricism, evocative imagery, metaphoric montage and compositional detail.

The narratives in Klahr's animations have been variously described by reviewers and critics as 'archetypal', 'compressed', 'discontinuous' and 'semi-abstract' (Atkinson 2000; Perry 2010; Klahr 2011). Gunning (1989–90) himself poetically remarked that 'plots stir just beneath the threshold of perceptibility. The sea swells of these subliminal stories align images into meaningful but often indecipherable configurations' (4). Indeed, one of the most striking aspects of Klahr's collage animations is that they provide viewers with a *feeling* of narrative without clearly communicating precisely what that narrative entails. My analysis of *The Pettifogger* is intended to go some way towards elucidating how the images' configurations might be indeterminable yet also meaningful.

Klahr works predominantly with cut-out images from mid-twentieth-century American magazine advertisements, comic books and other printed ephemera, and his signature style has evolved over time. The almost 50 collage films Klahr has made since 1987 offer a subtly diverse array of organisational principles and compositional techniques, ranging from more or less explicitly narrative, to musically and thematically centred, to highly metaphorical and ambiguous. For instance, many of the 12 films in Klahr's early four-part Super 8 series of collage films, *Tales of the Forgotten Future* (1988–1991), use advertising imagery to play freely with the generic tropes of Hollywood melodrama, sci-fi, film noir and documentary. Elements of these genres can be seen most clearly in his films *In the Month of Crickets* (1988), *For the Rest of Your Natural Life* (1988), *The Organ Minder's Gronkey* (1990), *Elevator Music* (1991) and the *Untitled* films (1991). With his 16mm series *Engram Sepals* (*Melodramas* 1994–2000) and *Daylight Moon and Other Constellations* (1999–2004), Klahr continued to explore more straightforward narrative, especially in films like *Pony Glass* (1997), while also venturing into more elusive and associational forms of storytelling, as in *Altair* (1994), *Engram Sepals* (2000) and *Daylight Moon* (2002). His more recent works, the series *Prolix Satori* (2009–2011) and *Sixty Six* (2002–2015), are varied in terms of theme, with many of *Prolix Satori*'s 'couplets' combining images with the lyrics of pop songs and the mythopoetic films of *Sixty Six* forming, in Klahr's words, more of a 'cohesive experience' or 'associational mindscape' (Cronk 2016) than an overarching narrative.

The Pettifogger is amongst Klahr's more overtly narrative works; however, it offers a mixture of poetic abstraction and narrative structure that encapsulates many of the most salient aspects of his filmmaking and storytelling aesthetic. This makes it a productive subject for close analysis, in terms of gaining a clearer understanding of Klahr's particular approach to collage animation, and as an example of the ways that artists play with modes of expression in experimental animation and cinema more broadly. In the case of *The Pettifogger*, the diffuse yet potent sensations that Gunning describes are due, in part, to the fact that the narrative appears elliptically in the work. First, *The Pettifogger* is elliptical in a way that recalls the art cinema of canonical filmmakers such as Federico Fellini and Michelangelo Antonioni, where the causal linking of events is often tenuous and contingent. In *The Pettifogger*, the main protagonist's narrative journey appears largely aleatory, and broad swathes of time are often elided and scenes jump from place to place. Borrowing from classical Hollywood cinema, one of the tropes Klahr often uses is the periodic display of changing calendar dates to act as short-hand for the passage of time. However, the work is also an elliptical narrative in the way John P. Powers (2011) describes the term, where 'the viewer may have difficulty accounting for all of the pieces but nonetheless intuits a strong organizing logic or sense of a narrative trajectory. This allows the filmmaker to retain the semblance of narrative while also subverting it to the associational flow of images' (101). One of the primary purposes of this chapter is to shed light on how 'the associational flow of images' in *The Pettifogger* interacts with its skeletal 'semblance of narrative'.

One of the most salient aesthetic features of Klahr's collage films is what Gunning (1989–90) described as their 'technical poverty' and 'total lack of illusionism' (5). Making his frame-by-frame animations in his garage studio without an animation stand, Klahr's films often look as if they have been cobbled together with images cut out of magazines and comic books placed incongruously, and often sparsely, on a variety of flat surfaces. Klahr 'heightens the stasis already inherent in cut-out animation' (2011, 396) by using a lower frame rate than traditional animation so that the movements in his films are at times pointedly jerky and jagged, a quality that is mirrored in some of the edges of his cut-outs. It is primarily for this reason that James Peterson (1994) aligned Klahr's early animations with what he called the 'bricolage' approach to collage animation, which led to the misapprehension that his work should not be interpreted 'centripetally', as in, where the 'pull of the "centering" new composition is stronger than the pull of the diverse intertextual references' (154).

On the contrary, Klahr's disjointed collage images consistently refer back to an intact diegetic world that the viewer can piece together and imagine as cohesive. As none of the cut-out figures he uses have articulable limbs, their movements are significantly limited; instead of moving realistically, their frozen gestures often float across the surface of the background. Nevertheless, Klahr has a keen sense of dramatic performance and his choices of figures often reflect a desire to capture a distilled representation of the physicality of a moment. This is enhanced by the figures he uses to represent his characters, which are often excised from pre-existing comic book narratives that provide a sense of drama and story *in medias res*, which he in turn bends to fit the needs of his own story. The expressive physicality of the figures is essential in providing clues as to the psychological and emotional states of the characters at a given time. In addition, their semi-abrupt movements, achieved by frame-by-frame animation, infuse the obviously motionless cut-out figures with a sense of agency. Their postures clearly suggest preceding and succeeding actions, and indeed, it sometimes feels as if examples of Gotthold Lessing's 'pregnant moments' were being shuffled around the frame. This distinctive, 'impoverished' style of collage filmmaking is one of the most expressively productive aspects of Klahr's work.

The semblance of narrative

One of the reasons viewers are able to intuit a sense of organising logic or narrative trajectory in *The Pettifogger* in particular is that it exhibits some of the characteristics of classical cinematic storytelling. *The Pettifogger* offers just enough narrative clues to enable us to gain a foothold into the world of the film, and if we further choose to apply a narrative interpretation to the film's poetically associational aspects, the results can fruitfully flesh out many of the details of that world. The film exhibits signposts, such as recurring characters and places, thematic objects, dialogue and musical cues, which suggest a narrative way of reading the film that draws directly from iconic genres of classical Hollywood cinema such as melodrama and the crime film. Narrative elements – what Gunning (1989–90) elsewhere described as 'barely graspable narrative events' (4) – most expressly manifest themselves in the film through the (partially) decipherable actions of its protagonist. These actions tend to take place in scenes that depict perspectivally coherent spaces and locations that are accompanied by more or less appropriate sound effects.

   The real difficulty, however, lies in recognising the collaged images as legible signposts. The restricted expression of his animation style on both an aesthetic and formal level sometimes makes it difficult to recognise his use of classic narrative cinematic tropes. Although Klahr's animations are primarily composed of flat background and foreground images, they nevertheless comprise distinct scenes and sequences whose transitions often mimic conventional editing techniques. A 'cut' between scenes is largely determined by a change in background. The backgrounds come to represent locations whereupon images are animated to move either according to a narrative/representational logic or a poetic/associational logic. Sometimes Klahr even mixes metonymy or synecdoche with realism in the same collaged image. An example of Klahr's use of realism and metonymy (the substitution of something for another thing with which it is associated) can be found in the placement of a cut-out of a folded shirt over a photograph of a bridge, signifying travel. An example of realism and synecdoche (where a part stands in for the whole or vice versa) occurs when a cut-out of a car bumper on a picture of a tunnel or train tracks stands in for a car driving through the tunnel or over train tracks (see Figure 8.1).

   Klahr also regularly and unexpectedly cuts from scenes that exhibit the fixed two-dimensionality of a pictorial plane, with more or less isolated cut-out images or objects placed on top of various types of non-representational backgrounds (see Figure 8.2), to scenes in which depth cues like linear perspective and overlap suggest multi-plane spatial relations between the figures and the background (for instance, where cut-out figures are arranged 'within' spatially depictive

FIGURE 8.1   Still: *The Pettifogger*, Lewis Klahr 2011. An example of realism and synecdoche. Courtesy of Lewis Klahr.

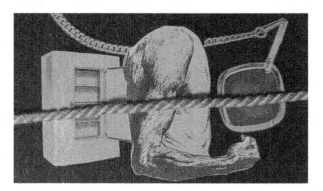

FIGURE 8.2   Still: *The Pettifogger*, Lewis Klahr 2011. An example of the fixed two-dimensionality of a pictorial plane. Courtesy of Lewis Klahr.

background images) (see Figure 8.3). Even within the latter kind of collaged shots that cohere spatially in a realistic way, Klahr often combines images from graphically dissimilar origins so that the illusion is never seamless.[8]

The difference in feeling between these two kinds of scenes is phenomenologically palpable; the first kind has a graphic quality that must be interpreted according to the combination of its discrete elements, while the second is much more immediately comprehensible as a unified image. These unified images function at points like establishing shots, allowing viewers to temporarily 'mentally construct a continuous, unified reality' (Pratt 2009, 111). In fact, it might be helpful to think of narrative in the film in terms of the distinction made by Russian formalists between syuzhet and fabula, where the syuzhet (or plot) refers to the ways in which the story is presented in terms of its order, emphases and logic and the fabula (or story) is, as David Bordwell (1985) notes, 'a pattern that perceivers of narratives create through assumptions and inferences' (49). In the case of Klahr's work, the syuzhet is presented as a spattering of informative moments, and viewers are left to construct the majority of the fabula for themselves.

FIGURE 8.3   Still: *The Pettifogger*, Lewis Klahr 2011. An example of three-dimensional spatial relations between the figures and the background. Courtesy of Lewis Klahr.

Sound plays a vital role in most of Klahr's collage films. In *The Pettifogger*, sound effects and location sound often offer clues to narrative events, although most often in an oblique way. The images and sounds most often run parallel to each other, with points of contact where the sounds and music seem intended to correspond directly to the images. This is most potent narratively when the sounds mimetically reinforce characters' movements so that they achieve what sound film theorist Michel Chion (1994) terms 'synchresis' (a combination of 'synchronism' and 'synthesis'), which refers to 'the forging of an immediate and necessary relationship between something one sees and something one hears' (5). With Klahr's work, music shapes the emotional mood of dramatic sequences as in classical Hollywood cinema, building suspense and indicating the tone of climactic moments. *The Pettifogger* also makes significant use of dialogue heard in voiceover, taken from an episode of the 1960s television programme *The Fugitive*. The dialogue is loosely attributed to the main characters, providing viewers with clues, for instance, regarding the various types of romantic and business relationships that the protagonist engages in. However, just as often the soundtrack acts as its own evocative sound collage, especially during the more visually abstract sequences, not only creating affective ambience but also inviting viewers to search for meaningful dialectical relationships between images and sounds. Viewers who are familiar with the original narratives imbedded in Klahr's source material will have access to additional layers of signification, where two narrative threads exist side by side and influence one another in complex ways.

The associational flow

Beyond the 'semblance of narrative' within Klahr's work, however, 'the associational flow of images' is an equally important aspect of its structure. Narrative scenes in *The Pettifogger* are punctuated by episodes of poetic imagery that can be seen to function according to a vertical (poetic) logic of expression rather than a horizontal (prosaic) narrative one. For filmmaker Maya Deren (2002), horizontal development encapsulated conventional film narrative's logic of actions, primarily based on a linear rationale of cause and effect which propels characters along a trajectory that takes place across a more or less determinable span of time. She conceived of vertical development in a film's structure as centripetal, where a core emotion or idea is approached via disparate images and scenes that contribute in their own distinctive ways to create a more complex expression of that central feeling or theme.

In *The Pettifogger*, the poetic resonances that can be drawn from various combinations of imagery might at times be understood to function descriptively, providing details regarding the mood of the film's world and its characters rather than depicting a straightforward narrative event. During these sequences, all of the compositional elements that make up a shot or sequence of shots may be in meaningful dialogue with any other elements of the work. These semantic and semiotic associative links can in turn simultaneously be based on an array of logics: Narrative, graphic, metaphorical, metonymic or mnemonic. Indeed, these poetic sequences can largely be interpreted according to the principles of polyvalent montage, as defined by Noël Carroll (1996):

> In this mode of editing, it is particularly important that each shot is polyvalent in the sense that it can be combined with surrounding shots along potentially many dimensions. That is, this style begins in the realization that a shot may either match or contrast with adjacently preceding or succeeding shots in virtue of color, subject, shape, shade, texture, the screen orientation of objects, the direction of camera or object movement, or even the stasis thereof.
>
> *(177)*

One of the fundamental heuristic methods that James Peterson (1994) suggests viewers use in order to decipher polyvalent montage in the poetic strain of the avant-garde is to 'look aggressively to establish coreference [...] whenever possible, even by using what might seem to be minor elements in the image' (42). Indeed, a productive way of approaching these poetic sequences is in making as many connections as possible between images, scenes and sounds. For example, the colour and texture of a particular background might offer an associative link to a particular filmic theme or character's mood, or the shape and placement of a single object on a non-representational background might have a narrative or metaphorical significance.[9] The animated movement of the object within the sequence often stresses this significance. The recurrence of these objects and images, presented in the same and in different combinations throughout a given work, reinforce their importance to its overall intention, even if that intention evades complete elucidation.

Klahr's use of associational logic in connecting images is part of what makes viewing his films such an intriguing challenge. The other major challenge lies in learning how to decipher the collaged images themselves. It is highly unlikely that viewers could meaningfully connect everything they see in *The Pettifogger*. It is sometimes difficult to recognise exactly what images and objects are, much less what they are meant to represent. At other times, the images seem to be based on moods or emotional resonances that express feelings that are difficult to articulate, or have a personal significance for Klahr that is inaccessible to viewers. Even the scenes and sequences in *The Pettifogger* that possess the most clearly narrative elements withhold vital information from viewers as to the exact nature of an action, preferring instead to offer hints and suggestions around central events, often achieved through vague exchanges of dialogue. This does not necessarily detract from the film experience; on the contrary, it is often the untethered, enigmatic elements of the work that evoke the strongest personal response by inviting viewers' emotions and imaginations to fill in the blanks. There are myriad possible readings of the film with regard to its specific narrative details, and there cannot be any single correct interpretation of it. Nevertheless, in what follows, I attempt to flesh out a reading of the skeletal narrative of *The Pettifogger*, pulling it up from 'beneath the threshold of perceptibility'.

Deciphering *The Pettifogger*

The first clue for entry into *The Pettifogger*, which is an essential part of how the film enables viewers to begin to construct a fabula through expectation, lies in the title. Coined in the early seventeenth century, the word 'pettifogger' has come to refer to 'a petty practitioner in any activity, a beginner, novice; *esp.* one who makes false claims to skill or knowledge, a charlatan, pretender' (Oxford English Dictionary, 1989, s.v. 'pettifogger'). This title prepares viewers not only to expect the film to focus on a central protagonist, but it also provides them with a clue as to its references to the conventions of the crime film genre. 'Pettifogger' also indicates that the nature of the crime that the protagonist is involved in will likely be on a minor scale (which is not to suggest that things could not escalate into more serious affairs). These expectations will not be easily met. However, they can function as a sort of touchstone (or decoder ring) by which the film's many disparate images may be interpreted.

The Pettifogger takes place over the course of a year in the life of an American gambler and con man. The film's 'semblance of narrative' elliptically follows his daily life as he evades debt collectors, argues with lovers, gambles at casinos and bets on boxing matches, has shady meetings with his older business partner or boss, goes on the road, succumbs to a delirious and amnesiac episode or injury-induced coma (as evidenced by the twenty-minute abstract sequence), ultimately recovers and continues his depressed life of delinquency. The protagonist is represented throughout the film by the comic book version of the actor Robert Vaughn from the popular 1960s television show *The Man From U.N.C.L.E.* (1964–1968). The continuity this creates between the various incarnations of Vaughn is enough to enable easy identification of the figure as the film's 'star'.

In addition to a recurring protagonist, the film offers a number of recognisable settings, some of which are returned to periodically over the course of the film. These are his and his girlfriend's domestic spaces, which are represented both mimetically and via synecdochic association; for instance, the mundaneness of his bathroom is encapsulated in a black and white image of a soap dish. In another scene a rack of coffee cups, a cuff link and a window sparsely define his kitchen. Lamps and couches indicate living rooms. At other points, travel is suggested when we see pictures of planes taking off either preceded or followed shortly by aerial cityscapes and iconic landmarks (San Francisco and the Golden Gate bridge, Las Vegas and casinos). Being on the road is symbolically represented by a steering wheel placed on top of a cut-out of the United States of America; different states' licence plates are shown in geographically sequential driving order, and a lone bumper (recognised as the Pettifogger's car) visits and revisits a photo of a gas station and a postcard of a motel.

The film begins with a twelve-minute prologue during which many of the images that will come to feature prominently in the rest of the film are condensed into an incomplete preview of what is to come. During this preamble a flashing message from a fortune cookie that reads 'Many possibilities are open to you, take advantage of them' seems to be directly speaking to its audience as well as indicating the pettifogger's opportunistic and nomadic lifestyle. The message might be understood as an instruction for how we should encounter the film, encouraging us to make as many connections between the elements as we can. As the clues in *The Pettifogger* that relate to particular aspects of the film's world are revealed intermittently and are interspersed with information regarding other aspects of that world, the film makes it frequently necessary for the viewer to connect details retrospectively, building a clearer mental scenario layer upon layer.

Due to the sketchy and partial nature of the depiction of the world in Klahr's film, we are obliged to recall certain pieces of information in order to orientate ourselves according to the narrative's temporal and spatial progression (such as keeping in mind which time of year is being represented, or where in the United States the pettifogger is at a given time). For instance, *The Pettifogger* reveals over the course of the prologue that it begins in the winter of 1963 by showing an image of '1963' imprinted on the granular leathery surface of a mechanic's guide to automotive parts, and then almost a minute later – after we have been introduced to his relationship with his lady lover and a mysterious transaction with the man in the green jacket – a sequence provides further details in the form of a cut-out circle inscribed with 'Jan 12' which circles an isolated milk bottle on another leathery surface. As if to emphasise this information, the next image is of a window with a heater underneath it with snowy trees outside, followed briefly by an image of a snow-covered car headlight. Often, the significance of something will not be revealed for a short period after it is introduced and thus must be retroactively put together.

The significance of sound

The soundtrack in *The Pettifogger* often corresponds rhythmically to the pacing of the scenes, and it also contributes information about the narrative that is unfolding, sometimes providing direct clues to the action and at other times serving a more atmospheric function (as with the ambient intervals of sounds of a billiards game and a long thunderstorm towards the end). The audio in the prologue is important in that it mimics the condensation of the story being conveyed in the visuals. For instance, the clearly edited sounds of a jazz bar which omits the performances, presenting applause and the indecipherable mumblings of the audience, mimics the formal properties of the film in two ways: It shows the elision of time that is being represented in the film as well as providing clues to an event without disclosing the essential information (in the case of the audio, intelligible words or the musical performance itself).[10] Also, the debt collection letters heard on the soundtrack establish that the pettifogger is most likely in financial trouble and under tremendous stress, and this is recalled again and again in the images of empty envelopes and library due date cards. It does not become clear that the voiceover regarding the outstanding debt is a dictation of a letter until the end of the prologue where the man's patronising, monotonous voice says 'sincerely yours'.

In other scenes, voiceover dialogue reveals the troubled nature of his romantic relationships. One humorous example of this occurs halfway through the film when, over images of billiard balls and boxers in a boxing ring, an excerpt of Dawn Upshaw singing 'What A Curse For A Woman Is A Timid Man' from Gian Carlo Menotti's radio opera *The Old Maid and the Thief* (1939) is heard. Upshaw trills, 'He eats and drinks and sleeps, he talks of baseball and boxing, but that is all!' This not only provides information regarding the obsessive nature of the gambling protagonist, but it suggests that these are some of the reasons for the pettifogger's romantic failings.

Some of the clearest narrative events that take place are depicted in conjunction with some form of dialogue, either through voiceover or in speech bubbles. Examples of this can be seen in the scenes in which the pettifogger vaguely receives instructions to 'get close to' unidentified people by the names of 'Palmer' and 'Callison'. Later on, a conversation takes place between the pettifogger and a brunette woman in front of a background image of a section of the Las Vegas strip where he invites 'Mrs. Callison' to his hotel for a drink (visible in handwritten speech bubbles). She refuses via speech bubble. It remains unclear whether she is the Callison the boss is looking for or the pettifogger is attempting to locate her husband. Later still, we see the first two figures (the boss and the pettifogger) in front of the same strip, where the boss says simply, 'Don't let him go!' before turning around to leave (cleverly shown in a quick succession of three cut-outs of the boss's face from different angles). Conversations like these convey an air of intrigue along the lines of the crime film genre and suggest that the pettifogger's actions will relate somehow to carrying out a criminal job.

Shifting perspectives and points of view

Klahr (2011) once explained to an interviewer that '*The Pettifogger* is a diaristic, first person montage full of glimpses, glances and the quotidian'. The film's tendency towards episodes of associational poetic imagery (especially under the unstable principles of polyvalent montage) means that it may be difficult to recognise that a first person point of view is at times being represented. However, Klahr's positioning of the figure of the pettifogger at the film's centre gives viewers the opportunity to interpret the images as representing variously objective and subjective views of the protagonist. In some scenes, we are invited to observe his actions and interactions from the outside and in others we are made privy to his subjective point of view. One example of this takes place early on in the film, where a vacillation between grainy black and white images of a part of a man's face and a shot of the pettifogger's face seen above the top of a hand of cards acts as a shot/reverse shot interaction between members of a card game who are scrutinising each other for signs of bluffing.

Recognising the possibility of interpreting these images according to the hermeneutic logic of the pettifogger's subjective experience unlocks the potential for many of the symbolic and associational aspects of the imagery to be interpreted with much greater narrative clarity. For instance, sequences in which a cigarette suddenly intrudes upon a scene (such as a baseball or poker game) may be interpreted as being seen from the point of view of the pettifogger while smoking. Poker chips hover over a picture of the bathroom; playing cards and drink stirrers appear everywhere, showing his obsession with gambling, which in turn is perhaps spurred by the constant reminder of his financial debt (connected tangentially to the voiceover debt letter by empty envelopes). This is not to say, of course, that these are the only ways of interpreting the imagery, and indeed, the same images can represent different aspects of the fabula over the course of the film. For instance, playing cards are a motif in the film that indicate his gambling habits, but it might equally be said that at points we are encouraged to identify the pettifogger hierarchically as the jack and the other man, his boss, as the king. The recurrence of scenes featuring play money may indicate straightforward financial transactions taking place, while also suggesting that the money may be counterfeit. Depending on the pettifogger's degree of villainy, the changing licence plates may also be interpreted as an indication that he is a serial car thief, stealing a new car in each new state, or else simply changing licence plates to evade detection.

The long stretch towards the end of the film where the image sequences grow increasingly abstract, interspersed with increasing intervals of blackness and accompanied by one long continuous recording of a thunderstorm, is a departure from the tone of the rest of the work, indicating a potential shift in perspective or consciousness. Single images (of cards, doors, bridges, suitcases, patterned paper, cigarettes, booze, tyres, casino chips, fabrics, naked women) flicker rapidly onscreen as if the elements that made up the film (and the pettifogger's life) up until this point are being digested in the depths of an unconscious mind. This interpretation is strengthened when, in the midst of this contemplative sequence, voices are again heard on the soundtrack and an image of a ceiling light viewed from below indicates a point of view shot of the pettifogger, just awoken. A voice, which seems to be that of a police officer, questions a man about how he came to be injured. Another man's voice recounts being struck when getting out of the car to get cigarettes. He states his name as Mr Browning (surely not his real name), and indeed the officers find no ID in his possessions. He has a mere 12 dollars in his pockets. Then the thunderstorm and the semi-erratic images return until the storm ends abruptly and an image of the pettifogger in motion is juxtaposed with the sounds of footsteps running on dried leaves (suggesting autumn) and alarm bells going off in the distance.

A subsequent image of a policeman suggests that the pettifogger has committed a theft or similar crime. Multiple images of fingerprints suggest that his crime is being investigated – perhaps that he is being pursued, and a phone conversation with a woman who says she's moving out indicates that the pettifogger hasn't woken to a more fortunate life. Airline tickets, aerial photographs of parking lots, flying geese and motel rooms suggest that he is travelling again. In the final sequences, the rainstorm returns and we see a picture of a Christmas ornament in a tree, perhaps suggesting that a full year has passed. The credits are followed by the sounds of a car driving and two final enigmatic images, ending silently on another glimpse of the image of the ceiling light seen from below. Linking back to the images of motel rooms and travel, I imagine the pettifogger waking up, yet again, alone in a strange room, doomed to repeat the same series of petty criminal actions until he finally ends up in jail (the threat of which has loomed throughout the work in the form of a floating square patch of wire mesh).

Conclusion

The potential for Klahr's experimental, and at times abstract, work to resonate differently for each viewer is part of the compelling power of *The Pettifogger*. The descriptions of obscured narrativity and meaningful indecipherability bear witness to the rich and nebulous experience of viewing his work for the first time – and arguably subsequent times as well. These qualities are integral to them, and it is doubtful, not to mention undesirable, that they would be completely clarified even after a hundred viewings. However, one of the benefits of studying a work as densely layered and cryptically composed as *The Pettifogger* is that the potential to recognise patterns, meaningful connections and expressive tropes has the opportunity to develop more fully from repeated viewings and close analysis. Klahr's sparse, semi-mimetic audio-visual configurations and his combined use of poetic and prosaic expressive logic require viewers to actively integrate the elements of his collage in order to arrive at a coherent narrative interpretation. By responding to aural cues, following the narrative signposts (however indeterminate) and interpreting the polyvalent graphical compositions of *The Pettifogger*, we gradually are able to bring our own versions of its 'submerged' narrative to the surface.

The amount of time and energy that goes into the making of experimental animation is often directly inverse to the amount of screen time they take up, as well as to the amount of critical attention they receive. It is my hope that the close reading provided in this chapter encourages others to engage in the formidable task of analysing experimental animations that are often staggeringly dense and difficult to describe. The benefits, I argue, are well worth the effort.

Notes

1 Up until quite recently, experimental animation has largely been addressed either as a subcategory or technique of avant-garde cinema (and, to a lesser degree, artists' film and video) or in isolated treatments within animation studies.

2 For instance, Russett and Starr's seminal text *Experimental Animation: Origins of an Art* identifies 'pictorial' and 'imagist' animators who produced narrative-based works, such as Lotte Reiniger, Berthold Bartosch, Alexander Alexeieff and Claire Parker, Harry Smith and Larry Jordan.

3 He is represented by Anthony Reynolds Gallery in London.

4 Part of this association, however enigmatic and oblique, can be traced back to P. Adams Sitney's quasi-narrative interpretations of American collage animators like Harry Smith and Lawrence Jordan in his highly influential *Visionary Film* (2002).

5 Suzanne Buchan (2010) refers to this feature as 'portmanteau images', where fragments of different images function 'like the lexeme fragments of different words' (187).

6 Other experimental animators working with collage include Stan VanDerBeek, Robert Breer, Carmen D'Avino, Martha Colburn, Janie Geiser, Jodie Mack, Kelly Sears, Jeff Scher, Frank Mouris, Paul Vester, Dalibor Barić, Kate Jessop, Amy Lockhart, Nathanial Whitcomb, Natalie Wilkin, Fritz Steingrobe and Hanna Nordholt, Virgil Widrich and Osbert Parker.

7 This refers to James Peterson's (1994) grouping of P. Adams Sitney's categories of American visionary film (namely, the 'trance film', the 'lyrical film' and the 'mythopoetic film'). Examples include Maya Deren's *Meshes of the Afternoon* (1943), Stan Brakhage's *Window Water Baby Moving* (1959) and Doug Haynes' *Common Loss* (1979).

8 Such a scene appears in *Elevator Music* (1991) where a photographic cut-out of an actress is shown fellating an illustrated male figure.

9 For instance, Klahr uses the colour green as a motif in *Daylight Moon* (which represents a character's subjective experience) or blue in *Altair* (which is a much more associational, metaphorical film).

10 Klahr is often obliged to edit his materials in order to avoid copyright infringement, which in turn provides opportunities to problem-solve and create creative storytelling techniques.

References

Atkinson, Michael. 'Culture Consumer Lewis Klahr: The Re-Animator.' *The Village Voice*. May 16 2000, accessed May 10 2018. www.villagevoice.com/2000–05–16/film/culture-consumer-lewis-klahr/.

Bordwell, David. *Narration in the Fiction Film*. Madison: University of Wisconsin Press, 1985.

Bordwell, David and Kristin Thompson. *Film Art: An Introduction.* 10th edition. New York: McGraw-Hill, 2012.

Brakhage, Stan. *Window Water Baby Moving* US, 1959. Film.

Buchan, Suzanne. "'A Curious Chapter in the Manual of Animation": Stan VanDerBeek's Animated Spatial Politics.' *Animation: An Interdisciplinary Journal* 5, no. 2 (2010): 173–196.

Carroll, Noël. 'Causation, the Ampliation of Movement and Avant-Garde Film.' *Theorizing the Moving Image.* Cambridge: Cambridge University Press, 1996.

Chion, Michel. *Audio-Vision.* Translated by Claudia Gorbman. New York: Columbia University Press, 1994.

Cronk, Jordan. 'Era Extraña: Lewis Klahr on Sixty Six.' *Cinema Scope Magazine,* Issue 66, 2016, accessed May 2018. http://cinema-scope.com/cinema-scope-magazine/era-extrana-lewis-klahr-sixty-six/.

Deren, Maya. *Meshes of the Afternoon.* US, 1943. Film.

Geiser, Janie. *Ghost Algebra.* US, 2009. Film.

Gunning, Tom. 'Towards a Minor Cinema: Fonoroff, Herwitz, Awesh, Lapore, Klahr and Solomon.' *Motion Picture* 3, nos. 1–2 (1989–90): 2–5.

Haynes, Doug. *Common Loss.* US, 1979. Film.

Huggins, Roy. *The Fugitive.* US, 1963–1967. Television series.

Jordan, Larry. *Sophie's Place.* US, 1986. Film.

Klahr, Lewis. 'A Clarification.' *The Sharpest Point: Animation at the End of Cinema.* Edited by Chris Gehman and Steve Reinke. Toronto: XYZ Books, 2005, 234–235.

Klahr, Lewis. 'Flotsam and Jetsam: The Spray of History.' *Animation: An Interdisciplinary Journal*6, No. 3 (2011): 387–398.

Klahr, Lewis. *In the Month of Crickets.* US, 1988. Film.

———. *For the Rest of Your Natural Life.* US, 1988. Film.

———. *Tales of the Forgotten Future.* US, 1988–1991. Film.

———. *The Organ Minder's Gronkey.* US, 1990. Film.

———. *Elevator Music.* US, 1991. Film.

———. *Untitled.* US, 1991. Film.

———. *Altair.* US, 1994. Film.

———. *Daylight Moon and Other Constellations.* US, 1999–2004. Film.

———. *Pony Glass.* US, 1997. Film.

———. *Engram Sepals.* US, 2000. Film.

———. *Daylight Moon.* US, 2002. Film.

———. *Prolix Satori.* US, 2009–2011. Film.

———. *The Pettifogger.* US, 2011. Film.

———. *Sixty Six.* US, 2002–2015. Film.

Lessing, Gotthold Ephrain. *Laocoön: An Essay on the Limits of Painting and Poetry.* Edited and translated by Edward Allen McCormick. Baltimore: Johns Hopkins University Press, 1984.

Lowne, James. *Our Relationships Will Become Radiant.* UK, 2011. Film.

MacDonald, Scott. "'Poetry and the Film: A Symposium" (with Maya Deren, Willard Maas, Arthur Miller, Dylan Thomas, Parker Tyler), 10/28/53.' *Cinema 16: Documents Toward a History of the Film Society.* Edited by Scott MacDonald. Philadelphia: Temple University Press, 2002, 202–212.

McGillicuddy, Louisa. 'Lewis Klahr's The Pettifogger: Collaging the crime – in pictures.' *The Guardian.* November 1 2011, accessed May 2018. www.guardian.co.uk/film/gallery/2011/nov/01/lewis-klahr-the-pettifogger-in-pictures.

Oxford English Dictionary. 2nd ed. 20 vols. Oxford: Oxford University Press, 1989. Continually updated at www.oed.com/.

Perry, Colin. 'Lewis Klahr.' */P Engine: Moving Image Transmission*. October 2010, accessed May 2018. http://web.archive.org/web/20160113122539/http://www.apengine.org/2010/10/lewis_klahr_by_colin_perry/.

Peterson, James. *Dreams of Chaos, Visions of Order: Understanding the American Avant-Garde*. Detroit: Wayne State University Press, 1994.

Peterson, James. 'Is a Cognitive Approach to the Avant-garde Cinema Perverse?' *Post-Theory*. Edited by David Bordwell and Noël Carroll. University of Wisconsin Press, 1996, 108–129.

Pitt, Suzan. *Asparagus*. US, 1979. Film.

Powers, John P. 'Darkness of the Edge of Town: Film Meets Digital in PhilSolomon's *In Memoriam (Mark LaPore)*.' *October* 137, Summer (2011): 84–106.

Pratt, Henry John. 'Narrative in Comics.' *The Poetics, Aesthetics, and Philosophy of Narrative*. Edited by Noël Carroll. Chichester: John Wiley & Sons Ltd., 2009, 107–117.

Russett, Robert and Cecile Starr. *Experimental Animation: Origins of a New Art*. New York: Da Capo, 1988.

Sitney, P. Adams. *Visionary Film: The American Avant-Garde 1943–2000*. Oxford: Oxford University Press, 2002.

Smith, Harry. *Heaven and Earth Magic*. US, 1957–62. Film.

Taberham, Paul. *Lessons in Perception: The Avant-Garde Filmmaker as Practical Psychologist*. Oxford: Berghahn Books, 2018.

Wrake, Run. *Jukebox*. UK, 1994. Film.

9

HOW TO BE HUMAN

The animations of Jim Trainor

Steve Reinke

Jim Trainor is an artist who works in film, video, comic strips as well as performances in which he narrates slide projection versions of his comic books to musical accompaniment. He is best known, though, for his animations, which he has been doing since he was 13. His favoured technique has remained constant, black felt-tipped marker on white typing paper, lately augmented with coloured paper and dots. The animations are, generally, representational narratives with voice-over narration. His work, like the work of Phil Mulloy and David Shrigley, employs a sophisticated naiveté that undercuts their sly transgressions with a seemingly 'innocent' humour and childlike directness. They can be viewed on his Vimeo channel.

When I first encountered Trainor's work, I liked it immediately. But I did not think of it as particularly important or profound. I mistakenly thought it proficient, but easy – seductive if not ambitious. This is a common reaction: It is very agreeable work. As my engagement with the work grew, it deepened. I began showing Trainor's animations, teaching them, thinking about them. I included the text from the voice-over of *The Moschops* in a book I co-edited with Chris Gehman, *The Sharpest Point: Animation at the End of Cinema*.

Over time, I began to think that the work was more than merely agreeable, more than simple and direct and charming with a disarmingly sly take on morality and transgression. And more, too, than incredibly funny and moving. But what is this 'more'? It is, I think, something that exceeds genre, something that uses animation to escape animation, something that points the way to new ways of being in the world. Or, if that is too much, new ways of making and watching cartoons.

The Fetishist (38 minutes, 1997)

The Fetishist (38 minutes, 1997) is a biopic of serial killer William Heirens, active in Chicago in the late 1940s and best known for the lipstick message he left on a victim's bedroom wall: 'For heaven's sake catch me before I kill more: I cannot help myself'. Trainor's longest animated film to date, it took 11 years to complete.

> Yes, it is true the "The Fetishist" took me eleven years. I chipped away at it very slowly. I piled up thousands of drawings for several years without even shooting them. My animation stand was disassembled and I had an odd disinclination to put it back together again, but I figured I could draw the pictures and find a way to film them eventually.
>
> *(Trainor, quoted in Rostron 2013)*

It is an odd turn of phrase: 'Find a way to film them eventually', for Trainor's animation technique – like his predecessor Winsor McCay's – leaves only one way to film any particular sequence of images/stack of drawings. One does not 'find' a way to film them, for the way to film them is built into the sequential drawing process. Yet Trainor does circumvent one of the usual attributes of this kind of animation: He does not storyboard. The processes of writing and drawing remain, if not quite improvisatory, open-ended as they are not tied to the tyranny of the storyboard. Consequently, there is a lot of – what one might call in a more industrial mode of production – waste. For the 38 minutes of *The Fetishist*, Trainor filmed almost two hours of animation. This 'waste' would be unheard of in, not only all of industrial animation, but most of artists' animation as well. Yet it is this excess, this surplus of not only labour but also thoughts, desires, possibilities that allows Trainor's works to remain alive, crackling with possibilities.

The story is told chronologically in a series of vignettes. Trainor augments his drawings by employing archival newspaper photographs as occasional background elements. Rather than disrupting the insular, childlike world of *The Fetishist*, these archival envoys from the world of historical reality shore it up. Unlike the bulk of contemporary American crime stories – whether fiction or documentary – this film does not attempt to mine the inner world of Heirens in order to 'get in the mind of a serial killer'. To quote the press material, 'It presents a world depopulated by the limitations of a psychopathic personality' (Reinke, n.d.). This rather obscure sentence means, I think, something more than eschewing the normalising/moralising tendencies of American popular culture, which would provide particular reasons for the development of the psychopathic mind (some childhood trauma, generally), and go to some lengths to assure us that the psychopath is fundamentally different from us.

Fetishism, as a concept, emerged in anthropology, particularly in relation to African material culture. Fetishism is the attribution of value or powers to an object: The fetish. Modern anthropology would more likely use the terms 'charm' or 'power object', in part to distance itself from the racist legacy of the fetish. (Hegel, for instance, theorised that primitive peoples needed fetishes because they were incapable of abstract thought.) (MacGaffey 1993). Though Trainor is well versed in anthropology, his use of the concept of fetishism is clearly the psychoanalytic version, in which fetishism is not part of a shared belief system, but an individual pathology. The classic articulation comes from Freud's 1927 essay, 'Fetishism' (Freud 2001, 152–159). Here, the (boy) child is playing at his mother's feet and, looking up, is alarmed to discover she does not have a penis. The child disavows this possible castration through a compromise: The simultaneous belief and non-belief in the maternal phallus: The fetish. This is why, according to Freud, the most common fetish objects are feet and fur (those things the child most likely sees when turning away, recoiling from the absent penis).

As the title suggests, Heirens' activities as a fetishist are emphasised over his assaults and murders. Fetishism is certainly easier to relate to than serial killing: Even if we are not fetishists, we generally have preferences, making the difference between fetishist and non-fetishist a matter of degree rather than kind. Fetishism is based on metonymy: It occurs when one's desire/fear (anxiety) in relation to a particular object (classically, the maternal phallus) is shifted to a proximal object (also the maternal phallus), in Heirens' case, women's undergarments.

Metaphors draw a similarity between two otherwise dissimilar things. They involve a kind of jump from one thing to another. In metonymy, there is no jump. There is a contiguity between two things, or between a single thing and an aspect of that thing. (Synechdoche, for instance, is the type of metonymy in which a part refers to a whole, or vice versa: 'Boots' for 'soldiers.') Metaphors involve a leap from one thing to another. In metonymy, things rub against one another. Metaphor selects, metonyms combine. In psychoanalytic terms, metaphors are involved in displacement, metonyms in condensation. Metaphors suppress/repress, metonyms combine/displace. As Jacques Lacan put it: 'It is in the word-to-word connection that metonymy is based', and then: 'One word for another: that is the formula of metaphor.' (Lacan 2006, 422)

The Fetishist eschews metaphor in favour of metonymy to marvellous effect. In particular, Trainor's depiction of body fluids – simple black drips, drops or puddles – form a particularly rich metonymic chain: Tear – sweat – blood – vomit – semen – urine – faeces – spit – bile – milk – phlegm – menstrual blood. Trainor plays around with this representational ambiguity, producing at turns humour, anxiety, dread, arousal, disgust: A general sense of physical abjection. Not only is it often unclear to us what a particular body fluid might be, it seems to me also unclear to Heirens, who may not care, or have the capacity to distinguish between particular fluids and whether they come from him or someone/something else. This ambiguity – as to where on the metonymic chain of body fluids a particular ink blob might lie – exists simultaneously within the world of *The Fetishist* (that is, diegetically) as well as extra-diegetically (the viewer's ability to recognise and name).

In this jittering animated world of crude line drawings and foleyed liquid plop sounds, bodies are reservoirs of various seeping, dripping or spewing liquids. If a body – a subjectivity, an identity – is represented by simple marker lines that delineate forms without volume, this body is under constant threat of dissolution through these fluids that escape it and gain volume aurally, through the sounds they generate hitting the ground. The fluid plop sounds are incredibly important to these dramas of physical dissolution, of the unstable boundary between self and world. Our fluids, whether vital or waste, gain dimension as they leave us.

The Bats (8 minutes, 1999) and *The Moschops* (13 minutes, 2000)

The Bats (8 minutes, 1999) and *The Moschops* (13 minutes, 2000) have a lot in common. They are part of the series *The Animals and their Limitations*, though the two components subsequently finished – *The Magic Kingdom* (2002) and *Harmony* (2004) – diverge from many of these commonalities. *The Magic Kingdom*, for instance, consists mainly of live-action footage of a zoo's monkey cage – though with short animated sequences. *Harmony*, discussed below, has multiple protagonists. Despite their titles, both *The Bats* and *The Moschops* have, respectively, a single particular bat and moschop as their protagonist.

Though the voice-over narrations for these two films are in the first-person, the films are not diegetically voiced by their protagonists. That is, they do not speak on-screen, but from a distance that is ambiguous, though at times seemingly becoming omniscient. Both the bat and the moschop are silent, incapable of speech. The jittering line animations face us mutely. They do not (cannot) address us directly from their worlds, but through narrators who adopt the first-person, confessional mode. Both films alternate between a male and female narrator, though the protagonists are indentified as being male.

In *The Bats*, the male narrator voices the unnamed protagonist bat's life story, including his death (January 4, 1361, of old age) and three visitations from God. Though God is identified as a male who appears, there is no visual depiction of him, and his words are narrated by a woman, who provides philosophy ('Sometimes you have to kill more than you can eat'), law ('You must only have sexual intercourse with your own species') and prophecy ('In another 900 generations, your lower-than-mid-pitches will become extinct'). Trainor describes *The Bats* as the 'story of life devoted to carnal pleasures and the avoidance of predators under the guidance of a prescient but ineffectual God'. (Reinke n.d.) So, the animation is not about bats at all, of course, except in the details, the biological specifics.

The moschops was a mammal-like reptile of the Permian era. It had a thick skull and short little hind legs. According to Trainor, 'Scientists believe the moschops was capable of interior tenderness, which it expressed, ironically, through incessant fighting' (ibid). (Scientists, of course, have not made such a claim.) In *The Moschops*, the narration alternates between a male and female voice. The male voice is identified with the protagonist, who tells the story of his life – fighting and fucking until he is fatally wounded – while the female voice speaks on behalf of the herd. Both narrators also speak in a voice that is primarily informational, the voice of a nature documentary. If there is anthropomorphism going on here – and, of course, there is, but a very strange anthropomorphism of shifting identities – it is one that simultaneously inverts that of the nature documentary and children's literature. The anthropomorphising force of the nature shown is one that attributes certain human abilities and motivations to creatures, but limits their consciousness. The creatures have a strictly demarcated interiority, trapped in instinct, limited to the fulfilment of basic drives. Cartoon animals are, in some respects, fully individuated: Human subjects in drag. Their assumed costumes limit them to functioning in a theatrical/allegorical manner. Cartoon animals are camp queens.

One of the things that marks Trainor's work is his developing uses of anthropomorphism, particularly in relation to narration and point of view. In *The Bats*, the relationship between narrators and protagonists is fairly straightforward. The male narrator speaks (first-person, in the past tense, from beyond the grave) on behalf of the mute protagonist, a particular lower-than-mid-pitch bat. In one sense, the protagonist exists completely within the register of the image, while the male narrator exists completely – and retrospectively – within the register of the textual/aural. This clean split allows the bat to be simultaneously mute and speaking/spoken, simultaneously not-anthropomorphised and anthropomorphised. (The female narrator speaking in the present tense as the voice of God is another kind of anthropomorphism, wherein supernatural or transcendent beings – gods – are given human characteristics.)

In *The Moschops*, these relationships are basically maintained, though in a more complex form. We still have a single protagonist who remains mute in the visual register while being spoken/speaking in the aural, as well as a male and female narrator. Both narrators speak in the first person, the male – identified with the protagonist – in the first-person singular ('I'); the female – identified with the herd – in the first-person plural ('we'). On the one hand, this social/sexual division makes it easy to read *The Moschops* as an allegory of male aggression and homosexual panic, which it certainly is. (What is homosexual panic? It's when you confuse aggression and intimacy. Not fight or flight, or even fight or fuck, but fight or snuggle.) On the other hand, both narrators equally perform as nature show hosts, providing factual commentary that exceeds their narrative function.

This is Trainor's sweetest work, his most directly affecting. Here, I'll show you. These are two sections of monologue from the work, one near the middle and the conclusion:

> You bashed a male with your head, but that night he'd be dozing right next to you. One little male never got to have sexual intercourse. I eyed him tenderly though my throat flared red with anger. I hit him 'til the females flipped over, all dreamy indifference.
>
> I wanted to tell them, all those battles, but I never hated anyone! The mud hardened across my eyes as I watched the world turn yellow and flat.

Were those males battling, or were they insects, stuck in sap? Nothing on earth has a right to live, only a chance, a chance.

(Trainor 2005, 270)

The Magic Kingdom (8 minutes, 2002) and *Harmony* (12 minutes, 2004)

The Magic Kingdom (8 minutes, 2002) is singular in the Trainor oeuvre. Masterfully shot by Ben Russell on beautifully grainy 16mm film and without a voice-over, or text of any kind (save for the titles), *The Magic Kingdom* looks like a structuralist film from the 1970s, save for the brief animated interludes in Trainor's usual style. And perhaps it is this surface of nostalgia for the avant-garde in experimental film that makes it, to date, the only one of Trainor's films to be featured in the Whitney Biennial (2004, curated by Chrissie Iles).

Here is Trainor's comically sardonic synopsis from Vimeo:

> In the blue-green light of the tropical rainforest, among the creeks and boulders and fallen trees, humankind's closest relatives drift in and out of meditative states. Also features a hippo and a tapir.[1]

The film does not take place in a tropical rainforest, but in the strange crepuscular landscape of an incredibly elaborate zoo. The primate enclosure doesn't strive for realism (and if it did, it would be the realism of the savannah as much as the rainforest) but instead presents over-designed forms that mimic rocks and trees. And the animals behave as seemingly healthy animals, swinging happily in their ever-darkening sci-fi playground, not exhibiting the withdrawn or repetitive behaviour one might expect from zoo psychosis. In other words, at no point do the animals 'drift in and out of meditative states'.

Within the body of the film (that is, apart from the titles) there are eight short animations, – some two or three seconds, most six or seven – simple unregistered line drawings, with coloured backgrounds and a coloured dot or dots. The black lines jiggle, but only the dots move. Initially, it is quite apparent that each inserted animation has been directly motivated by the live-action shot before it. A black line drawing, for instance, might refer to a tree structure from the previous shot, and the coloured dot moving along one of the lines, the monkey we have just seen climbing the structure. Lines, then, are structures, either indicating barriers or, more often, possible lines of flight. And dots are creatures, individual creatures from the previous shot. But by the time we get to the fourth and fifth animations, the visual relationship between the animation and the preceding shot becomes difficult to discern. The same activity seems to be taking place: An abstraction of the previous shot, a simplification which seems to also be a kind of analysis. But the effect is strangely unnerving: We do not know what we are looking at exactly, even if we are fairly sure it has been derived, in some way, from the previous shot.

If there are meditative states in *The Magic Kingdom*, they do not appear in the animals, who are blissfully immune to interiority, but in the distance between the live-action shots and the brief animations that simultaneously remap, analyse, illustrate and abstract these relations of creature to structure. There is a strange empathy here. The animations are not meditative in the least. They are simple, crude, somewhat satisfying formally, but pathetically inadequate at commenting on the previous shots. The work, care, meditation and empathy are not in the animations in themselves, but in the distance from the truly inscrutable being of the creatures as depicted in the live-action shots and the conceptual, affective and representational inadequacies of the animations derived from them.

Trainor's synopsis of *Harmony* doesn't describe the work so much as provide a particularly perverse extra-textual bracketing of it.

> A male god bestows upon animals the gift of self-awareness, which they promptly use to express guilt for their behavior. This moral breakthrough is somewhat undermined by the appearance of humans, whose inversion of magical belief systems degrades the whole of Nature.

Nothing of the sort happens in *Harmony*. No god appears in the film, there is no bestowal of self-awareness, no moral breakthrough, no invention of a magical belief system. What Trainor describes here aren't the narrative events of his film. Rather, he is describing a kind of extra-textual allegory of his own role: Artist as both anthropomorphiser and (to coin a truly awkward term) counter-anthropomorphiser. If there is a god bestowing upon animals the 'gift of self-awareness' (with this phrase, Trainor's irony drifts toward an uncharacteristic sarcasm) it is Trainor himself as that particularly limited creator of worlds: The animator.

The film presents ten scenarios, ten characters, seven animals who speak as the protagonists of *The Bats* and *The Moschops* speak, displaying agency even though their behaviour is 'natural', species-determined and three humans, the first with an individual sin, the second cultural, the last – The Woman Who Ruined Everything – zooming off to myth. In order of appearance: The Spotted Hyena ('I killed my identical twin sister'.), The Lion ('I killed my girlfriend's children, which is to say I killed all the children of all my girlfriends'.), Short-Faced Kangaroo Man ('I killed my totemic animal'.), The Boreal Chickadee ('I mated with a man who was not my husband'.), The Pygmy-Chimpanzee ('I rubbed my clitoris against the clitoris of my own mother'.), The Hunting Leopard ('I caused her pain with my backwards-facing barbs'.), The Lartna Men ('We cut a little boy's penis open'.), The Deep-Sea Angler-Fish ('I let my husband kill himself'.), The Woman Who Ruined Everything ('I had my menstrual period and I prepared food'.), The Bottle-Nosed Dolphin ('We raped her. We all raped her'.).

Although there is some variation with individual sections, they follow a basic model. First, the character is introduced in a headshot (or what would be roughly equivalent to a head shot). Affect is central to these introductory shots: Our characters are sympathetic and even, sometimes, cute. It is while they are being presented to us in pleasing close-ups that the narrator, speaking in first person, outlines their transgressions. This is followed by a middle section in which the narrative aspects of their transgressions are represented in animations reminiscent of the interludes in *The Magic Kingdom*. Line drawings and dots, the dots usually corresponding to the characters, the line drawings to the environment. But these abstracted sections, while using the same formal techniques, work quite differently. They hit hard as narrative content: The murders, rapes and mutilations are here straightforwardly represented; it takes little effort to make these abstractions representational. The final sections of each episode return us to the world of the first shot, but this world has been degraded, the characters slump in medium long shots, forlorn (except for the rape-loving dolphins, who provide admirable closure to the parade, and The Woman Who Ruined Everything, who has already moved to the realm of the mythic).

Harmony is not so much concerned with the difference between the human and the animal, but what might constitute the human itself. Slavoj Žižek, in his usual combination of Hegel, Lacan and the Marx Brothers, puts it like this. If at the zero level of subjectivity, the Lacanian real, 'the subject is confronted not with constituted reality but with the spectral obscene proto-reality of partial objects floating around against the background of the ontological Void', – which sounds like the description of a Fleischer Brothers cartoon, or cartoons in general – how does the human appear? On the level of the individual:

> as the 'minimal difference' on account of which an individual is never fully him/herself, but always only 'resembles him/herself.' The Marx Brothers were right: "You look like X, so no wonder you are X ... " This means, of course, that there is no positive-substantial determination of man: man is the animal which recognizes itself as man, what makes him human is this formal gesture of recognition as such, not the recognised content. Man is a lack which, in order to fill itself in, recognizes itself as something.
>
> *(Žižek 2006, 44)*

All of Trainor's work activates this minimal difference, but perhaps none so sharply as *Harmony*, which remains the artist's favourite among his own works. It also marks a specific step in his development, from the quasi-psychoanalytical approach to interiority and transgression (*The Fetishist*); to one which deploys a particularly complex set of anthropomorphisms, a humanism of becoming-animal that replaces agency with ritual and instinct, dispensing with psychoanalytical concerns (as much as they can be dispensed with); to work like the 'The Woman Who Ruined Everything' section of *Harmony*, which moves from instinct/ritual to the mythic and returns us, as I argue in the next section, back to individual interiority, to a psychoanalytical engagement with the death drive.

Presentation Theme (14 minutes, 2008)

Apart from a few smaller projects (such as a music video for the band Ice Balloons) 2008's *The Presentation Theme* is the most recent animation we have from Trainor. After winning the Alpert Award in 2010, Trainor began work on a 71 minute live action feature, *The Pink Egg* (2016).

The Moschops takes on masculinity and homosexual panic in a somehow sweet narrative of fragility, of mortality. The world of *The Presentation Theme* is much more claustrophobic, combining a remarkable number of themes in its seemingly slow-paced 14 minutes. This journey – which is simultaneously mythological and subconscious, equally personal and cultural, though the particular culture/ religion seems distant, remote – has multiple destinations: Sacrificial mutilation, transfiguration, death, dual primal scenes (vaginal and anal). There is no after-life: There is no spirituality to this religion.

The animation has two voices, a female narrator and our protagonist, 'You', who has but a few short lines and is voiced by the artist. The narrator addresses us in the second person: Not only is the protagonist You, but we, the audience, are you, too: Anxious, bewildered. The one good thing about religious ceremonies seems to be that they can restructure our psychic lives, turning anxiety into awe. Spiritual belief is not necessary, just some fundamental trauma.

And this trauma is introduced in the pre-title section in which we see a baby under a curved checkered rectangle (later identified as a blanket, though, as we'll see, all representations in this work are tentative, shifting, contingent). The nar-rator says:

> You used to think you were the center of everything. You thought you were the center but you were mistaken. More on that later.

This positions the work as a narrative of the trauma of the unbounded narcissism of the infant entering into language, into the symbolic realm. Which it certainly is, but I should note that Trainor comes to psychoanalytic thought through the back door, so to speak: through his profound engagement with anthropology.

After the title sequence, our protagonist, You, is an adult. The narrator continues:

> You find yourself in an unbounded landscape. And you are walking.

In the remaining dozen or so minutes, this empty, unbounded landscape gets filled in, though sometimes it is unclear exactly what is delimiting it. The initial delimiter is somewhat abstract: two horizontal lines, for which the narrators offer no description. We do not know what they represent, apart from a boundedness that is simultaneously comforting – finally something to delimit the void! – and anxiety-provoking why are those lines bounding me in?

The narrator tells us, in a seemingly straightforward way (though little by lit-tle, elaborating through repetition) what we are seeing. The simple drawn marks are identified for us (unlike in the *The Fetishist*, where they could sometimes float in a metonymic chain).

> We know that the dots are blood, because they are concentrated around your nose and mouth, and these are the parts of you that are bleeding.

Yes, we see the dots and they are concentrated around You's face, so he is bleeding, though how and why this blood is being aspirated is not clear. And soon it becomes clear that blood is coming from other sources: Limbs and heads strewn about, perhaps the landscape itself. In this way the dots do and do not represent blood and the blood they represent has ambiguous origins (it comes from You, but also others, and also the landscape and the religious ceremonies) as well as an ambiguous form (it sometimes seems gaseous, aspirated through breath, sometimes larger liquid drops.

Trainor does a similar thing with You's genitals. Initially they are his genitals, with a certain level of anatomical detail (penis and testicles protruding), but very soon they become flattened, seemingly inverted. And we discover other acolytes, identified by their nakedness and exposed genitals, which are, we're told, a sign of their subjection. But some of them do not have exposed genitals. Instead, their genitals are simply drawn on their sides and these drawings function equally well in their humiliation.

In the earliest work discussed here, *The Fetishist*, Trainor uses metonymy, a metonymy that is at play through all his work. The semiotics he employs in *The Presentation Theme* is even more sophisticated. An individual dot may be blood that metonymically slips and calls forth breath, disease, spirit, semen and milk, but also a sign that simultaneously exists in the registers of the Symbolic and the Imaginary, gesturing toward the void of the Real. Trauma is not primarily psychological, but mythic: Inescapably horrifying and grounding.

Note

1 Available online at: https://vimeo.com/248045011

References

Freud, Sigmund. *The Complete Psychological Works, Volume 21*. Vintage: London, 2001.
Lacan, Jacques. *Ecrits: The First Complete Edition in English*. Translated by Bruce Fink. Norton: New York, 2006.
MacGaffey, Wyatt. *Astonishment & Power, The Eyes of Understanding: Kongo Minkisi*. Washington National Museum of African Art: Smithsonian Books, 1993.
Reinke, Steve. (n.d.). Self-published program notes.
Rostron, Edwin. 'Jim Trainor'. *Edge of Frame*. October 23 2013. http://www.edgeofframe. co.uk/jim-trainor/
Trainor, Jim. *The Fetishist*. US, 1997. Film.
_____. *The Bats*. US, 1999. Film.

_____. *The Moschops*. US, 2000. Film.
_____. *The Magic Kingdom*. US, 2002. Film.
_____. *Harmony*. US, 2004. Film.
_____. 'The Moschops.' In *The Sharpest Point: Animation at the End of Cinema*, edited by Chris Gehman and Steve Reinke. Toronto: YYZ Books, 2005.
_____. *Presentation Theme*. US, 2008. Film.
_____. *The Pink Egg*. US, 2016. Film.
Žižek, Slavoj. *The Parallax View*. Cambridge: MIT Press, 2006.

PART VI

Interviews C

C1

MARTHA COLBURN

USA

Please give us a brief summary of your work, including, if possible, a description of your creative process (e.g., how your creative ideas first appear and take shape).

I make stop motion animated films, comprising of cut-up paintings, paper, found materials and occasionally handmade paper dolls. My work has spanned music videos, book commercials, clips for documentaries, found footage films, political animations and more. I approach my films much like a fashion designer or art director would, through compiling sketchbooks, which include text, colour palettes, historical research and references and sometimes personal photos.

One element of my process is to analyse a sport, dance, physical activity or routine that resonates with the individual film, this in turn becomes a rehearsal for the motions in the animation. Without this phase, the process becomes too static, my films need to be rhythmically balanced and constitute a whole 'world'. The suspension of disbelief cannot be broken, even if the subject explores an act of obliteration that creates a floating afterlife of images, the world has to retain a believability. The images require a certain strength; that's why the images are often so striking. My work does not originate from an office chair and a desk lamp. I make work that explores my personal limits.

How would you define your animation practice in terms of its relation to fine art traditions, experimental animation or the (historical) avant-garde? Its relation to commercial industry? Who/what are your strongest influences?

As contemporary artists, we are the continuation of a story. As far as I am concerned, my work and I have no relationship to the commercial industry.

Nor do I feel that my work fits into one particular genre, like avant-garde, art naïve or fine art as my work encompasses so many elements. I listen and look to music, theatre, literature, history, fashion, nature and other people's stories as influences because what I make is personal. As an experimental animator – I understand that my work is in the background of the 'more important arts' like music, fine art, theatre and literature. Animation can be seen in the streets as in the work of the artist Blu, on the internet, in a New York Times Op-Ed section, in a Radiohead concert or in an orchestra hall. As an art form it stands alone, and this autonomy allows it to evolve and take on a number of different forms.

Why animation?

For me, animation is effortless. It is one of the few activities in my life that does not feel laborious. Keeping the rest of my life in order, for example organising papers, keeping a roof over my head, maintaining the wheels of my suitcase, re-heeling my shoes, all feel like work. However, when I have an idea, it is so easy for me to visualise and quickly get to work on an animation. For all its physical tedium, it is somehow the least tedious task on my list. Animation is compressed time, it represents the compression of time we're experiencing as a society now. I was always told my films were too fast (pre-internet), and now I never hear that.

Is material or media a particularly important component of your practice? How does it operate in your work?

I was raised as an outsider by outsiders in an outsider population of American-Appalachia, where funnily enough everyone was and still is sceptical of outsiders, if not despising of them. So, it's the 'outsider who is an insider' effect, and that has always resonated with me because that is exactly what being an experimental animator is. Animators, especially experimental animators are a very disparate and loosely organised group so it is no surprise that I, and others, assimilate the other arts.

What is your work's relation to experimental form and technique? Is there something you want to articulate with your work that can't be expressed through conventional narrative means?

My ideas form in individual frames. The idea of frames flipping through a shutter at 24 frames per second (back in the day when we shot film), gives me some kind of anxiety. I also find the way in which time passes in real life to be tedious and too slow. I want it to be edited and sped up, coloured and cut like my films. In this way, making my films is a way of expressing this vision of what I think to be an 'engaging world'; one in which there is no time to catch a breath and flashes of events and impressions flutter past and are almost felt in the body. It is a bit like an alternate spirit world, and this is not something I could adapt to a narrative because narratives involve the gradual build-up of an idea, rather than an impression of a world outside of that. It is not a 'Post-' anything or a 'New' anything; creation for me falls into the 'Other' category.

How do you see your work operating culturally? Politically?

I believe I contribute culturally through the animation workshops I lead and through screening my films. I think that learning anything is empowering to people, and empowerment can lead to political actions, to opinions and eventually to changes in our society. I like to be able to offer these kinds of experiences to those who are either disinterested or not in the right position to go to a University, which is a system based on advantage.

C2

MASHA KRASNOVA-SHABAEVA

Russia/the Netherlands

One of the first memories of my childhood is of my father's paintings, in which he tried to describe some kind of worldwide catastrophe – anthropogenic, I believe. Grey skies, enormous, deserted, unpopulated spaces. Only tumbledown buildings, still impressive in their greatness, remind us that this wreckage was once a stronghold of an unknown powerful state. Now I understand that my father's post-apocalyptic fantasies reflected very precisely the public mood of that time. I should mention that my childhood fell during a very complicated period in the history of Russia. The huge utopia called USSR was rapidly collapsing; it was a time of ruins. I believe that my fascination with utopias and dystopias (in my case feminist), and subsequently my little post-apocalyptic world that I try to describe in my artworks, grew out of these memories of my father's paintings and also reminiscences of my hometown Ufa, the centre of Russia's chemical and engineering industry situated somewhere in the wilds between Moscow and Siberia.

In my work I'm constantly re-examining my childhood impressions and feelings: The world that I was living in, where fantasies and dreams were as real as reality itself.

I've been always captivated by certain architectural images of Soviet and Post-Soviet periods. It was a time of ruins, abandonment, devastation, emptiness and mutation. When I look at photos of deserted Pripyat and Chernobyl, they seem to resemble my home town in the 1980s and 90s. I clearly remember weeds taller than me growing from the cracked pavement in the centre of the city; I remember tumbledown houses, broken windows and ramshackle fences. My interest isn't architectural but, in a sense, psychotherapeutic. These images are still chasing me. At the time it seemed to me that this atmosphere was alive, that those ruins and houses had organs and circulatory systems. They became a part of nature, wilderness, they were acquiring personality and becoming monsters. Somehow, I always wanted to express this feeling in my work. To tell the story of a little girl, impressed by all of this.

For years I've been searching for the right medium to tell my stories. I think that about seven years ago this process crystallised into something real: Books/ zines and animation are the two genres that I feel can help me achieve the effects that I wanted to achieve. Sometimes I think of myself as a comic artist who can't even draw a comic page properly, or an animation artist who doesn't know how to draw a storyboard. For now, it's important for me to avoid any linear plots. My books and animations are more of a window to another world. On every page of a zine, in every video you just get a peek of what is going on there; there is no narrative. I like the freedom that those two media give me.

I still consider myself a beginner at animation. My first two shorts *The Lake* (2011) and *The Classroom* (2012) were rather an experiment – an attempt to translate my stories into this new medium. My future pieces will definitely involve more complex storytelling. A few of my biggest influences in animation are Suzan Pitt, Bruce Bickford and Priit Pärn.

The Lake was my first experience as an animator. Before that, I had worked on other animations (mostly advertising) as an illustrator, but I had never tried to do it on my own. *The Lake* was made as a part of my earlier series 'The Silent Earth', which included drawings, a book and a few small sculptures. It was supposed to be my personal show in one of Rotterdam's galleries. I wanted *The Lake* to be some sort of a looping visual and sound background for the whole show. The whole subject of this series was life after the end of the world, some sort of life after death. So, I wanted to express this feeling in my animation in the most primitive ways possible, because I didn't have much time to produce this short.

In October 2011, I started to work on my new series 'The School Diary'. I've had this idea for some time. I've always been interested in different educational systems. Every authoritarian state needs to control people in all aspects of their life. Of course school is an ideal place where you can teach people what they can be and can do, and what they can't. School in Russia is a totalitarian system with a clear hierarchy. At least it was when I was growing up. If you're a student, you're a lower being, just an extension of the teacher. You don't have any right to express yourself if it doesn't meet certain requirements. In my animation *The Classroom,* I'm trying to compare the school to a dysfunctional family, which are in many ways very similar, but different in terms of scale. It's also very personal for me because my family was not functional at all.

Both videos were made in collaboration with my husband Timur Shabaev. He's an architect, but sometimes he helps me with some technical issues I have in my work. For example, in these two films he helped me a lot with the animation process and sound. It's really nice to have a person at home who is interested in what you're doing and with whom you can discuss your ideas and problems.

Our approach to the making of the sound was kind of amateurish. For *The Lake* we just went to the forest and recorded the sounds using a dictaphone. For the second one, I used a fragment of a song from my home country. It's a song in the Bashkir language, which is the main ethnicity in our region, and I'm also half-Bashkir. The name of the singer is Flura Kildiyarova. I also recorded some sounds with my phone: water flowing, singing, etc. We built everything up after the visual part was ready.

I've always wanted to tell stories about women and for women. But in my early (and even not so early) days in Russia, I was told constantly that this kind of art is too 'girly', not serious, etc. I didn't give up, but it took some time to realise that what I am doing is right. I hope that my experience as an artist and my works will help young female artists know that their stories deserve to be told.

References

Krasnova-Shabaeva, Masha. *The Lake*. Netherlands, 2011. Film.
_____. *The Classroom*. Netherlands, 2012. Film.

C3

DIEGO AKEL

Brazil

Please give us a brief summary of your work, including, if possible, a description of your creative process (e.g., how your creative ideas first appear and take shape).

What is your work's relation to experimental form and technique? Is there something you want to articulate with your work that can't be expressed through conventional narrative means?

I've been messing with animation since 1998, and I've made dozens of short films and commissioned pieces. I've participated in animation festivals and events all over Brazil and in several other countries as well, presenting my films, giving lectures, workshops and engaging with people from the field.

An experimental approach is definitely my preferred choice. My exploration usually starts with sensations, diverse things that move or inspire me somehow. At some point these small observations transform themselves into ideas, the work begins to grow organically, and I begin really living it. This means: Listening to music, watching tonnes of reference films, drawing and painting in my sketchbooks (I like to devote an entire sketchbook for this purpose), and so on. The film initiates its animation process pretty much without me noticing. It's like tricking myself into it: working on the ideas, not on the film. Before I notice, the film is running on its own account, and in a few blinks of an eye, it's done.

I also work mostly alone, doing the conception, animation, photography, editing and post-production myself. I use both analogue and digital methods – I know this will sound like a cliché, but the digital is really just a tool. Of course, a strong, 'pumped-up' tool, but nevertheless only that. It helps me reach my artistic goal, but isn't the main objective in itself, otherwise the work would become empty. For me the benefits of the digital are to explore different aspects of the spectrum; to create a film on the go, drawing on the telephone screen, for instance. To be able to digitally compose two different physical techniques together. Experiment in a way that isn't possible with another medium.

How would you define your animation practice in terms of its relation to fine art traditions, experimental animation or the (historical) avant-garde? Its relation to commercial industry? Who/what are your strongest influences?

Is material or media a particularly important component of your practice? How does it operate in your work?

My practice in animation is very much guided by instinct. That said, every artist or art movement that operates in a similar fashion can influence me. In the beginning, my two biggest animation influences were Mike Jittlov – his feature *The Wizard of Speed and Time* (1988) blew my mind when I saw it the first time when I was 10 years old – and Norman McLaren. The simplicity, playfulness, yet strong personality in his films continues to speak to me.

I would also name Oskar Fischinger from Germany, Ishu Patel from India (although he produced animation in Canada) and Len Lye from New Zealand. I greatly admire Juan Camilo González' animations, and we have been in contact over these last few years. He has selected my films for screenings throughout the world, alongside several incredible works by Latin-American animators. From Brazil my influences come mainly from painters and drawers, such as Iberê Camargo, Newton Mesquita and Carla Caffé. I like the atmosphere and personality in their work. I think that above all I most admire the personality of one's work. The true feeling of it.

The Fundamentals of Animation (2006), by Paul Wells, is a book that really opened my eyes, in the way that it respects every part of the animation process. Some books on animation only focus on the technical aspects, and list only the best-known films as case studies. Wells explores other areas and places great value on the artist animator, with chapters such as 'The Animator as Performer' and 'Working as an Independent'. In the chapter 'Alternative Methods' he has put together a brilliant essay on the possibilities of alternative approaches, going beyond the general term of 'experimental animation'.

I always look for character and personality in works, and much of this can be found in the Polish School. I admire their animation a great deal, as well as that of Eastern Europe in general. Recently, at the StopTrik festival in Slovenia, I met Miloš Tomić in person. The man is a genius, whose personality flows beautifully into his films. The bottom line for me is that we always have so much to learn from each other's works and culture. For me the ultimate personal question is: How can a film be made that truly comes from the heart? A vibrant work emanating directly from one's soul? Without any barriers from industry and medium standards, but using every technique and approach needed for it to come into being?

I'm also inspired by everything in life that happens in a natural, unpredictable way, even if it is not 'art'. I view animation as a way of living rather than an 'industry' or 'market'. Actually, I hate those two words. To be able to see the beauty of movement and rhythm, joyfully executed in time, is the main thing. I'm constantly experimenting with different art media, and old and new ideas quickly find their way into my experimentations.

Why animation?

Animated art is really an extension of life. I love searching for these kinds of works and talking to the people who make them. I really enjoy this great, limitless and 'nationless' world of experimental animation.

I like that quote that says something like 'you do not choose things; they choose you'. Almost 20 years after my first contact with animation, and 12 years of making short films, I still get excited and mesmerised when I see things moving in my films. It is as if some divine entity has come down and put a soul in things, creating movement from nothing, life from stillness. Every time is like the first time.

To be able to experiment with techniques, materials, approaches, and to put visions and crazy ideas into animated form is really addictive. Each new work is a journey into the unknown, and such a delicious one.

How do you see your work operating culturally? Politically?

Brazil is notoriously a country with a lot of character. It's so vast and diverse that I always feel as if each state is a country in itself. We are currently experiencing a creative surge in animation, and Brazil is in the spotlight this year, at the Annecy Festival 2018. However I think that we are still to really show the world our true spirit and energy. We are naturally born with an impromptu ability which has become more than a cultural feature. It is like we really see things. We learn by doing, we make things and invent stuff, and these are all great skills for creating animation. It is really just a matter of time until the world witnesses the rich diversity of our animation.

In Brazil we have had some outsiders in animation, who have made brilliant direct-on-film works from the 1950s through the 1980s (Roberto Miller, Rubens F. Lucchetti, Bassano Vaccarini and Firmino Holanda). Nowadays very few – almost no one – dedicates him/herself to a more experimental approach. Apart from the more auteur-type animators – who make brilliant work that I admire greatly – a lot of people here are dedicated to producing industry-oriented works.

One Latin-American artist-animator in particular who is more than a reference and has become a friend is Tomas Welss, from Chile. I first saw his films when there was a screening of Chilean animations some years ago at a festival here in Fortaleza, and met him in person in 2015, in Santiago. Tomas' work is very strong and has a unique personality, like very few others. He has created his own world, with his own distinctive style and tempo, using timing and loops in a fashion I haven't seen before. He has just finished a new film, *Magic Dream* – created with the motion painting technique – and it is really awesome. Today we are close friends and we chat almost every day, often exchanging our thoughts on the animation scene in South America.

Culturally, the best way that I can see my work operating is in really moving someone. In an ideal world, inspiring them. Making them see things in a different way, provoking turmoil inside their soul, to the point where this person has to respond artistically, and create something. Give their best to the world. And his or her work can in turn move somebody else, and so the thing goes on. At least, that's what happened to me. All the incredible things that I see or experience in life urge me to do something, and it is such a joy to do so.

References

Jittlov, Mike. *The Wizard of Speed and Time*. US, 1988. Film.
Wells, Paul. *The Fundamentals of Animation*. Lausanne: AVA Publishing SA, 2006.
Welss, Tomas. *Magic Dream*. Chile, 2018. Film.

PART VII

Science and the cosmos

10

ANIMATING THE COSMOLOGICAL HORIZON

Between art and science

Janine Randerson

Cinematic art experiences can approximate the optical intensity of distant stars in the night sky or the powerful light of the sun. Philosopher of light Paul Virilio once described the starry sky itself as 'never more than an illusion, since no astronomer knows if the remote source of their light still exists' (2000, 46). From the mirage of atmospheric images produced by optical effects of light, to the frame-by-frame animation of contemporary satellite or telescopic images, this chapter will consider a body of artists' techniques for cosmological representation. The first section focuses on experimental film-maker Jordan Belson's radiating astronomical imagery in films such as *Allures* (1961), *Samadhi* (1967) and *Momentum* (1969) that grew out of the Vortex concerts at the Morrison Planetarium in San Francisco in the 1950s. In the latter part of the chapter I introduce contemporary Australian artists Joyce Hinterding and David Haines' installation *Earthstar* (2010), an installation that includes an animation produced by a hydrogen-alpha telescope fixed on the sun; and American artists Sarah and Joseph Belknap's animation *12 Months of the Sun* (2014), which uses imagery sourced from NASA's Space Weather Media viewer app. I position these artists as inheritors of Belson's cosmological visual language, while examining my own artistic connection to Belson through my video installation artworks such as *Report to Darmstadt* (2007), *Aerosphere and Atmosphere* (2011) and *Albedo of Clouds* (2012). In each of these works I animate and reprocess remote satellite images to imagine an expansive cosmological horizon.

Virilio's term 'cosmological horizon' describes the visibility cone of astronomical appearances, where light is visible even before the objects or phenomena that it illuminates (2000, 45). In Jordan Belson's oeuvre of films in the 1960s, the cosmic illusion of the sky collides with mystic temporalities drawn from Eastern philosophy, and embodied, inner space. Today, an altered sense of space-time, combined with speed, is opened by the sharing of digital data with science in collaborative processes within artists' experimental animation. This discussion of contemporary animated visions of the cosmos is prefaced by an historical reflection on intersections between scientific apparatuses for sequential recordings of the sun. Galileo Galilei, for instance, developed a method of projecting the sun's image via a telescope to draw the sun's path at approximately the same time of the day; these early experiments are positioned here as a speculative forerunner to one-stop animation.

The naked eye, historical apparatus and our closest star

The sun's searing light harms the naked human eye, so we always approach our closest star obliquely through instruments and imagination. A deeper history of solar imaging and projection are situated here as precursors (in spirit) to the digital animation of solar bodies by contemporary artists. The basic principles for harnessing the sun through a pin hole camera obscura device were first recorded in China in the fifth century BC by philosopher Mo-Ti. Meanwhile in Greece, Aristotle investigated the nature of sunlight in his natural philosophy. In Book XV, Aristotle describes how he uses his own hands and available material to study the sun. He ruminates, 'Why is it that an eclipse of the sun, if one looks at it through a sieve or through leaves, such as a plane-tree or other broadleaved tree, or if one joins the fingers of one hand over the fingers of the other, the rays are crescent-shaped where they reach the earth?' (Hammond 1981, 5). The sun is a projected light source that is animated by his hands. The human body therefore becomes an embedded part of the solar viewing apparatus, breaking down the distinction between instrument and phenomena, subject and object and the 'knower and the known' phenomena (Barad 2007, 138).

In the European Renaissance, entire architectures became apparatuses for projecting the sun and allowing a solar image to form. In 1475 the Renaissance mathematician and astronomer Paolo Toscanelli placed a bronze ring with an aperture in the window in the cupola of the Duomo in Florence. Intense sunlight through the hole allowed a solar image to form on the cathedral's floor. At noon, the solar image bisected a 'noon-mark' on the floor to mark the time (Renner 1995, 6). The changing light of the projected sun over time allowed the viewer a new closeness to this distant body. By 1611, German scientist Christoph Scheiner invented the *heliotropii telioscopici* (heliscope) with coloured lenses to view the various faces of the sun (Reeves 2010). While Scheiner pre-dated Galileo's recorded observations of sunspots through a lens-based apparatus, Galileo's drawings of sunspots reveal the progress of sun spots across the sun's surface over time as separate 'frames', that suggest the sequential image in animation.

During the summer months of 1612, Galileo let the sun's light through the eyepiece and projected an image onto a piece of paper, following the process one of his students had developed, rather than blind himself by looking directly through his telescope at the sun. He made drawing after drawing at the same time each day in a sequence that demonstrates change in sunspot activity over time. The foreshortening of the sunspots on the edges of the sphere and their movement from left to right was the first evidence that the sun was a spinning sphere (Green 2016, 77–78). In 1613 the drawings were published in *Istoria e Dimostrazioni Intorno Alle Macchie Solari e Loro Accidenti Rome* (History and Demonstrations Concerning Sunspots and their Properties). Researcher Albert Van Helden has animated the images online on his webpage *The Galileo Project* (1993) in what he calls a 'flip-book' type sequence. In Enlightenment science the 'triadic structure of words, knowers and things' began to solidify into separate entities (Barad 2007, 138). Galileo takes on authority as the knower, the things (apparatus) and the sun spots (the phenomena) became represented as findings published (words), and he became intensely competitive with Scheiner. Yet philosopher of science Karen Barad reminds us that with every measurement using an instrument in which we 'peek inside' a phenomenon, our measuring mark entangles with the phenomenon being measured (345). When contemporary artist-animators engage with scientific phenomena the distinction between phenomena, knower or observer and the primacy of the written word begins to dissolve again. This sense of the inseparability of instrument, phenomena and observer resonates with the creation of the solar image in Belson's experimental film-making practice.

Belson's apparatus, beyond the heliocentric universe

By the 1960s, knowledge about the sun and the cosmos was advancing rapidly with the advent of observation satellites, and the static, heliocentric universe of enlightenment scientists was replaced by the knowledge of an ever-expanding, infinite cosmos. Belson used circular radial motifs as archetypal images of both interior (psychological) space and physical 'outer' space. Belson's most active period of film-making and animation spanned the period of the space race, as well as nuclear testing in the Pacific, and his films reflect many developments in space technology and science. His well-known amorphous, gaseous circular images evolved from the Vortex Concerts at the Morrison Planetarium in the late 1950s. The Vortex concerts were widely attended by enraptured audiences in San Francisco, with viewings occurring two or three times a night at their peak, over a three-year period. Belson developed techniques of merging abstract images to suggest solar phenomena, along with rhythms of kaleidoscopic geometric forms and oscilloscope streak dots and slowly fading lights, synced with music by electronic sound composer Henry Jacobs (Brougher 2005).

As a ten-year-old child I visited San Francisco's Morrison Planetarium in the Golden Gate park on a family trip from Auckland in the 1980s. I was awed by the cosmic projections in the hemispheric dome and the accompanying scientific experiments in the museum. No earlier experience for me compared to the marvel of a flash of light that left a rainbow-hued outline of my body against a white wall, recalling Newton's experiments with a prism of glass to reveal that white light was made of rainbow colours. Strangely this experiment also recalls the shadow left after the flash of nuclear light in Hiroshima. I didn't know at the time how this image-sensation was created, yet looking back, this moment embodied the legacy of the experimentation in the Vortex concerts at the planetarium that continue to the present. My own experience resonates with Barad's performative account of scientific practices that unsettle the separation between the human body and phenomena, in this case of phenomena of light. Barad writes that a performative account of scientific practices, 'takes account of the fact that knowing does not come from standing at a distance and representing but rather from a *direct material engagement with the world*' (Barad 2007, 49). She comments that little exchange has happened between science studies and social and political theorists about the nature of the 'real' in quantum terms. Yet I argue that a dialogic relationship exists between experimental animation, digital art practice and the sciences that bring the body into the act of sensing how matter transforms.

In the light projection technology of the Vortex concerts, Belson discovered slow fades and zooms as an effective means of creating movement compared to his early frenetically paced animations. He states, 'After working with some very sophisticated equipment at Vortex I learned the effectiveness of something as simple as fading in and out very slowly' (Youngblood 1970, 162). Rather than conceiving animation as one frame at a time, he made cycles of images built from multiple exposures, dissolves and fades. With a full rotary-controlled set of projectors Belson tested 'making the whole dome very dark red and then we introduced the full starfield into the dark red' before fading out again (Macdonald 1998, 73–74). There is one sequence where the glowing red circle in the far distance slowly shifts closer that suggests the approach of a solar body. I speculate that Belson's evocation of the red light connects to the cosmological 'redshift' in physics which evidences our ever-expanding universe. Sufficiently distant light sources show a redshift corresponding to the rate of increase in their distance from earth. Virilio writes that the theory of the expanding universe, suspected as early as 1922 by the Soviet Physicist Alexander Friedman, and proven by Edwin Hubble in 1929, informs our 'cosmological optical illusion' where there is no beginning or end to the cosmos beyond the earth. He continues, 'The general flight of heavenly bodies, and the famous red shift in the light of galaxies, certainly leads to a perceptual vanishing point' (Virilio 2000, 43). Belson's slow fades into nothingness reflect this illusion-producing, ever-expanding universe.

Belson regards *Allures* (1961), a collaboration with Jacobs, as his 'space-iest' film after the Vortex concerts at the Morrison Planetarium which creates the feeling of a gravitational pull towards a deep void of the cosmos. He connects *Allures* to the mind-expanding moment of cosmogenesis with the most direct connection to the experience of the (unrecorded) Vortex concerts at the Morrison Planetarium (Youngblood, 160). Belson ascribed his inner eye with the ability to perceive cosmic truths that he only much later saw represented in scientific astrophotography. Light is a phenomena that becomes the subject of his films in itself; rather than as a tool for illuminating objects, light emanates from interior bodily experiences as well as from external cosmic light. For Belson inner space was discoverable through Mahayana Buddhism and yoga; and outer space through interstellar and galactic astrophysics (Youngblood, 159). In an interview with Larry Sturhahn, Belson stated, 'The distinction between an external scene perceived in the usual way and the scene perceived with the inner eye is very slight to me. The screen is just that – a screen. Who's to say that what you see on it is only perceived with the eyes' (Sturhahn 1975, 27). This sensing beyond sight, is also important to Joyce Hinterding and David Haines, as discussed in the later part of the chapter.

Allures is described by Belson as 'a combination of molecular structures and astronomical events mixed with subconscious and subjective phenomena' (Youngblood, 160). Less than two minutes into the film we slowly fade in to a pulsating red solar image. A low base tone in the soundtrack accompanies the changing colours of the central orb. The expansion and compression of matter feels endless, generating and generative, recalling Barad's understanding of the material conditions that enfold phenomena, apparatuses and our bodies together (Barad 2007, 244). We feel the sound resonating through our bodies and the pulsing light radiates through our retina, agitating our internal rhythms. The ever-changing interference patterns in *Allures* evidence the agentive properties of mattering as a differentiating process; where 'spacetime is an enactment of differentness, a way of making/marking here and now' (Barad, 137). Belson enfolds external 'space-time' into the body and into flows of matter in a way that resonates with Barad's philosophy. Her posthumanist undoing of the common representation of the body 'as a natural and fixed dividing line between interiority and exteriority' (Barad, 136) is materially present in Belson's collapsed vision of inner, bodily space-time in co-relation with the vastness of galaxies in his films.

In Belson's most productive period, Gene Youngblood's wild, 'paleocybernetic' interpretative lens on his oeuvre also recognised a closeness between artists' and scientists' vision of the 'transinfinite'. For Youngblood (1970), an expanded consciousness emerges through mescaline, meditation or both, to reach our primitive 'paleo' brain, along with the 'practical utopianism' of the cybernetic age of expansive networks of telecommunications. He proclaims, the 'Paleocybernetic age witnesses the concretization of intuition and the secularization of religion through electronics' (Youngblood, 41). In addition to a radical reassessment of inner space, the new age is characterised by the 'wholesale obsolescence of man's historical view of outer space' (Youngblood, 137). P. Adams Sitney also notes Belson's temporal commitment to the 'all-consuming present', as a 'meditative quest through the radical interiorization of mandalic objects and cosmic imagery' (Sitney 2002, 258–259). In a later interview with Scott MacDonald, Belson plays down the effects of hallucinogenic drugs and focuses on his inner journey to self-enlightenment through meditation and yoga. In the howling tones of *Samadhi* (1967), Belson's inhaling and exhaling can be heard, in accompaniment to changes in colour and intensity of the solar spheres.

Belson's film-making table, based on a converted X-ray stand, is an elusive figure in the three major discussions of his practice by Sitney, Youngblood and

MacDonald. They each note the filmmaker's reticence in revealing the technical aspects of his work. Belson saw the instrument as less important than the film's meaning, countering the techno-determinist rationale for his film-making. Belson's optical bench for animating in San Francisco's North beach is described by Youngblood as 'essentially a plywood frame around an old X-ray stand with rotating tables, variable speed motors and variable intensive lights' (158). This set-up allowed Belson to create films out of intensities, ebbs and flows of light effects that he developed in the Vortex concerts. After his collaboration with Jacobs ended, Belson also synthesised his own sound on home equipment. The close relations between the film-making-table instrument to the phenomena being produced and the light phenomena represented fuses material concerns of abstract art and the similar questions pursued within the science of optics.

Belson comments that it was not until after *Samadhi* when he made *Momentum* that he started researching solar phenomena in earnest. During the 18 month period when Belson was making *Momentum*, the artist stated,

> All the material [for *Momentum*] was similar if not identical to solar phenomena, photosphere phenomena, chromosphere phenomena, sun spots, plasma storms – I was even getting in to some interesting speculation of what goes on inside the sun. And I realised the film doesn't stop at the centre of the sun, it goes to the centre of the sun and into the atom. The end shows the paradoxical realm in which subatomic phenomena and the cosmologically vast are identical.
>
> *(Youngblood, 176)*

Momentum reveals the dark centre of the sun awash solar storms. *Samadhi*, made prior to Belson's acknowledgement of the close relation of his films to scientific solar imaging, also features flaming wave effects and a darkness that suggests, to me at least, the imagery of nuclear detonation from above. Of the Vortex concerts, Belson commented that he aimed to achieve 'Beautiful and terrifying sensations and feelings' (MacDonald, 75). Both these affects suffuse these films.

There is little mention, however, of the impact of the terrifying visual spectacle of nuclear detonation in commentary on Belson's oeuvre. Images of waves of radiation and glowing orbs of destructive force must have loomed large in the consciousness of liberal-minded occupants of San Francisco in the post-Hiroshima period and throughout the continuing experiments at Bikini Atoll. Media historian Douglas Kahn argues that the spectacle of the series of tests at Bikini Atoll in 1946 became the most photographically and cinematically recorded event in history (Kahn 2013, 171). In images of the United States' Castle Bravo test on 1 March 1954, the sun appears as a blinding white light that turns the sky red. The size of this explosion far exceeded expectations and spread radioactive material throughout the globe. A bluish light as a secondary ring radiates out from other Bikini Atoll images, just as secondary rings surround a central orb in Belson's *Samadhi*. While the flashes in *Allures*, produced by a near white-out of the frame, bring to mind the white nuclear flash against a red sky. The rumbling, threatening sounds in *Samadhi* evoke the dark undercurrent of the atomic age, as one of the paradoxes of the search for individual freedom in the era of 'Hippie Modernism' (Blauvelt et al. 2015).

Many of the artists who work at the intersection of art and technology from this period were motivated to generate an alternative vision as a reaction to the destructive effects of the bomb. The age of the space race, and a burgeoning ecological consciousness occurred in parallel with the threat to the planet of a nuclear event. Elizabeth DeLoughrey notes that in American post-war propaganda, 'weapons of mass destruction were naturalised by likening them to harnessing the power of the sun, and their radioactive by-products were depicted as no less dangerous than our daily sunshine' (2011, 236–237). DeLoughrey argues that the persistent use of solar metaphors for understanding nuclear weaponry have been vital to naturalising global militarisation. Belson would surely have been well aware of nuclear imagery and its frequent comparison to the sun's force. Solar imagery accrues powerful affects by association with nuclear explosion, just as today, the sun is synonymous with the encroaching threat of global warming.

Joyce Hinterding and David Haines: Earthstar

In 2011, the year of Belson's death, I came across the sound and video installation *Earthstar* at ACMI (Australian Centre for the Moving Image) in Melbourne, and I was immediately transported back to Belson's archetypal solar forms. Joyce Hinterding and David Haines describe the work as a visual and aural 'portrait of the sun'. The animated hydrogen–alpha sequence of the sun in Haines' *Earthstar* video projection is made from thousands of composite images animated at 25 frames per second to form a four-minute long sequence. The animation sequence commences with a bright white orb of the sun, almost too bright to look at, against a red background. The next phase is a black orb with a circular red frame which is the hydrogen stretching out – flaring frequently. The final sequence shows the yellow orb flecked with red solar activity. The colour phases depend on the length of exposure of each image, with the longest exposures at two minutes. Haines made creative decisions around the lengths of exposure and frame-rate of the animations to simulate the movement of sunflares.

Each image leaves an imprint on the retina; a perceptual effect that suggests the intensity of looking at the sun with the naked eye, similar to the effects produced by Belson's *Samadhi*. These are raw frames with little post production, although they are false colour images, shot in monochrome. The dynamic range of the image is a composite of many exposures to get the final outcome. Rather than suppressing the role of the instrument in the observation of nature as classical physicists once did, the instrument that creates the sound to accompany this animation is laid out in the gallery space. To form the pulsating images of the sun for *Earthstar*, Haines experimented with a hydrogen–alpha telescopic lens for his camera. This newly available lens enabled solar activity to be observed by the layperson, through the detection of the major gas in the sun's make-up: Hydrogen. Viewing the sun through the telescope produces a red solar disc by shifting the ultraviolet light to the red part of the visual spectrum.

The electromagnetic frequencies from the sun that drive Hinterding's sound composition are produced by the same type of radiation as ultraviolet light revealed by the hydrogen alpha telescope, although with differences in wavelength and frequency. In the *Earthstar* installation, custom-made radio antennae wrapped with coils of copper wire capture the electromagnetic energies of the sun. Energy is converted to sound in the form of crackles and hisses and pops on these long instruments lying on benches in the gallery.

Hinterding and Haines' recent work *Sound Ship (descender 1)* (2016), is described by the artists as the first artist-launched site-specific artwork in the stratosphere. The artists attached several GoPro cameras and various instruments to a weather balloon to capture the ascent to the sun as well as a reverse perspective back to earth. The sun's lights flare around the edge of the images, as if animated by the solar body. In science, such effects are regarded as optical aberrations made by the instruments and they would be 'cleaned up' from the recorded account. Like Belson's *Re-entry* (1964), *Sound Ship (descender 1)* is structured around literal ascent into space, the close images of the sun and a hurtling descent as the camera crashes back into the Earth made from a real-time imagery of space travel. Belson's early films were composited through optical effects and video mixing, whereas in a later film *The Astronaut's Dream* (1981), Belson drew on NASA material such as rockets taking off and mixed it with his own material. The reversed image of the sun from the countervailing perspective of a rocket ship, or from camera's drifting on a weather balloon, in Hinterding and Haines case forges a connection to our closest star.

Sarah and Joseph Belknap: 12 Months of the Sun *(2014)*

While Haines uses his own images taken with a hydrogen-alpha telescope, the Chicago-based partnership Sarah and Joseph Belknap draw on scientific images for animating the sun that are freely available to consumers. The artists animate remote satellite technology by accessing free images from NASA's mobile app Space Weather Media Viewer (2011). Telescopes at NASA's satellite-based Solar Observatory take ten highly detailed images of the sun's atmosphere every twelve seconds and give us images well beyond the scope of visible light. The data generated by the instruments from the observatory adds 1.5 terabytes of data to our picture of the solar atmosphere every day (Green 2016, 2). Through the Space Weather Media Viewer, the distant light of stars can be held in our hands, mediated by technology, where Aristotle once looked at the sun through his fingers.

In the Belknaps' multichannel installation *12 Months of the Sun* (2014), exhibited at the Museum of Contemporary Art, Chicago (2014–2015), a range of animations of the sun from the Space Weather Media Viewer app are animated. The visualisation decisions of the NASA team are highlighted in a multi-screen arrangement of monitors, where each contains a different, false-colour image of the sun; from the yellows of Atmospheric-Assembly images to the red, large angle Spectrometric Coronograph images. The Belknaps profess a curiosity about the filtered seeing of instruments that I also share. The artists delight in the scientists' use of false colour, emphasising its purpose as follows: 'it allows us to see things that the human eye cannot see. It is both real and faked/mediated. The enhancement and modification is not done to deceive but rather to show what we cannot see' (Picard 2014). Scientific images of the sun and universe are made up of the sensors of instruments designed by engineers, mathematical formulae, and digital computation of abstract information yet there is also an element of imagination in colour choice. Kahn parodically describes scientists' space visualisations as vibrantly colourful, 'jewel-encrusted bling' that paints the universe as if 'the cosmic egg were from Fabergé' (Kahn, 227). The artists use this 'false' colour aesthetic with an ironic nod to the riotous palette of many animated scientific visualisations.

The animation in *12 Months of the Sun* is also deliberately clunky because the artists used an idiosyncratic method to decide on which images to animate. As a reflection of the couple's inner states, whenever one of the artists thought about or mentioned the sun to each other they would download an image to become part of the sequence to animate (Lund 2014, 2). The result is that many frames are 'missing' in the sequences. Like Belson, there is an irreverent fusion of so-called objective, scientific methods and intuitive 'artistic' or psychological methods of making. The scientist's observation of the sun is regulated while the artists produce an animation with humorously irregular time-lapses. Rather than a seamless, high-tech screen system, the animations are also presented on a teetering stack of televisions, in a homely distillation of advanced scientific imaging.

Belson, intermedia, the cosmos and I

Like Belson, Hinterding and Haines, and the Belknaps, I am drawn to the space instruments that generate visions of the cosmological horizon. In the late 1990s I studied Intermedia at the Elam School of Fine Arts at the University of Auckland, under the energetic and visionary sound artist and filmmaker Phil Dadson. I didn't realise until later that our 'Intermedia' department was named after Youngblood's radical inflection of the term *intermedia* in *Expanded Cinema*. Youngblood used *intermedia* to signal how the 'entire environment' is suffused with elements that draw from art as well as science, rather than simply to describe the inter-mixing of technical forms or disciplines (Youngblood, 347). The artist as ecologist was very much part of both Youngblood's and later Phil Dadson's interdisciplinary vision. Our student performance events included trips to the summit of Maungawhau, the local volcanic cone, with custom-made sound-making instruments to celebrate Winter Solstice, linking the earthly and the planetary.

Like Belson, Dadson's visual and sound-based artistic language, developed in the 1960s and 1970s, was inspired by a rich cultural milieu that included readings of the I Ching, meditation and environmental activism, including a political resistance to nuclear testing in Mururoa Atoll in our Pacific neighbourhood. Youngblood defined ecology in cybernetic terms, like Gregory Bateson, as 'the totality or pattern of relations between organisms and their environment' (Youngblood, 346). His insight that the artist's role is the revelation of 'previously unrecognised relationships between existing phenomena' still resonates with my own art practice. As a student I was also consuming experimental abstract film, including available works by Belson from the comprehensive video library managed by animator Greg Bennett (interviewed in this book) and Roger Horrocks, one of the key authors on experimental filmmaker Len Lye at the University of Auckland in the 1990s.

Circular forms and an engagement with environmental science and astronomy emerged in my artworks from an early stage. I not only made experimental films from 16 mm film stock, VHS video tape and 'vision mixers', and later digital cameras and software such as After Effects, but I also made circular screens from resin discs onto which to project my orb-shaped abstractions. In 2005 I developed a 1.5 metre, curved, round Perspex screen that was suspended horizontally above a crowded group lying below in *Report to Darmstadt* (Auckland, 2005). This work was my first animation using satellite imagery in an outdoor sculpture event at night at Corban Art Estate. I negotiated with Landcare-Research NZ to use weather satellite images above the Southern hemisphere that would otherwise be discarded as excess data, once the particular weather data became obsolete as commercial information. The curved screens, I envisioned, were enlarged instruments in which one could drift inside an imagined cosmos. The soundtrack in *Report to Darmstadt* included publicly available sound recordings from the atmosphere of Mars that was transmitted back to the European Space operations centre in Darmstadt in Germany. Although I was unaware of it at the time of making my work, Belson's film *Re-Entry* (1964) also included dialogue of astronomer John Glenn's first flight into orbit. Belson comments, 'If you listen very carefully to the soundtrack, you actually hear John Glenn's voice mumbling something about passing over Perth, Australia' (MacDonald, 76). *Re-Entry* is also a film structured around an imaginary departure from Earth, a speculative glimpse into an aspect of the cosmos not visible from Earth and then a re-entry into its atmosphere (see Figure 10.1).

By 2006 I began using multiple hemispheric-shaped acrylic screens for animating MTSat-1R satellite imagery which I downloaded frame by frame with permission from the Japanese Meteorological Association and the Australian Bureau of Meteorology in Melbourne. Although the negotiation to legally use satellite data for an artist's animation was complex, the animating of computer-generated imagery is much faster in digital form than in Belson's time. However,

FIGURE 10.1 Janine Randerson, *Remote Senses, Storms Nearby* (Shanghai Festival of Art and Science, Shanghai, 2007). Multi-channel installation (perspex, custom-formed screens), with animated satellite images of weather patterns over China and Aotearoa New Zealand.

like Belson, to supplement the graphic satellite images I used layers of real-time video images, including flames of fire, shifting shafts of light reflected on walls or light bouncing off oscillating pot lids to provide a greater depth to what I perceived as the flatness of the graphics of Adobe After Effects. Belson used seven or eight layers of imagery including lasers, optical printing, liquid crystals, a mixer from a television broadcasting studio, as well as some found footage. For the dual projection installation *Aerosphere and Atmosphere* (2011), Hungarian artist Nina Czegledy and I collaborated on projections on the exterior of a remote wooden observatory dome in Taranaki on the West coast of New Zealand. We projected and animated scientific images of the north pole of Mars and the Antarctic pole of earth.

Albedo of Clouds

My engagement with the animation of satellite imagery deepened with *Albedo of Clouds* (2012). This work concerns the sun's light, although my animations are made from the opposite perspective to Belson. The two-screen installation, also using the custom-made round screens described above, was conceived as a conversation between an artist and a meteorological satellite. A late nineteenth century experiment by Australian astronomer P. Baracchi for two cloud observers and their instruments underpins the compositional logic of the installation. In this period of astronomy and a nascent meteorology, observing practices of the heavens drew on both aesthetics and natural history to measure distance with early photographic and telegraphic technology. Baracchi's report 'Cloud Observation in Victoria' published in the *Australian Association for the Advancement of Science Report* (1898, 259–273) was written in response to the late call in 1897 for Melbourne Observatory to participate in an international cloud observation project to generate material for a cloud atlas.

The experiment required two astronomers communicating by telegraph to photograph the same cloud at the same time from different points in Melbourne. Later the two plate photographs were superimposed by 'shadowgraphing' them onto one plate. Using an alignment of the two zenithal points of the cameras it was possible for them to determine the height and velocity of the cloud under scrutiny. Baracchi discusses in detail the 'beautifully paired' Zeiss anastigmat lenses and a small dish containing mercury which was placed between the camera and the telescope. The observers were sometimes forced to use yellow screens over the lenses 'principally intended to deal with the higher clouds, some classes of which are sometimes barely visible against the deep blue sky' (Baracchi 1898, 263–64). Baracchi's report provides illustrations of pairs of photographs produced on Ilford chromatic plates developed slowly by Metol-hydroquinone with enlargements of the negatives on bromide paper.

To collect cloud images for my installation, I set up a camera in the same ground-based observing position as Baracchi in Melbourne. My view from below the clouds is matched with a satellite-based image of the same clouds from above, in collaboration with a Mike Wilmott, a satellite meteorologist at Melbourne's Bureau of Meteorology (BoM). Although *Albedo of Clouds* is a quasi-scientific account of a historical experiment, the project speculates on why clouds reflect and how different technologies 'see' clouds through human and non-human modes of observation. BoM derives its weather data from MTSat-1R, a Japanese weather satellite in geosynchronous orbit with the earth's equator. The binary code that makes up the distributed weather images of cloud passes through space via the scans of the MTSat-1R satellite through trans-governmental agreements to be disseminated through popular weather news media in Australia (Randerson et al. 2015, 16–24). The spatial mobility of the satellite has been situated as an agent for circulating remote community engagement and creative activity, such as the trans-global performance art pioneered by Nam June Paik. Despite the substantial history of creative access to satellite media, to access state-controlled meteorological satellite information as raw data was still a sensitive negotiation (Figure 10.2).

A four-month period of interviews and archival research at BoM helped to shape my concept for *Albedo of Clouds*. Wilmott provided interpretations of the satellite data and cyclonic movement so I could understand how to animate the thousands of images generated daily. As an employee at the Australian bureau for 40 years Wilmott had a historical overview of satellite meteorology since its inception. He had been present through the development from analogue to digital satellite forecasting when the first weather images were delivered from television cameras attached to satellites in 1966. Wilmott demonstrated basic techniques of animating satellite data for weather broadcast, using cuts between images rather than dissolves. We discussed colourisation processes of the meteorological maps and how the choices of colour are determined. The data is processed using a data-ingester and some images are created in 'false colour' using software such as Maquaris or Paintshop Pro. I discovered the extent that the

FIGURE 10.2 Janine Randerson, *Albedo of Clouds* (Hermitage Education Centre, St Petersburg, 2018).Two channel installation (with perspex, custom-formed screens), with animated satellite images of synoptic weather patterns.

colour choices for satellite images are subjectively determined, or based around common identifications such as the representation of the land mass of Australia as red. The digital images are transferred onto digital linear tape and often the outline of the map of Australia is overlaid onto these images. Over several days, Wilmott extracted the data that allowed me to generate the remote observational perspective of the same clouds that we recorded with surface-based observations. He gave me a data file containing many thousands of images.

In Belson's film *Light* (1973), the subject is the electromagnetic spectrum with infrared light on one end, ultraviolet light at the other and visible light in the middle (MacDonald, 77). Piano music in the soundtrack gives way to the sub-sonic roar of our cosmic beginnings. The progression of the animation sequence is structured on a scientific basis, shifting from solid forms and fields of colour to particles of light that ebb and flow and ultimately become fiercely intense, almost burning up the frame. I was also concerned with the role of both the heat and light of the sun in forming images in *Albedo of Clouds*. Three different instrumental means of sensing clouds via satellite were animated in my studio in from the data sets Wilmott gave me; first, visible images where the visible sunlight scattered or reflected towards the satellite from the Earth and clouds are recorded. In the animated visible images sequences there is an observable shift from night to day. Clouds play a crucial role in reflecting a certain amount of the Sun's short wavelength (visible light) radiation back into space. The proportion of radiation reflected by a substance is called its albedo. The lower and denser the cloud, such as stratocumulus cloud, the higher the level of albedo. The possibility of producing artificial clouds drives many geo-engineering schemes to counter the effects of global warming through this albedo effect. The second sequence in the installation is animated from infrared images that are produced from the temperature of the underlying surface or cloud that radiates thermal-infrared wavelengths where cloud albedo is contrasted in black and white. The darkest areas of the infrared image are the hottest; the Australian continent can be discerned beneath the clouds as it heats and cools. The third sequence consists of water vapour images that are produced by radiation emitted by water vapour when it is taken as the dominant absorbing gas. The albedo of clouds stands out against its shadowed negative, the darkness.

The editing process for *Albedo of Clouds* drew together the surface-based live recordings of the clouds and the space-based recording of the satellite. I slowly animated the visible, infrared and water vapour satellite images given to me by Wilmott over several weeks. To achieve the speed of dissolves for the animated satellite images, I went through a series of tests in After Effects, using the techniques I had developed in *Areosphere and Atmosphere* and *Report to Darmstadt*. As each image was an hour apart in real time, I simulated a pace of animated dissolve between stills for the viewer to approximate the movement of the live video-recorded clouds. I intuitively selected a speed of 12 still frames per second; 1200 stills comprise nearly two minutes of animation. While the meteorological data began as documentary information, a lengthy post-production instilled a particular pace to the piece as an artwork. Like Belson, I was interested in how slow fades in and out could also become a form of animation.

For the spatial composition of the installed projection screens, the stereoscopic nature of Baracchi's experiment suggested that I use a pair of hanging screens to show these differing perspectives. Baracchi's (1898) description of the circular 'beautifully paired' lenses, the small dish containing mercury and the roundness of the satellite images of the globe led me to return to a circular shape. Through tracking in and out of animated satellite images, I hoped to approximate an expansive sense of looking up at the cosmological optical illusion underneath the curved screen. I formed my constructed round screens as a counterpoint to the rectangular film frame, which I connect in retrospect to Belson's abstract films. His preference for the circular over the rectangular may have emerged from his light experiments on the interior curve of the planetarium roof in the Vortex concerts.

By chance, the satellite images from BoM recorded an extreme weather event that had occurred in the same week of filming from the ground. On 7 May 2008, during the week selected for Wilmott to extract the satellite data, severe cyclonic storm Cyclone Nargis hit Burma. The cyclone made landfall at Ayeyarwady Province. The category four cyclone caused environmental destruction and over

138,000 people perished. The movement of the cyclone can be traced in the MTSat-1R images with a clearly defined eye by 1 May 2008. The cataclysmic event of Cyclone Nargis and the Burmese government's obstruction of the international relief effort became a tragic part of the embedded animation in the *Albedo of Clouds* installation. As an inadvertent record of Cyclone Nargis, the animated satellite imagery of the *Albedo of Clouds* project became more explicitly connected to the current climate crisis and our increasingly severe storms. The reflected light of the sun opens onto speculation about the future of the earth's atmosphere and the potential of clouds to protect us from the ferocity of the sun's light. There is also a potent political context in the threat of nuclear annihilation in Belson's work, just as the implicit issue of the climate crisis hovers over Hinterding and Haines and the Belknaps' solar artworks.

For Youngblood the new instrumental capacities of lunar observatories and satellite telescopes radically affected a leap in human knowledge and an expansion of consciousness within the intermedia environment that had 'become as nature' (Youngblood 1970, 137). Belson was undoubtedly aware of scientific forms of representation of the cosmos, yet conversely the pulsing waves and showers of particles produced in Belson's films and the Vortex Concerts at the Morrison Planetarium have also had a pervasive effect on aesthetics of the 'cosmos' in animated scientific visualisation. *Allures* was widely seen in the 1960s, and Belson was invited to represent the cosmos in scientific documentaries such as the PBS documentary *The Creation of the Universe* (1985). While it is outside the scope of this chapter to try and make a concrete narrative of influence, I speculate that the concerts and Belson's filmmaking informed the intense colourisation of scientific visualisations of solar and astro-phenomena. Contemporary astronomical animations are as much aesthetic images as those made by experimental filmmakers or artists when they represent data sets of phenomena that are invisible to the naked eye.

The making of optical illusions of the cosmos in experimental animation parallels the augmentation of our senses with astronomical instruments. From optical animation tables that emulate cosmic matter, adaptive reuse of telescopes, to custom-made round screens, artists imagine the cosmological horizon, with scientific knowledge as a departure point. Virilio suggests that there is no part of the heavens that does not show some angular deformation that is, in part, produced by viewing apparatus such as telescopes and satellite sensors; he writes, 'the sky of astronomers and astrophysicists is never more than a gigantic refraction effect, a cosmic illusion due to the relativity of celestial motion', that is shaped by our viewing apparatus of the telescope' (Virilio, 47). Artists have also contributed to our imaginings of the cosmos by producing new ways to experience light as a spatio-temporal phenomena. In Belson's work in particular we encounter ever-expanding light as an experience of space-time, rather than through solid planetary bodies, or any heliocentric version of the cosmos. Although the 16 mm medium prohibited ongoing loops of Belson's films, his works build and loop images internally, and his sound and image repertoire become raw materials that are shared from film to film. The contemporary art-animations discussed in this chapter operate in ongoing looped sequences in installations where there is no beginning or end, just an elastic sense of being constantly present inside an expanding universe. In the sensory intuitions of cosmological time produced in these artworks, our bodies become sensitive to cosmic energies and momentums, from wave-particles to the molecules of our own DNA.

References

Baracchi, P. 'Cloud Observation in Victoria.' *Australian Association for the Advancement of Science Report* 7 (January 1898): 259–264. Museum Victoria.

Barad, Karen. *Meeting the Universe Halfway.* Durham, NC: Duke University Press, 2007.

Belknap, Sarah and Joseph. *12 Months of the Sun.* US, 2014. Film.

Belson, Jordan. *Allures.* US, 1961. Film.

Belson, Jordan. *Re-entry.* US, 1964. Film.

Belson, Jordan. *Samadhi.* US, 1967. Film.

Belson, Jordan. *Momentum.* US, 1969. Film.

Belson, Jordan. *Light.* US, 1973. Film.

Belson, Jordan. *The Astronaut's Dream.* US, 1981. Film.

Blauvelt, Andrew, Greg Castillo and Esther Choi. *Hippie Modernism: The Struggle for Utopia.* Exhibition catalogue. Minneapolis: Walker Art Centre, 2015.

Brougher, Kerry. 'Visual-Music Culture.' In *Visual Music: Synaesthesia in Art and Music Since 1900,* edited by Kerry Brougher, Jeremy Strick, Ari Wiseman and Judith Zilczer, 88–179. London and New York: Thames and Hudson, 2005.

DeLoughrey, Elizabeth. 'Heliotropes: Solar Ecologies and Pacific Radiations.'. In *Postcolonial Ecologies: Literatures of the Environment,* edited by DeLoughrey Elizabeth and George B. Handley, 235–253. Oxford: Oxford University Press, 2011.

Ferris, Timothy. *The Creation of the Universe.* 1985. Film.

Green, Lucie. *15 Million Degrees: A journey to the Centre of the Sun.* London and New York: Penguin, 2016.

Hammond, John H. *The Camera Obscura. A Chronicle.* Bristol: Adam Hilger Ltd., 1981.

Hinterding, Joyce and David Haines. *Earthstar.* Australia, 2010. Installation.

Hinterding, Joyce and David Haines. *Sound Ship (descender 1).* Australia, 2016. Installation.

Kahn, Douglas. *Earth Sound Earth Signal.* Berkeley and Los Angeles, CA: University of California Press, 2013.

Lund, Karsen. *Eyes on the Sun, Hands on the Moon.* Exhibition catalogue. Chicago: Museum of Contemporary Art, 2014.

MacDonald, Scott. *A Critical Cinema 3: Interviews with Independent Film-makers.* Berkeley and Los Angeles, CA: University of California Press, 1998.

Picard, Caroline. 'Sarah and Joseph Belknap Translate the Solar System for Earthlings.' *Artslant,* 2014, accessed April 20 2017. www.artslant.com/ny/articles/show/41488

Randerson, Janine. *Report to Darmstadt.* NZ, 2007. Video installation.

Randerson, Janine. *Aerosphere and Atmosphere.* NZ, 2011. Video installation.

Randerson, Janine. *Albedo of Clouds.* NZ, 2012. Video installation.

Randerson, Janine, Jennifer Salmond, and Chris Manford. 'Weather as Medium: Art and Meteorological Science.' *Leonardo* 48 no. 1 (February 2015): 16–24.

Reeves, Eileen and Albert Van Helden. *On Sunspots: Galileo Galilei and Christoph Scheiner.* Chicago: University of Chicago Press, 2010.

Renner, Eric. *Pinhole Photography. Rediscovering a Historic Technique*. Boston and London: Focal Press, 1995.

Sitney, P. Adams. *Visionary Film*. Oxford: Oxford University Press, 2002 [1972].

Sturhahn, Larry. 'Experimental Filmmaking: The *Art of Jordan Belson*: An Interview with *Jordan Belson*.' *Filmmakers' Newsletter 8*, no. 7 (May 1975): 22–26.

Van Helden, Albert. The Galileo Project, 2017, accessed April 20 2017. http://galileo. rice.edu/sci/observations/sunspot_drawings.html

Virilio, Paul. *Polar Inertia*. London: Sage, 2000.

Youngblood, Gene. *Expanded Cinema*. New York: E. P. Dutton & Co, 1970.

11

WHERE DO SHAPES COME FROM?

Aylish Wood

Where Shapes Come From (2016) is a recent work by Semiconductor, the artist duo Ruth Jarman and Joe Gerhardt. Using 3D-computer-generated (CG) animation software, they create the abstract shapes of lattice diagrams and animate the motion of atoms arrayed within these three-dimensional crystalline lattice structures.[1] The CG elements sit against live-action footage filmed during a residency at the Mineral Sciences Laboratory at the Smithsonian Institute. The whole is accompanied by a soundtrack comprised of three elements: A voice-over, ambient sound from the lab and seismic data of earthquake tremors converted into sound. As Semiconductor (2017) explain their work: 'They depict interpretations of visual scientific forms associated with atomic structures, and the technologies which capture them [...] By combining these scientific processes, languages and products associated with matter formation in the context of the everyday, they become fantastical and strange encouraging us to consider how science translates nature and question our experiences of the physical world'. Semiconductor's strategy for asking their audience to question our experiences of the physical world draws on experimental animation techniques. Combining 3D-animation of abstract shapes with live-action footage, and juxtaposing the animated events with a voice-over, they add layers of competing imagery to live-action footage, Semiconductor reveal gaps between artistic and scientific languages by avoiding any seamless integration of the two.

My interest in *Where Shapes Come From* lies in what it also reveals about digital materiality. Although an intangible thing, digital materiality is part and parcel of our everyday life. Any device that operates using digital technologies, Amazon's Alexa for instance, has the capacity to alter the way we live in our spaces. With a voice-activated functionality relying on software, Alexa changes the active dimensions of a space so that touch and movement are no longer needed to switch things on or search for information, speech is enough.

Physically, a location looks the same, but now has a digital materiality founded on computation that facilitates the ways in which many users engage with Alexa. As digital devices continue to become increasingly pervasive, and artists experiment with what they offer, there is a lot more to say about the digital materiality of their work. In design theory, Johanna Drucker has introduced the concept of performative digital materiality to explain digital objects by paying heed to their associations and connections with people, processes and cultural domains (Drucker 2013). In this essay, I take abstraction, a familiar term from discussions of experimental animation, and expand it via the idea of performative digital materiality. My aim is to offer an analytic tool connecting algorithms used by artists (and other kinds of image producers) to the technological and cultural systems within which they work.

Underpinning any computational work, whether experimental or not, is a process of abstraction. To illustrate, I begin by connecting the idea of abstraction in animation to its usage in computer science, and move to then establish a link to Drucker's conceptualisation of performative digital materiality. With these connections in place, I draw comparisons between *Where Shapes Come From* and *Category 4 Hurricane Matthew on October 2, 2016* (2017), a visualisation of Hurricane Matthew created by the Godard Science Visualization Studio, part of NASA. Using 3D-animation, the visualisation depicts the complex cloud formation, winds and rain patterns associated with 48 hours of Hurricane Matthew as it traversed the Caribbean. Through this comparison I show that an artwork or visualisation's performative digital materiality is context specific. *Where Shapes Come From* and *Category 4 Hurricane Matthew* each use data – seismic data in the case of the former and precipitation data for the latter – to drive the motion of CG elements in the animations. Consequently, while both pieces are overtly concerned with events taking place in physical environments, they also rely on algorithms to facilitate motion. Though they share this same technique, tracing out their different associations and connections shows their very different performative materialities. The algorithm facilitating motion in *Category 4 Hurricane Matthew* is linked to consensus building across the different components behind data gathering and processing, whereas that used for *Where Shapes Come From* maintains the interrogative gap essential to the experimental animation's engagement with scientific discourse.

Opening up abstraction

The first step of this essay is to move from abstraction to performative digital materiality. Both *Where Shapes Come From* and *Category 4 Hurricane Matthew* use visual abstractions as a mode of depiction. In Semiconductor's work, the crystal lattices are abstract configurations of atoms, and in NASA's animation colour coding is used to map rather than show rain density. Taken broadly, abstraction can mean various things, whether in relation to artistic movements, grammar, ways of thinking, mathematics and also computing. Despite the differences in detail across these domains, the word abstract denotes a similar condition, which is to do with idealised as opposed to concrete qualities. In animation studies, definitions of abstraction can be found in the work of both Maureen Furniss and Paul Wells. For Furniss, 'abstraction describes the use of pure forms – a suggestion of a concept rather than an attempt to explicate it in real life terms' (Furniss 1998, 5). This definition mobilises a distinction between an idealised version of something versus a particular version of that thing. Although referring to rhythm and movement, Paul Wells relies on a similar distinction when he states: 'Abstract films are more concerned with rhythm and movement in their own right as opposed to the rhythm and movement of a particular character' (Wells 1998, 43). Abstraction in these definitions is both a descriptor of a type of visual imagery and a conceptual process.

These definitions of abstraction offer avenues for thinking about imagery on the screen, but they do not say much about digital matters in any obvious way. The same distinction, between an idealised and concrete version of something, is also, however, relevant to computing. At first sight a computational definition of abstraction might seem to offer little to our interpretation of images, but once linked to performative materiality it becomes a conceptual model for thinking through how artists connect with processes and cultural domains through the technologies of animation software. Turning first to computer science, abstraction is understood as a process of filtering out, a setting aside of the characteristics of patterns not essential or relevant to the computational solution of a problem. Computer scientists Peter Denning and Craig Martell draw parallels with abstraction in computing and as a mode of thought: 'Abstraction is one of the fundamental powers of the human brain. By bringing out the essence and suppressing detail, an abstraction offers a simple set of operations that apply to all cases' (Denning and Martell 2015, 208). The process of defining something through its essential characteristics often involves rule building that necessarily includes and excludes characteristics based on whether they are general rules. Elaborating further, Denning and Martell add a further and very useful distinction when they compare the explanatory abstraction of classical science and abstraction in computing: 'Abstractions in classical science are mostly explanatory – they define fundamental laws and describe how things work. Abstractions in computing do more: not only do they define computational objects, they also perform actions' (208). Touch-sensitive screens for instance, rely on abstractions. Rather than having to provide input as variable parameters, such as position, we simply touch the screen and an algorithm carries out an action.

There are two important points to open out further here: Abstraction as rule building and as a performance of actions, with the latter especially helpful to thinking through performative digital materiality. Rule building, whether in complex or simple algorithms, relies on a series of simplifications, informed choices and assumptions about what is or is not an essential characteristic, and these are where cultural, social and political influences have the potential to come into play. When the process of rule-making is described as a pulling back from concrete examples, details about the wider situation in which a digital object operates or exists are left out. A statement such as 'the essence of abstractions is preserving information that is relevant in a given context, and forgetting information that is irrelevant in that context' (Guttag 2013, 43), suggests that while rule-making is embedded in technological circumstances, it remains aside from cultural ones. But, as software studies scholars point out, coding is not neutral (Mackenzie 2006; and Chun 2011). Similarly, the implementation of code is not neutral either, but happens via interactions with systems, people and objects. The claim that code lacks neutrality will be unlikely to surprise animation scholars; we are after all used to thinking through questions around the simplifications, choices and assumptions, or rule building, which inform and underlie the politics of representation when it comes to depictions of people and things on the screen. It is probably fair to say, though, that how we translate those kinds of insight into the world of coding and its implementation becomes less obvious when faced with the simulated rain patterns of *Category 4 Hurricane Matthew* or the crystal structures of *Where Shapes Come From*. Johanna Drucker's approach to digital materiality as performative offers a conceptual scaffold to connect ideas about rule building with the images on-screen. Through Drucker, adding back detail to the abstractions of algorithms means taking notice of the associations and connections active in an image-making process. When thought of in this way, algorithms remain connected to their cultural operations as well as their computational ones.

The important move made through performative digital materiality is that digital objects and their materiality are linked to what these objects do, or how they perform actions, in the world. Rather than only thinking in terms of what an algorithm is (a line of code, say), we can pay attention to the difference an algorithm makes to a situation. There is a useful conceptual echo between Denning and Martell's view of computational abstractions performing an action and algorithms making a difference to a situation. The latter places actions in a wider context, and a performed action grasped and given meaning through a range of associations. For instance, when changing an input into an output, a computation can be understood as performing an action. When framing this act in terms of its digital materiality, the action is not limited to a specific set of operations. So, rather than simply saying an algorithm drives the motion of an animation, the wider context in which that algorithm is working becomes important too – how it makes a difference within a large network of collaborators working with high-end technologies or a duo of artists critiquing science from their perspective as experimental animators. Any performed action ripples outwards since a software or algorithm is part of a wider situation in which something takes place. An algorithm which drives motion performs the further actions of enabling consensus across a network or maintaining an artistic challange. This perspective is informed in part by Paul M. Leonardi's description of digital things: 'When [...] researchers describe digital artifacts as having "material" properties, aspects, or features, we might safely say that what makes them "material" is that they provide capabilities that afford or constrain action' (Leonardi 2010). Leonardi takes digital objects not only to be coded entities, but digital artefacts or objects which make a difference to activities in the world. Their actions can facilitate activities or obstruct them, they are mediators in the sense meant by Bruno Latour (2007, 72). It is also informed by Drucker, who argues too that digital materiality be associated with what something does. Introducing the additional word 'performative' to signal the doing of digital objects, Drucker says: 'Performative materiality suggests that what something *is* has to be understood in terms of what it *does*, how it works within machinic, systemic, and cultural domains' (emphases in original) (Drucker 2013). The final link between abstraction and algorithms is that algorithms are where abstractions become active in any given situation. As Ed Finn puts it: 'The algorithm deploys concepts from the idealised space of computation in messy reality, implementing them in what I call "culture machines": complex assemblages of abstractions, processes, and people' (Finn 2017, 2).

In this section I have moved from familiar ideas about abstraction and experimental animation, to computational abstraction and performative digital materiality. At the heart of these different ways of thinking is the same distinction between an idealised and a concrete version of something. Where algorithms and their abstract thinking are often placed outside social, political and cultural concerns, performative digital materiality puts algorithms right back in the middle of things. Drawing out the performative digital materiality of *Where Shapes Come From* and *Category 4 Hurricane Matthew* involves tracing out associations and connections surrounding the production of both pieces through a focus on the 'precipitation algorithm' in the case of *Category 4 Hurricane Matthew* and for *Where Shapes Come From*, how Semiconductor use Autodesk 3ds Max. I will claim upfront that the following makes no attempt to go into the detail of algorithms. Instead, I draw out how they perform as an active element within the creative process of each piece of work, part of the complex assemblage of abstractions, processes and people co-participating in a production.

Cloudy with digital materiality

Category 4 Hurricane Matthew is an animated visualisation showing the rainfall and wind generated by Hurricane Matthew on 2 October 2016 as it moved in from the Atlantic towards the Caribbean Islands before making landfall in South Carolina. It combines several kinds of visual depiction to create an apparently coherent whole. A proof of concept work for a larger scale piece, the visualisation can be broadly taken as an experiment. Even so, because its many elements are coherently combined, it does not share the same traditions as the experimental animation techniques discussed later for *Where Shapes Come From*. Comparing the two allows me to show how the differing contexts of the animations generate distinct performative materialities.

Starting with a satellite-type view of a hurricane swirl, *Category 4 Hurriance Matthew* transitions to a visualisation of the internal precipitation structure of the storm, and finally a static view of wind fields (as described in the text accompanying the visualisation: https://svs.gsfc.nasa.gov/4548). The internal precipitation is first shown as a 2D rain density map beneath the cloud mass of the hurricane, which then reconfigures into a 3D slice revealing the precipitation structure of the storm as a 'rainfall curtain' (see Figure 11.1). The 2D and 3D elements draw on abstract and diagrammatic conventions of colour coding to show rain density (reproduced here in greyscale gradations), whereas at first sight the hurricane cloud looks to be a copy of a natural event. Seeing the hurricane for what it is, a simulation of a complex entity crafted from a multiplicity of perspectives, opens up a place to introduce the digital materiality of the animation. The precipitation algorithm, which computed the data used in depicting the rainfall, is central to the visualisation's digital materiality, and I approach the algorithm by looking at how it performs within a wider set of assocations triggered by imagery of hurricanes.

The image of the storm which opens *Category 4 Hurricane Matthew* is not an optical record, though as the animation begins it has the appearance of one. Since 1961, when the first images of hurricanes were recorded by television cameras on board Tiros III (Bandeen et al. 1964), the top-down perspective of satellite photos of hurricanes has entered into popular currency. The animation leverages that currency to visually establish the phenomenon, while also placing it in a specific geographical location. With the pattern of the hurricane

FIGURE 11.1   The 2D rainfall pattern is the foreground with the 3D rain curtain in the background of the image. Also visible are height and distance markers, which show the rain curtain to be over 10km in height. Image: NASA's Scientific Visualization Studio Data provided by the joint NASA/JAXA GPM mission.

secured through its recognisable shape and location, the animation shifts per-spective by moving from the top-down view associated with the high altitude of a satellite, to a more parallel view. As the imagery of the rain curtain is drawn back, the 2D colour scale pattern of rainfall becomes visible. Once this happens, the image of Hurricane Matthew is clearly a simulation of the hur-ricane tracking across from the Atlantic Ocean to the Caribbean created using Autodesk Maya. With the digital status of the cloud obvious we can begin to think through the ways in which the imagery is, as Martin Kemp suggests, 'both consistent and inconsistent with our normal ways of viewing things' (Kemp 2006, 63). In *Category 4 Hurricane Matthew*, the consistency lies in our everyday familiarity with clouds as well as the swirl patterns of hurricanes. The inconsistency comes from the use of a 2D convention of colour scale to depict rainfall, and the more novel colour scaling of the 3D simulation of the rain curtain. By using the word inconsistent, Kemp is calling attention to how data, when used to generate the imagery, embodies features we would not normally see. Writing specifically about Landsat mapping, Kemp suggests soil moisture and the vigour of vegetation growth as things we would not normally see. For *Category 4 Hurricane Matthew*, equivalent features would encompass the amount of snow at the top of a cloud stack, rainfall on a wide area of ground and the wind patterns as they occur in and under the rainfall curtain.[2] Given what I have said about digital materiality, we can go further than features only found in physical reality and consider how the visualisation embodies a performative digital materiality too.

First, I will briefly outline the monitoring system used to gather the data that drives the visualisation, giving insight into the assemblage of people and processes involved. As materials on NASA's website, publicity information and papers published in science journals describe, rainfall data is captured on the Global Precipitation Mission (GPM) Core Observatory, whose instruments collect observations that allow 'scientists to better "see" inside clouds'.[3] The GPM Core Observatory, part of a constellation of satellites, is described on a factsheet thusly:

> The GPM Core Observatory will measure precipitation using two science instruments: the GPM Microwave Imager (GMI) and the Dual-frequency Precipitation Radar (DPR). The GMI will supply information on cloud structure and on the type (i.e., liquid or ice) of cloud particles. Data from the DPR will provide insights into the three-dimensional structure of pre-cipitation, along with layer-by-layer estimates of the sizes of raindrops or snowflakes, within and below the cloud. Together these two instruments will provide a database of measurements against which other partner satel-lites' microwave observations can be meaningfully compared and com-bined to make a global precipitation dataset.
>
> *(GPM factsheet)*

There are many places to begin interrogating this system, and my focus here is on how the global precipitation data set referred to in the quotation is generated. Undertaking the comparisons and combinations necessary to make a data set entails integrating observations across the satellite network with ground-based data gathering, and converting numbers registered on observational devices into data about precipitation. Central to this process is the precipitation algorithm (Kidd et al. 2012). George Huffman, head of the multi-satellite product team for GPM, describes working with algorithms designed to relate the numbers generated by the satellite instruments to the rain, snow and other precipitation within the cloud and on the ground. He states: 'Algorithms are mathematical processes used by computer programs developed by the science team that relate what the satellite instruments measure to rain, snow and other precipitation observed throughout the cloud and actually felt on the ground' (Space Daily Writing Team 2014). Information is gathered from current precipitation satellites, routine ground validation efforts, and focused field campaigns to capture the variety of rainfall and snowfall in different parts of the world. Getting this data together into information relies on the precipitation algorithm whose role is to: 'Intercalibrate, merge, and interpolate "all" satellite microwave precipitation estimates, together with microwave-calibrated infrared (IR) satellite estimates, precipitation gauge analyses, and potentially other precipitation estimators at fine time and space scales for the TRMM and GPM eras over the entire globe' (Huffman 2015). From Huffman's detailing of the algorithm, the necessity of a large and varied group of supporting personnel, a network of satellite and land-based sensors, the simulation is evidently comprised of a multiplicity of perspectives. From this description, we can see how the precipitation algorithm sits at an intersection of spaces, and through exploring further the associations relayed via those intersections I show it has a performative materiality based around generating consensus.

The precipitation algorithm performs this materiality in complex ways. Enabling the cultural system of meteorological visualisations, it participates in reconfiguring global precipitation data into scales comparable to human perception and cognition. It also generates the data used to drive the simulation of the rainfall curtain and the colour coded precipitation patterns created in the 3D-animation software Autodesk Maya. The hurricane, neither copy nor optical record, is an explanation realised in a simulation. As Sherry Turkle notes: 'Simulation makes itself easy to love and difficult to doubt. It translates the concrete materials of science, engineering, and design into compelling virtual objects that engage the body as well as the mind' (Turkle 2009, 7). At the same time, by thinking in terms of abstraction and performative materiality, simulations are revealed as mathematical explanations. In her research into computer-generated visualisation practices in biological sciences, Annamaria Carusi argues: 'Briefly we can say that if the visual images used in visualisations represent data, they do that by modelling rather than copying it, and what they represent is meant to be the mathematical 'explanation' of data rather than the appearance of data' (Carusi 2011, 308). Outlining what is meant by a mathematical explanation, Carusi makes a distinction between modelling an explanation and enabling something to appear. I want to suggest that performative materiality emerges in the gap between explanation and appearance, complicating both terms so that neither explanations nor appearances occur without being weighted by associations of some kind. To explain, generating an explanation from raw data requires a series of manipulations in which the data is in some way translated, and that comes with both losses and gains in the available information. George Huffman, who I quoted above explaining that the precipitation algorithm intercalibrates, merges and interpolates data from various sensors in the observatory network, gives a more everyday account of the algorithm for an interview in *Science Daily*. Riffing on the idea of *raw* data he uses a metaphor of cooking soup, with vegetables standing in for data:

> "They're all vegetables, and so you have to wash them, peel them, take out the bad spots – that's a really important step, since you don't want your soup to taste bad," Huffman said. "Maybe you sauté some things, and you boil other things, and you put it all together. When you get done you have to taste-test it to make sure you have the seasoning right. So each of those steps, in a mathematical sense, is what we have to do to take all the diverse sources of information and end up with a unified product, which the user finds to be useful.
>
> *(Space Daily Writing Team 2014)*

Huffman's soup analogy effectively indicates the degree to which data is smoothed, edited and manipulated before it becomes the basis for a simulation, which entails running the data through another set of complex algorithms. For the latter, GPM data is processed to create the data swathe geometry, volumetric brick maps and textures used in the Autodesk Maya/Renderman pipeline of a 3D-visualisation process (email conversation with Alex Kekesi, 2017).

Across the varied processes described above, we can see the more abstract and idealised spaces of mathematical explanations and computation coming into contact with the practicalities of available computational power, conventions of good or bad data, perceptions of what constitutes an artefact, styles of visualisations, the storytelling needs of the visualisation. Here we see algorithms as Ed Finn's culture machines, as complex assemblages of abstraction, processes and people, a perspective resonating with Drucker's performative digital materiality. Both descriptions understand digital entities – in this case, algorithms – as a material thing operating as part of a series of relations with people and systems. No longer only rule-based and theoretical descriptions of the essence of a problem, algorithms are a material-cultural entity where abstraction gets down and dirty and returns to the fold. We can go further: The computations of the precipitation algorithm perform not only by generating data within this assemblage, but also by generating consensus. Writing again about bioscience and visualisation, Annamaria Carusi claims: 'Visualizations of computational simulations are common currency among the members of successful collaborations being used for analyses, in the context of workshops, and in publications' (Carusi 2011, 308). As common currency amongst a successful collaboration, visualisations are based on consensus, a series of agreements operating across all levels of the project: The multinational team agreeing the terms of the project, the cross-disciplinary negotiations around conventions and visualisation practices, the calibrations of data, and agreements between data. The performative materiality of the precipitation algorithm, through its associations and connections with the animation software, the people on the visualisation and geophysics team, and all the conventions of visualisation practices, emerges as it gives the appearance of a seamless integration based on creating a consensus of both people and data.

Between a rock and software

Exploring *Where Shape Comes From* reveals a different performative digital materiality. The work of Semiconductor has always been to shake up the kind of consensus seen around *Category 4 Hurricane Matthew*, to destabilise the certainty of the metaphors used when nature is constructed through scientific language. With Autodesk 3ds Max they create 3d-animated crystalline structures whose spatio-temporal timescales sit in dialogue with the mineral science discourse of the live-action elements of the work. This interplay of spatio-temporal scales can be described as asymptotic, they are in dialogue but never converge.[4] The performative digital materiality of Semiconductor's use of 3ds Max intersects with and makes possible this asymptotic logic.

Instead of allowing language, whether that of words, pictures or moving images, to readily stand in for an accurate description of natural phenomena, Semiconductor disrupt scientific conventions by suggesting alternative possibilities. In the following combined quotation, Semiconductor say: [Joe Gerhardt:] 'we try not to create metaphors, we are trying to actually allow you to feel things [...] [Ruth Jarman:] about the material, it's always about the material whatever we're doing' (Semiconductor, in interview with the author). Semiconductor use animation to restage encounters with nature through an interpretive reimagining of scientific discourse, exposing how nature is mediated. When talking about what they mean by mediation, Gerhardt commented:

> We were interested in how science educates our idea of what nature is and, of course, it's one step away from the thing itself. And the science is then a mediation of nature itself and a lot of what we take for granted as being reality is actually an interpretation in scientific language.
>
> *(Semiconductor, in interview with the author)*

Gerhardt's use of the word language here crosses between spoken language, the language associated with techniques of measurements and visualisations of the results of those measurements. In *Where Shapes Come From*, these different facets of language are present and in conversation with Semiconductor's interpretative approach. The spoken language of a mineralogist (Jeffrey Post) is heard on the soundtrack explaining crystal formation. The location for the live-action footage, the Smithsonian Mineralogy Laboratory, is full of pieces of equipment, and the image lingers for a while on the abstracted language of geological mapping. The animation of the crystals draws on diffraction patterns generated using the technique of X-Ray crystallography (see Figure 11.2). Combined with a second sound track based on seismic data, the animation plays off these different languages. The artwork not only resists the kind of consensus found in *Category 4 Hurricane Matthew*, but actively challenges it too. This challenge is present in much of Semiconductor's work, leading Lilly Husbands to describe it as a philosophical critique of scientific representation (Husbands 2013).

When talking about Semiconductor's aim to create an experience of nature, Jarman says:

> We are always trying to get as close to the material as possible and that's why we've ended up questioning science so much. We're so interested in matter and how we experience matter. When you look at an amazing picture from outer space the Hubble space telescope has taken, outer space doesn't look like that. The image is hundreds of images put together and loads of colour put on it, and everything is still quite inaccessible in terms of how you experience something. When it comes down to our work, we're trying to create experiences of nature, but there's always science getting in the way of the thing you are looking at.
>
> *(Semiconductor, interview with the author)*

One of the ways Semiconductor creates an experience of nature is by exploring the possibilities of expanding spatio-temporal scales through animation.

FIGURE 11.2 Still: *Where Shapes From* (Semiconductor, 2016). The atoms of a crystal are arrayed in a lattice structure based on a typical diffraction pattern generated using the technique of X-Ray crystallography. Courtesy of Semiconductor.

They aim to make the invisible visible, which 'sometimes requires a transformation in scale or another shift in the realms of human perception' (Hinterwäldner 2014, 16). Commenting in an interview about their earlier film *Magnetic Movie* (2005), Semiconductor remark on the capacity of animation to enable their transformations of scale: 'Animation was a useful tool for the way we wanted to explore man's relationship to an experience of the natural environment, allowing us to manipulate and control time beyond human experience and scales larger and smaller than us' (Selby 2009, 171). In *Magnetic Movie* Semiconductor created animations of magnetic waves and composited them within still photos of lab spaces, using CG animation to bring these invisible waves into visibility. Recently Paul Dourish has argued that 'the material arrangements of information – how it is represented and how that shapes how it can be put to work – matters significantly for our experience of information and information systems' (2017, 4). In *Where Shapes Come From* Semiconductor use Autodesk 3ds Max to generate 3D-digital crystals. How these shapes are put to work in challenging the conventions of scientific representation lies not only in how they look but also how they enter into a dialogue with the other elements of scientific discourse in the animation. Through this process a version of materiality emerges, and which is experienced by the viewers of the artworks. The materiality that emerges is, however, as much digital as it is physical.

Semiconductor have consistently, though not exclusively, used the 3D-animation software 3ds Max to model CG shapes and create movement (for *Earthworks* (2016), Semiconductor worked with Houdini). Autodesk 3ds Max was originally released in 1990 as 3D Studio. In a 2010 interview with CGPress, Tom Hudson, one of the early developers of the software, says that he 'wanted software that [he] could make movies with' (Baker et al. 2010). This design aim has been privileged and built into the software with toolsets for rendering and lighting continuing to evolve and get better at delivering photorealistic results. In the context of Semiconductor's experimental work, the software design of 3ds Max is flexible enough to enable alternative associations and connections than those seen in animation for commercial sectors. Speaking of their early work with 3ds Max, Jarman recalls how they actively engaged in breaking down the conventional materiality of the then new software:

> When we first went into 3ds Studio Max we would spend all the time turning things off. It was developed as a tool to make things look realistic, so we'd go in turning shininess off, everything off. Because we were doing experiments in the early stages, we were trying to understand the material nature of the software and how we could develop our own language [...] As we've progressed, I guess that hasn't remained so important. It was a way of developing our own language, stripping everything back and we could build on it from there.
>
> *(Semiconductor, interview with the author)*

As Jarman describes, in experiments such as *A-Z of Noise* (1999), Semiconductor set themselves against the primary visual language of the software by designing experiments to explore and expose both the limits and possibilities. This kind of experimentation connects Semiconductor to a growing body of artists, including Alan Warburton and Claudia Hart, who engage with a range of software to create images and challenge conventional usage. In his work *Primitives* (2016), Warburton explores the possibilities and limits of crowd simulation software, putting into practice a 'close reading of software and its attendant aesthetic and political biases' (Warburton 2016). Hart, in her mixed media installation *The Dolls House* (2016), combines 3D models with algorithmically generated patterns. Adapting the forms and the software normally used to create 3D shooter games, Hart describes how she challenges existing conventions: 'By creating virtual images that are sensual but not pornographic within mechanised, clockwork depictions of the natural, I try to subvert earlier dichotomies of woman and nature pitted against a civilised, "scientific" and masculine world of technology' (Claudia Hart, artist statement). Like Semiconductor, these experimental animators are artists who interrogate the language of the software not only to generate images but to also provoke a deeper understanding of what software contributes to creative practice.

In their early experiments, Semiconductor created associations and connections that generated their own language. The animation software has a performative materiality in this process too, it makes a difference, performs actions via the controllers designed as part of the software's functionality and the possibilities for manipulation they offer to artists such as Semiconductor. The performance continues to emerge in both Semiconductor's imagery of atoms and crystals and the audio-control of molecular motion. Gerhardt says one of the reasons Semiconductor continue to work with 3ds Max is its capacity to let them both expand the scales of world they are exposing and also build their story in the ways they want:

> One of the reasons we work with 3ds Max still, and one of the first reasons we came to it as well, is you could technically make anything in it. You can build a world on any scale in it. When we first started out as artists and couldn't have afforded a studio that was hugely beneficial situation. But you can also build the ways that you can tell your story. Like using certain connections of controllers and inputs. And that's allowed us to develop a kind of signature in a way.
>
> *(Semiconductor, interview with the author)*

This combination of scalar expansion and story building is seen in the modelling and movements of the crystals. With *Where Shapes Come From*, Semiconductor use the software not simply to depict 3D animated versions of crystal lattice structures based on the abstracted visual language of X-Ray patterns, but also craft a relational sense of atoms coming into being as they move through that structure. Gerhardt observes that the relationality of the atoms is informed by ideas in quantum mechanics:

> We play with the nature of animation in our work and so what is also happening is that these things that look like atoms are more like fields and the shapes are moving through the fields of atoms. It's like quantum mechanics where a particle has a place and a vector at the same time. Things don't come into existence until they have a relationship with something else. These shapes are actually moving through something that is there but is also not fixed. It is a play with those relationships.
>
> *(Semiconductor, interview with the author)*

As 3ds Max is used to animate atoms, some of which seed to crystals and then grow, the spatial and temporal scales of the work proliferate. Jeff Post's live-action audio uses the language of scientific information to talk about an atomic scale and a timescale of thousands of years, and the video shows a man grinding a stone, an old piece of matter in this timescale. All the while, CG atoms oscillate and transition across the fields, at times coalescing through relations that precipitate into crystalline forms. As someone used to looking for patterns and degrees of coherency, a facet readily recognisable in *Category 4 Hurricane Matthew*, it seems reasonable to try and see these digital transformations of scale as a new ordering, an imagined spatio-temporal congruence where the microscopic has its own seamless system set against the macro-scale of a lab. But that is not the case as neither the atomic oscillations nor the growing crystals are of the same order of scaled space or time. Consequently, CG adds competing scales to the flow of images in *Where Shapes Come From*. As a visualization, *Category 4 Hurricane Matthew* presented a consensus around multiple perspectives. In contrast, Semiconductor bring multiple perspectives into proximity through different audio-visual elements, and then maintain a gap between them. The relations across the audio-visual elements are asymptotic, coming close enough for dialogue but never converging to a singular point or perspective.

The spatio-temporal complexity of imagery in *Where Shapes Come From* always holds a gap in place, and the way Semiconductor utilises seismic data brings another dimension into the (audio) mix. Semiconductor have used seismic data in several of their artworks, including *Worlds in the Making* (2011), *The Shaping Grows* (2012), and *Earthworks* (2016), and describe sound as a sculptural tool through which to add time and motion to microscopic worlds (Semiconductor, artists' statement). Of using seismic data Jarman says: 'when we first started working with seismic data we saw it as a tool for revealing events that took place over geological time frames long time ago'. Gerhardt adds: 'When you listen to the seismic data you feel what's actually happening in the earth. It sounds like what it is. It's not a metaphor of something else' (Semiconductor, interview with the author). In *Where Shapes Come From*, the audio track created using seismic data from the Mariana Trench sounds like the earth creaking and cracking as it subtly shifts deep beneath our feet. It is tempting to hear this audio track as only bringing a more direct experience of nature into the work, when in fact it also introduces another dimension of digital materiality. When used as a procedural software, 3ds Max can be programmed through its controllers, essentially mathematically-defined algorithms allowing the timing of movements in an animation to be automated. Seismic sound, converted back into a waveform, can be input into an audio controller adding motion to specific parameters in the models of lattices and crystals, the motion of a particular atom, for instance. Through this process, the audio and the visual become inseparable since sound sculpts motion. As Gerhardt explains, without further adjustment to the motion, this would quickly look rather repetitive and so a noise controller is used to add randomness to the motion:

> A lot of the time, say with matrices and lattices, if everything just moved up and down in the z-axis, then it wouldn't be very interesting. We have to then transfer that one-dimensional or rather two-dimensional wave, you know time and axis, into movement of noise so that the sound then goes into a noise controller that would then affect all the different points in different random ways so that the amplification of the noise is what's happening. It allows variation, everything is moving in a different way.
>
> *(Semiconductor, interview with the author)*

The underlying motion remains based on the seismic waveform, but the detail of the motion for different points within a model is randomised, creating a wave-like motion punctuated by jumps and rotations.

The complexity of the mixed materiality of physical sound and algorithmically generated noise is intriguing, and another place where performative digital materiality emerges. Seismic sound is used to sculpt motion, suggesting an experience closer to a natural phenomenon. At the same time, a digital element literally comes into the picture through the noise controller. The algorithm of the noise controller in 3ds Max creates Perlin noise, designed to reduce the unnatural smoothness of CG elements by imitating the appearance of texture and motion in nature. By creating random movement at points partly described by the seismic waveform, another asymptotic relationship becomes active in the animation. The gap runs through the materiality of the artwork, and via this gap performative materiality emerges. Every point of motion in an atomic array or a growing crystal has the possibility of being a combination of seismic waveform and a randomly defined point. In the flow of the animation, the origin of motion cannot be said to be either physical or computational, it is both. Like the counterpoint between Jeff Post's audio track and the different spatio-temporal scales introduced by the CG animated atoms and crystals, these two drivers of motion can never coincide. Through *Where Shapes Come From*, Semiconductor challenge their audience to rethink their understanding of the world and its material nature. They do this by not only posing questions about how nature is mediated by scientific language, but also through the emergent performative digital materiality of 3ds Max and the Perlin noise algorithm.

Conclusion

With digital techniques increasingly accessible, artists are able to create experimental work using software, and in doing so they often explore and push against the materiality it offers. Since the materiality of software is intangible, expanding with any depth on this idea has not been an easy matter. In this essay, I propose a way forward. Using two case studies, one an experimental animation and the other a proof of concept visualisation, I have taken Johanna Drucker's idea of performative digital materiality and linked it to the work of algorithms via the idea of abstraction. This linkage relies on excavating the complex assemblage of abstractions, processes and the people involved in making animations. By comparing *Where Shapes Come From* and *Category 4 Hurricane Matthew* I have shown performative digital materialities as concrete, they emerge in specific situations. Placing software and algorithms in their situation allows us to see two things: How the material arrangements of information alters our experience of information, and, algorithms are active in the cultural politics in which those arrangements evolve. Finally, returning to the title of this paper, where *do* shapes come from? Shapes happen at the intersections of complex assemblages, in the relations between the materials and technologies with which they are conceived, such as CG software, the histories and conventions of a discipline (say, animation, geometry or art history), in arenas of production or debate, and through the imaginations of people. As some or all of these happen together, the things we call shapes emerge.

Notes

1 Atoms in a crystalline structure form a regular repeating pattern known as a crystalline lattice. A lattice diagram depicts the repeating pattern in 2D or 3D. Semiconductor create 3D lattice diagrams.
2 A cloud stack is a term used to describe storm clouds that rise to dramatic heights.
3 GPM: 'Global Precipitation Measurement,' accessed 11 July 2017, https://eospso.nasa.gov/missions/global-precipitation-measurement-core-observatory.
4 An asymptote is a mathematical term used to describe a straight line that continually approaches a given curve but does not meet it at any finite distance. I use it here more metamorphically to describe visual and audio imageries that come close but never resolve into a single coherent whole.

References

Baker, Dave, Neil Blevins, Pablo Hadis, and Scott Kirvan. 'The History of 3D Studio.' *CGPress* (2010). Accessed July 11 2017, http://cgpress.org/archives/cgarticles/the_history_of_3d_studio.

Bandeen, W.R., V. Kunde, W. Nordberg, and H.P. Thompson. 'Tiros III Meterological Satellite Radiation Observations of a Tropical Hurricane.' *Tellus XVI* (1964): 481–502.

Carusi, Annamaria. 'Scientific Visualization and Aesthetic Grounds for Trust.' *Ethics and Information Technology 10* (2008): 243–254.

Carusi, Annamaria. 'Computational Biology and the Limits of Shared Vision.' *Perspectives on Science 19*, no. 3 (2011): 300–336.

Chun, Wendy H.K. *Programmed Visions: Software and Memory*. Cambridge, Massachusetts: The MIT Press, 2011.

Denning, Peter J., and Criag H. Martell. *Great Principles of Computing*. Cambridge, Massachusetts: The MIT Press, 2015.

Dourish, Paul. *The Stuff of Bits: an Essay on the Materialities of Information*. Cambridge, Massachusetts: The MIT Press, 2017.

Drucker, Johanna. 'Performative Materiality and Theoretical Approaches to the Interface.' *Digital Humanities Quarterly 7*, no.1 (2013). Accessed July 11 2017, www.digitalhumanities.org/dhq/vol/7/1/000143/000143.html.

Finn, Ed. *What Algorithms Want: Imagination in the Age of Computing*. Cambridge, Massachusetts: The MIT Press, 2017.

Furniss, Maureen. *Art in Motion: Animation Aesthetics*. Barnet: John Libbey Publishing, 1998.

Godard Science Visualization Studio. *Category 4 Hurricane Matthew on October 2, 2016*. US, 2017. Video.

GPM: Global Precipitation Measurement. Accessed July 11 2017, https://eospso.nasa.gov/missions/global-precipitation-measurement-core-observatory.

Guttag, John V. *Introduction to Computation and Programming Using Python*. Cambridge, Massachusetts: The MIT Press, 2013.

Hart, Claudia. *The Dolls House*. US, 2016. Film.

Hinterwäldner, Inge. 'Semiconductor's Landscapes as Sound-Sculptured Time-Based Visualizations.' *Technoetic Arts: A Journal of Speculative Research 12*, no.1 (2014): 15–38.

Huffman, George. 'NASA Global Precipitation Measurement (GPM) Integrated Multi satellite Retrievals for GPM (IMERG).' NASA (2015). Accessed July 2017, https://pmm.nasa.gov/sites/default/files/document_files/IMERG_ATBD_V4.5.pdf.

Husbands, Lilly. 'The Meta-Physics of Data: Philosophical Science in Semiconductor's Animated Videos.' *Moving Image Review and Art Journal 2*, no. 2 (2013): 198–212.

Kemp, Martin. *Seen|Unseen: Art, Science, and Intuition from Leonardo to the Hubble Telescope*. Oxford: Oxford University Press, 2006.

Kidd, Chris, Erin Dawkins and George Huffman. 'Comparison of Precipitation Derived from ECMWF Operation Forecast Model and Satellite Precipitation Datasets.' *Journal of Hydrometeorology 14* (2012): 1463–1482.

Latour, Bruno. *Reassembling the Social: An Introduction to Actor Network Theory*. Oxford: Oxford University Press, 2007.

Leonardi, Paul M. 'Digital Materiality? How Artefacts without Matter, Matter.' *First Monday 15*, no. 6 (2010). Accessed July 11 2017, http://journals.uic.edu/ojs/index.php/fm/article/view/3036/2567.

Mackenzie, Adrian. *Cutting Code: Software and Sociality*. New York: Peter Lang, 2006.

Semiconductor. *A-Z of Noise*. UK, 1999. Film.

_____. *Magnetic Movie*. UK, 2005. Film.

_____. 'Magnetic Movie.' In *Animation in Process*. Edited by Andrew Selby, London: Laurence King Publishing, 2009, 170–175.

_____. *Worlds in the Making*. UK, 2011. Film.

_____. *The Shaping Grows*. UK, 2012. Film.

_____. *Earthworks*. UK, 2016. Film.

_____. *Where Shapes Come From*. UK, 2016. Film.

Space Daily Writing Team. 'GPM Mission's How to Guide for Making Global Rain Maps.' *Space Daily* (2014). Accessed July 11 2017, www.spacedaily.com/reports/GPM_Missions_How_to_Guide_for_Making_Global_Rain_Maps_999.html.

Turkle, Sherry. *Simulation and Its Discontents*. Cambridge, Massachusetts: The MIT Press, 2009.

Warburton, Alan. *Primitives*. UK, 2016. Film.

Warburton, Alan. 'Spectacle, Speculation, Spam.' Video essay (2016). Acccessed January 3 2018, http://alanwarburton.co.uk/spectacle-speculation-spam/.

Wells, Paul. *Understanding Animation*. London: Routledge, 1998.

12

NASA'S VOYAGER FLY-BY ANIMATIONS

Sean Cubitt

A preliminary ambition of an eco-poetic approach to cinema is to establish that eco-criticism can give a radically new understanding of film and video. Part of the cultural work of experimental animation is to demand just such radically new readings. This chapter offers an eco-poetic/eco-critical reading of a group of films that appear to have no connection to environmentalism, and which are in every sense of the word experimental. In this sense the chapter is itself an experiment. As befits a philosophy of connection and interconnection, the eco-poetics of cinema has many genealogies. Among them, we should respect the genealogies of science and engineering that underpin the moving image in general and animation in particular, not least since it is in them that we first encounter the technique of experimentation. The rise of modern science in the Renaissance is a familiar story, perhaps too familiar and therefore unexamined (though see Koyré for an already more nuanced account). Science is composed not only of things known but someone or something who knows. For science to exist, it was first necessary to invent Man. In many respects, this is an invention that remains to be completed: Indeed, its incompletion is surely a contributory feature in the notion of experimental media. The invention of the human that occupied the luminaries of the history of science and engineering – Galileo, Leonardo and Alberti among them – was conducted in a theological era, an era that lasted at least until the time of Newton. Yet our commonest narrative about the foundation of the scientific worldview is one of struggle with and escape from God. It might even be thought, in this tradition, that the struggle to secularise is integral to science and, like science itself, also unfinished. If science is incomplete, then the subject of science, the one who knows, is also still under construction. James Blinn's NASA animations of the Voyager space mission, coming at a particularly interesting moment in this history, are both experimental in their own right and accounts of an experiment in science and engineering in which the question of how the human can be extracted from the divine are particularly in play. To understand how this experiment contributes not only to space flight and space science but to the unfinished project of inventing the human, this chapter proposes to trace some of the missing theological genealogies of modern science. Animation constantly plays at the border of what it is to be human: Blinn's animations still reverberate as some of experimental animation's most moving expressions of what lies beyond the human, perhaps casting light on what the *anima* of animation might be.

To define experiment in animation would risk losing its impetus. Yet the choice of 'experimental' rather than 'avant-garde' or 'artistic' as an adjective indicates a trajectory of work, one that attempts, tries out, explores and perhaps verifies an idea. It suggests an enquiry about what animation might achieve that it has not already, and perhaps about what kind of knowledge it might produce. The series of animations undertaken by James Blinn at the Jet Propulsion Laboratory (JPL) with Charles E. 'Charley' Kohlhase, Jr and the assistance of Alvy Ray Smith between 1978 and 1983 – when Blinn was awarded both the NASA Exceptional Service Medal and the SIGGRAPH Computer Graphics Achievement Award – surely merit the term, both for their development of then brand-new techniques in digital animation and for their application to one of the most daring engineering/science projects of its time. Several features make these short films (they circulated on 16mm) experimental.

Launched in 1977, the two Voyager spacecraft had yet to reach their first major planets, Jupiter and Saturn, when Blinn arrived at JPL from Ivan Sutherland's formative computer graphics programme at the University of Utah. NASA engineers provided Blinn with the projected flight data, which gave him the armature on which the animation would be built. In a 2014 interview, Kohlhase gave a sense of the complexity of these flight plans.

> 1977 was the 'Goldilocks' opportunity. In '76, since Jupiter is moving faster around the Sun than Saturn, it 'trails' Saturn, so to speak. You can still do a gravity assist on the trailing side of Jupiter, but you have to fly very close to get enough deflection to get to Saturn, which is further ahead. In '77 the arrangement was perfect for flying through the region of the Galilean satellites ... . Then we wanted to fly by Io, which orbits Jupiter every 1.7 days, so we started dividing the encounter dates at Jupiter into 1.7-day increments. Titan goes around Saturn every 16 days, and we divided up the encounter at Saturn in this way too, but we also wanted to encounter Titan before we crossed the ring plane, rather than afterwards – we called these 'Titan-before' encounters ... . we knew we could use "patched conics" – ellipses, parabolas, hyperbolas and so forth – to approximate the integrated trajectories, so we basically developed software that could approximate and run hundreds of cases overnight on a computer. We picked those which satisfied all engineering constraints, then asked the science teams which ones best suited their needs, for example close flybys of certain satellites.

> Finally, through this process, out of the 10,000 or so possible trajecto-
> ries, we targeted 110 with the Titan-Centaur launch vehicle, and finally
> launched on two of them.
>
> *(Starr 2014)*

Significantly, the trajectories plotted by the flight engineering team led by
Kohlhase were projections, in the dual sense of projective geometries, especially
in the case of the conic section geometry of the curved trajectory round planetary gravity wells, and in the sense that they projected the navigational trajectories forward in time. Accuracy in both modes of projection was essential, since
each Voyager satellite carried only a tiny amount of fuel for course corrections,
and an equally tiny 8Kb computer, mainly dedicated to the scientific mission
rather than navigation: Chances to fix launch errors were extremely limited.
Mercifully, the calculations proved accurate: By the time of its 1989 encounter
with Neptune's moon Triton, the error was of the order of one kilometre per
billion. But at the time the animations were being done, the vast majority of
the flight lay ahead. They are then exemplary of the deep principles of vector
graphics: They indicate constantly changing direction over time extending into
the future.

Equally significant is the application of data to the animation. While the
computer-generated models of the Voyager craft were basically polygons of a
kind already familiar in computer graphics, the orchestration of their movements
was entirely derived from the geometry of Kohlhase's conics. The animating
principle – the design of the motion – was then not the free, individual, creative
act of the animator but a collaborative effort. In this, the animation is informed
by and informs the collective subject of Science as the collective knower of scientific knowledge. Despite its dramatic setting, the films are by no means products
of artistic fantasy: On the contrary, they are documentary in at least the sense
that they document a complex engineering project, a certain kind of truth. In
this, the fly-by animations are precursors of CADCAM and architectural fly-
throughs: Intermediaries between a plan and its actualisation. Their order of
truth is projection – here based on the escape velocity, direction of launch and
interactions with heavenly bodies: Predictable, within reason, but nonetheless
an experiment. When we watch them today, we see the uncertain past of a now
certain future that was still in the act of becoming. Where we see an actuality,
Blinn, Kohlhase and their team could only descry potential.

This raises the unusual question – for animation – of realism. By the time the
two Voyagers had completed their journey past the outer planets, the trajectories
translated from flight planning data to animated flight had become real, and
remain that way from that moment on. The trajectories have become real, in the
sense that the projection has become a record of the two flights transcribed into
animated film. For Blinn at his work desk, back in 1978, that real was not yet
already actualised: It was the *idea* of the flight. In philosophical terms, this is a
perfectly acceptable variant of realism. Opposed to 'nominalism', the theory that

only particular objects exist, an older definition of 'realism' (rooted in mediaeval Scholasticism) proposed that the world is a presentation of underlying truths that do not make themselves immediately (without mediation) apparent to us humans. Ideas like Being, Truth, or for that matter conic sections are real, and our various media, as much as the phenomena of the world that we observe with our ordinary senses, are simply expressions of them. In the immense void of the space between Mars and the outer planets, the planned paths of the satellites existed only as idea. Yet by the Scholastic definition, that idea of the trajectory, with its complex gravitic slingshots, was already real. It was only a question of the animation expressing it, which it did before it was expressed a second time by the Voyager craft. Now that Voyager 1, hotly pursued by Voyager 2, is further from us than any human-made artefact has ever travelled, passing the demarcation line between the Solar System and interstellar space on the 25th of August 2012, it can no longer exist in any unmediated way for us left here on Earth. This was equally true of the period of their fly-bys of Jupiter and Saturn. They exist, therefore, not only as material objects whose speed and direction evidence their terrestrial origin, but as ideas made real. At the same time, unless you want to reach for some truly stupefying conspiracy theory, there is no reason to doubt that they are out there at the further reaches of the heliosphere, transmitting sporadic messages, and carrying with them the famous golden record in hopes of proving to some far-future alien species that we too once existed.

The golden record designed by Carl Sagan (with whom Blinn would collaborate on the successful TV mini-series *Cosmos: A Personal Voyage* [1980]) captured public attention and a degree of controversy. NASA's almost permanent funding crises have consistently driven them to media spectacles, from the 'Blue Marble' (Lazier 2011, 602–630) and live pictures of the Moon landing to Hubble Space Telescope imaging of deep space (Chaisson 1994). The golden record was one such stunt, whatever its scientific purposes: A collection of greetings in 55 living and extinct languages, 115 images, 27 music and 21 other audio tracks, and a recording of brain activity on a pair of phonographic discs, one for each Voyager. The controversy came from the nude portraits of two strongly Caucasian figures, the male greeting, the female passive; and from the inclusion of Chuck Berry's 'Johnny B. Goode' among the music tracks (Steve Martin joked that the first reply from the aliens would be 'Send more Chuck Berry'). Sagan's showmanship would be a major boost to NASA's popularity. The Voyager fly-by animations belonged to the same platform of popular appeal, over the heads of the government, directly to the taxpayers funding adventures in space.

Such, perhaps cynically, is one possible account of the rationale for sending a phonographic disc into outer space. Alternatively, the determining factor of popular support in its turn enabled the Voyager animations to express the peculiar silence of digital animation, which, unlike film, did not imply at the very least the chatter of a projector, and unlike analogue video of the period, is not simultaneously a sound-and-image medium. The silence of digital animation is more absolute than the absence of soundtrack on either film or video. It is entirely appropriate to the airless, vibrationless, soundless zone of interplanetary space. Once transferred to film, and of necessity (at least the necessity of professional practice in broadcast news) when transmitted, the animations acquired a soundtrack. In at least some instances, that soundtrack would have included samples from the golden discs. Which in turn begs the question: Why send sound recordings into interstellar space? Recalling John Cage's experiments in the anechoic chamber, where in the depths of silence he heard the sounds of his breathing, his heartbeat, the blood rushing in his veins and finally the thin, high whine of his central nervous system, where there is a body there is no silence (Cage 1957, 6–12). In deep space, there can be no body, for the same reason that there is no sound. To send sound is to evoke a body that is absent, left behind. There is a kind of congruence between the silent travel of discs full of sounds (themselves of course silent until some alien intelligence decodes the instructions on how to play them) and another delightful and thought-provoking quality of the animations, whose success with audiences and policy-makers as well as among the small but growing band of specialists in computer graphics was boosted by the inventively fluid camerawork of Alvy Ray Smith and his colleague David DiFrancesco (Sito 2013, 49).

If the flight plans anchored the animation in maths, science and engineering, Smith's moves with the virtual camera introduced a choreography that transformed the mute documentation into a recognisably embodied experience. In his phenomenological study of *Bodies in Technology*, Don Ihde recalls Galileo's experiments with the telescope, noting that though the astronomer and optician was focused on the objects he could observe – the surface of the Moon and later the moons of Jupiter – he might equally well have observed his own involuntary movements constantly reframing the remote objects as they pursued their course through the turning sky (Ihde 2002, 58–60). For Ihde this mutual approximation – movements of the body equated with the movements of its objects; bringing the Moon and the moons close to him and him closer to the Moon and the moons – is a permanent state of scientific observation. As a thermometer popped into boiling water changes the water's temperature in the act of measuring it, or even more like Einstein's observer on a moving train, all observation is necessarily relative, and therefore necessarily embodied. While modern science strives either to minimise or to incorporate this bodily presence, Smith's mobile views into the mathematical universe Blinn had built restores to it Ihde's sense of a human body engaged by and indecipherable from its observing.

The quasi-embodied state of quasi-phenomenological scientific instruments is implicit in the combination of flight plan and improvised camerawork. And yet the implicit body is not the familiar gravity-bound body of normal perception. Its strangeness blossoms in the evocation of zero gravity, a pleasurable vertigo like diving, the liberation of moving in three dimensions, while at the same time taking us into zones where no human could survive. The effect is of a non-human embodiment, an out-of-body embodiment, an intimation of posthumous existence that lays a gloss of spirituality over the hard engineering of the underlying data. That posthumous aura rhymes with the eternity of the Voyagers' flights into space beyond the Solar System and into time beyond the galaxy, a finite but barely conceivable duration played out in several fiction films including *Star Trek: The Motion Picture* (1979), where Voyager returns freighted with knowledge gathered through centuries of travel. Curiously, if the hard data gives a sense of the animated fly-bys as realist, these camera moves return them to nominalism. By specifying a view which is almost human, and whose motions emulate the processes of suture that stitch shots together in classical découpage (inviting us to want to see, and then supplying the view we wanted), these camera moves establish each of the satellites as a particular and unique object of perception. But at the same time, they instigate the same instability that gave realist theologians the basis for attacking nominalism. The virtual camera moves make clear that what we see are appearances, apart from the essential existence of the particular thing, so that as a particular object, it fails the test of self-identity which, since Aristotle, has defined the being of being. The animation's realism produces the animated satellite as a symbol of something that exists as independent entity; superadding movement demonstrates that it is nonetheless both being and appearing, that it is inscribed in the field of the visible, and as such dependent on a universe in which, even in this posthumous or posthuman perspective, it is always there not only in its own right, but as object of perception, even if not to be perceived by humans; its mission not only to discover but to be discovered, not only to see but to be seen. Smith's moves on the one hand make it the object of human gazes – the millions of TV viewers in the United States and around the world – and at the same time of a more-than, less-than or other-than human perception in the cold, silent, weightless vacuum of outer space.

This weightlessness is an entirely appropriate evocation of Smith's three-dimensional camerawork, its swooping, circling, effortless and alluring vertigo. The embodiment of the camera implicit in its quasi-human perception of the satellites is at the same time an out-of-body experience. The camerawork takes the viewer from the domestic sitting room where she would ordinarily be watching the footage on the television set to an extreme of human perception which is both intensely mediated and, through its mobility, intensely present. At the same time, it de-domesticates the body, specifically the suburban (taken here to mean the level below the urban occupied by domestic space in urban environments), plugging it into the enormous capabilities of electronic networks that now, in 1978, extend beyond the terrestrial, beyond even the ionosphere that had formed part of radio technology since its wireless origins, to parts of the universe wholly inimical to human being, but now ostensibly immediately available to human vision. This distance from the domestic distinguishes the gendered body of the TV viewer circa 1978 from the genderless human body of the animated camerawork, incidentally also distinguishing it from the more presumptively gendered Man of the Renaissance origins of science and its project. The body of outer space is beyond biological sex, socio-cultural gender, affect and desire. Equally, while space explorations can easily be argued to be continuations of the imperial design of the Renaissance on cosmic scales, they are at least equally emblems, not of the settler, but of the refusal to remain indigenous to this little blue ball of Earth. These sacrifices of gendered and placed domesticity, on the other hand, like Galileo's telescope in Ihde's optic, allow the films simultaneously to extend the body to interstellar dimensions while bringing remote planets into physical reach. Much as we say that glamour is a function of the contradiction between apparent proximity and real distance (apparent intimacy combined with the irreducible distance between on-screen close-up and the viewer's body), so the Voyager fly-bys enact a profound contradiction between the graspable vertigo of Smith's roving point of view and the unutterable distance of the flight trajectories away from every familiar reference point barring a displaced, degendered, disembodied *idea* of the human.

The missions were tasked with sending back the first close-range imagery and data from the planets and their moons. Since, at this stage, there were no images, simulations of their likely appearances had to be provided by space artists Don Davis and Rick Sternbach (Starr 2014, 196–209). Later, as the craft sped past the gas giants, NASA substituted actual imagery for the artists' impressions (Seymour 2012). The animations continued to evolve in line with the science. Blinn had however added something to the artists' impressions of the likely surfaces of these distant bodies: Bump maps. Blinn introduced the technique of bump mapping in 1978. This involves altering the reflective properties ascribed to a smooth surface, without actually changing the surface itself, to give the impression that light is reflecting from it at a variety of angles, just as it would from a pitted surface. These apparent elevations and depressions, applied to the otherwise smooth spheres drawn by the artists from data caught by telescopes, gives the surfaces of the moons of Saturn and Jupiter the kind of texture that we expect from our knowledge of the Earth and the Moon.

As the flights progressed, the combination of artwork and bump maps were replaced with actual data from the spacecraft. The likely – the potential surface textures of the moons – was replaced by the actual, as observed by the satellites. Like the flight plans, the new data exists in the animation as metadata: As a scarcely visible alteration to the projections Blinn's team brought to the first purely animated versions, yet now carrying the weight of scientific measurement. This move from mediated projected to mediated instruments marks a move from realist to nominalist positions in the history of the fly-by animations as they developed from their first animated iterations to the newer versions incorporating the Voyager data. The supplement of the photographic observations of the outer planets and their moons added to the space art representations initially placed in the animations marks the arrival of knowledge sought and gained, the achievement of knowledge as the result of work. At the same time as it indicates the removal of the last traces of artistic fantasy, and with it of an older humanist individualism, replacement indicates both the unfinished quality of the experiment and its place as a process which involves both projection and labour.

At the beginnings of modern science lies the figure of Nicolas of Cusa, also known as Cusanus, theologian and mathematician (Cassirer 1963, 7–45). Cusanus set out to reconcile nominalism and realism through *docta ignorantia*, learned ignorance, whose founding principle was that 'the infinite, qua infinite, is unknown; for it escapes all comparative relation' (Cusa 1981, 3). Comparison was, for Cusanus, always a matter of measurement: Of size, mass or distance. But in the realm of God, such measures are meaningless. On this principle, we cannot know God; but we can know what we can know: And therefore by discovering the limits of knowledge, come to understand where the Absolute, and therefore our ignorance, begins. The Voyager missions indicate the outer limit (c. 1977–83) of what might be known; beyond lies what Cusanus called the Absolute Maximum. This is the indefinite distance of the further galaxies (a secular infinity, a scale so vast that we cannot live long enough to know whether the Voyager craft ever make it there). But it marks also, critically, a sense that the unknown of space travel is also the infinite that has been left behind – not the human, which travels with it, but the planetary environment, and with it the fixed embodiment of our ordinary perception.

It is useful here to distinguish two complex terms whose evolution parallels much of the development of Western philosophy: *Logos* and *nomos*. For the Scholastics immediately preceding Cusanus, *logos* recalled the first line of St John's Gospel, 'In the beginning was the word [*logos*]'. The word of God permeated His creation: This is the underlying principle of mediaeval 'realism' as belief in the reality of concepts. *Nomos*, the Greek for 'law', is also the principle of order, but order as a strictly human product, even if dedicated to and oriented towards God. The strictly algebraic flight data and its numerical expressions underpinning the animated spacecraft comprises the logic, the *logos* of the films; the 'handheld' camera the *nomos* that ties it to the regime of a human body. However, we should also add a more contemporary sense of *logos*. The ecological principle of the connectedness of everything with everything, is a theory of mediation. Everything connects through something; everything mediates. Grass mediates sunlight, cows mediate grass, humans mediate cows … We restrict the word 'media' to human and often only technological forms of mediation; yet for environmental thought, mediation is the universal principle. This thesis is itself a reinterpretation of the ancient Stoic philosophy of *logos* as the primal wisdom of the world. On the other hand, the severance of human from nature, and the restriction of mediation to human communication, which are themselves the foundation of law, of *nomos*, are also historical realities, indeed foundational of history as such, if we agree that history begins with the distinction of human from nature, and even more particularly with the conscious telling (that is communication) of history as stories and eventually written records. The challenge faced by Cusanus in reconciling realism and nominalism equates then to the more contemporary challenge of reconciling primal mediation as the *logos* of nature, and communicative *nomos* as the quality of the human.

In a first move, the animations reconcile the cardinal (counting) numbers used in constructing the polygon representations of the satellites and the real numbers used in vector graphics and the algorithms used to plot the trajectories (vectors) of the spacecraft, where 'real numbers' include the infinitesimals that lie between counting numbers (1.1, 1.12, 1.121, 1.1211111, ...). By including both polygon and vector graphics, the films reconcile not only two modes of depicting but two orders of mathematics, indeed two modes of infinity (the infinity of counting numbers lying at the end of the series 1, 2, 3, 4, ... ; but the infinity of infinitesimals always being as great between 1.1 and 1.2 as it is between 1.11111 and 1.11112). Because the Voyager expedition engages with the Absolute Maximum, it is only correct that its depiction should also establish the limits of its own capacities by introducing these ostensibly irreconcilable infinities in the medium itself. At the same time, through the addition of observed data, in numerical as well as photographic form, into the evolving pictures of the moons, the films also reconcile these Absolutes with the measurable realm. In a third moment, the videos then assimilate the human, in the form of the movements of the camera, to these disparate series and discrete modes of picturing. The problem is however that this can only be achieved by abstracting all of these domains from the messy involvement of the ecological intermediation of everything. At this stage, we are still in the bind addressed by Cusanus: The restriction of knowledge to what can be quantified; to the exclusion of the green world that gave birth to, and still lies unreconciled with, the extreme technology of space flight. Save only that these voyages do involve and evoke worlds, even if not our own but the worlds Cusanus would have known as the Wandering Stars.

Labour, as already noted, is a feature of both the journey and the animations: Labour is the necessary precondition for the production of the kind of knowledge that produces the documentary impulse of the project. It is important to clarify what is meant by labour here, since labour is a central category of materialist thought. This is not the indifferent, undifferentiated labour subsumed into exchange value at the heart of the commodity form: It is not itself the commodity form of labour. Rather this labour is the undertaking characteristic of humans (*homo faber*): To make and to pursue knowledge out of sheer curiosity. As Cassirer says of Cusanus,

> when he explains that all knowledge is nothing but the unfolding and explication of the complication that lies within the simple essence of the mind, he is referring not only to the basic concepts of logic, of mathematics, and of mathematical natural science [that is the innate knowledge that Socrates persuaded his interlocutors to reveal and the drive to compare through quantitative evaluation that Cusanus himself focused on], but also to the elements of technical knowledge and technical creation.

> *(Cassirer 1963, 57)*

and as Cassirer continues to explain, Cusanus believes

> Because he is the representative of the universe and the essence of all its powers, man cannot be raised to the divine without simultaneously raising the rest of the universe by virtue of and within the process of man's own ascension. The redemption of man, therefore, does not signify his liberation from a world worthy of being left behind because it is the inferior realm of the senses. Rather, redemption now applies to the whole of being.
>
> *(ibid., 64)*

The work of discovery is a labour of redemption; and though today we are less Platonic, no longer believing that basic syllogisms and the idea of number are born innate in the mind, those who were inspired by the animations were illuminated, however subliminally, by the mutuality of discovery, of the universe discovering the Voyagers and humanity as a condition of our discovery of the universe. That mutuality is precisely the secular redemption of the ecological movement. Equally significant, the labour involved is neither commodified nor productive of commodities. Presenting itself as pure science – as adventure, as imagination and as acquisition of knowledge without application – its labour is not a part of commodity relations but the goal of any work: To create wealth, of course, but not for its own sake: rather in order to discover the good, wherever it may lie. This is what wealth is for. To create art and science is in its way wasteful; but all social organisation is wasteful in the sense of requiring expenditure. Nor is this waste in the sense that warfare, the absolute waste of deliberate destruction, is the integral waste of a capitalist system which requires this abject destruction in order to fuel its self-destructive compulsion to growth without end, endless overproduction, which we now know to lead, ironically or cynically, to the end of all growth.

And yet there is no denying that from the point of view of human suffering and environmental degradation, this is a cost that could have been deployed – better – in bettering the condition of humans on this planet. Its artistry, its status as art, then, belongs with the question of what human life is for, and so, theologically speaking, with the Four Last Things, the *quattuor novissima* of Death, Judgement, Hell and Heaven. Launching and depicting the Voyagers' voyages in this ambivalently post-human way is the act of a species that already considers itself as if dead, and offers itself to eternity's judgement. It considers itself posthumously, in its silence and in the out-of-body embodiment of the virtual camera. Posthumous here implies not only the death of all life on Earth (or indeed its survival as the recipient of the heavenly return message from the future or the hell of a silent universe). The death that the Voyager project offers to survive is the death of consciousness. It is then the last act of a species which considers itself uniquely conscious in local space; and which nonetheless believes that somewhere, elsewhere, the universe will repeat the experiment of consciousness. The desire for infinity and the desire for posthumous existence are the theological ambitions of a secular age (it is almost possible Kohlhase, Blinn or Smith might have encountered Cusanus through their studies – Cassirer's book came out in English in 1963, early enough to have been available to their teachers if they ever took electives in History and Philosophy of Science).

In the third book of the *docta ignorantia*, Cusanus' Christology, puts Christ at the crux between the measurable, comparable world of experience and the Absolute Maximum of the Godhead. It is in Christ that we perceive the limit and the origin of the human. The same position in scientific modernism is occupied by the terrestrial ecology – the incomprehensibly complex, which produces consciousness, and specifically the Voyager project and its expression as animation, as a purpose, a teleology: To understand consciousness's place in the universe. What results is not the absolute and maximal knowledge of the entire cosmos but more an understanding of our place in it, in line with Cusanus' belief that by discovering its own limits, the mind could intuit what lies beyond them. At the same time, since we are in the realm of the Last Things, it is also quite possible, in place of the deification of the scientific impulse, to read the whole project – satellites and animations – as an expression of shame at the failure of the species to ensure its own survival.

And yet, the Voyager mission does fulfil one posthumous action: To preserve the subject of science, the *concept* of humanity. Once again, the theological origins of the scientific project as a whole reveal something of what is at stake in this. In the opening narrative of his *Oration*, Pico della Mirandola describes the unique position of humans among the rest of creation:

> upon man, at the moment of his creation, God bestowed seeds pregnant with all possibilities, the germs of every form of life. Whichever of these a man shall cultivate, the same will mature and bear fruit in him. If vegetative, he will become a plant; if sensual, he will become brutish; if rational, he will reveal himself a heavenly being; if intellectual, he will be an angel and the son of God. And if, dissatisfied with the lot of all creatures, he should recollect himself into the center of his own unity, he will there, [having] become one spirit with God, in the solitary darkness of the Father, Who is set above all things, himself transcend all creatures.
>
> *(Pico della Mirandola 1956, 8–9)*

The key phrase here is 'the center of his own unity'. Pico sets humanism against pantheism, against all temptation to be swept into union with the *logos*, against all mystical dispersals of the self. For us, maintaining this self is no longer, as it was for Pico, necessarily about preserving a personal, individual subject. Instead, today, Science is the collective subject that knows, a subject which has gained through collaboration and socialisation but in the process sacrificed its gendered, placed and embodied position, transcending, as Pico suggested, his created nature. This subject, like Pico's 'Man', is however still engaged in the struggle to produce *nomos*, an order that would enable it to find the centre of its own unity, even if that order can only be achieved by alienating itself, in the form of this posthumous vision made so explicit in Blinn's animations, from the *logos*, the ecology that gives it birth. At the end of the Renaissance project to become human by knowing humanity, Voyager is the unhuman human at the edge of projection. It accepts, even embraces the cost of alienation from the world, precisely in order to overcome its self-alienation. For Pico, to be fully itself the human must transcend itself. To know, and thereby to be, humanity, science must sever its integration into nature. It is this severance that, in its structural absence, produces the tragic edge to the yearning expressed in the Voyager fly-by animations. At the same time, as Lucien Goldmann describes Pascal's wager: 'Risk, possibility of failure, hope of success, and the synthesis of the three in a faith which is a wager are the essential constituent elements of the human condition' (Goldmann 1964, 302). This is the experiment at the heart of these animations: Not simply to gamble on the success of the missions, but to bet that there is indeed a purpose to consciousness, to the conscious-ness which came to its concentrated peak between 1977 and 1983 in the sci-ence and engineering of the Voyager project and the computer graphics, still in their most experimental phase, that became their most iconic expression. Sending sounds into space is a pledge that somewhere, beyond the human and its extinction, there will be bodies to sense them; that there will be a body, and the environment (air, matter, vibration and therefore time) to support it. If in retrospect we reapply Cusanus' principle of learned ignorance, we may well find the hubris and waste of the project is at least in part repaid by the discovery of what is revealed, in negative, by the documentary knowledge that the films became: That the human is defined not by its extinction in the vast-ness of duration and of space but by the ecology that space flight by definition exiles it from.

References

Berry, Chuck. 'Johnny B. Goode.' US, 1958. Song.

Cage, John. 'Experimental Music.' Music Teachers National Association, Chicago, Winter 1957. Reprinted in liner notes to *The 25-Year Retrospective Concert of the Music of John Cage*. [1958]; Mainz: Wergo Schallplatten, 1994. 6–12.

Cassirer, Ernst. *The Individual and the Cosmos in Renaissance Philosophy*. Translated by Mario Domandi. Chicago: University of Chicago Press, 1963.

Chaisson, Eric J. *The Hubble Wars: Astrophysics Meets Astropolitics in the Two-Billion-Dollar Struggle over the Hubble Space Telescope*. New York: Harper Collins, 1994.

Cusa, Nicholas of. *On Learned Ignorance (De docta ignorantia)*. Translated by Jasper Hopkins. Minneapolis: Arthur J. Banning Press, 1981.

Goldmann, Lucien. *The Hidden God: A Study of Tragic Vision in the Pensées of Pascal and the Tragedies of Racine*. Translated by Philip Thody. Preface by Michael Löwy. New York: Brill, 1964.

Ihde, Don. *Bodies in Technology*. Minneapolis: University of Minnesota Press, 2002.

Koyré, Alexandre. *From the Closed World to the Infinite Universe*. Baltimore: Johns Hopkins University Press, 1957.

Lazier, Benjamin. 'Earthrise; Or, The Globalization of the World Picture.' *The American Historical Review 116*(3), 2011. 602–630.

Pico della Mirandola, Giovanni. *Oration on the Dignity of Man*. Translated by A Robert Caponigri. Introduction by Russell Kirk. Chicago: Henry Regnery Company, 1956.

Sagan, Carl. *Cosmos: A Personal Voyage*. US, 1980. Television series.

Seymour, Mike. 'Founders Series: industry Legend Jim Blinn'. *Fxguide*. July 24 2012. www.fxguide.com/featured/founders-series-industry-legend-jim-blinn/

Sito, Tom. *Moving Innovation: A History of Computer Animation*. Cambridge, MA: MIT Press, 2013.

Starr, Chris. 'Charley Kohlhase Has Been Our Ambassador to the Planets'. *RocketStem*. October 17 2014. www.rocketstem.org/2014/10/17/charley-kohlhase-has-been-our-ambassador-to-the-planets/

Wise, Robert. *Star Trek: The Motion Picture*. US, 1979. Film.

PART VIII
Interviews D

D1

TIANRAN DUAN

*Translated by Lili Mei, English version of
text edited by Dr. Janeann Dill*

China

Please give us a brief summary of your work, including, if possible, a description of your creative process (e.g., how your creative ideas first appear and take shape).

My artwork is grounded in philosophy. For example, the art piece that is both an animated film and a gallery installation, *Maze of Noumenon*, is directly borrowing the idea of 'Noumenon' from Immanuel Kant's *Critique of Pure Reason*. Kant's writing about the relationship between 'Phenomenon' and 'Noumenon' is inspiring as two words that appear in relationship to or in contrast with each other. Noumenon is 'the thing-it-self' and exists outside our human senses or perceptions. We, as human beings, can't 'see' noumenon's material evidence in physical form. Kant's idea inspired the making of my film, *Maze of Noumenon*.

I usually start creating from a point, a thought or an idea. I begin with an image. For the *Maze of Noumenon*, I had an image of a zebra in my mind. I begin to think about small things that seem unconnected to each other. When I have a number of those images, I feel the need to have a structure to connect them. These small images eventually grow into an artwork.

How would you define your animation practice in terms of its relation to fine art traditions, experimental animation or the (historical) avant-garde? Its relation to commercial industry? Who/what are your strongest influences?

I draw a line between my artwork and the commercial industry. I don't make art for commercial purposes and I don't expect people from the commercial world to use my art. I consider all my works to be self-exploration. Making animations and installations is a way for me to discuss my responses to a thought or an idea that I read in philosophy or art criticism and theory.

Why animation?

My work is not limited to animation. The word 'animation' poses limits to the medium. I like to think of my work as 'moving images' which is the literal translation of 'animation' in Chinese. In Chinese, we translate animation '动画 (dong hua)' but '动 (dong)' means 'moving' and '画 (hua)' means 'images'.

Usually when film history is being referenced, the element of 'time' in live action film exists in the past. They are always the past. Animation is wholly created in the present. The element of time is created by the animator and doesn't exist in a past history, like live action does. This freedom to create time in animation allows me freedom from limitations.

Is material or media a particularly important component of your practice? How does it operate in your work? What is your work's relation to experimental form and technique? Is there something you want to articulate with your work that can't be expressed through conventional narrative means?

Material and media are important components for all works of art. Discovering the quality of a material or taking the action of choosing certain types of materials is also an art form.

For me, material and media are not separated from my creative process.

How do you see your work operating culturally? Politically?

I am not a utilitarian artist when it comes to my point of view about art making; meaning, I don't expect to bring cultural or political changes to the cultural or political environment. My works are diaries which record or reflect the questions I explore or the ideas I am interested in during a particular period of time. My concerns are not how to bring about changes or provide solutions to problems in society. I believe that art is meant to only raise questions. Philosophy is meant to answer questions. I would rather raise universal questions than give answers. Culture and politics are not my first consideration.

References

Duan, Tianran. *Maze of Noumenon*. China, 2017. Film.
Kant, Immanuel. *Critique of Pure Reason*. Penguin Classics, 2007.

D2

DAVID THEOBALD

UK

Please give us a brief summary of your work, including, if possible, a description of your creative process (e.g., how your creative ideas first appear and take shape).

I work with computer animation. Advances in imaging technology have the potential to stretch the limits of our senses and what we are capable of perceiving, but much CGI and game technology instead appears directed towards anthropomorphism and a pre-canned form of wish fulfilment. In contrast, I've developed a body of work that often combines elements such as a static virtual camera, restricted viewpoint and repetition to create something that has sometimes been described as 'anti-animation'. The intensive labour that goes into these animations is perversely used to produce images of objects and experiences that we normally go out of our way to avoid seeing and experiencing. I think that the 'durational experience' of viewing my work, with ample time to explore the unchanging areas of the image, is more akin to viewing a photograph than a conventional film or animation – the image 'posing' rather than 'passing' in front of our eyes.

I will often structure works as continuous loops rather than conventional films, so there is no real beginning or end – one can start watching at any point. I think that this kind of 'flat' narrative structure works well in gallery or public spaces allowing what Walter Benjamin referred to as 'reception in distraction' where multiple fragmented viewings allow casual passers-by to build a view of the whole loop over time.

My ideas tend to take shape slowly. I often will read around subjects that I'm interested in, looking for an angle or a way in or maybe looking for an overarching concept that combines several ideas in one piece. Some ideas will arise through 'play', where I am learning something new and experimenting – it's all about making the connections. Even then, I might have the kernel of an idea for 12 months or longer before I take a decision to invest in it and try to make something. Much of this conceptual thinking about new ideas will be done while I'm actually making something else. From the initial decision to make something to the completion of a new work usually takes about three months, but a lot of that time will be used playing around with different visual ideas and structures. This will include a lot of visual research as well as the 'how can I do that?' aspect where I experiment to see how I might technically achieve certain visual ideas. The actual 'making part', where I am intensively modelling, rendering and editing, usually takes around four to six weeks. This is a pretty creative period and the final product is often a bit different from what I might have been thinking about when I embarked on the process. Often this search for a final structure can suddenly resolve itself very quickly and the multiple elements fall into place in a way that I think works.

How would you define your animation practice in terms of its relation to fine art traditions, experimental animation or the (historical) avant-garde? Its relation to commercial industry? Who/what are your strongest influences?

I think of my work in terms of a conceptual art practice that happens to be built around digital animation. At the heart of each piece is an idea, or set of ideas, that I am trying to bring together both through content and form using a visual rather than textual medium. I am obviously utilising the techniques of industrial computer animation, but to create work that I think is quite different. That's not to say I'm not influenced by commercial animation – I spend a lot of time looking at mainstream movies and commercials. For example, I might use visual cues that could have come straight out of the world of Pixar as I think this creates an effective way for the audience to access my work, as they will understand the visual language that I am working with. I also think my work has a relation to structural film-makers. I'm interested in the dematerialised nature of digital animation and how it relates to and reflects the tools used in its creation, and I think you can see this is my work.

I feel that some of my strongest influences have been writers and philosophers. For example, the writings of Gilles Deleuze, Brian Massumi and Bruno Latour have all had some impact on the way I think about the world. In terms of artists, I find the work of Mark Wallinger and Rodney Graham interesting, particularly the way they utilise humour within their work.

Why animation?

When I first went to art college I thought that I wanted to be a painter. However, I became increasingly frustrated with using paint as a means to express or explore a particular idea or concept. I found that moving images offered me much more flexibility. I could add whatever sound, colour or movement I wanted and if I stopped the film it became a photograph. To me it seemed like a 'super-medium' as it was multi-sensory – each element could be directly manipulated to generate effect. Further, with animation you get complete control over the image – I could represent anything I wanted as I was not reliant on needing to have the physical subject standing in front of the camera. Digital editing and computer animation took this one step further, allowing the direct manipulation of the pixels to potentially generate photo-realistic imagery of anything. That in turn opened up the opportunity to explore ideas around perception and the potential failure of digital images – the so-called 'uncanny valley' where our brains sometimes appear to reject hyperreal digital perfection.

Is material or media a particularly important component of your practice? How does it operate in your work?

My choice of medium is a key aspect of my practice – to me it just seems natural to use 'digital materials' to make work about contemporary subjects. CGI and digital animation underpin almost every advert and movie that we see so it seems apt to utilise the same medium and visual language to make art, albeit with a different objective – perhaps foregrounding the technology that is usually intentionally hidden. It also opens up certain strategies that are hard to pursue in other media. For example computer simulation allows one to meticulously recreate experiences that are hard to access or even no longer accessible, such as events from the past – a technique common in role-play video games.

What is your work's relation to experimental form and technique? Is there something you want to articulate with your work that can't be expressed through conventional narrative means?

A key form that recurs many times in my work is 'the loop'. I'm interested in loops both as a metaphor and also as a durational experience. The loop is the fundamental control structure that forms the basis of pretty much every computer programme, including those I use to create my animations. Many of our daily processes in the workplace and in our leisure time are structured by the technology that we use, and the control loop is a key part of that. If we think about globalisation and the myriad of supply chains and systems that we use to manage that, none of these would be possible without the loop. Hence, I'm interested in the loop as a metaphor for both technology and contemporary existence itself. At the same time, I'm interested in loops in a material sense. The seamless temporal loop is a structure that seems unique to animation as it requires direct control over the image to ensure that the start and end conditions are identical, something that is hard to achieve with live action film-making. Loops have unique durational characteristics in that a viewer's narrative is constructed from where they start and stop watching – once the loop has started there is no beginning or end. Conventional narrative flow and causality can even be reversed depending on the point at which the loop is entered and exited. Hence, it allows an exploration of ideas around repetition and memory as each iteration of the loop will be informed by those that we have viewed previously.

How do you see your work operating culturally? Politically?

I use humour quite a lot in my work as I think it encourages people to make new connections. However, there can be a price to pay in terms of accessibility as humour can be very culturally specific and my desire is to try to create something that is 'open'. Still, I understand that my practice is a product of a specific set of cultural forces – that's just the way it is. The contemporary art that most interests me encapsulates some criticality about the society that I live in – in some way it interrogates my contemporary existence. As you can probably gather from my previous answer, I believe that technology is a key aspect of that and so I'm interested in it both as a subject in itself and as a vital material for artists. Today, location is not so much defined by geography, but by our position within the complex web of processes that make up contemporary society. My work attempts to capture such a situation, caught in a perpetual state of transit where increasing complexity is often presented as the illusion of 'progress'. I see technological development as deeply political – each innovation directly impacts how we structure our society and how we relate to each other and 'the world' – the idea that technology is in some way 'neutral' is a myth – I think there's some value in exploring this idea. If we think of politics in the terms of the ongoing creation of multiple collective subjectivities, technology directly impacts that and so I think it lies at the heart of twenty-first century politics.

D3

GREGORY BENNETT

New Zealand

Please give us a brief summary of your work, including, if possible, a description of your creative process (e.g., how your creative ideas first appear and take shape).

I have worked exclusively with 3D animation software since 2003, primarily with Autodesk Maya. My work is created and built up using a generic 3D male figure, which is animated using an array of looped movement cycles. This figure is duplicated and multiplied, often forming a range of movement clusters.

These can suggest choreographic forms, performance, ritual or simply randomised crowd behaviour.

These figures are staged within environments which rotate or pan past the viewer, situated in a kind of metaphysical 'no-space' reminiscent of a video game environment. These can be read as a series of psychological spaces, as representations of hermetic digital colonies – depictions that fluctuate between the utopian and dystopian – or as a staging ground for figures enacting some enigmatic ceremonial.

Figures, objects and 'natural' phenomena move in synchronous and asynchronous time: Loops, cycles, intervals and durations are both moving forward and concurrently held in a kind of dynamic stasis. The distortions of one-point perspective are rejected – perspectival space is flattened out to orthographic projection, recalling the representational systems employed in Japanese art and architectural drawings.

I take a meta-creational approach which might at times appear to mimic the appearance of a living system, but is in fact dependent on a range of virtual processes and simulations. This provides a staging ground for a variety of both passive and active interactions between the figures and their often unstable geographic and architectural settings.

As mentioned, my primary tool is the 3D animation, modelling, simulation and rendering software Autodesk Maya, a high-end 3D computer graphics software developed for and used extensively in the film and games industries.

Starting with the looped actions of the generic male figure as a base, animation is built up adopting a modular approach. Multiple units of cyclic animated and sometimes motion-captured bodily movements are developed, generating a database of elements that can be combined and recombined in manifold ways.

I adopted 3D animation software as my creative primary tool in 2003 when it became technically possible (and affordable) to run relatively advanced 3D animation software on a personal computer.

It was then that I started to work directly into the 3D software itself – eschewing any preparatory conceptual processes such as storyboarding, or previsualisation typically employed in industry animation and visual effects pipelines. Instead I embraced the medium for its own intrinsic qualities. 3D had a reputation as a labour-intensive and time-consuming process (often in the service of creating photo-realistically rendered outputs). My aim was to be able to harness the software for more rapid generation of work, embracing generic and the preset in the various tool settings, minimising render times and preserving a creative spontaneity in the making process while acknowledging the medium itself rather than effacing the base digital aesthetic behind the lure of the photoreal. Creative ideas emerge through and out of this process of direct engagement with the 3D medium.

How would you define your animation practice in terms of its relation to fine art traditions, experimental animation or the (historical) avant-garde? Its relation to commercial industry?

My animation work is very much embedded in fine art and experimental approaches to practice. In terms of presentational modes, my work is staged in a range of non- or extra-cinematic ways including screen, projection and installation-based works in art galleries, as projection or projection-mapped pieces on large scale public screens or architectural façades, or as online work.

When I first encountered 3D animated work in the mid-1980s I was very interested and excited in the possibilities this new medium offered for the artist in co-opting an industrial production tool for experimental exploration and creation, particularly its ability to create a fully realised and navigable 3D 'world', and its as-yet unrealised potential as an expressive artistic tool beyond the commercial and aesthetic imperatives of mainstream entertainment. To paraphrase 3D artists Claudia Hart and Rachel Clarke: Creating content which embraces the traditions of avant-garde and the legacy of art history rather than commercially-driven aesthetics of Hollywood feature films and first-person shooter video games.

As an artist I also choose to engage directly with the medium itself, rather than employing technical specialists to realise my concepts, or employ a typical industry pipeline process with distributed specialist roles (e.g., modelling, rigging, animating, rendering etc.). Finding unique 'ways in' to the software, and distinctive working methods I felt would be important to the creative discovery process within a new and developing medium, and also to help create outputs distinguishable from a media environment already saturated with commercially produced synthetic 3D imagery.

Who/what are your strongest influences?

I would describe my influences in both form and content as a somewhat diverse spectrum from fine artists to animators to Hollywood filmmakers. I have an enduring fascination and love of pre-cinematic era of moving image representation nineteenth century optical toys: The various Phenakistoscopes, Zoetropes, Praxinoscopes etc., and the photographic experiments of Eadweard Muybridge and Étienne-Jules Marey. In their employment of the loop, and the abstraction of human movement, and metamorphic transformations, they strongly connect in my mind to the extraordinary movie choreography of 1930s Hollywood director and choreographer Busby Berkeley, another key influence in his use of de-individualised (mostly) female figures to create vast and complex fantasias of movement 'ornaments', composed with a virtuosic eye for the cinematic camera. The contemporary artist Michal Rovner also had a profound effect on me when I encountered the video works in her installation in 2002 in the Israeli Pavilion at the 50th Venice Biennale. In particular the formal ways in which she used moving figures in various configurations: As crowds, small groups, or rows and lines, the figure itself reduced to an absolute de-individualised essence, but retaining an uncanny sense of life. The sculptural psychological spaces created by Louise Bourgeois are also greatly influential, as well as the isometric landscapes and environments in the drawings of Paul Noble. I would also have to name check a number of the great auteurs of animation: Jan Švankmajer, the Brothers Quay, Yuri Norstein, Len Lye, Norman McLaren and Robert Breer. Apart from their achievements in creating distinctive and visionary bodies of work within animation they also are great role models for auteurist practice outside the mainstream.

Why animation?

For me animation has always had a kind of fundamental magic appeal – the ability to create the illusion of life with even just a small sequence of still images is endlessly appealing to me. This appeal also is tied to the absolute control you have in creating an autonomous world.

Is material or media a particularly important component of your practice?

Currently digital 3D animation software is absolutely central to my practice.

How does it operate in your work?

It is core to my creative engagement with animation and my fascination with, to quote 3D artists Claudia Hart and Rachel Clarke again, the 'artificial "xyz" space, the non-referenced, non-indexical synthetic image/object, … [and] … the specific qualities of the virtual camera that records it'.

What is your work's relation to experimental form and technique?
Is there something you want to articulate with your work that can't be expressed through conventional narrative means?

Although my work formally deals in figurative rather abstract imagery, it does reject conventional moving image narrative structure and filmic grammar in cinematography and editing, and notions of character development and narrative advancement. It has more in common with sculptural practice and installation in the way its components are literally 'sculpted' in 3D, and arranged and presented in an integrated and continuous, albeit virtual, space. In terms of my approach to narrative, and of the loop and the database as an underlying narrative mechanism, I acknowledge the resonance of Lev Manovich's characterisation of the loop in new media production as an 'engine' which puts narrative in motion. Loops retrieved from the 'database' are a 'multitude of separate but co-existing temporalities' (Manovich, 2001): Units which do not so much replace each other in an ordered flow, but rather are already-activated elements which are composed in one of any possible sequential chains. This allows me to explore and question notions of narrative progression and temporal integrity, with the loop allowing for the concurrent arrest and advance of time, a place where there is motion but not necessarily progression.

How do you see your work operating culturally? Politically?

I would say that any cultural and political content within my work operates in an implicit rather than explicit fashion. On one level it presents open-ended imagery which can be read as utopian and/or dystopian visions, but which personally is also informed by my own psychological reservoirs. In some ways these works are a response to, and inverse of, Busby Berkeley's all-female utopian fantasies, where a potentially infinitely duplicated male figure is subject to the repetition compulsion of the loop, endlessly enacting and performing within structures of what philosopher Siegfried Kracauer coined as the 'mass ornament'.

Reference

Manovich, Lev. *The Language of New Media*. Cambridge: MIT Press, 2001.

INDEX

Page numbers in *italics* refer to figures. Page numbers in **bold** refer to tables.

AANAATT (Hattler) 98–99, 165
absolute 37–49
Absolute Film, Der 42
Absolute Maximum 253–254, 256
abstract art 30–31
abstraction 21–22, 97–98, 229–232, 243
abstract stop-motion 98
Abstronics films (Bute) 53
Accident (Engel) 95
Adventure Time 128
Aerosphere and Atmosphere (Randerson)
    211, 221, 224
aesthetic diversity 119
Afrofuturism 144
Against the Grain (Chong) 99
Aids Quilt 75
Akel, Diego 8, 120, 205–208
Albedo of Clouds (Randerson) 211–212,
    221–225, *223*
Alexa 228–229
Alexeieff, Alexandre 92
algorithms 229, 230–233, 243
Allahyrai, Morehshin 127–128
Allen, Rebecca 135–136
All New Gen 140
All Stars (Mack) 154
Allures (Belson) 27, 211, 214–217, 225
Altair (Klahr) 172
alteration-de-la-voix (Kim) 145
Álvarez Sarrat, Sara 119

Amanita Studio 121
Amazing World of Gumball, The 21
Analytical Engine 139
Anger, Kenneth 170
Animals and their Limitations, The
    (Trainor) 189
Animate! Channel 4 5
Animated 'Worlds' (Buchan) 5
Animation in the Home Digital Studio
    (Subotnick) 119
Anomalies of the Unconscious
    (Behrens) 107
anthropomorphism 190
Antonioni, Michelangelo 173
Antonisz, Julian 7
Apollinaire, Guillaume 40
Appadurai, Arjun 95
Arabesque (Whitney) 45, 48
Aristotle 212
Art in Motion (Furniss) 20–21
artist: role of 24, 27–30
artists' film 104
Ascher, Robert 105
Asparagus (Pitt) 169
associational flow of images 176–178
Astronaut's Dream, The (Belson) 218
Attie, Shimon 74
avant-garde filmmaking 102–104
'avant-pop' 51–52, 58, 64
A-Z of Noise (Semiconductor) 240

Babbage, Charles 139
Babble on Palms, The (Woloshen) 110
Baglight (Ross) 108
Balsom, Erika 5–6
Bang! (Breer) 26
Baracchi, P. 221–222, 224
Barad, Karen 213–215
Baret, Julien 59
Barratt, Virginia 139–140
Bass, Saul 52–53, *55*, 56–58, 64–65
Bateson, Gregory 220
Bats, The (Trainor) 189–192
Battey, Bret 49
Bears on Stairs 95
Beecher, Carol 105
Behrens, Jon 107
Belknap, Sarah and Joseph 211,
    218–219, 225
Bellona (after Samuel R. Delany)
    (Lislegaard) 123–124
Belson, Jordan 9, 20, 26–28, 38, 43–46,
    125, 163, 165, 211, 213–217, 223,
    225–226
Benjamin, Walter 121
Bennett, Gregory 8, 127–128, 220,
    267–270
Bergson, Henri 118
Berkeley, Busby 165, 269–270
Bickford, Bruce 203
Big MOMA (Schwartz) 135
Bikini Atoll 216
Biophilia 125
Bjork 125
Black Lake (O'Reilly) 32, *32*
Blake, Jeremy 116
Blanket Statement [s] #1 and #2
    (Mack) 155
Blinn, James 246–248, 250, 252, 255–256
Blutrausch (Fleisch) 108
*Bob Monroe 24/7 Out of Body News
    Network, The* (Couillard) 126
Bode, Lisa 117
Bodies in Technology (Ihde) 250
body: artist's 108; feminism and 138,
    140–141, 144
Body I (Gagnon) 138
boiling lines 88
Bolter, Jay 114–115, 129
Bond, Mark Evan 39
Bond, Rose 9, 73–75, 120
Bordwell, David 175
Boris Karloff's Thriller 57
Borowczyk, Walerian 72, 80
Bors, Sabin 121

Bottle (Lepore) 90
Bourgeois, Louise 269
Brady Bunch, The 57–58
Brakhage, Stan 105–106, 108–109
Bras, Luis 8
Breer, Robert 4, 20–21, 26, 28, 32–33,
    88, 154, 269
Broadsided! (Bond) 75
Brose, Lawrence 110
Buchan, Suzanne 5, 118
bump maps 252
Burr, Peter 126, 128
Bus Stop 57
Bute, Mary Ellen 19, 42, 52–54, 59, 61
Butler, Octavia 144

Cabonik, Laboria 143
Ça Ce Soigne? 53, 59–61, 63–65
Caffé, Carla 206
Cage, John 161, 250
Calculated Movements (Cuba) 162
Camargo, Iberê 206
Cameron, Donna 108
Camilo González, Juan 8, 206
Cantrill, Arthur 106
Car Craze 122
Carré, Lilli 145
Carroll, Noël 171, 177
Carusi, Annamaria 235–237
Cassirer, Ernst 254–256
*Category 4 Hurricane Matthew on October 2,
    2016* 229, 231, 232–234, 237–243
Cavell, Stanley 118, 134
cel animation: materiality and 86
Children's Television Workshop
    (CTW) 4–5
Chinese Series (Brakhage) 109
Chion, Michel 176
Chong, Jonathan 99
Chua, Daniel K. L. 40–41, 47
Cinema-16 54
circular imagery 44–45, 220
Citron, Jack 47
Cixous, Hélène 137–138
Clarke, Rachel 268
Classroom, The (Krasnova-Shabaeva) 203
Clowes, Simon 52, 64
Colburn, Martha 9, 199–201
Coleman, Jeremy 105
collage animation 171–174; *see also
    Pettifogger, The* (Klahr)
Collagist, The (Lockhart) 88, *88*
Collision (Hattler) 165
commercial animation 20–21, 33

commercialisation 62–64
Composition in Blue (Fischinger) 33
computer animation: cyberfeminism and
    132–147
Concerning the Spiritual in Art
    (Kandinsky) 30
Conner, Bruce 170
Cook, Nicholas 39
Coomaraswamy, Ananda 46
Cooper, Kyle 63
cosmos 211–226, 246–257
Couillard, Jeremy 126
counterpoint 30–31, 41, 55, 57, 59–61
Cox, Paul 9, 80
Creation of the Universe, The 225
Critique of Pure Reason (Kant) 261
Crossroads (Krumme) 93–94
Cuarón, Alfonso 123
Cuba, Larry 4, 9, 42, 125, 161–163
Cubitt, Sean 115, 124
Cusanus (Nicolas of Cusa) 253–257
cut-out animation 87–88, 91–92, 172
cyberfeminism 132–147
Cyberfeminist Manifesto for the Twenty-First
    Century 140
Cyberflesh GirlMonster (Dement) 141
Cyborg Manifesto (Haraway) 137
Czegledy, Nina 221

Dadson, Phil 219–220
Daniel, Kathleen 145
Danse Macabre (Saint-Saens) 60
da Rimini, Francesca 139–140
Dark Matter (Allahyrai) 127–128
Darnell, Eric 91
Davis, Don 252
Daylight Moon and Other Constellations
    (Klahr) 172
de Beijer, Evert 120, 122
de Bruyn, Dirk 118
decontextualization 98
Deep, The (PES) 96
deep remixability 116, 122
Deirdre's Choice (Bond) 74
de León, Tania 8
Deleuze, Gilles 118, 126, 264
DeLoughrey, Elizabeth 217
Del Pieve Gobbi, Rena 105
Delusional Mandala (LuYang) 144
dematerialisation 119
Dement, Linda 139–141, 144
Denning, Peter 230–231
Deren, Maya 40, 177
Dery, Johanna 107–108

'developmental' animation 21
Dhalgren 123
Diacono, Estaban 127
Diakur, Nikita 127–128, *128*
DiFrancesco, David 250
digital ephemerality 123–126
digital experimentation 114–129
Digital Harmony (Whitney) 46
digital simulations of materiality 90–92
Dimensions of Dialogue (Švankmajer) 89
direct animation 61–62, 102–110
Disney, Walt 53
distribution 5–6, 24
Divisional Articulations (Hattler) 165
Dolls House, The (Hart) 240
Dourish, Paul 239
Dragelj, Zoran 105
Draves, Scott 49
Drucker, Johanna 229, 231–232, 236, 243
Dumała, Piotr 80
Duras, Marguerite 138
Dusty Stacks of Mom (Mack) 153

Earth Shiver (Hughes) 90
Earthstar (Hinterding and Haines) 211,
    217–218
Earthworks (Semiconductor) 241
Eastern religions 43
Eco, Umberto 58–59, 61
écriture féminine 137–140
Edwards, Gareth 122
Eggeling, Viking 19, 21, 30, 37–38,
    41–43, 46–44, 54, 105, 165
Eisenstein, Sergei 74
Elder, R. Bruce 42
Elevator Music (Klahr) 172
Elsaesser, Thomas 115, 119–121, 126
emotional expression: digital animation
    and 115–117
Emshwiller, Ed 4
End of Eating Everything, The (Mutu) 144
Energie! (Fleisch) 32
Engel, Jules 19, 21, 154
Engram Sepals (Klahr) 172
environmental animation 90
ephemeral materiality 92–95
Errai 81
essentialism 142
Etyma (Sorenson) 136
Everything (O'Reilly) 124, 128–129
evocation versus explicit statement 17
Expanded Cinema (Youngblood) 74, 219
Experimental and Expanded Animation
    (Smith and Hamlyn) 5

experimental animation: accessibility of 5–7, 18; context for 1; critical attention and 33; cyberfeminism and 132–147; defining 17–34; definitional flexibility of 1; digital experimentation and 114–129; global context for 7–9; motion graphics and 51–65; overview of discussion of 9–11; parameters for 23–24; plan for discussion of 33; production techniques and 85–100; as term 2–3; visual music animation 37–49; women and 132–147
Experimental Animation (Russett and Starr) 2–4
exposure of materials/medium 17, 31–32
External World, The 23

fabula 175, 181
Fantasia 60, 61
Fellini, Federico 173
feminism 132–147
Fetishist, The (Trainor) 186–189, 195
film: as medium 102–104
Film Ist Rhythmus (Richter) 56
Final Fantasy 117
Fincher, David 122
Finn, Ed 232, 236
Fischinger, Oskar 19, 21, 33, 38, 42–43, 47–48, 54, 59, 105, 163, 165, 206
Five Film Exercises (Whitney and Whitney) 43
Fleisch, Thorsten 32, 108
Flusser, Vilém 118
formal diversity 119
form and space 119–123
For the Rest of Your Natural Life (Klahr) 172
found-object animation 88–90, 95–97
Fragrant Portals, Bright Particulars and the Edge of Space (Gatten) 109
Friedman, Alexander 214
From Point to Pixel (Hoy) 124
Fugitive, The 176
Fundamentals of Animation, The (Wells) 206
Funny Games (Haneke) 125
Furniss, Maureen 20–22, 89, 115, 119, 126

Gagné, Michel 33
Gagnon, Madeleine 138
Gaia's Dream (Bond) 73–74
Gajjala, Radhika 141–142
Galileo Galilei 212–213, 250, 252
Gallese, Julian 8

Garden of Earthly Delights (Brakhage) 108
Gascoigne, Damian 121
Gas Planet (Darnell) 91
Gatten, David 109
Gehman, Chris 5, 186
Geiser, Janie 170
Gerhardt, Joe 228, 237, 240–242
Get Real! 122
Ghost Algebra (Geiser) 170
Gibson, Sandra 104–105
Gillie, Johnathan 32, 125
Glabicki, Paul 154
Glass, Philip 43
Glenn, John 220
Glistening Thrills (Mack) 154
glitch effects 128
glitch feminism 144–145
Glitch is a Glitch, A 128
Global Precipitation Mission (GPM) Core Observatory 234–235
Goehr, Lydia 38, 41
Golden, William 57
golden record 249–250
Goldmann, Lucien 257
Gondry, Michel 121
Graham, Rodney 264
Gravity 123
Greenberg, Clement 31, 40, 46
Grusin, Richard 114–115, 129
Gunning, Tom 171–172, 174
Gurevitch, Leon 117

Hadid, Zahar 122
Hagener, Malte 119
Haines, David 211, 215, 217–218, 225
Hamlyn, Nicky 5
Haneke, Michael 125
Hanslick, Eduard 37, 39–42
Harada, Goh 105
Haraway, Donna 137
Hardstaff, Johnny 119
Harlequin (Mack) 155
Harman, Graham 96
Harmony (Trainor) 189, 191–193
Hart, Claudia 115, 117–118, 121, 127, 240, 268–269
Hart, Emma 108
Hattler, Max 8, 89, 98–99, 125, 164–166
Hautnah (Fleisch) 108
Hay, Meredith 115
Hays, Ron 52, 59
Heaven and Earth Magic (Smith) 169
Heaven and Hell (Hattler) 165
Hébert, Pierre 109–110

Heidegger, Martin 96–97
Heirens, William 186–188
Her (Jonze) 120, 126
Hertz, Betti-Sue 119
Hester, Helen 143
Hillbilly (Daniel) 145
Hilton, Stuart 17, 88
Hinterding, Joyce 211, 215, 217–218, 225
Hoffmann, ETA 39
Hofmann, Hans 40
Hollywood Flatlands (Leslie) 119
Hommage à Paul Klee, 13/9/65 Nr. 2 (Nake) 134
Horrocks, Roger 220
Hosea, Birgitta 115, 118, 122
Hoskins, Courtney 105
Hoy, Meredith 124
Hubble, Edwin 214
Hudson, Tom 239
Huffman, George 235–236
Hughes, John 'Hobart' 90
Husbands, Lilly 25, 29–30, 127, 238

Idealism 44, 47
identity 85–100
Ihde, Don 250, 252
Illumination No 1 (Bond) 74–75
Illusionist, The 23
imaging board: art as 24–27
Inception 123
Indian classical music 44–46, 49
individualism 17–18
In My Gash (Dement) 141
Institute Benjamina 118
Interception (Del Pieve Gobbi) 107
International Animated Film Association (ASIFA) 4
intersectionality 142
intertextuality 58–62, 64–65
In the Month of Crickets (Klahr) 172
IntraMuros (Bond) 75
Introspection (Yonesho) 158
Irigaray, Luce 137
Islamic art 48
Ito, Takashi 7
It's Such a Beautiful Day 23
Iturralde Rúa, Víctor 8

Jackson, Peter 116
Jacobs, Henry 213–214
Jacobs, Ken 170
Jafri, Faiyaz 120, 126
James, David E. 43
Janetzko, Christophe 110

Jarman, Ruth 228, 237–241
Jeu de Paume (Mosley) 123
Jill (Carré) 145
Jingle Bells (Theobald) 29
Jittlov, Mike 206
Jonze, Spike 120
Jordan, Lawrence 20, 170
Joy, A (Mack) 154
Jukebox (Wrake) 170

Kahn, Douglas 216, 219
Kamler, Piotr 9, 80
Kandinsky, Wassily 30, 40–41
Kant, Immanuel 261
Kantor, Tadeusz 80
Kawamoto, Kihachiro 159
Kebab World (Theobald) 29, *29*, 127
Kefali, Joel 121
Kemp, Martin 234
Kennedy, Jason 127
Kentridge, William 9, 31, 77–78, 80, 102, 118
Kenworthy, Richard 61, 65
Kijowicz, Mirosław 80
Kildiyarova, Flura 204
Kim, Wednesday 145
King Kong 116
Kitson, Clare 5
Klahr, Lewis 169–183, *175*
Klee, Pauol 30, 40
Kohlhase, Charles E., Jr. 247–248, 255–256
Kovalyov, Igor 72
Kracauer, Siegfried 270
Krasnova-Shabaeva, Masha 8, 202–204
Krauss, Rosalind 118
Kravitz, Amy 125
Krumme, Raimund 88, 93–94
Kucia, Jerzy 9, 72, 80
Kumar, Annapurna 120
Kupka, František 30
Kuri, Yōji 7, 72
Kurokawa, Ryoichi 125

Lacan, Jacques 188
Lachaise, Gaston 135
La Coda (Toccafondo) 33
Lake, The (Krasnova-Shabaeva) 203–204
Land (Leiser) 90
Landreth, Chris 127
landscape animation 90
Language of New Media, The (Manovich) 104
Lapis (Whitney) 45

La Pista (Toccafondo) 33
Larkin, Ryan 23
Latour, Bruno 232, 264
Laughton, Kim 127
Leaf, Caroline 72–74
Legend of the Boneknapper Dragon 21
Le Grice, Malcolm 18, 134
Leiser, Eric 90
Lenica, Jan 80
Leonardi, Paul M. 231–232
Lepore, Kirsten 89–90
Lesage, Augustin 165
Leslie, Esther 119
Lessing, Gotthold 174
Let Your Light Shine (Mack) 154
Light (Belson) 223
light-drawn animation 92–93
Light Magic (Pruska-Oldenhof) 107
light-stick animation 95
Lillemon, Geoffrey 28, 126
Lilly (Mack) 155
Line films (McLaren) 43–44
Liotta, Jeanne 107
Lislegaard, Ann 116, 123–124, 128
Lissitzky, El 165
Lockhart, Amy 88, *88*
logos 253–254, 256–257
loops 265–267, 270
Lorenzo Hernández, María 119
Loretta (Liotta) 107
Lovelace, Ada 139
Lowne, James 170
Lucky (Prendergast) 92
Lucy 122
LuYang 126, 144
Luyet, Claude 71
Lye, Len 8–9, 19, 21, 31, 33, 59, 61, 80,
    106–107, 125–126, 154, 206, 220, 269

MacDonald, Scott 215–216
Macha's Curse (Bond) 74
Mack, Jodie 8, 153–156
Madden, Paul 5
Magic Dream (Welss) 208
Magic Kingdom, The (Trainor) 189,
    191–193
Magnetic Movie (Semiconductor) 239
Mamidipudi, Annapurna 141–142
Man From U.N.C.L.E., The 178
Manovich, Lev 104, 115–116, 118,
    121–122, 270
Man with a Movie Camera 78
Man With The Golden Arm, The 52–53,
    56–58, 60, 64–65

Marey, Étienne-Jules 269
Marks, Laura 118
Martell, Craig 230–231
Mary and Max 23
Massumi, Brian 264
material identity 95–99
materiality 85–100, 119–123, 127–128,
    229, 231–237, 239
Matisse, Henri 31
Matrix III (Whitney) 48
Maxwell, Stephanie 107, 125
Maya 121–122, 124
Maze of Noumenon (Tianran) 261
McCafferty, Larry 51, 58, 64
McCay, Winsor 187
McLaren, Norman 9, 19, 33, 42–44, 61,
    72–73, 78, 102, 106, 163, 206, 269
Menabrea, Luigi 139
Menotti, Gian Carlo 180
Merleau-Ponty, Maurice 118
Mesquita, Newton 206
metaphor 188
metonymy 174, 188, 195
Mihailova, Misha 117
Mission Impossible 57–58
Mitchell, W.J.T. 104
mixed-media 21
Mizue, Mirai 121
Mizushiri, Yoriko 7
Model Starship: Unclear Proof (Hattler) 165
Modernism 51–52, 54, 57–58, 64, 125
modernist art 31
Modern Wonder (Theobald) 127
Moholy-Nagy, László 165
Mollaghan, Aimee 27
Momentum (Belson) 211, 216
Monaghan, Jonathan 126–127
Mondrian, Piet 31, 40
Mood of the Planet (Sorensen) 137
Moonlight (Neubauer) 108–109
Moritz, William 37
Moschops, The (Trainor) 186,
    189–192, 194
Mosley, Joshua 120–121, 123
Mothlight (Brakhage) 108
Mo-Ti 212
motion graphics 51–65
Mountain (O'Reilly) 124
Mounument Valley 124
Mouris, Frank 154
Movie-Dome (VanDerBeek) 4
Moving Gods (LuYang) 144
MTV 4–5
Mulloy, Phil 186

Murata, Takeshi 116, 126
music: absolute 37–39
musicality 21–22, 30–31
music videos 33, 121
Musique Non-Stop 136
Mutu, Wangechi 144
Muybridge, Eadweard 269

Nachtmaschine (Hattler) 165
Nake, Frieder 134
Nam June Paik 155, 222
narrative: as hermeneutic 170–171; Klahr
    and 172–176; role of 22–23
Nash, Adam 115, 126
*Natural History of Harris Ave, Olneyville
    (RI), The* (Dery) 107–108
Neubauer, Bärbel 105, 108–109
New Fancy Foils (Mack) 154
Newman, Barnett 46
Nexus (Bond) 73–74
Nicolas of Cusa (Cusanus) 253–257
Night Light (Theobald) 29
Noble, Paul 269
No Kill Shelter (Mack) 154
Nolan, Christopher 123
nominalism 248–249, 253–254
nomos 253–254, 256
Norstein, Yuri 72, 87, 128, 269
Novak, Shannon 125
nuclear imagery 216–217
Numerical Engagements (Walton) 106

Ocelot, Michel 87
Odell, Jonas 120–121
Old Maid and the Thief, The 180
1:1 (Reeves) 105
On the Musically Beautiful (Hanslick) 37
Oration (Pico della Mirandola) 256
O'Reilly, David 23, 32, 115, 120,
    124–125, 128–129
Organ Minder's Gronkey, The (Klahr) 172
Ouroboros 107
Our Relationships Will Become Radiant
    (Lowne) 170
Outer Limits, The 57
Owl Who Married a Goose, The (Leaf) 74

Pajek, Marta 7
paleocybernetic interpretative lens 215
Paley, Nina 105
Panic Room 122–123
Papamargariti, Eva 126
Parker, Claire 92
Pärn, Priit 203

Pascal's wager 257
Passage (Neubauer) 108–109
Patel, Ishu 206
Pelletier, Mike 127
pencil on paper animation 88, 91, 93–95
performative digital materiality 229,
    232–237, 243
Permutations (Whitney) 45, 48
Persepolis 23
Persian pattern construction 48
Persian Pickles (Mack) 155
persistence of vision effect 94
Pervasive Animation (Buchan) 5
PES 89, 95–96, 99
Peterson, James 171, 173, 177
Pettifogger, The (Klahr) 169–183, *175*
Picasso, Pablo 31
Pico della Mirandola 256–257
Pierce, Julianne 139–140
Pink Egg, The (Trainor) 194
Pitt, Suzan 169, 203
Plant, Sadie 139, 143
Please Say Something (O'Reilly) 124–125
Plumb (Wood) 31–32
Point de Gaze (Mack) 155
polyvalence 171–174, 177, 182–183
Pony Glass (Klahr) 172
Post, Jeffrey 238, 241–242
Posthaste Perennial Pattern (Mack) 155
Potter, Ralph K. 53–54
Poulette Grise, La (McLaren) 102
Power (Sink) 94, *94*
Power, Patrick 115, 119, 121
Powers, John P. 173
Practice of Light, The (Cubitt) 124
Precarious Path (Givson) 105
Prendergast, Darcy 90, 92–93, *93*
'present-at-hand' objects 97
Presentation Theme (Trainor) 193–194
Priestley, Joanna 88
Primitives (Warburton) 240
Prince, Stephen 121
process: experimental 85–100
Prolix Satori (Klahr) 172
Prudence, Paul 125
Pruska-Oldenhof, Izabella 107
Pythagorean conception of harmony 46–47

Quay Brothers (Stephen and Timothy)
    20, 89, 116–118, 269
quotation: contemporary 58–62

Rad Plaid (Mack) 155
raga 45

Randerson, Janine 125
Ratatouille 33
Razzle Dazzle (Mack) 155
'ready-to-hand' objects 96–97
realism 62–64, 248–249, 253–254
Recreation (Breer) 32
Re-entry (Belson) 218, 220
Reeves, Richard 105
reflexivity 119, 126–129
Reich, Steve 43
Reihana, Lisa 8
Re-Imagining Animation (Wells and
    Hardstaff) 119
Reinhardt, Ad 17
Reiniger, Lotte 87
Reinke, Steve 5
Remediation: Understanding the Media
    (Bolter and Grusin) 114
Remote Senses, Storms Nearby
    (Randerson) *221*
Report to Darmstadt (Randerson) 211,
    220, 224
Rhythmus 21 (Richter) 31, 42, 52,
    56–57, 65
Richter, Hans 19, 30–31, 37–38, 41–44,
    46–48, 52, 54–57, 65, 105, 119, 165
Riefenstahl, Leni 165
Riley, Terry 43
Rippled (Prendergast) 90, 92, *93*
Road Runner cartoons 22
Robin Hood 33
Robinson, Marcus 107
Rojas, Bibiana 8
Romanticism 37–39, 41, 48
Romney, Jonathan 123
Rope Dance (Krumme) 93–94
Rosenbaum, Jonathan 25
Ross, Rock 108
Rossin, Rachel 126
Rostron, Edwin 33
Rovner, Michal 269
rule building 230–231
Russell, Ben 191
Russell, Erica 23
Russell, Legacy 144–145
Russett, Robert 2–4, 30, 86, 169
Ruttmann, Walter 19, 30, 37, 43, 48, 54,
    59, 105, 119, 165
Rybczynski, Zbigniew 72

Sagan, Carl 249
Saint-Saens, Camille 60
Samadhi (Belson) 46, 211, 215–217
Scanimate 4

Scheiner, Christoph 212–213
Schelling, F.W.J. von 38–39, 44, 47
Schlesinger, Leon 51
Schopenhauer, Arthur 38–39, 41
Schulnik, Allison 31
Schwartz, Lillian 4, 135
Schwizgebel, Georges 9, 71–72
science: art and 211–226
Scott Pilgrim Vs. the World 33, 59, 61–65
Seidel, Robert 125
Self Song/Death Song (Brakhage) 106
Semiconductor 228–229, 232,
    237–243, *238*
Sensology (Gagné) 33
Separate States (Gillie) 32
'Sesame Street' 4–5
Seven Year Itch, The 55
Sexual Saga (Brakhkage) 106
Shabaev, Timur 203–204
Shankar, Ravi 44
shapes 228–243
Shaping Grows, The (Semiconductor) 241
Sharits, Paul 32, 154
Sharpest Point, The (Gehman and Reinke)
    5, 186
Shift (Hattler) 165
Shiri, Mehdi 121
Shrigley, David 186
Silly Symphonies 22
Sims, Robert 44
Sin City 116
Sink, Dana 94, *94*
Sitney, P. Adams 215–216
Sixty Six (Klahr) 172
Skin Film (Hart) 108
Smith, Alvy Ray 247, 250–251, 255–256
Smith, Harry 20, 106, 165, 169
Smith, Jack 170
Smith, Vicky 5
Snibbe, Scott 125
Snow White and the Seven Dwarfs 24
Sobchack, Vivian 115–117
Social Life of Things, The (Appadurai) 95
Sophie's Place (Jordan) 170
Sorenson, Vibeke 125, 136–137
sound and sound effects 176, 180,
    241–242
Sound Ship (descender 1) (Hinterding and
    Haines) 218
South Park 91–92
South Park: Bigger, Longer and Uncut 91
Sowa, Robert 8–9, 79–81, 120
Spin (Hattler) 165
Spinoza, Baruch 126

Standing Women (Lachaise) 135
Starewicz, Władysław 80
Stark, Scott 154
Starr, Cecile 2–4, 86, 169
Starrs, Josephine 139–140
Star Trek: The Motion Picture 251
Stauffacher, Frank 57
Stein, Gertrude 128
Steinkamp, Jennifer 125, 155
Sternbach, Rick 252
stop-motion animation 91, 95, 97–99
Stop the Show (Hattler) 165
Street of Crocodiles (Quay Brothers) 89
Sturhahn, Larry 215
Subotnick, Steven 119–120
Sundén, Jenny 145
Sun Ra 144
surface details 30–31
Suter, Daniel 71
Švankmajer, Jan 7, 9, 20, 28, 89,
    116–117, 269
Svirsky, Sasha 121
Symphonie Diagonale (Eggeling) 41
synaesthesia 54–55, 62–64
Sync (Hattler) 165
'synchresis' 176
synchronisation 55–56, *55*, 61, 63
synecdoche 174
syuzhet 175
Szczechura, Daniel 7, 80

Tabaimo 7
Taberham, Paul 127, 171
Tablecloth (Gibson) 105
Take Me Out 121
Tales of the Forgotten Future (Klahr) 172
Tanaami, Keiichi 7
Tarantella (Bute) 52–53, 61
technical image 118
Tezuka, Osamu 7
Themerson, Franciszka 7, 80
Themerson, Stefan 7, 80
Theobald, David 28–30, 127, 263–266
Thorstensen, Gina 121
3/78 (Objects and Transformations)
    (Cuba) 162
3D printed characters 95, 127
Tianran Duan 9, 261–262
Time Machine 124
Time Tunnel, The 57–58
title sequences 51–53, 56–58, *59*–64
Toccafondo, Gianluigi 33
Tom and Jerry 22
Tomić, Miloš 206

Torn, Katie 28, 126
Toscanelli, Paolo 212
totalization of illusory solids 92
T:O:U:C:H:I:N:G (Sharits) 32
Toy Story 115, 120
Trainor, Jim 186–195
Treasure Planet 21
Trębacz, Ewa 81
Triangle (Russell) 23
Trinka, Jiri 87
Trois Inventeurs, Les (Ocelot) 87
Trois Visage (Schwartz) 135
Turkle, Sherry 235
12 Months of the Sun (Belknap and
    Belknap) 211, 218–219
Twilight Zone, The 57–58
Two Hundred Feet (Mack) 154
Two Space (Cuba) 162
Typhoid Mary (Dement) 141
Tzara, Tristan 41

Ugly (Diakur) 128, *128*
Uman, Naomi 110
Understanding Animation (Wells) 20–21
Undertone Overture (Mack) 154–155
Unititled films (Klahr) 172
Universelle Sprache (Richter and
    Eggeling) 41
Upshaw, Dawn 180
Urbański, Kazimierz 80
Ustwo Games 124
Uterus Man (LuYang) 144

Vaevae, Veronica 8
VanDerBeek, Stan 4
Van Helden, Albert 213
Vaughn, Robert 178
Vertigo 52
Vertov, Dziga 78
Virilio, Paul 211, 214, 225
visualisation of music 18
visual music/visual music animation
    37–49, 52–54, 56, 60, 63–64
VNS Matrix 139–140
von Rebay, Hilla 42, 55, 57
Vortex Concerts 213–214, 216, 224–225
Voyager 246–257

Wada, Atsushi 7
Wagner, Richard 39
Walking (Larkin) 23
WALL-E 116
Wallinger, Mark 264
Walton, Chelsea 106

Waltz with Bashir 81
Warburton, Alan 127, 240
Wees, William C. 43
Weidenaar, Reynold 4
Wells, Paul 20–22, 89, 97, 115, 119, 126,
   206, 230
Welss, Tomas 207–208
Western Spaghetti (PES) 95–96
Where Shapes Come From (Semiconductor)
   228, 231–232, 237–243, *238*
Whitehead, Alfred North 98
white space: empty 93–94
Whitney, James 20, 38, 43–46, 165
Whitney, John 4, 9, 19–21, 38, 42–43,
   45–48, 52, 163
Wiesing, Lambert 97
Wilding, Faith 139, 141
Williams, Christopher 62–63
Wilmott, Mike 222–224
Wimbledon 63–64
Wittig, Monique 137
Wizard of Speed and Time, The (Jittlov) 206

Wodiczko, Krzysztof 74
Woloshen, Steven 110
Wood, Aylish 115, 117, 123–124
Wood, Caleb 31–32
Worlds in the Making (Semiconductor) 241
World Trade Alphabet (Cameron) 108
Wrake, Run 170

xenofeminism 143–144
X-Men: First Class 52, 64

Yantra (Whitney) 44, 45
Yard Work is Hard Work (Mack) 155
Yonesho, Maya 8, 158–160
Yong-Baek, Lee 155
Young, Lamonte 43
Youngblood, Gene 27, 74, 215–216,
   219–220, 225

Zeros + Ones (Plant) 139, 143
Žižek, Slavoj 193
Zurkow, Marina 126